# Integrating Research Into Pr
## A Model for Effec

**Cynthia D. Bisman**
*Bryn Mawr College*

**David A. Hardcastle**
*University of Maryland*

**Brooks/Cole • Wadsworth**

I(T)P® An International Thomson Publishing Company

Belmont • Albany • Bonn • Boston • Cincinnati • Johannesburg • London • Madrid
Melbourne • Mexico City • New York • Pacific Grove • Scottsdale • Singapore • Tokyo • Toronto

Sponsoring Editor: *Lisa I. Gebo*
Marketing Team: *Liz Poulsen, Margaret Parks*
Editorial Assistant: *Susan Wilson*
Production Coordinator: *Nancy L. Shammas*
Production Service: *Matrix Productions Inc.*

Manuscript Editor: *Victoria Nelson*
Cover Design: *Roger Knox*
Typesetting: *Omegatype Typography, Inc.*
Cover Printing/Printing and Binding: *Webcom Limited*

*For more information, contact:*

WADSWORTH PUBLISHING COMPANY
10 Davis Drive
Belmont, CA 94002
USA

International Thomson Publishing Europe
Berkshire House 168-173
High Holborn
London WCIV 7AA
England

Thomas Nelson Australia
102 Dodds Street
South Melbourne, 3205
Victoria, Australia

Nelson Canada
1120 Birchmount Road
Scarborough, Ontario
Canada M1K 5G4

International Thomson Editores
Seneca 53
Col. Polanco
11560 México, D. F., México

International Thomson Publishing GmbH
Königswinterer Strasse 418
53227 Bonn
Germany

International Thomson Publishing Asia
60 Albert Street
#15-01 Albert Complex
Singapore 189969

International Thomson Publishing Japan
Hirakawacho Kyowa Building, 3F
2-2-1 Hirakawacho
Chiyoda-ku, Tokyo 102
Japan

Printed in Canada

10  9  8  7  6  5  4  3  2  1

**Library of Congress Cataloging-in-Publication Data**
Bisman, Cynthia
     Integrating research into practice : a model for effective social
work / Cynthia D. Bisman, David A. Hardcastle.
          p.   cm.
     Includes bibliographical references and index.
     ISBN 0-534-36215-X
     1. Social service.   2. Social service–Research–Methodology.
I. Hardcastle, David A.   II. Title.
HV40.B542   1998
361–dc21                                    98-35449
                                                CIP

# Contents

# 7  Data Collection: Gathering Information for Decision Making   107

# 8  Designs and Practice Plans   134

# 11 Populations, Samples, and Sampling: Getting the Units 173

# 12 Analyzing the Data: What Do You Know about the Success of the Practice Plan and How Do You Know You Know It? 191

## 14  Using Research Methodologies for Practice Effectiveness    230

# Preface

A house divided against itself cannot stand.

*Abraham Lincoln, 1858*

Responding to the rift in social work between practitioners and researchers as well as divisions among researchers, this book teaches an integrated approach to practice and research. In our model students learn to function as practitioners with research skills integral to their practice.

Practice and research are two primary curriculum areas in master's and bachelor's social work degree programs. Practice courses present theories, principles, and techniques of intervention, and research courses offer epistemology and methods to develop knowledge and evaluate practice. While the intent is unity, the curriculum is generally bifurcated and often dichotomous, reflecting a house divided. In this book we argue the necessity of research skills for BSW and MSW practitioners, not to make them researchers but to make them more effective practitioners.

A long history of such divisions has characterized the social work profession in debates about its mission, curriculum, terminal practice degree, cause and function, and even whether it is a profession (Austin, 1983; Schwartz, 1969; Popple, 1985). Yet the purpose of social work is too important to continue this myopic and parochial approach. Issues in society and troubles of individuals (Schwartz, 1969; Ehrenreich, 1985) have become ever more complex and are crying out for good social work practice skills.

Currently, social work students are taught research as if they anticipate careers as researchers or social scientists. However, most social work labor force data and surveys of social workers' research interests indicate that few social workers do research as their primary or significant secondary professional activity (Williams & Hopps, 1990, Hardcastle, 1987). And still fewer social workers, including social work researchers, engage in experimental research (Kirk, 1990). Consistently over the years research has not been held in high regard by social workers (Dunlap, 1993; Kirk, Osmalov, & Fischer 1976; Rosen & Mutschler, 1982). Reviews of student and alumni surveys evaluating curriculum areas and their contributions to practice indicate that research is not viewed as a popular and helpful part of curriculum (Dunlap, 1993). Furthermore, knowledge in social work or even in most scientific disciplines often does not come from classic experimental designs.

Yet the crux of the research enterprise—systematic inquiry to discover facts, theories, and applications—is central to practice. Social workers must be able to systematically gather data, formulate case theories, and plan and develop interventions. Moreover, to evaluate the relevance and effectiveness of their practice, social workers must articulate what they are doing, monitor that this is what they set out to do, and decide whether to continue the applications with this and other clients. In order to achieve these goals, clients must also be able to recognize what was done with and for them and describe the change.

There are different approaches to conceptualizing research and practice. In one, practice is a source for contributions to the social sciences. Many doctoral dissertations, theses with no direct practice application, fall into this category. In the second, research is a means to develop knowledge for practice. Social research and development models along with behavioral approaches are good examples. The focus tends to be on testing limited behaviors that are more precise and readily measured. Though useful, both of these approaches are either too abstract and conceptual, or too narrow and behavioral, in offering much guidance for those engaged in direct practice with clients. In our model we espouse a third conceptualization, in which research skills are part of practitioners' development of their practice knowledge and skills. Use of research methodologies as practice techniques encourages more rigorous case theories and better designed interventions, resulting in improved practice.

Council of Social Work Education (CSWE, 1992) standards require social work curriculum to educate students in research knowledge and skill. These accreditation guidelines are meant to assure that social work practitioners can develop and evaluate their practice. Yet most often schools have translated this curriculum standard into discrete courses on statistics and general research methods, not directly related to or seen by faculty or students as practice courses.

In the current model of teaching research in the social work curriculum, research design and data analysis courses present research as something separate and distinct from practice. With this bifurcation, researchers, at times lacking understanding of what practitioners actually do, try to fit practice into their definition of research, conducting research that does not match the totality of the practice enterprise.

We offer an alternative approach that is non-dichotomous with a broad conception of empir-ical methods. This model presents the teaching of research in practice and research courses using the contributions of research epistemologies and methodologies to analyze, develop, and enhance practice with the client system. Instead of studying about practice and research as distinct components, we present research methodology and epistemology as integral ingredients of social work practice ending this division that has long plagued the profession. All practitioners, including those in direct service, management, and community organization, need research methodologies as practice skills. For example, survey methods are basic tools of social planners who use the methods in their practice role of planners, not researchers. Research skills are part and parcel of practitioners' development of their knowledge and skills as practitioners. Research methodologies are practice techniques. Needs of practitioners and the professional domain determine the research epistemology and methodologies.

Although professions draw from the natural and social sciences, they are not the same as science and cannot rely solely on the scientific method, just as not all sciences equally rely on a particular method for knowledge development. Whether attention is directed to individuals, families, groups, communities, organizations, or policies, social workers intervene to create change among these systems to improve problems in social functioning, a territory that encompasses issues of morality, values, and ethics. To cover the complexity and breadth of this domain, we advocate attention to multiple approaches of research, including qualitative and quantitative methodologies as well as approaches beyond the social sciences.

Note that throughout the book we use bold type to highlight major points and illustrate the integration of research into practice.

## Acknowledgments

We wish to thank our students over the years for motivating us in writing this book and particularly the following social workers for their inspiration and contributions to the case material when they were students in the MSS program at Bryn Mawr College Graduate School of Social Work and Social Research: Cynthia Clarke, Mia Martin, Darcy Seagraves, Jacqueline Stahl, Janine Wettstone. Other practice examples come from our professional experiences.

The continuing support of our editor, Lisa Gebo, was a most important contribution and we sincerely appreciate her excellent ideas, passionate commitment, and warm encouragement. Brooks/Cole, as usual, has been a fine publisher, and we thank Merrill Peterson and Nancy Shammas for their patience and editorial contributions.

For their thorough reading of the manuscript we especially thank Kathy Pottick, Rutgers University; Dan Harkness, Boise State University; and Rona Levy, University of Washington, for their perceptive and relevant suggestions. We are grateful to the reviewers for their comments: James Drisko, Smith College; Daniel Harkness, Boise State; W. David Harrison, University of Alabama; C. Aaron McNeece, Florida State University; Goutham Menon, University of South Carolina; and Kathy Pottick, Child Services Research Group.

We also acknowledge the support of our deans, Jesse Harris of The University of Maryland and Ruth Mayden of Bryn Mawr College.

Our spouses are not acknowledged because they are us. By integrating our skills of practice and research we hope to benefit the profession for which we have together committed almost three fourths of a century.

We acknowledge our debt to all those who have preceeded us, many cited in this book, and to those who will follow us, devoted to improving social work practice effectiveness. We especially acknowledge the late William Gordon, a dedicated theoretician and scholar of social work, who was both a mentor and a friend.

# CHAPTER ONE

# Professions and Science

While most persons probably agree that scientists engage in research, such unanimity is likely missing when describing professionals. Because professionals practice by providing *expert services* to the community, they are considered practitioners of a body of knowledge. Doctors provide medical services, lawyers practice law, social workers engage in social work. The highly visible provision of these services may make it easy to ignore the centrality of research to the work of professionals.

Yet, research is central to the work of both professionals and scientists. Considered by some "the activities of scientists" (Dubin, 1978, p. 17), the *Random House Dictionary* defines research as a "diligent and systematic inquiry or investigation into a subject in order to discover or revise facts, theories, applications" (1996, p. 1219).

In considering this definition, we can see that research is also the activities of professionals. Their *practice is a careful study of each client to discover facts, develop a case theory* (in medicine called a *diagnosis* and in social work an *assessment*), *and conduct an intervention* (to cure an illness or ameliorate a problem in social functioning).

That professionals and scientists are both researchers, however, does not also mean that professionals are scientists. Science increases understanding of some small part of the world captured by a discipline; practitioners change the world in some small way encompassed by their profession's domain.

Kilty and Meenagham (1995) explain:

> Disciplines are primarily concerned with knowledge, the professions are primarily concerned with doing something to promote some activity or change. (p. 446)

Professions, they note, use scientific knowledge and methods for their particular area of intervention:

> The profession is normatively oriented to some chosen goal being achieved or some expectation being met, and within this context, scientific inquiry is helpful.... *Technology* is the selective application of science.... technology is the purposeful attempt to apply science to shape and, at times, manage the environment, or at least specific components of it. Technology is inherently driven by the norm of utilitarianism. (p. 446)

Professions also use technology and techniques but go beyond it:

> Technology as professional behavior and practice is also guided by professional values and ethics and client desires.... Both outcomes [dependent variables or "effects"] and interventions and "means" [independent variables or "causes"] are value guided and constrained, rather than pure utilitarianism. (p. 446)

Professional intervention relies on knowledge to plan and implement change, whether to build a bridge, heal a broken arm, or create a safe home environment for an abused child. *Application of knowledge for the purpose of change* is the primary task of professionals, whereas scientists focus on the *development of knowledge*. Both may use the scientific method in addition to other forms of knowledge development.

In this chapter we distinguish functions of professions from those of science, discuss approaches to research including the scientific method, examine different assumptions of reality, and consider various means of building knowledge. We lay the foundation for our model that directly links research and social work practice, removing the dichotomy between them.

## Knowledge

Kuhn's seminal presentation in 1962 on paradigms, and later work by French philosophers such as Foucault (1969) and Derrida (1972), challenged disciplines to reconsider the kind of knowledge they needed and the means used for its development. Questions about the traditional approaches of modernity to theory development and research affect not only the natural and social sciences but also the humanities.

The *positivist approach to knowledge development*, with a belief in a rational world knowable through empirical evidence, dominated the period of modernity. Here the function of science is uncovering the laws of nature through strict adherence to the scientific method. Nature is not random but operates under laws of cause and effect that are free from time, context, and our ideas. The task is to predict and control this reality.

A major assumption of modernity is that "our knowing of something" lies in how it is measured, existing in the measurement and the operational measurement applied only, not in the language and ideas of our construction. "Red" is, therefore, not an idea or impression; people do not mean the same thing when they say

something is colored "red," but rather all individuals point to the same spot on the color chart when they see a particular color.

Hudson, a social work positivist, reflects the ultrapositivist position with his statement that "if you can not measure the client's problem, it does not exist. If you cannot measure the client's problem, you cannot treat it" (1976, p. 65). While it may be difficult to measure many of the problems social workers address, such as those experienced by some parents who abuse their children, or the resulting feelings in those abused, these are, nevertheless very real feelings and problems for the clients and their social workers. Moreover, though the problems may not exist for the social worker, they are still faced on a daily basis by the clients.

Positivism considers that the only true propositions about nature are *empirical*, which they equate with *measurable*, a departure from the philosophical rationality position that reason is the path to true knowledge. From the positivist perspective, the only valid source of truth is experience and measurements. If true reality is not discovered, it is because the measurements or the processes of measurement are deficient, the appropriate tools have yet to be invented, or they are inappropriately used.

> Empirical knowledge is knowledge derived from what is sensed and what is discovered through the senses, from induction rather than deduction.... Logical positivism, a modern form of empiricism, suggests that it is only scientifically verified experience that is the reflection of truth. (Souflee, 1993, p. 325)

This brand of empiricism rejects metaphysics and ethics on the grounds that their assertions are "over and above the world of experience" and therefore nonsensical (Passmore, 1967). Hempel, considered a founder of this philosophical approach to science, believed that concepts in psychology and the social sciences were "basically the same character as...used in the natural sciences" (1965, p. 171).

*Positivism relegates values to their holder's prefer- ences and wants: what the holder wants things to be, but not reality.* They dismiss any inherent role of values in (1) determining a phenomenon's im- portance, (2) formulating questions, and (3) de- veloping measures. Yet it is the values and ethical code of the social work profession that guide its practice and form the basis for its existence.

*Empiricism,* however, deals with the real world, not our fantasies, and is not limited to the narrow definition of positivism. Practice experi- ence and wisdom is empirical. The issue is whether the practitioner does a good job in ex- plaining reality, whether the practitioner's con- structions fit the client's real problems.

Positivism is the predominant paradigm among social work academics, including among others Bloom and Orme (1993), Briar (1990), Fis- cher (1993), Hudson (1982), and Rubin (1993).

*Postmodernism,* on the other hand, skeptical about any true essence, *takes a relativist position.* Believing that knowledge is constructed within a social context, postmodernists attend to *process* and *issues of language and meaning.*

Some postmodernists adhere to a naturalist paradigm, critiquing what they consider positiv- ist shortcomings: reflexivity, general limits on developing usable knowledge, inability to pro- duce the universal laws that positivism touts, and incapacity to operationalize a true value- free position in its theory and methodology. They argue that positivism's constricted concep- tion of empiricism loses sight of the meaning of objects and behavior, which they believe are crit- ical in human interaction.

*Postmodernism assumes that knowledge, though transient, is derived from many sources: knowledge is not rooted in a specific measurement approach but is socially determined.* Not existing in nature apart from social constructions, knowledge is bound by time and context. Thus the search for knowl- edge is a search for meaning, a value question. Knowledge and values influence thoughts as well as the methods for gathering and interpret- ing things.

A task in postmodern knowledge develop- ment is to recognize the relevance and impact of values. Social work critics of positivism such as Imre (1984) hold that science, especially all the social sciences, is value laden rather than value free. Other *naturalists* in the social work litera- ture include Goldstein, (1986), Heineman Pieper (1989), Rodwell (1987), Saleebey (1979), and Ty- son (1994). Many draw from Gergen (1985), a professor of psychology. A major criticism they level at the social work positivists is that much, if not most, of science and knowledge, is not based on large-scale surveys, experimental and quasiexperimental designs, and elegant statisti- cal and analytical methodologies. Often, rather, *knowledge is based on a very wide range of experi- ences in natural settings* (see the table on p. 4).

Postmodernists, however, often sound reac- tive against the rationality and scientism of the positivists and thereby dismissive of the very real problems that practitioners confront. Peile and McCouat (1997) worry that social work's de- velopment of substantive knowledge will suffer from this rise in relativism. Although emphasis on process and attention to values and meaning makes good sense, social workers practice with real life-and-death situations. In assessing the safety of a child at risk of abuse in the home, so- cial workers need more than attention to their ethic of parental confidentiality. They also re- quire some means of measuring that risk prior to deciding on removing the child or terminating parental custody or continued stay in the home. Social workers in child welfare and other prac- tice settings need specific tools to understand, measure, and intervene.

In his *Making Science,* Cole (1992) describes the divisions among the social constructionists and traditional positivists. Pointing to contribu- tions by both groups, Cole agrees that *social fac- tors influence knowledge development* and at the same time *that measurement can provide valid and useful information.* It is our position in this text that the mixture advocated by Cole is the most fruitful for building relevant knowledge and

Contrasting Positivist and Naturalist Paradigm Axioms

| Axioms About | Positivist Paradigm | Naturalist Paradigm |
|---|---|---|
| The nature of reality | Single, tangible, fragmentable | Multiple, constructed, holistic |
| The relationship of the knower to the known | Independent, separate, dualistic | Interactive, inseparable, unit |
| The possibility of *generalization* (theory) | Time- and context-free generalizations (*nomothetic statements*) are possible. | Only time- and context-bound working hypotheses (*idiographic statements*) are possible. |
| The possibility of *causal linkage* (determinism or positivism) | Real causes are temporally precedent to or simultaneous with the effects (nature is not random). | All entities in nature are in a state of mutual simultaneous shaping, making it impossible to distinguish causes from effects. |
| The role of values | Inquiry is (should be) value free (objective). | Inquiry is value bound as part of culture. |

Adapted from *Naturalistic Inquiry* by Y. B. Lincoln and E. G. Guba, p. 37. Copyright © 1985 by Sage Publications. Reprinted by permission of Sage Publications.

theories for social work practice. Support among social work academics for this synthesis include Peile (1988), Gibbs and Gambrill (1996), and Zimmerman (1989).

The positions of the positivists and postmodernists reflect fundamental differences in understanding the nature of science, reality, and the development of knowledge. A good source about modernism including its conceptualization and leading thinkers is *The First Moderns*, by Everdell (1997). Professions draw from the natural and social sciences but cannot solely rely on the scientific method, just as not all sciences are equally able to rely on this method for knowledge development. Sole reliance on a narrow interpretation of the scientific model is inappropriate to the purpose of the profession and to the education and preparation of its practitioners to address problems in the real world. At the same time, attention only to process, meaning, and values leaves practitioners without tools necessary for responsible practice.

## Assumptions about Reality

Lincoln and Guba (1985, pp. 82–85), believing that naturalist and positivist paradigm adherents have basic differences in their perceptions of reality, group conceptions of reality into four models. Positivists generally assume a putative reality exists apart from any observer, while naturalists assume that even though putative elements exist, the whole is the observer's social construction.

1. The **objective reality position** (naive realism) maintains the existence of a *tangible reality that is fully knowable*. Physical, temporal, and social reality all exist apart from any observer; with sufficient time and reasonable investigatory techniques, inquiry can converge on those realities, although individual studies may only approximate it. Reality and the world exist apart from our knowledge of them, and observers' selection of concepts and constructs will not alter that reality.

This is the conception of reality inherent in positivism, although mitigated to some degree with the positivists' emphasis on measurement. If reality is indeed determined by the measurements used, then reality is limited by its measurement or perception. Measurement is valid when it fits or captures putative reality according to its own methodological rules.

2. The **perceived reality position** asserts that *reality is never fully knowable but only can be appreciated from particular vantage points.* Knowledge of reality is always limited to our perceptions of it. For any individual, reality can only be a partial picture of the whole because of reality's complexity. Understanding a "thing" reflects a mere slice of reality, dependent on our vantage point and perceptual-measurement tools.

Both perspectives, objective and perceived, posit a putative reality, already existing apart from the observer. They differ, however, on how it can be known and what is knowable. The objective reality position assumes that ultimately reality is fully knowable, and on this basis its critics label it "naive" realism. While in the perceived reality model, since not all of reality is observable, it is never possible to fully perceive, know, or comprehend all of reality.

How we select concepts and constructs to examine and explain reality will influence our perception of it. The perceived reality position is accepted by some positivists and naturalists as a bridging position.

3. The **constructed reality position** holds that *reality is a construction in the minds of observers, drawn from putative information, stimuli, and data from the environment and shaped by observers' values, culture, and experiences.* While elements of a putative reality may be there, we can never know or experience it except in our constructions. No amount of inquiry will produce total convergence with a culture-free truth or a reconstruction that is truly reality, just as no amount of inquiry will free us from our experiences.

Constructions are always dependent on observers' experiences, assumptions, collected data, and perceptual filters. Selection of concepts and constructs determine the construction of reality. In research and theory building, the constructions should explain the tangible entities and putative elements, offer a possible internal logical contradiction of the position, but not assume a single reality or fulfill objectivism criteria. Constructions in science should represent the multiple constructions of individuals and account for and use all the information. This standard appears to represent the general theoretical construction requirement of intersubjectivity and the development of a shared construction of reality. *Intersubjectivity* is the agreement on, or a sharing of, meaning. Meaning is the major consideration in the constructed reality model.

4. The **created reality position** proposes that *reality exists only as it is created.* Reality is "ego centered" and appears to relate more to the observer's interpretation of reality than to the existence of a putative reality or even the shared social constructions of the constructed reality perspective. Most contemporary scientists and philosophers reject extreme versions of this posture.

The familiar and trite "tree falling in the woods" analogy—does the tree make a sound if no one is there when it falls?—illustrates these different perspectives of reality. Objectivists would answer: "Yes, or at least the sound waves exist and are measurable. Sound waves emanate from the tree striking the ground." Perceived realists would respond: "Probably so, if some device is there to measure the sound, but it will vary by measurement device, location, and sensitivity." The constructionists, meanwhile, would argue: "though the mass of the tree striking the mass of the earth probably creates the sound waves, the important questions are: What does it mean for the tree, the ground, and the observer?" Conversely, the created realist might respond: "Sound is what the observer wants it to be. If the observer does not want it be sound, it is not sound."

Positions 3 and 4 are similar in their basic assumptions about reality—that it does not exist for the collective and individual participants as a co-herent whole until it is constructed or created by the actors or participants. The issue is not *corre-spondence* with an assumed putative reality, as in objective or naive realism, but *coherence* of the construction or creation of the theory of reality—does it account for the phenomena and the effects of the phenomena? For these two approaches a single reality does not exist, although the ele-ments may, apart from our selected concepts, con-structs, and theories be used in its construction.

The concept of race is a good example of con-structed reality. Neither a biological nor genetic construction, "what constitutes a race and how one recognizes a racial difference are culturally determined.... There are no objective (i.e. biolog-ically scientific) boundaries to set off one subspe-cies from another" (King, 1981, pp. 156–157). Though we can cluster physical attributes, most biologists agree these traits do not constitute a taxonomy of race.

Yet race as a concept does seem to exist for most people. Its existence is a social construction of physical and social characteristics rather than a biological construction, since biological race does not exist (King, 1981; Spickard, Fong, & Ewalt, 1995). What constitutes the taxonomy of race has varied temporally and across cultures. The existence and meaning of race is more anal-ogous to the concept of religion than to that of gender, a concept that biologically and socially is also in the process of reconceptualization.

In the social work profession, practitioners must not only understand the client's construc-tion of reality but develop a shared construction with the client. As Bisman (1994) and Rodwell (1987) assert, client assessment is a measurement task involving understanding the client's con-struction of reality within a social context involv-ing quantitative data, qualitative information, and the meaning assigned by the client. We take the "constructed reality" position that practice constructs new realities from the array of tangi-ble pieces of realities. A significant part of treat-ment is thus *assisting the client in constructing a new reality of change and helping the client achieve coherence with the new reality.*

## Functions and Attributes of Science

As we work to understand the nature of science, we recognize the influence of these debates. The *Random House Dictionary* defines science as "a body of facts or truths systematically arranged and showing the operation of general laws... systematic knowledge of the physical or mate-rial world" (1996, p. 1279). Imre (1984) points out that science is development of knowledge by fol-lowing specified methodologies. She quotes Gordon (1965 p. 41) to clarify the prevailing sci-entific approach to knowledge,

> Knowledge...denotes the picture man [sic] has built up of the world and himself as it is, not as he might wish it or fantasy or prefer it to be. *It is a picture derived from the most rigorous interpreta-tion he is capable of giving to the most objective sense data he is able to obtain.* [emphasis original]

Gibbs and Gambrill offer a broader definition of science as "a process designed to develop knowledge through critical discussion and test-ing of theories" (1996, p. 24). They present science as a systematic problem-solving process that em-phasizes the critical (i.e., empirical) testing of claims to acquire information about a subject. For them, science includes correlational, case, and naturalistic studies and other nonexperimental approaches. Favoring parsimony, other things equal, they advocate fewer concepts and propo-sitions accompanied by a skeptical attitude (1996, pp. 18–19).

For Gibbs and Gambrill, truth is as equally tentative and transitory as knowledge. Some-thing is true "if it corresponds to, or agrees with, the facts" (1996, p. 25). Scientific knowledge is "problematic and tentative guesses about what may be true" (p. 24). Truth, they believe, is never permanent or fully established: *Some assertions, propositions, or theories are closer to the truth than others by their correspondence with and accounting for the facts.* Facts are beliefs that "have been critically evaluated and/or tested" (Gibbs & Gambrill, 1996, p. 17). While facts are only beliefs, or the acceptance of something as true evidenced by a willingness to act as such, we can distinguish scientific facts and beliefs through testing with scientific methodologies.

Beliefs other than scientific, such as religious and moral, are not scientifically testable. Possible as facts, though not as scientific facts, we can consider them unscientific knowledge. Before we reject all beliefs as false that do not adhere to the testing of science, however, we must be aware of the fallacy of *naive scientism,* or "a slavish adherence to the methods of science even in a context where they are inappropriate" (Gibbs & Gambrill, 1996, p. 25).

Science consists of two general parts: (1) **Epistemology** is concerned with the construction or structure of knowledge approximating nature. This part of science approaches philosophy. (2) **Methodology** specifies the rules and procedures for finding out about nature and providing the information used in the construction of knowledge. Research falls within this part of science.

*Interdisciplinary research,* or the mixing of epistemologies and methodologies of diverse scientific disciplines, represents an effort to complete a view of nature from multiple perspectives. *Disciplines* focus on distinct features of the world and may have different perspectives on the same features. Inherent in the concept of a discipline is the assumption of adherence to a prescribed logic and process of thought, or both epistemology and method. A scientific discipline denotes order, restraint, regimen, and indoctrination in thought and methods to understand some piece of nature.

We review here the main components of science. Most accept that science provides *description, explanation,* and *prediction,* while professionals also accept these as necessary attributes of their work. Later in this and other chapters, we discuss why these characteristics are problematic and not always achievable.

## Description

*Classification of dimensions* is the easiest to achieve since concepts, persons, rocks, or social systems can usually be specified and organized through typologies. Problems in determining typologies involve selecting criteria to use. To accomplish *exhaustiveness,* it must be possible to classify all phenomena in a domain; *mutual exclusiveness* demands complete clarity and no ambiguity about each item's classification (Reynolds, 1971).

## Explanation

Specification of *relations between dimensions* is usually possible only after first achieving description because one needs identification of the parts to explain their relationships (Fawcett & Downs, 1992).

## Prediction

The highest level of science involves *forecasting events in the future based on explanation of those in the past and present.* Statements posed as *if/then,*— if I do *a,* then *b* will occur—must be independent of historical time. In other words, there is applicability to both past and future statements, with a focus on outcomes. The most difficult, and probably most important, purpose of science is to focus on *processes of interaction.* Reynolds believes that this goal is achieved only when "the causal mechanisms that link changes…in concepts (the independent variables) with changes in other concepts (the dependent variables) have been fully described" (1971, p. 7). He also poses other desirable characteristics of scientific knowledge, including abstractness, intersubjectivity, and empirical relevance.

### Abstractness

*Independence of time and space* is necessary for applicability of statements about one situation to others in the past or future. This effect is related to explanation: if a statement is unique to a particular time, then it cannot be used for predictions to another time and does not meet one of the purposes of science.

### Intersubjectivity

Without *shared agreement* about the meaning of and relationship of concepts, logical rigor is not possible—that is, there is no agreement about prediction and explanation.

### Empirical relevance

Confidence in usefulness of theories is based on comparison with objective research of others, that which is *observable* or *testable* in the real world.

We return to these attributes of science after a discussion of professions.

## Functions and Attributes of Professions

As with scientific disciplines, we distinguish professional occupations by their epistemology and methodology—the ways they structure their knowledge and the means they use to construct that knowledge. Different perspectives explain professional occupations, including the classic attitudinal and structural model of Carr-Saunders & Wilson (1933) and Greenwood's (1957) attribute framework.

We define **professions** as *occupational groupings possessing the characteristics of a body of knowledge, professional authority, self-regulation, code of ethics, and a service commitment.* Since no profession captures all attributes to the same degree, the concept of profession is considered an ideal, a model to describe and understand behaviors of this work.

### Systematic Body of Knowledge

Professionals use an internally consistent body of knowledge, and their *skills emerge from and relate to that knowledge.* For Abbott (1988) it is the abstract knowledge system that provides professions with legitimation, research and instruction, but also shapes its vulnerability to outside interference. While much is made about theory and skills, many occupations rely on specialized knowledge to carry out their work. For example, diamond cutters and cabinetmakers utilize information in developing their highly refined skills.

### Professional Authority

"Professionals profess to know better the nature of certain matters, to know better than their clients what ails them" (Lynn, 1963, p. 2). Because of their specialized competence, clients accede professionals a *monopoly of judgment* as experts. Though it is not unusual to shop around for professional services, clients, unlike customers, are not free to return purchases, although legal suits are becoming more frequent when services cause harm. Abbott (1988) alleges that professional authority derives from control and application of knowledge, while Haber (1991) emphasizes that the marketing of knowledge helps explain the professions' special status in society. Krause (1997) raises concerns that professional control in the workplace is increasingly more precarious.

### Self-Regulation

Professions *control their training institutions through accreditation and restrict membership with educational requirements, internships, certification, and licensure.* Each professional group sets its own standards for curriculum and entry into the profession. As Haber (1991) points out "professionals sold their labor but not the right to be commanded" (p. 360). For a thorough discussion of social work licensure, see Hardcastle (1990).

### Regulative Code of Ethics

Related to their service mission and body of knowledge, professionals *guide themselves by a code of ethics that is informed by values of the profession and larger society.* The Hippocratic oath guides behaviors of physicians, while informed consent and self-determination, among other values, guide social work practice. In Chapter 3 we review the social work code of ethics within the context of the profession's values.

## Service Commitment

The original meaning of *profess* is to take vows, to accept a calling. Professionals are *called* to their work by a moral commitment to serve the community and work toward a greater good by creating change in some public phenomena such as illness, social disorder, or education. This is the single feature that most distinguishes professions. *Service* to the society, shaped by the profession's values and ethics, is unique to professional occupations.

### The service mission

Professions exist, enjoy public protection and sanction, because of their benefit to communities, the public, clients, and the common good. Professions require a *vision of and commitment to ends to be served and not just the techniques practiced* (Howe, 1980; Lubove, 1977). The service is not only to the individual clients, but to "a larger whole, to a larger good...of the community" (Gustafson, 1982, p. 512). Research, as distinct from the service professions, serves the public good in the provision of knowledge.

*Altruism,* though perhaps hidden by high incomes for some professional groups, is a basic tenet of professions. While professionals receive remuneration for services, they are to provide services when clients need them, not to earn more money or gain power.

*Ethics and the service mission* rather than knowledge and skill define and separate professions from occupations. A profession is more than an occupation using sophisticated techniques. The National Association of Social Workers' (NASW) 1979 Code of Ethics held that the service mission was the primary ethical obligation of the professional, with the first service obligation to the client:

I. The Social Worker's Conduct and Comportment as a Social Worker
  C. Service—The social worker should regard as primary the service obligation of the social work profession.
II. The Social Worker's Ethical Responsibility to Clients
  F. Primacy of Clients' Interests—The social worker's primary responsibility is to clients. (p. 1)

The service imperatives are maintained as the primary ethical principles guiding the revised code passed by the NASW's Delegate Assembly in August 1996 (Code of Ethics Revision Committee, 1996):

Value I: Service; Ethical Principle: Social worker's primary goal is to serve.

1. Social Workers' Ethical Responsibilities to Clients

1.01 Commitment to clients

Social workers' primary responsibility is to promote the welfare of clients. In general, clients' interests are primary. However, social workers' responsibility to the larger society or specific legal obligations may on limited occasions supersede the loyalty owed clients and clients should be so advised. (Examples include when a social worker is required to report that a client has abused a child or threatened to harm self or others.) (pp. 19, 21)

Gustafson (1982) agrees with the centrality of service in professional occupations. "A *calling* without professionalization is bumbling, ineffective, and even dangerous. A profession without a calling, however, has no taps of moral rootage" and cannot "envision the larger ends and purposes of human good that our individual efforts can serve." For Gustafson, professions "exist to serve human needs. Needs do not exist to serve the interests of a profession" (p. 514). Critical in Gustafson's perspective on professions is their base in morality. Values and the profession's vision for a greater good shape the kind of knowledge needed and the skills utilized, determining the curriculum for educational programs and degrees.

## Professionals and the Scientific Method

While we might like to include the characteristics of science we discussed at the beginning of this chapter as the repertoire of professionals— that they can describe, explain, predict and understand their phenomena—we begin to see that the subject matter and nature of their work make this very difficult.

In order to achieve the easiest level of science, that of description, typologies would be unambiguous about placement of events and the criteria would not omit any case that belongs. To predict which clients will respond to certain interventions, explanations of past histories would be provided and cases grouped into like categories. For example, when confronted with a case of an abused child, our ability to classify this client with others of like characteristics would provide support for the typology of child abuse. The prognosis would be based on knowledge of past events in the life of the child, and from that we could determine the likelihood of continued abuse if the child is not removed from the home. Or consider a third grader who cannot read. Again, applying the components of science, we need to classify this child with a like group of third-grade nonreaders and explain the factors resulting in the nonreading behavior. Reducing reading readiness to the simple *if/then* format allows us to predict that, following a certain set of behaviors, the child's reading ability will improve.

But there *are* ambiguities in the real world of practice, and professionals are not easily able to make these classifications or predictions. Even the simpler level of description is not easy for professionals because their domain usually does *not* allow for unambiguous classification. With the interaction of so many variables, classifications that are mutually exclusive are extremely difficult. To illustrate, let us continue with the ex-ample of the abused child. This behavior cuts across lines of race, class, age, and gender, resulting in confusion about which category fits a particular client.

Meyer (1993) asserts:

> While classification is important, it is also extremely complex in fields like social work and mental health, because the human condition does not lend itself easily to discrete analysis, where one is able to select particular units or variables that describe complex bio-psychosocial phenomena in reliable ways. (p. 4)

These difficulties in the simplest task of description compound those of explanation and prediction. Child abuse can be related to social factors such as loss of housing or employment, marital discord, or physical illness. While patterns exist across generations, not all people who were abused become abusers, and some abuse with no previous abuse experience. Without clarity about the interactions among these factors, the practitioner has no basis to predict that change in one of them will result in stopping the abuse.

Moreover, the *function* of professions and science is different. As we have stressed earlier, using knowledge to create change is the professional's primary task, while the scientist focuses on development of knowledge. Creation of change relies to some extent on ability to control events, but science has no such charge. Even for sciences such as geology, with typologies and explanatory statements more sophisticated than those currently available in social work, control is not expected. We do not compel seismologists to control earthquakes, nor think less of them because they cannot, although we may read with great interest about fault lines and even make decisions about where to reside based on such figures.

Science can limit its prediction to generalizations. Professions deal with particular phenomena and events—*this* client in *this* situation. Generalizations in science are more advanced than the capacity of professionals to control specific phenomena. While it may be reasonable and just to expect social workers to create change, they are not currently able to control the specific social phenomena such as physical or sexual abuse, substance abuse, and delinquent behavior, although at times they may be able to describe these events. The inability of geologists and astronomers to control their phenomena is understood. Yet expectations of control are applied to social workers who are immersed with the turbulence of volatile human beings interacting within a constantly changing world, where interventions are not available for all diagnoses.

Nevertheless, we do count on our professionals to create change and influence events—that is the reason for their existence. Some professionals are better able than others to apply scientific knowledge to their object of change. For example, we can reasonably expect structural engineers to use knowledge from the sciences of geology and seismology to build bridges and buildings that may withstand earthquakes.

A serious difficulty for the professional is integration of accrued knowledge with current demands and future needs. Applying what has come before while treating each case as a unique and new area of inquiry challenges professional practice. It is clear to us that when we visit our physicians we are not expecting them to develop new generalized knowledge from our case, but rather to apply what is known about a problem to alleviate our discomfort. Any knowledge generated is case specific. Likewise, when engineers agree to build a bridge to get us from one side of the valley to the other, we expect that bridge to get us safely across. While the terrain and geologic conditions may be somewhat unique, again we expect the building of this bridge to be significantly similar to other such constructions—that there is available knowledge to draw on in order to build a safe bridge. If not, we would expect the engineers to turn down the job.

Professionals desire to replicate behaviors deemed helpful. While each client is unique, building on previous knowledge is essential to responsible and efficient practice. Whether we confront a heart condition or a troubled adolescent, we want the professional to be knowledgeable about previous successes and failures with these problems. For the same reasons, professionals must utilize generalizations and typologies and plan interventions with some understanding of relationships among treatments and outcomes.

## Multiple Methods

We argue that the scientific method through systematic inquiry is central to knowledge development for professions, including social work. Reliance solely on a *single* scientific paradigm, however, results in an overly narrow approach to knowledge and neglects the many ways professionals confront their practice.

Assumptions of linearity in the positivist paradigm ignore the complexities inherent in professional practice—engaging with real people who live in a turbulent world, often behaving in ways that are unpredictable. These difficulties are recognized in the sciences. As Gleick (1987) explains in his provocative book *Chaos*, "nonlinearity means that the act of playing the game has a way of changing the rules" (p. 24). As all who have had direct practice experience know, each client brings a unique twist to what may be a common situation and the practitioner/client interaction modifies that situation in ways that may be hard to discern. Moreover, as we discussed earlier, classification in professions is often problematic.

Additionally, the art versus science division can apply to professional practice as well as the practice of scientists. Dyson (1995, p. 33) believes scientists are inherently rebellious and that "science is an art form and not a philosophical method" flourishing "best when it uses freely all the tools at hand, unconstrained by preconceived notions of what science ought to be." Hilts (1997) asserts that medicine, despite technological advances, is still as much art as science, while Jones in his review of Pinker's challenging book, *How the Mind Works,* announces that "psychology is a journey from the arts to the sciences and then back again" (1997, 13). Social workers argue that their profession is both art and science (Martinez-Brawley & Mendez-Bonito Zorita, 1998).

Short of rejecting clients who present an unclear set of symptoms, *professionals need multiple means of knowledge development and research,* which may better capture the complex range of phenomena they treat than reliance on sole scientific method.

Biologists, working with animate matter, share with professions serious limitations in prediction with individual organisms. Noted biologist Stephen Jay Gould (1983) believes that heavy reliance on a scientific method is a misconception of the nature of science:

> The problem lies with our simplistic and stereotyped view of science as a monolithic phenomenon based on regularity, repetition, and ability to predict the future. Sciences that deal with objects less complex and less historically bound than life may follow this formula.... Organisms...are directed and limited by their past. They must remain imperfect in their form and function, and to that extent unpredictable since they are not optimal machines.... *Notions of science must bend (and expand) to accommodate life.* The art of the soluble...must not become shortsighted, for life is long. [emphasis added] (p. 65)

Since they lack a unifying theoretical framework, professionals must rely on multiple theories, bodies of knowledge, and scientific paradigms. Medicine draws from anatomy, physiology, chemistry, and biology; engineers utilize knowledge from geology, physics, and quantum mechanics. Natural sciences such as biology, the behavioral science of psychology, and the social sciences of anthropology, sociology, political science and economics all inform social work practice.

Moreover, professionals need more than knowledge of the physical world. Influenced by the primacy of action to create change, their distinguishing feature is the *inherent relationship among skills they use with the multiple bodies of knowledge from which they draw and the values that shape their targets of change.*

While service commitments direct their practice, professions lack a science paradigm, what Kuhn (1986) defines as "the entire constellation of beliefs, values, techniques, and so on shared by the members of a given community...and...the concrete puzzle-solutions which, employed as models or examples, can replace explicit rules as a basis for the remaining puzzles"(p. 144). An overarching framework, such as social work's "person and environment," combined with the profession's code of ethics, offers a service rather than a disciplinary science paradigm. To share a paradigm requires understanding of "the manner in which a particular set of shared values interacts with the particular experiences shared by a community of specialists to ensure that most members of the group will ultimately find one set of arguments rather than another decisive" (p. 164). Social workers, like other professionals, often do not share a similar method in the same way as chemists or physicists, where "communication is relatively full and professional judgment relatively unanimous" (p. 146), but they do adhere to a shared code of ethics and a set of values.

Focus on problems in the real world—engineering highways to withstand unpredictable earthquakes, guiding a 16-year-old unwed mother to self-sufficiency, medicating a 21-year-old suicidal college student—results in serious epistemological and methodological difficulties for the professional. There are no standard models or the operation of general laws for these problems, and the concrete puzzle solutions (the means of intervention) may radically differ depending on the unique circumstances of the clients.

Moreover, to practice effectively with clients, professionals continually struggle with *effects of meaning and process.* Interactions with clients shape the content discussed, often making understanding of an objective reality mostly illusory. Meanings that clients and professionals attach to feelings of pain, or word usage, vary greatly, so that agreement or shared understanding becomes problematic.

This complexity in professional practice is further exacerbated by the need for contemporary relevance in problem solving and sensitivity to current mores and values. Social workers today practice with issues unlike those of the early 1900s. Changes in women's employment outside the home and increases in options of lifestyles for both men and women demand different theories and techniques. Justice Oliver Wendell Holmes states in *The Common Law:* "The life of the law has not been logic; it has been experience.... In order to know what [the law] is, we must know what it has been, and what it tends to become" (1881, p. 1). Values shape professional practice, from the profession's own overarching values and vision for the common good and through the society in which it is practiced.

At the same time that professions are deeply rooted in the current world by changing certain ills and maintaining social order, they connect a society to its past. Professional knowledge draws from theories that have emerged from long traditions of philosophical and scientific inquiry. Transmitting these continually changing bodies of knowledge, professions reflect and teach societal values and norms.

Methods of inquiry must be appropriate to the subject matter under investigation. Berlin urges that the nature of phenomena under examination determine the research method (1990). This long-held assumption of scientific inquiry is relevant and applicable to professions and their methods of research and knowledge development.

## Summary

Through discussions of research and knowledge along with assumptions of reality, we distin-guished between professions and the sciences, reviewing their functions and attributes. Emphasizing the centrality of the service mission to professional occupations, we considered limitations of the scientific method for professional knowledge, arguing professionals' need for multiple methods relevant to their practice domain.

Sciences inherently differ from professions. Professions may use the epistemology, methodology, and tools of sciences in practice. Sciences often pursue questions of interest to professions. Both have ethics that share similar canons. Nevertheless, professions are not sciences. The sciences have as their principle objective the search for knowledge about nature or some part of it. Professions go beyond knowledge to changing nature or some part of it. Professions are not sciences but use scientific knowledge and methods for the particular reason of intervening to create change in their domain.

Practice in a real world, not a laboratory, results in practice wisdom. Not merely anecdotal, it consists of experiences with and observations of clients, which are all empirical.

Guided by professional values and ethics and client desires as well as using scientific knowledge, epistemology, and methodology, a profession's knowledge and truths extend beyond the transitory scientific knowledge, truths, and facts of a single paradigm or era to beliefs rooted in values and preferences. These beliefs are not subject to empirical scientific testing.

## Preview of Chapters

The following chapters present the inherent relationship between research and social work practice.

What is the purpose of research in social work? Why do we include research in bachelor's, master's, and Ph.D. social work degree programs? We respond to these questions and offer a model of research education for social work practitioners. Through examination of certain basic questions, we can relate research directly to the needs of the field.

Our goals for readers of this book are (1) to alter thinking about research—that they conceptualize an inherent relationship between research and what social workers do in practice with clients; and (2) to expand their abilities to include research as a practice skill.

The book is divided into two main sections. In the first, consisting of Chapters 1 through 4, we consider relevance of research to social work practice, establish the need for critical thinking and epistemological skills by social work practitioners, and present ethical considerations.

The second set of chapters, 6 through 13, present and apply research methodologies as necessary practice skills. These methodology chapters follow the standard linear process of research texts yet through discussions and examples emphasize the use of research methodology in practice.

In this first chapter we established a foundation for understanding professions and science and the nature of research and knowledge development. We continue this discussion in the next chapter, focusing specifically on the social work profession's particular needs for knowledge. Chapter 3 extends examination of the profession with discussion of the connections among ethics, values, and research.

Theory building is the subject of Chapter 4, examining the construction of case theory and its relationship to intervention.

Chapter 5 offers an integrated model of research methods applied to the range of social work practice components, including relationship, communication, practitioner observation, and intervention.

The next eight chapters are methodological and cover measurement, data collection, design, single-case designs and practice plans, intervention control and measurement, sampling, analysis, and reporting. In the final chapter, 14, we illustrate practice using all the methodologies covered in the book.

## Discussion Questions and Exercises

1. In small groups of three, discuss professional occupations and how you distinguish them from other types of work. Why is research important to professions? to the sciences?

2. In ten written pages, identify the components of science and attributes of professions.

3. Compare and contrast the naturalist and positivist positions and evaluate their utility for professional practice.

4. Present the four sets of assumptions about reality. Identify the strengths and limitations of each in developing knowledge for professional practice.

5. In a class discussion, consider Gustafson's seminal article on professions (1982), highlighting the following passage:

   A *calling* without professionalization is bumbling, ineffective, and even dangerous. A profession without a calling, however, has no taps of moral rootage" and cannot "envision the larger ends and purposes of human good that our individual efforts can serve." For Gustafson, professions "exist to serve human needs. Needs do not exist to serve the interests of a profession." (p. 514)

   Discuss the bases on which professions practice, including state laws of licensure, professional certification procedures, agency function, and professional mission.

# CHAPTER TWO

# Social Work and Knowledge Development

The social work profession has unique needs for specific kinds of knowledge, theory, and practice interventions. We present here the vast domain of social work and argue for approaches to knowledge building that better fit the extraordinary breadth and depth of its professional practice. In discussing differences between doctoral research courses and those in practice degree programs, we review social work education and the purpose of social work. We consider the challenges to traditional means of knowledge development and the contributions to social work knowledge from the social sciences and humanities.

## Purpose of Social Work

All professions focus on changing some small piece of the world. Medical workers seek alleviation of illness and acquisition of health, teachers strive to turn ignorance into knowledge, social workers improve social functioning. Though disputes continue among both academics and practicing social workers about the relative worth of individual change versus social reform, all can agree that *change in social systems* is the goal of social work. Whether attention is directed to individuals, families, groups, communities, organizations, or policies, social workers intervene to create change among these systems to improve problems in social function-

ing, target services to the poor and oppressed, and enhance social justice.

Beginning with the friendly visitors and settlement house workers during the late 19th and early 20th centuries, social workers have intervened to create multilevel change. Individuals, families, small groups, and communities are targets of change as well as organizations, policies, and programs. Depending on their chosen specialization, social workers may do social casework where their thrust is on change of individuals, or they may practice family therapy, group work, community organization, or program planning and policy development. Tied together by the social work mission to improve social functioning, to "help individuals navigate through their society, and to help society provide resources to its citizens" (Bisman, 1994, p. 11), social work practice attends both to individuals and to the larger society.

Sharing a core framework of person and environment, emphasis differs depending on the chosen specialization. For social casework, according to Bisman (1994), "Person and environment means the consideration of individuals within context of the community and its resources, societal policies and regulations and the service delivery of the organization" (p. 27). Yet individual change cannot be achieved without considering community resources, organizational service delivery, and policies. Likewise, effective community organizers must be attentive to problems and needs of those individuals residing within the community as well as to organizational service delivery and policy regulations.

While the framework and mission are clear, specificity of interventions and goals are not. Dependent upon values, culture, and current mores, definitions of good social functioning vary. The goals and even the substantive areas of social work intervention reflect changing norms, agency function, and individual preferences. During the early years of the profession, for example, normative roles for women were wife and mother. Divorce was not common, abortion was illegal, and women were to stay home to care for children and keep house. Towards the end of the 1990s, many women work outside the home, divorce rates are stabilizing, and while states differ in their abortion regulations, the Supreme Court decision in the mid 1990s reaffirms a woman's right to choose.

Yet because of continuing societal dissension about abortion, some social service agencies do not present it as an option while others specifically offer abortion with other family planning services. New divisions arise in the debate about welfare versus work. The worth of child care by mothers is questioned if it comes at taxpayers' expense, and good day care services remain limited. Social work practice with women, children, and families continues to reflect changing roles of women, work, and welfare.

## Social Work Curriculum

Social work programs at the doctoral level educate future scholars and educators of the profession. Emphasis is on research, knowledge of theories and theorists, and expertise in a specialized area of inquiry. Covered as a domain of the profession, practice is discussed in terms of theories and effectiveness of intervention; advanced practice skills are not included in most traditional social work doctorates. Instead, students learn to design and conduct research, add to knowledge and theory development, shape policies and im-

plement programs, and improve practice effectiveness. Ongoing intellectual development of the profession is the responsibility of doctoral education. Critical analysis is taught to enhance conceptual abilities for teaching, writing, and researching the profession's principles and skills.

At the BSW and MSW levels, conversely, the primary objective is educating practitioners. Foundation courses emphasize general knowledge. Responding to the broad domain encompassed by social functioning, the four foundation areas for BSW and MSW degrees include human development, social policy, research and practice. Electives develop expertise in practice specializations by provision of information about particular populations such as practice with children and adolescents, or fields of practice such as mental health and child welfare.

Reflecting like most professions the need for a wide range of knowledge, social work depends on a range of sciences. Medicine, upon which social work has modeled itself, draws from anatomy, physiology, chemistry, and biology; engineers utilize knowledge from geology, physics, and quantum mechanics.

Courses on human behavior within the social environment cover theorists and theories from psychology and sociology. These provide a theoretical foundation to understand individual and community development, basing interventions on normative theories of individual, group, and social behavior.

Social policy courses present history, basics of the social welfare system, and policy analysis for students to connect policies, programs, and individuals. Here they learn legislative specifics, advocacy, and a history of social welfare.

Research classes include statistics (sometimes a requirement of admission) and research design. Teaching research methodologies is intended to help students learn to critically read research efforts and wisely choose from research to inform their practice. As discussed throughout this book, we argue for changing the current model and present research here as a central ingredient of practice.

Reflecting the function of the BSW and MSW degrees to teach practice to students, the greatest proportion of required courses are those in practice. A minimum of four semesters is standard, usually consisting of two semesters in foundation followed by two semesters of concentration either in clinical practice or in program development, planning, administration, or community practice. Foundation practice courses offer variations on the basic components of relationship, assessment, communication methods and skills, practitioner observation, intervention, and evaluation (Bisman, 1994). Socialization into the profession is achieved through discussion of social work values and code of ethics and presentation of diversity issues, including differences in class, gender, race, ethnicity, sexual orientation.

Elective courses provide specialization in the student's chosen area of practice. Casework students might enroll in courses of family therapy or practice with children, while those in community practice would tend to take courses in advocacy and fundraising.

Doctoral students learn to conduct research, whereas master's students acquire skills to intervene with clients. The profession's terminal practice degree is the master's, while (just as for most disciplines) the terminal degree for research and scholarship is the Ph.D.

Courses in each of these degree programs should reflect differences in program objectives, and, for the most part, this is the case. Behavioral and social science courses at the doctoral level emphasize critical and conceptual analysis and construction along with development of theories. Doctoral students acquire the ability to contribute to the existing literature. Emphasis for master's students, however, is on acquiring the skills that allow them to base practice decisions on theoretical knowledge. Master's students learn theories so that their assessments and interventions are informed and shaped by tested interventions.

Research courses, however, do not meet the degree objectives for master's students. Instead of focusing on practice and evaluating the validity and effectiveness of interventions, master's

research content often appears as something watered down from the doctoral level. In her survey of schools of social work, Dinerman found that the first curriculum objective for research was to make students "intelligent consumers of research" (Dunlap, 1993, p. 298). But the objective for master's students is not to conduct research projects, or to merely be consumers, but rather to use research thinking and skills in practice. For this, they need research methods and skills directly tied to their practice, including the populations and problems they confront. The profession, however, has not developed the kind of research needed by practitioners. Reflecting the position of scientism, in which achieving science is considered a justifiable end, social work researchers have traditionally focused on research *qua* research, and their interest in practice was purely its contribution to research. Research became the end, rather than a means to an end.

## Knowledge Development

A primary goal of social work research is the fostering of successful social work interventions. To accomplish this goal, *research must relate directly to the needs of its field of inquiry*. For social work, those needs reflect many aspects of the human condition.

### Social Work Knowledge

Social workers address the complexities of behavior at the level of individuals, communities, and societies. As we have just discussed, in merely two years social work curriculum at the master's level covers a vastly broad domain, including social and behavioral theory; policy; practice with individuals, families, groups, communities, and organizations; and research. In addition to this foundation, students acquire specialization around a particular population, such as the elderly, or problem, such as substance abuse. Justification for such breadth of curriculum is that the social work domain of social functioning demands an array and range of knowledge and skills.

*Just as social science cannot be the only source of knowledge for practicing social work, it is also insufficient as the means of researching the practice.* Using only one social science model as the research base of social work is not realistic and hinders the development of useful and relevant knowledge.

We should keep in mind the relative newness of the social sciences. As Dorothy Ross (1991) points out, although John Adams used the label as early as 1785, it was not until the 19th century that a proliferation of disciplines, including sociology, political science, and economics, addressed issues of society, previously covered only by philosophers. During medieval times Christian explanations for historical events centered on divine action or random variations. With modernity, intellectual inquiry broadened to include a contextual view of world events, combined with making all things rationally understood through the scientific method. Though replacing divine laws, the laws of science continued the search for uniformity and predictability.

Because they were modeled on the natural sciences, the social sciences made use of the same deterministic principles of the scientific method, predominantly used with disciplines such as physics and chemistry. The task of inquiry was to unfold these principles. The world existed in some finite ways, and science would uncover and explain them.

As we discussed in the first chapter, since the 1960s postmodernists have questioned the validity and relevance of this method throughout the humanities, social and natural sciences, and professions. Debate about the nature of social work knowledge began in earnest during the early 1980s with publication of Fischer's presentation of Kuhn's paradigms (1981). Eloquent appeals by scholars like Gordon (1959, 1983) have called for closer examination of social work practice, questioned the narrow definition of what is empirical, and advocated that "research enterprises …contribute to the understanding of practice issues" (Fanshel, 1980).

Researchers and practitioners are obligated to work together to develop the knowledge that directly relates to the needs of professional practice. Time and talent that could be better spent relating research methodologies to needs of the field is wasted on an interminable dialogue between academic researchers. Similarly, divisions among practitioners about the nature of social work practice leaves little time for concern about questions of effectiveness. Their drift toward practicing therapy with the "worried well" and abandonment of traditional social work fields like child welfare (Specht, 1994) has not fostered the building of linkages between practice and research.

## Multiple Methods, Sources, and Traditions

Following our position established in Chapter 1, we argue that *a single limited approach to knowledge development is inadequate to the breadth of the social work domain.*

A historical perspective is necessary to understand effects of oppression and learn from previous failures to ameliorate poverty. Literature enhances compassion and sensitivity just as study of the English language gives social workers writing skills. Philosophy teaches logical rigor while philosophy of science presents epistemology and questions relevant to the development of knowledge. Ethnography, a well-respected field of study for anthropologists, has much to offer social work research, as does closer study of practitioners to better understand the art of practice. Communication, the sending and receiving of messages, is central to understanding human interaction. Sociology, already well represented in social work curriculum, provides information about behavior of individuals in groups and communities.

We now briefly explore these disciplines for their relevance to social work practice and knowledge building, comparing social work to other professions such as law and medicine. It is very important for social workers to recognize that they are not alone in their struggle for relevant sources and types of knowledge. All disciplines and professions are facing challenges to the assumptions of modernity. Most utilize multiple methodologies to knowledge development, while some have been more successful than others in integrating divergent traditions.

## English and Literature

To maintain agency records and reports and to present assessments and intervention plans, social workers need *writing skills*. Knowledge of grammatical rules, spelling, and styles of written communication enables practitioners to present their information in a format understandable to others. Poor writing not only can result in dismissive reactions to the written report, but can generalize to the writer, agency, and profession.

Social workers rely heavily on written communication to identify the roles they performed and outcomes that were achieved and to explain the nature of their clients' problems. Lacking the laboratory report format of medicine or the achievement tests used by teachers, one of the primary tools social workers have is the narrative and case summary information. Here again, we turn to language skills and literature as sources and models of good storytelling.

James Baldwin's *Notes of a Native Son*, originally published in 1955, continues to capture the feelings of Americans from African descent. A recent selection of Baldwin's essays, novels, and short stories is edited by Toni Morrison (1998).

We can learn much from good fiction and nonfiction about universals of the human condition. Social workers need knowledge and understanding of the human spirit with its heights and depths, foibles and wonders. We argue that works by D. H. Lawrence, William Faulkner, or Nadine Gordtimer offer us greater insights and explanations for human behavior than many texts in the behavioral and social sciences. For example, consider how enlightening it is to distinguish between the homelessness depicted in the novel *The Grapes of Wrath* by John Steinbeck (1939) and in *Travels with Lizbeth*, a memoir by Lars Eighner (1993). Appreciating the differ-

ences in the social work role with Eighner (homeless and traveling with his dog, Lizbeth) during the 1990s from a hypothetical practice with the Joads in the 1930s also encourages appreciation of how social context shapes practice. At the same time, we can recognize the consistency and relevance of the basic practice components, including relationship, assessment, and the ethical code. Or consider the poignant memoir by Sidney Winawer, a gastroenterologist specializing in cancer, of his wife dying from intestinal cancer (1998). Another memoir, postumous by Gale Warner, beautifully details her courage in facing both life and death (1998).

Another example comes from Karen, a social worker who works in child welfare.

．．．．．．．．．．．．．．．．．．．．．．

*When Karen was in her child welfare practicum and MSW practice classes she read Toni Morrison's **The Bluest Eye** (1970). The very poignant portrayal of violence in the home and powerful affects of racism forcefully shaped Karen's comprehension of parental abuse, sexual abuse, and societal oppression. She is able to draw from both the compassion and horror depicted in the book for sustaining her commitment to help families and children in her role as child welfare social worker.*

*Karen credits Morrison for helping to shape her orientation as a social worker with commitment to serve oppressed and vulnerable populations. More recently she read Richard Powers's new novel, **Gain,** a compelling narrative detailing the frightening connections of a corporation's growth and the deteriorating health of a family exposed to its chemicals. She tries to live her life by ideas articulated in Ibsen's play, **An Enemy of the People.** Ibsen has the main character, Peter Stockmann, stand alone for his principles, risking great harm to himself and his family. Ibsen's plays often address struggles between the individual and the society. Karen is White, grew up in poverty, and tries to consider both issues of class and race. She knows that to be an effective social worker she must take a stand and believe that she can make a difference. In personal and professional interactions Karen* *speaks out against injustice. Through regular reading of fiction and non-fiction that address issues of class, race, poverty, and oppression Karen enriches her performance as a social worker.*

• • • • • • • • • • • • • • • • • • •

Even the humanities have not escaped the modernist/postmodernist debates. Just as for other disciplines, there are divisions among academics about the proper study of literature. Literary analysis that emphasizes structure and meaning is being supplanted by the postmodernists' concern with intention and context. Literature departments in colleges and universities reflect these differences, along with lack of agreement about assigned readings and required texts. Concern for cultural diversity has broadened the range of literature read by undergraduate students. While the University of Chicago still emphasizes Western civilization, many other prestigious universities no longer require immersion in the great books of a single culture through reading Shakespeare, Milton, T. S. Eliot, or Dickens.

These different perspectives are tolerated together in some departments, while others employ only one methodology in the study of literature. For our purposes, we ask that social workers be aware of the wide-ranging questioning now taking place into the proper mode and object of inquiry. Those who teach and study language skills also struggle with integrating different perspectives about the nature and purpose of their discipline's inquiry and presenting good writing that is relevant to daily life. In *Doubletake*, a new magazine, the editors attempt to find a bond between social concern and everyday life through special photographic features, inclusion of fiction and non-fiction works, and coordination with books and films.

## Historical Inquiry

As members of a professional occupation, social workers need *historical perspective* about their profession and the types of problems their predecessors confronted. To redress oppression and

poverty and achieve social justice, social workers require a knowledge of history. This includes specific instances of these themes in other periods of time and past successes in achieving the goal of social justice.

Likewise, to address social reform, social workers need information about previous policies and regulations, ones that worked and why, effective strategies in implementing new policies, and successes and failures of social movements.

In formulating assessments, social workers gather historical information. This may include data about past events in the lives of individuals and communities or about the evolution of policies. Social workers then engage in *historical narrative* as they construct case theory about client systems or develop case studies to better understand passage of legislation and the construction of social problems.

Some practitioners press for detailed historical information as a necessary aspect of family treatment.

• • • • • • • • • • • • • • • • • • •

*Concerned about the multiple generations of families she sees in child welfare, the social worker Karen regularly uses genograms, a tool developed by Bowen (1978) to portray family patterns across several generations. Engaging Sharra (an 18-year-old mother of her 9-month-old daughter, Trish) in drawing a genogram covering three generations, they both clearly see patterns of young single motherhood, severe parental abuse and neglect, sexual abuse and substance abuse, and unemployment. Utilizing this graphic chart to highlight the persistence of these problems for Sharra's family in the past and present, Karen motivates Sharra to consider different choices beneficial for both herself and her daughter.*

*The historical perspective is not deterministic, but rather a tool for better understanding one's present condition in order to more purposefully create new and better options in the future.*

• • • • • • • • • • • • • • • • • • •

Facing problems similar to those of social work in knowledge development, historians struggle with interpretation, biases and distortions, communication, categorizing, generalization, seeking patterns and understanding. Often lacking definitive proof about the accuracy of the information they obtain and their interpretation of it, historians acknowledge that determining the significance of the information and articulating guiding principles are ultimately issues of judgment.

In the classic treatise on historical inquiry, Strayer (1943) states:

> History, at least in its final stages, is more of an art than a science, and historians, like artists, have seldom been able to describe their work in purely intellectual terms. In both cases there is a belief that a certain arrangement of carefully selected facts will illustrate some aspect of universal truth, and a feeling that this belief can never be fully justified by purely rational arguments. (pp. 3–4)

Accumulating and connecting facts to discern patterns, according to Strayer, requires that the historian "must be accurate and honest…possess sympathy, imagination, and understanding" (pp. 16). Also like social workers, historians require certain traits and modes of education. Specific solutions are not taught; rather, study and reflection are emphasized to develop balance and proportion with skills of judgment and writing. Unlike the world of mathematical formulas, historians conduct their work on real life as perceived by ordinary individuals.

> Barzun (1943) affirms that historical observation differs…from the mathematico-physical reasoning we in this century are most inclined to admire. The historian indeed is *no* more a scientist than the navigator or the doctor. His historical reason, like their diagnostic power, is part subjective and part hypothetical, but its results are nonetheless tangible and true. (p. 51)

Both history and social work require systematic and critical approaches to inquiry, but historians more readily accept, perhaps even relish, their need for an approach to knowledge development that uniquely fits historical inquiry. Schlesinger explains that "there has always been a gap between practicing historians and philosophers of history" (1996, A 31).

Social workers need to draw from historical works to better understand the societal conditions they address in practice. For example, a book by Spiegel (1996) on slavery, racism, and animalization raises disturbing questions germane for all social workers practicing with diverse populations. At the same time social work professionals can learn from the historian's approach to knowledge development and reporting.

## Anthropology

Anthropology, like history, studies people and life events, but instead of solely the past it focuses on living cultures both past and present. Since culture includes beliefs, traditions, and behavior patterns of a group's way of life, anthropological inquiry must obtain information directly from individual members of the group under study.

Social workers use the same term for their internships—*fieldwork,*—that anthropologists use to describe their approach to study. Anthropologists engage in fieldwork by going to where people live and asking them questions about their daily living patterns while observing their eating, interacting, play, and work. Fieldwork results in an *ethnography,* the goal of which, according to Malinowski (1922), is "to grasp the native's point of view, his relation to life, to realize his vision of his world" (p. 25).

Because culture is a paradigm that is inferred, not observed directly, anthropologists have developed systematic means to conduct ethnographic interviews, including achieving language competence, engaging with informants (local residents who teach the ethnographer), observing actors (those observed), holding to ethical principles to protect informants' rights and privacy, and using systematic approaches to reporting the information.

Many of these terms that anthropologists use to describe their domain—interviewing, observation, narrative communication, engagement, ethical principles, reporting information—apply also to social work. To obtain rich narratives of the culture under study, anthropologists ask descriptive questions to expand their knowledge. Expecting their written reports to communicate meanings of the culture to those unfamiliar with it, anthropologists view themselves as translators. Emphasizing steps in writing the ethnography, they teach skills of participant observation—their strategy for listening to people and watching them in natural settings (Spradley, 1979).

Social workers also learn communication methods and skills for asking questions and have designed formats for their assessment reports and plans of intervention. Continually revised codes of ethics establish principles to guide practice behaviors, including informed consent and respect of privacy. Practitioner observation is the strategy used by social workers to address bias in understanding and reporting (Bisman, 1994).

Methodological and analytical problems exist in anthropology. Is it really possible to understand a culture highly distinct from one's own, and determine the effects of biases on findings? Can the ethnography written in a different language from that of the culture studied fairly capture the nuances of that culture? Is there a changeless essence of a people, or is this an illusion?

At the same time, subdisciplines within anthropology tackle a range of questions. Some cultural anthropologists believe that nurture rather than nature explains differences among persons, and, just like DNA, creates the tissues of living bodies (Rosaldo, 1989). Spiro (1987), on the other hand, supports a psychic unity as the basis of transcultural understanding.

•  •  •  •  •  •  •  •  •  •  •  •  •  •  •  •  •  •  •

*Karen, the social worker in child welfare we discussed earlier, is aware that biases may affect her understanding of Sharra's mothering and that it may not be possible to really understand the patterns in Sharra's family history. Nevertheless, she formulates her case theory and plans her intervention seeking to balance the weight of both environ-*

*mental and biological explanations for behaviors in this family.*

*She visits families in their home, observing their interactions and living conditions. Karen also explores the neighborhood, determining community resources and safety, while meeting extended members of the family.*

•  •  •  •  •  •  •  •  •  •  •  •  •  •  •  •  •  •  •  •

Just like anthropologists, social workers study cultures, employ some methods similar to those in anthropology, and attempt to answer questions about "how they know what they know." These questions about methodology and epistemology lie at the heart of this book as we come to see that social work shares problems with the humanities and social sciences.

## Philosophy

The nature/nurture debate was resolved by Noam Chomsky, a philosopher and radical political theorist (1968), in opposition to some of the cultural anthropologists, on the side of nature. Believing that humans are distinguished by a primal grammar, Chomsky posits an innate linguistic ability. Other philosophers, such as Derrida (1977), emphasize meaning and context in language.

Teaching the generation, interpretation, and logic of ideas, philosophy considers the major questions of humans and their existence and analyzes these fundamental questions. Philosophers have long pondered many of the issues now addressed by the social and physical sciences. In the 19th and 20th centuries, linguistics, psychology, and philosophy separated as disciplines. Yet recent advances in understanding the brain and thought processes have once again linked them, now with the fields of physiology and neuroscience.

Philosophy focuses on thought and abstractions, while social work addresses living in the real world. Yet even this oldest discipline incorporates differing perspectives on the development of knowledge and theoretical perspectives of reality. Some philosophers are positivists, trained in the analytical tradition, and stress logic and the scientific method. Others address issues of aesthetics and ethics, while the French tradition is postmodern.

In *Truth and Progress: Philosophical Papers, Vol. 3*, Richard Rorty (1998) discusses many of the themes we emphasize. He criticizes the search for truth, presses for moral progress through expansion of stories and human interaction, and encourages use of imagination and creativity in the advancement of knowledge.

Philosophers utilize a range of methods to further develop their complex domain—the foundation of knowledge. Questions raised by philosophers are also of interest to social workers—the meaning of living well in society, the nature of knowledge, ethics and values and their relation to individuals and societies.

## Communication Theory

As a separate field of inquiry, communication is relatively recent, beginning in the late 1940s and early 1950s with the work of Deutsch (1952), Bateson (1972), and Birdwhistell (1973). Prompted by social science inquiry into human interaction, these early theorists carved out a field concerned with individuals and information processing.

Birdwhistell (1973) defines communication as "a structural system of significant symbols (from all the sensorily based modalities) which permit ordered human interaction" (p. 95). For Birdwhistell, "a human being is not a black box with one orifice for emitting a chunk of stuff called *communication* and another for receiving it. And, at the same time, communication is not simply the sum of the bits of information which pass between two people in a given period of time" (p. 3). Miedaner (1981) says "communicating…is converting private ideas into the common currency of signs in patterns" (p. 107).

Communication consists equally of *process* and *content*. While structure is used to convey meaning, the meaning intended may not be the one received or even the one sent. Involving a system among persons that is not always acknowledged, feelings and experiences influence both the manner and content of communication, at times without the awareness of those engaged.

Judith Nelson (1980) developed a communications framework as a **metatheory** through which to translate practice theories and models. Considering communications theory to be similar to systems theory, she believed it provided social workers a means of organizing knowledge with relevance for micro and macro practice and social work research.

In social work practice (Bisman, 1994) communication methods and skills are the tools used to transmit information. While we discuss communication further in Chapter 5, here we present communication theory as one of the areas of inquiry relevant when we attempt to understand the complexity of social work practice. We are not dealing with chemical experiments in a lab, but rather the conveyance and receipt of information. *Different meanings attached to words, cross-cultural issues, and unintended messages sent through behaviors and bodily mannerisms all shape the management of that information.*

• • • • • • • • • • • • • • • • • • • • • •

*In another case example, Elana, a social worker in practice with Bill and Sharon, describes her frustration when working with a domestic violence case:*

*I used listening checks constantly with Bill and got back very little. It is difficult for me to talk with someone who can't find words. Though I'm good at reading others intuitively, I dare not misunderstand a client. I have to learn what Bill means. I suspect that he hit Sharon because he had difficulty describing in words his feelings to her.*

*He told me that the arrival of their baby changed everything in his relationship with Sharon, but has never discussed this with anyone. I have to model with him how to choose words to express his emotions, while also teaching him that he must use means other than striking to communicate.*

• • • • • • • • • • • • • • • • • • • • • •

We see in this example the centrality of communication in practice. It is not only the content or specific words that transpire between worker and client. The message or intent that shapes the content, the meaning or interpretation by participants may differ. Moreover, the mode of communication among family members may be responsible for the very patterns they are seeking to change.

Whether we agree with the postmodernists that reality is socially constructed, meaning is central to all knowledge, and existence involves communication—which is always an interaction.

## Symbolic Interactionism

For some, interaction is primary. According to Blumer (1969), *human interaction does not merely express human conduct, but is a process that forms it.* While the world consists of objects—things that are either physical, social, or abstract—the meaning of things is a function of interaction. A social creation, interaction is learned and transmitted through a social process.

In Blumer's model, humans are acting organisms and possess a "self," an object to which they attribute meaning, attributions, and definitions of symbols. Assigning the meaning in this indication of self, the individual is not merely the mathematical product of forces, "not a mere responding organism but an acting organism—an organism that has to mold a line of action on the basis of what it takes into account instead of merely releasing a response to the play of some factor on its organization" (p. 15).

**Symbolic interaction** involves *interpretation*, or ascertaining the meaning of actions of the other person, and *definition*, or conveying indications to another person about how to act. Participants fit their own acts to the ongoing acts of others, and guide one another through this process (Blumer, 1969, p. 66).

The symbolic interaction model rests on the following three premises: (1) humans act toward things on the basis of the meanings that the things have for them; (2) the meaning of such things is derived from the social interactions they have with their fellows; and (3) these meanings are handled in, and modified through, interpretive processes they use in dealing with the things encountered. *It is not the things themselves, but the meaning of the things, that is important and constitutes reality:* "The meanings that things have for human beings are central in their own right"(p. 3).

The association of people with one another is a process in which they interpret each other's indications and assess the situations confronting them. Interlinkages of acts that comprise organizations, institutions, divisions of labor, and networks of interdependency are moving and not static affairs (p. 50).

In contrast to Chomsky's views about language, symbolic interactionists such as Blumer believe individuals interpret instead of merely responding based on their native capacities. A person "has to construct and guide his action instead of merely releasing it in response to factors playing on him or operating through him. He may do a miserable job in constructing his action, but he has to construct it" (p. 15).

Likewise, in the creation of norms and values, though the result of social interaction, they are also used by the individual to construct meaning. "It is the social process in group life that creates and upholds the rules, not the rules that create and uphold group life" (p. 19). If they are not used, the rules are meaningless.

Blumer is critical of the role of empirical science in positivism. He believes that empiricism means to look at the world as the world sees itself, but that much laboratory social and behavior science research is not a true "look at the world" (pp. 22–23). For Blumer, research methodology should be self-evident and not mystified in extreme and obscure scientism, statistical quantification, and mathematical rationalism that loses meaning and makes results—or knowledge—irrelevant because it has no meaning to the real world. Blumer does not reject prior theory, but rather requires it (p. 24); the theory or "picture," however, is tested in terms of how it fits the world. Concept formation is critical, and concepts need clarity, not the commonly used ambiguous ideas. Concepts are the constructions of research to understand the world, but they are not synonymous with the world (p. 150). It is the concepts, the ideas with their linkage to empirical indicators and referents, that move philosophy into becoming science.

We share Blumer's understanding of concepts, and it is the framework through which we present theory building in later chapters (see Chapter 4). The issues raised by Blumer relate to practice as well as research about practice. Behavior is generally the result of a highly complex set of things, not the relationship of a few "variables," no matter how sophisticated the analytical model. It is our task to understand the meaning for all participants. While things exist, the construction and meaning of the whole is a social expression and must receive attention along with examination of the things.

· · · · · · · · · · · · · · · · · · · · · · ·

*Consider again Elana's practice. While she needs to help Bill change his specific behaviors of striking Sharon, she also needs to consider with them their dynamics as a family. This includes not just what the striking means to each of them, but the norms for behavior in each of their families of origin and the rules followed by family members. Moreover, social norms continue to change. By the mid 1990s many no longer considered it macho for a husband to strike his wife, but rather an act of weakness or even cowardice.*

*In working with clients, Elana **must be aware of the meaning they attach to events, attend to the content of behaviors and give equal attention to the meaning of those behaviors to the clients, and to the larger society.***

· · · · · · · · · · · · · · · · · · · · · · ·

Elana needs to understand the meaning of the interactions to Bill and Sharon in order to understand and help them alter their behavior. Vigilante (1993) elaborates on the relevance of symbolic interactionism or constructionism in social work practice, assuming that systematic

data gathering cannot accurately reflect the complexities of human functioning. For her, the client and worker continually frame and reframe the client's story until coherent and shared meanings are achieved (p. 184). Greene and Saltman (1994) agree and argue that social workers cannot formulate assessments without attention to meaning.

## Legal Education

Law schools are also now questioning the appropriate content for their students. Some wish to emphasize traditional legal knowledge, while others want courses in economics to better cover relationships between businesses, and language and literature skills to teach writing and the universal conditions of humans. Turow (1988) and others criticize lawyers' lack of preparation to practice with clients, which some law schools do not respect and barely cover.

Preparation in most law schools remains the **Socratic method,** based on a set of assumptions that law is a special sort of reason known only to lawyers. Socrates believed in natural law (something discovered rather than created) that students should learn through the case method, reasoning via analogy. This case model approach emphasizes acquisition of a particular approach to the law, including a set of legal materials and vocabulary.

Though acknowledging the value of this immersion in judicial opinions, Posner (1990) criticizes the lack of analytic training. In his view, the case study approach, in which students learn to "think like a lawyer," overemphasizes specific practice cases and neglects larger philosophical questions about the nature of the law and methods of reasoning.

For Posner, lawyers need to learn about communication, meaning, and interpretation and to understand the impact of mores and politics on the law. While we earlier acknowledged that these areas are also important in social work education, there are further similarities. Both professions struggle in balancing the case study approach to teaching practice with developing specific knowledge and skills, and both lack clarity about the consequences of professional decisions. A fundamental question for each profession, law and social work, concerns the nature of the enterprise: Is there a set of natural laws (about the law or about social functioning) that can be observed and learned, or is the subject matter ever-changing and therefore ill served by training that overly emphasizes the formal and scientific aspects of professional practice?

In his treatise about how professionals think in action, Schon (1983) stresses the importance of **tacit knowledge**—the spontaneous, intuitive, or unconscious basis for professional behaviors. Posner (1990) affirms that "tacit knowledge is important in legal reasoning" (p. 109), while Schon states that "knowing is *in* our action" and is the basis of professional day-to-day decisions (p. 49).

• • • • • • • • • • • • • • • • • • •

*As we saw earlier, the social worker Elana was able to intuit things about Bill prior to his telling and before she articulated them. Schon believes that professional practitioners also engage in a process of reflection-in-action, the thinking on one's feet needed when confronting unique client situations. Experienced practitioners like Elana may reflect-in-practice, basing practice decisions partly on previous experiences while remaining attentive to the unique and present circumstances of the current client. This is the art of practice, relevant for all professional occupations.*

• • • • • • • • • • • • • • • • • • •

## The Medical Profession

Some consider physicians to be scientists. Yet even though they learn the scientific method, many physicians condemn it as reductionist and too narrow in scope, neglecting relevant factors more readily observed by some of the holistic, alternative approaches to medicine. In some medical schools little attention is paid to values and the art of medical practice. Informed by

dramatic advances in technology, medical education is still based on the teachings of Flexner who stressed lectures, memorization, and laboratory study with a split between academic work and clinical training.

This same Flexner has continued to influence social work education. Instead of being one approach among many, his became the only model. Responding to his 1915 critique that social work lacked methodology, Mary Richmond and others in the Charity Organization Societies attempted to make social work scientific and developed social diagnosis as its unique method. As Richmond (1917) stated:

> Social evidence, like that sought by the scientist or historian, includes all items which, however trifling or apparently irrelevant when regarded as isolated facts, may, when taken together, throw light upon the question at issue; namely as regards social work, the question what course of procedure will place this client in his right relation to society? (p. 39)

Interestingly, though Richmond compared social workers to both historians and scientists, it was the scientists who came to represent the ideal, and science that social work borrowed from and continues to use as a model for practice and knowledge development.

The medical profession also struggles with linking research and practice. "Evidence-based medicine" relies on data bases of treatments that were helpful to large groups of patients. Proponents of this new approach to decision making believe it will assist physicians to rely less on familiar methods and their own habitual behaviors, and more on empirical evidence. Critics worry that the emphasis on statistics will impede physicians' ability to treat the individual patient under their care. As Dr. Sandra Tanenbaum states "I don't understand how you can use probabilistic thinking when you are working on one patient at a time" (Zuger, 1997, C 1, 7).

While we all value the knowledge obtained by physicians through memorization, most of us have experienced problems when doctors do not look at the "whole person." Sole trust in laboratory tests can often ignore significant factors about bodily functioning. Good physicians have easy access to their tacit knowledge and rely on a range of methods for their professional judgments. Like social workers, they rely on historical data and information about functioning. Yet issues of meaning and communication are central to accurate diagnoses. Just like the results of blood work and cat scans, eliciting valid information about a patient's feelings, experiences, and behaviors will influence effective treatment.

## Other Disciplines

We tend to see art and science as separate and distinct endeavors, yet, as we have seen, art is present in professional practice, and systematic rules exist in various art forms. Painters know how to achieve effects of light by shading, composers need knowledge of musical notes, and singers learn how to capture particular sounds through control of their vocal cords. Moreover, different fields encounter challenges to their ways of knowing. Batchen (1997) argues that early photographers were deconstructing reality and representation, illustrating their false dichotomy. This is in opposition to the modernists' position that photography is an imprint of nature, and to the post modernists who see photography solely as a product of a changing culture. Lewis and Wigen (1997) point to the biases of mapmakers and replace "continents" with the concept of "world regions" for less distorted and more respectful diagramming and labeling.

We have reviewed only some disciplines and professions for similarities and contrasts with social work. Many others are also highly relevant. Economics is increasingly offered in social work curriculum. Biological explanations for behavior and pharmacological treatments are basic in many social work cases, as we illustrate in examples covered in later chapters.

Work in the sociology of knowledge directly fits with the symbolic interactionists and the postmodern perspectives from other disciplines.

Berger (1966) presents reality as a social construction, with a dialectic between social reality and individual existence. He argues that in dealing with issues of people, sociology is humanistic and "must be carried on in a continuous conversation with both history and philosophy or lose its proper object of history" (189). The same may be said of social work.

## Summary

Social work shares with other disciplines and professions confusions about the best approach to knowledge development and the types of knowledge needed. To practice successfully, social workers follow the scientific method but not a limited view of science. At the same time that they establish a historical perspective in data collection and assessment formation, they challenge the meaning they ascribe to events, producing a rich understanding of individuals within communities. Social work draws from a liberal arts and humanities perspective with compassion and respect for others, sensitivity to cultural differences, tolerance for different ideas, openness to different lifestyles, and use of multiple theories to explain social behavior. It is a social and moral profession.

Limitations exist in reducing phenomena to simple explanations, a fact not recognized by those favoring a single social science model (Fischer, 1981; Briar, 1990). Bernard (1994) indicates that the scientific method is barely 400 years old and has been applied to human behavior for only 150 years, with social work barely 100 years in existence. Yet some researchers in social work, through narrowly defining what constitutes creditable research and rejecting other models of discovery consider this the only valid way of knowing. Process has been ignored for a solely linear approach and empiricism has been defined narrowly to mean one approach to knowledge generation.

As in other professions, the domain of social work is the real world. It is not possible to practice or do research or scholarly inquiry in social work and not be immersed in the empirical world. These difficulties are readily acknowledged by some in the hard sciences, such as Gould in biology and noted physicist Mitchell Feigenbaum, who states: "I truly do want to know how to describe clouds. But to say there's a piece over here with that much density, and next to it a piece with this much density—to accumulate that much detailed information, I think is wrong.... Somewhere the business of writing down partial differential equations is not to have done the work on the problem" (Gleick, 1987, p. 187).

We agree with Blumer (1969). All social sciences represent a construction and hence an ideology. In addition to the ambiguities of morality, meaning is critical in the social sciences. Meaning is a social product, arising in the process of interaction between people. At the same time, without some degree of determinism, there is little reason for intervention. In order to be professionals, we have to assume that interventions will do some good and are not merely part of a random cluster of behavior. Berlin (1990) rightly argues that dichotomous thinking about complex phenomena leads to replacing one pole for another. We need to reconceptualize social work knowledge and reach beyond an incorporation of the positivists and the naturalists.

Accompanying the vast technological advances in such areas as global communication via the Internet, human organ transplants, and observing locations in the brain that control emotions is an emphasis on multidisciplinary study. Social work must recognize that it cannot keep pace with the changing world by holding to only one or even two models for developing social work knowledge.

## Discussion Questions and Exercises

1. In small groups of three, differentiate the three degree programs in social work. What is the purpose of research in each of these programs? In what ways is it important, or not, for you as a practitioner to conduct research?

2. How will you as a practitioner develop and use knowledge in your practice?

3. Compare the role and methods of social workers to those of historians and anthropologists.

4. What is the role of communication in social work?

5. Compare the professions of law, medicine, and social work, considering their balance of art and science.

6. Discuss the major tenets of symbolic interactionism. What are Blumer's concerns about empiricism? Where would you place Blumer in the four models of reality discussed in Chapter 1?

### For a writing assignment:

7. In ten pages, trace some of the debates about knowledge development in the humanities and the natural and social sciences. How has the social work profession responded to these trends?

8. Choose a work of fiction that you have not read (consider any of the authors mentioned in this chapter or discuss with your professor). In a 10 page paper, identify problems in functioning and examine contributions a social worker could offer.

# CHAPTER THREE

# Social Work Ethics, Practice, and Research

Professions maintain the social order through reflecting and teaching societal values and norms while also serving to ameliorate certain ills. The social work domain of social justice, improving social functioning, and furthering the social welfare is value based and driven, requiring those who practice to continually address questions of morals, values, and the nature of objectivity.

Social work practice focuses on "doing good" in a world filled with good and evil, interacting with enigmatic individuals, turbulent communities, chaotic organizations, and changing policies. As we have discussed, the primary focus of professions, including social work, is not defining and explaining, which are the objectives of the social sciences (Durkheim, 1938), but maintaining and changing (Horton, 1966). *Professional practice derives from normative or moral theory* and "deals with moral values and social norms, with conduct that is socially good, obligatory, and normal, or that is bad, offensive, and deviant" (Siporin, 1975, p. 64).

Values are institutionalized through **social norms,** the rules and criteria we use to decide on behaviors of ourselves and others (Blake & Davis, 1964). As the basis for social rules, they guide us to socially acceptable actions, sanctioned by society. Violation of norms, behavior labeled *deviant,* can result in various forms of punishment including isolation, imprisonment and, in some U.S. states, the death penalty. Social

norms do not usually result from a participatory decision-making process; rather, they evolve from values. Yet sharing the same value will not necessarily produce the same behavior. For example, the broad value of respecting the dignity and worth of individuals may be used by both opponents and proponents of abortion, by those advocating that women stay home to raise their children as well as by those pushing for women to work outside the home.

Different interpretations of the primacy of the individual result in particular policies and services. Concern in the 1960s with creating equal opportunities and access to resources led to a myriad of antipoverty programs and affirmative action laws. However, emphasis in the late 1990s on less government intrusion in the lives of individuals thrust the United States into more restrictive services, with attention to cost and elimination of some affirmative action regulations.

## Morality as a Foundation

McCormick (1961) explains that people's social functioning is a response to social values within social relationships, while Frankel (1966) further emphasizes that the concept of welfare involves moral decisions and cannot be morally neutral. Warnock (1971) conceives of morality as contributing to the betterment of the human predicament through extending sympathetic perspectives. Promoting the betterment of society, especially social functioning and social relationships, is Rescher's (1972) definition of social welfare.

Upholding belief systems and values orientations, with a mission to change the moral behavior of individuals and society, *social workers cannot practice without continual attention to issues of right and wrong.*

Mead (1930) believes that social workers serve as moral agents and in that role develop a service orientation to those they are helping. Implicit in the social work helping process is appeal to an ideal social structure and criticism of conditions responsible for the suffering. Gustafson (1982) points to the centrality of morality to professional practice. "A profession without a calling…has no taps of moral and humane rootage to keep human sensitivities and sensibilities alert" (p. 514).

Rawls presents a theory of justice (1971) based on natural rights, and Witkin (1998a, b) contends that human rights are inseparable from social work theory and practice. Leiby (1985) argues that morality provides a firmer basis for social work decisions and a more solid justification for social services than natural or legal rights. Yet in recent decades social workers have shied away from using morality as a basis for their profession, arguing from a politically liberal position that it is the responsibility of government to protect the natural rights of its citizens.

Nevertheless, the most compelling case for more equal access to and availability of resources, especially for the poor and those excluded through prejudice and discrimination, is that *it is the right thing to do.* Accompanying our individualistic ethos are societal values for compassion and generosity. Emphasizing that rights bring responsibilities shifts focus to strength of community, a social work value not commonly articulated. With erosion of the legal basis through the 1996 welfare reform legislation and

growth in conservative political philosophies, only the moral argument remains.

Social work is a **normative profession,** motivated by its values. Perhaps as Reamer (1995a) asserts, it is the most normative of professions in that "social work's mission has been anchored primarily, although not exclusively, by conceptions of what is just and unjust and by a collective belief about what individuals in a society have a right to and owe to one another" (p. 5).

Goals of social work practice include the *creation of a common good* and *social justice.* Bellah and colleagues (1991) consider whether American institutions reflect a good society, while Etzioni presents his communitarian vision of shared community responsibility (1993).

These are not new themes for social workers who simultaneously address needs of individuals and problems in society. Pioneers in the profession were concerned with issues of social interdependence and responsibility, as well as social ethics. As the forerunners of social casework, the Charity Organization Societies (COS) followed the tradition of religious charity. Conceiving their role as that of helping individuals become self-sufficient, they believed this in turn would strengthen communities. For them, community meant "a group of people held together by sentiments of personal and social responsibility" (Leiby, 1984, p. 527). Personal responsibility in this context meant persons helping themselves or others, while social responsibility was help offered by family, neighbors, or community leaders.

Though they placed greater emphasis on the responsibility of society through legislation and services, settlement house workers shared with COS workers an interest in creating a good society. Best epitomized by Jane Addams (1902), they concentrated on integrating immigrants and improving social conditions—on both "democracy and social ethics."

**Altruism** is attending unselfishly to the welfare of others. Though social workers, like all professionals, receive remuneration for their services, their code of ethics requires that they base decisions to provide services on client needs, not on agency needs for funds. Facing increasing conflicts with changes to a managed care payment approach for services, the social work code of ethics nevertheless places primacy on clients' needs for services over reimbursement.

As we discussed earlier, all professional occupations share a commitment to service and altruism. *Social work, perhaps more than other professions, deals directly with values and morality,* imbued as it is with concerns for welfare, issues of well-being and caring for individuals and societies. Cohen (1958) went so far as to describe social work as "humanitarianism in search of a method" (p. 3).

• • • • • • • • • • • • • • • • • • • •

*As we learned about the social worker Karen in chapter 2, her commitment to social justice and righting inequities is central to her orientation as a social worker. Drawn to social work because of its* **person and environment** *perspective, Karen is acutely aware that the problem of individuals and families cannot be understood out of context of the immediate neighborhood, extended family, social supports, community resources, and the services delivered by the agency. She is focused on helping her families and the children, while also improving the society where the families live.*

• • • • • • • • • • • • • • • • • • • •

Ricoeur (1987) states that "morality has to be prescriptive and not merely evaluative" (p. 106). This is evident in practice decisions. In removing children from abusive homes, for example, the value of protecting children from abuse supersedes the rights of parents. A community's norms, along with state and county regulations that emerge from those norms and values, influence judgments about preserving biological families versus foster care placement or termination of parental rights.

While social work strives for the common good, agreement is lacking about what constitutes a good community. Most persons would not disagree that responsible communities consist of responsible individuals or that in moral communities there is love, duty, caring, and sharing. Specificity is much more difficult and will vary at different times. In the 1960s, responsible communities meant, for some, the provision of finances and services to those not able to care for themselves. This period saw the initiation of antipoverty programs, with federal government responsibility for maintenance of income levels, health care, and access to resources. During the late 1990s, responsibility is on states and local charities, with greater emphasis on individuals and family. These beliefs resulted in welfare reform with strict time limitations for receipt of welfare, cutbacks in health care funding, and increasing disparity in access to resources for the poor versus the well-off.

## Relationship of Knowledge and Values

As Gordon (1965) insists, there is a distinction between values and knowledge "what social work wants for people (values) and what it knows about them (knowledge) (p. 54). Not only do *preferences* affect what we will do about what we know, but *values* may also shape what we know. This outcomes occurs in very basic ways by influencing funding and research or, as the social constructionists claim, by controlling the primary discourse. Even more fundamentally, values shape people's lives and the kinds of problems people have in functioning—changing women's roles affect family life, which in turn creates workplace needs for services such as homes for the elderly and day care. Demands follow for knowledge to understand, explain, prevent, and treat these problems and to develop relevant and effective services and treatments.

### Values

Values are defined as "those enduring beliefs we hold about what is to be preferred as good and right in our conduct and in our existence as human beings" (Lewis, 1982, p. 12). They refer to goals that benefit individuals and the collective. In her search for a common base to the social work profession, Bartlett (1970) explains that values "refer to what is good and desirable. These are qualitative judgments; they are not empirically demonstrable. They are invested with emotion and represent a purpose or goal toward which the social worker's action will be directed" (p. 63).

Values "are generalized, emotionally charged conceptions of what is desirable; historically created and derived from experience; shared by a population or group within it; and they provide the means for organizing and structuring patterns of behavior" (Reamer, 1995a, p. 11). Values motivate behavior, and should direct the nature of social work's mission, the relationships, obligations, and duties social workers have for clients, colleagues, and the broader community. Along with technical and research-based knowledge, the profession's ethics provide criteria for selecting actions and making judgments regarding intervention methods.

As we emphasize throughout this book, intervention is not totally a matter of empirical science, nor is the social work profession merely an amalgamation of technology. The profession and its interventions should reflect a set of coherent values capturing the service orientation.

Social work's basic value configuration is the result of many forces and orientations that shaped and continue to influence the profession. Reamer (1993, pp. 18–20) and others (Gustafson, 1977; Lubove, 1977; Spano, 1982; Wenocur & Reisch, 1989) offer some adjectives describing the orientations and forces buffeting the profession and forging its values, including: paternalistic, social justice, religious, clinical, defensive (protecting the profession and the professional from attacks by the radical political left and right), and amoralistic (contemporary forces and growing "scientism" that reject a strong value base of normative concepts and emphasize technical and "scientific" knowledge as the exclusive guide to intervention).

Social work values derived from these orientations (Levy, 1976; Reamer, 1979, 1993) include some configuration of the following:

1. The dignity and worth of the individual is the primary concern of society; individuals have a right to privacy and to be secure in themselves.
2. Individuals and groups in a society are interdependent.
3. All people have social responsibility for one another.
4. While each person is unique, people also share common attributes.
5. Society is responsible for removing obstacles and assisting individuals in reaching their full potential.

While these values are at variance with the currently prevailing political culture, they remain nevertheless the profession's values.

## Ethics

Values are general and abstract, whereas ethics are rules of conduct that direct behavior. While still general, ethical codes provide means to enact the more overarching values. Ethics rest on, but are not themselves, values. Professional (Drucker, 1974, pp. 368–369) and research (Bailey, 1996, p. 13) ethics rest on the imperative "First do no harm." Drucker (1974) argues

"Above all, not knowingly do harm." No professional…can promise that he will indeed do good for his client. All he can do is try. But he can promise he will not knowingly do harm. And the client, in turn, must be able to trust the professional to not knowingly do him harm. Otherwise he cannot trust him at all. And *Primum non nocere*, "not knowingly to do harm," is the basic rule of professional ethics, the basic rule of ethics of public responsibility. (pp. 368–369)

Professionals have a *fiduciary relationship* (Kutchins, 1991) with clients and research subjects. Clients have the right to expect professional competence—that the professional possesses current and valid knowledge and skills necessary to intervene in client's problems, recognizes limitations, and *primum non nocere*—"Above all, not knowingly do harm."

Although the National Association of Social Workers (NASW) holds that its code of ethics "does not represent a set of rules that will prescribe all the behaviors of social workers in all the complexities of professional life" (NASW, n.d., p. v), ethics are generally viewed as prescriptions for professional standards used to guide professional behavior. Ethics deal with right and wrong, good and bad in a moral sense (Reamer, 1993, p. 42; 1982, pp. 27, 31) and provide the basis for defining professionally appropriate and inappropriate behavior (Lewis, 1982, p. 83). Without the capacity to guide and judge appropriateness of behavior, ethics are meaningless. A profession's ethics are usually codified in its code of ethics.

## The Profession's Code of Ethics

There are many codes of ethics from the various societies for social workers, including those from the Clinical Society, the National Association for Black Social Workers, and the National Association of Jewish Social Workers. Knowledge of the code from NASW, the largest association of professional social workers, is the responsibility of all practitioners, students, and educators. We focus on the NASW code in the remainder of this chapter because it is the one often used by state licensure boards. Code standards specify obligations to clients, the profession, colleagues, and the community. Professions continually evaluate and revise their codes to stay relevant with changing norms and values. In 1996, after years of work, NASW agreed on major revisions for its social work code of ethics.

The NASW Code of Ethics (1996) serves six purposes:

1. Identify core values on which the mission is based.

2. Summarize broad ethical principles that reflect the profession's core values and establish *a set of specific ethical standards that should be used to guide social work practice* [emphasis ours].

3. Help social workers identify relevant issues when professional obligations conflict or ethical uncertainties arise.

4. *Provide ethical standards that the general public can use to hold the social work profession accountable* [emphasis ours] (an essential feature of a profession is its willingness to regulate itself and to establish standards by which the public can judge its performance).

5. Socialize new practitioners to the profession's mission, values, and ethical principles and standards.

6. Articulate standards that the profession can use to assess the ethical and unethical behaviors of its professionals. (p. 2)

NASW's ethical standards argue against an unambiguous set of rules that prescribe how social workers should act in all situations. Rather, specific application of the code must take into account the context in which it is considered and the possibility of conflicts among the code's values, principles, and standards. Ethical responsibilities flow from all human relationships—from the personal and familial to the social and the professional (NASW, 1996, p. 3). While the primary obligation remains service to clients, this obligation is weakened by placing public law over professional ethics.

Growing out of values are the practice requisites of confidentiality in communication and respect for the individual's privacy; commitment to create change; separation of personal feelings from professional obligations; belief in and respect for the dignity of each individual and social grouping; self-determination and empowerment; commitment to social justice and the social and economic well-being of all members of society; the physical, emotional, and mental health of all people; and commitment to professional standards of behavior to promote these ends and create opportunities for all people. The value configurations result in social work's "simultaneous commitment to individual well-being and to the welfare of broader society" (Reamer, 1993, p. 27). This commitment is an obligation for the profession and for each individual professional, regardless of practice or field of service specialization.

Values are translated to behavior by ethical standards, represented by ethical codes. The ethics may be deontological or utilitarian. **Deontological ethics** emphasize the inherent goodness of an action. The assumption is that they cannot be superseded by a utilitarian good. **Utilitarian** and **teleological ethics,** on the other hand, are based on whether the consequences of the ethical behavior will produce a future good. If the consequences are good, then the behavior is justified as ethical.

The NASW Code of Ethics rests its over 125 specific ethical statements of standards on six value statements and ethical principles:

> Value: Service; Ethical Principle: Social worker's primary goal is to help people in need and to address social problems.
> Value: Social Justice; Ethical Principle: Social workers challenge social injustice.
> Value: Dignity and Worth of the Person; Ethical Principle: Social workers respect the inherent dignity and worth of the person.
> Value: Importance of Human Relationships; Ethical Principle: Social workers recognize the central importance of human relationships.
> Value: Integrity; Ethical Principle: Social workers behave in a trustworthy manner.
> Value: Competence; Ethical Principle: Social workers practice within their areas of competence and develop and enhance their professional expertise. (pp. 5–6)

Contrary to NASW's position that ethics are relative, in our view ethical codes cannot be too relativistic and ambiguous if they are to have any meaning in guiding professional behavior and holding the profession accountable. Ethical guidelines serve as substitutes for the individual

professional's morality and judgments of virtue. As such, ethical codes need to be approached with a degree of firmness. We should not justify codes exclusively on a utilitarian and teleological basis because, as we will see, there may be little such evidence supporting the profession's most cardinal ethics.

## Shared Ethics of Research and Practice

As part of their fiduciary responsibility, social work practice and research share the two cardinal ethics of **informed consent** and **confidentiality.**

### Informed Consent

Informed consent is fundamental to the values of client self-determination and client empowerment. An ignorant client is neither empowered or capable of self-determination. NASW's Code of Ethics (1996) states that:

> Social workers should provide services to clients only in the context of a professional relationship based, when appropriate, on valid informed consent for services delivered to them. Social workers should use clear and understandable language to inform clients of the purpose of the services, risks related to the services, limits to services because of the requirements of a third party payer, relevant costs, reasonable alternatives, clients' right to refuse or withdraw consent, and the time frame covered by the consent. Social workers should provide clients with an opportunity to ask questions. (p. 7, 1.03)

In five subsequent sections the code elaborates the informed consent requirements for clients not literate, those with communication difficulties, involuntary clients, and the use of electronic media.

Requirements for informed consent exist in every practice situation. Involuntary clients have the right to informed consent including information about the ramifications of not participating in the intervention. Limitations on confidentiality and duty to warn are included in the information provided to clients to obtain informed consent. Obtaining true consent is possible only after the client is fully informed.

### Guidelines for practice and research

Social research is equally rigorous with informed consent of subjects (Bailey, 1996). *Just as*

#### Fully Informed Consent Check Sheet

*Clients have been provided with the following in a manner understandable to them:*

| Item | Yes | No |
|---|---|---|
| 1. Correct descriptions of the accuracy in assessment or diagnosis methods. | | |
| 2. Sound estimates of the likely success of recommended procedures. | | |
| 3. Descriptions of alternative methods and their likely success. | | |
| 4. Explanations of the time, cost, risk, and effort in the proposed interventions. | | |
| 5. Likelihood of positive and negative side effects of the intervention plan. | | |
| 6. Truthful information about any helper's (social worker and others) competencies to offer services of the intervention plan. | | |
| 7. Absence of coercion or undue influence. | | |
| 8. Information provided in writing. | | |
| 9. Arrangements made to involve the appropriate guardians to obtain informed consent using the above guidelines when the client cannot emotionally, intellectually, and legally provide informed consent. | | |

Adapted from Gibbs & Gambrill (1996, p. 190); Reamer (1994, pp. 71–79).

*covert practice interventions should be limited, if not prohibited,* the requirement for informed consent in research limits covert research. **Covert research** occurs when subjects do not know they are research subjects and/or the nature of the research. **Covert practice and intervention** occurs when the clients either do not know they are clients and/or the intervention's nature, risks, and benefits.

Not all covert research is prohibited, nor is informed consent always required (Bulmer, 1982). Observational research involving truly public behavior of subjects, such as in public meetings, may not require informed consent. Protection of human subjects from detrimental repercussions of the research, however, is always required.

Continuing issues include: Is informed consent necessary when personal life events are analyzed? When does the inclusion of others in the analysis extend it beyond the personal? Other, more marginally acceptable covert research efforts include bogus commitments to mental hospitals and experiential studies of service delivery systems with pseudo and real patients. Generally, however, covert research or use of deception in practice violates informed consent and the subject's or client's privacy. Questions about discarding informed consent, ethical behavior, and the rights of subjects and clients include: Who decides, and at what point does the need for and importance of the research or intervention supersede these rights and principles? In the research enterprise it is generally not a decision of an individual researcher but requires peer and ethics panel preview.

We believe social work practice needs a similar review protocol to emphasize the importance of this ethic and help practitioners with difficult decisions. Currently, it is too common for social work practitioners to espouse this ethic in principle only. Violations occur even in very basic behaviors such as failure to introduce oneself as a student or to explain the reason for obtaining family background information. Clients who see social workers are often involuntary or incapacitated through physical or mental illness, yet they should not lose their right to informed consent.

The Department of Health and Human Services' National Commission for the Protection of Human Subjects (Mark, 1996) hold that informed consent is the core of research ethics and the essence of truly voluntary participation in research. Informed consent requires three conditions:

1. Competence of research subjects to give informed consent
2. Provision of information by researchers that is understandable to the subjects so that their participation is truly informed.
3. The individual's consent to participate is truly voluntary[1] (p. 41)

Guidelines for informed consent in research resemble those required for practice. They generally include the following specifications, which state that subjects must be told

1. That they are participating in research, the purpose of the research, the procedures that will be followed, what is expected of them, and an estimate of the amount of their time required.
2. About any possible risks to them or discomfort that they may experience. Risks and discomfort include physical, psychological, and social.
3. Of any physical, psychological, and social benefits to them or to society that may result from the research.
4. About alternative procedures or treatments that may be beneficial to them.
5. How confidentiality will be protected, whether subjects are anonymous, and limits to confidentiality.
6. Of contact people, procedures available to them for answering questions, including any they may have after their participation is completed.

7. That participation is voluntary, that they can withdraw at any time without consequences or what the consequences of withdrawal will mean to them, and that refusal or withdrawal will not affect any other benefits to which they are entitled.
8. Of any possible compensations or treatments to cover risks that they may be exposed to and how the compensations and treatments can be obtained. (Bailey, 1996, p. 11; Mark, 1996, p. 41)

· · · · · · · · · · · · · · · · · · · ·

*Consider Elana's practice from Chapter 2. In contracting with Bill and Sharon to engage in a therapeutic process, Elana should inform them about different approaches used with domestic violence. These might include meeting with them as a unit or individually, bringing in extended family members, obtaining extensive family background, and contracting about specific behavior changes.*

*Constructing the genogram (a tool for family assessment) should involve all of them in this family project and directly link the family to Elana's ideas about the nature of their problems. Moreover, she must discuss possible outcomes of the treatment, including their marital breakup, continuation and escalation of the abusive behaviors, or a marital relationship free of physical abuse.*

· · · · · · · · · · · · · · · · · · · ·

## Confidentiality

Confidentiality is another principal ethic of social work practice and research. Derived from the values of self-determination, respect for the individual, and the individual's privacy rights confidentiality rests on four premises: (1) human autonomy regarding personal information, (2) respect for relationship, (3) respect for promises, and (4) benefits to society and those in need of advice and aid (Bok, 1982; Rhodes, 1991).

The 1996 NASW Code of Ethics has eighteen sections related to confidentiality and its limits:

Social workers should respect clients' rights to privacy. Social workers should not solicit pri-

---

[1]Does the payment of money to poor subjects for their participation in medical research have ethical implications for informed consent and truly voluntary participation?

vate information from clients unless it is essential to providing services or conducting social work evaluation or research. Once private information is shared, standards of confidentiality apply. (pp. 10–12, 1.07)

Agencies, law enforcement officials, and often a range of participants in a client's social network may have the legal and ethical right to acquire client information and communications. Social workers need to distinguish and understand the difference between *privileged communication*, a legal right afforded to clients to limit disclosures of possibly damaging information in court proceedings, and *confidentiality*, an ethical responsibility of the professional imposed by the profession.

Social workers argue on utilitarian grounds that confidentiality is necessary so that clients will impart personal information essential for the intervention's success. But "no one has established (1) that confidentiality is essential to effective therapy or (2) that restricting confidentiality decreases the benefits of therapy" (Rhodes, 1991, p. 64). Better, more defensible justifications for professional confidentiality and client privileged communication are (1) legal protection of clients from self-incrimination and the need for self-protection, (2) client autonomy, and (3) a person's right to privacy.

The utilitarian argument is dangerous because it rests on an assumption, as yet untested, that confidentiality and privacy are necessary and contribute to better practice outcomes, or a better quality of information from the client. If confidentiality does not contribute to better outcomes based on better information, a utilitarian argument supports discarding confidentiality.

### Guidelines for practice and research

The utilitarian teleological arguments, including violating confidentiality when it will produce a greater good, such as social protection and the protection of others inherent in the duty to warn, should not rest on utilitarian grounds but on deontological grounds—that is, that people have a right to be secure from harm from others. If a cli-

ent represents a threat to a person's right, then the duty to warn (discussed next) comes into play because the client is affecting the autonomy and rights of another person. An individual's right to basic well-being takes precedence over another individual's right (the client), to self-determination. If clients, however, are a threat to themselves in their own behavior, and are rational—recognizing and understanding the threat posed by the behavior—should confidentiality and client privilege communication be violated? Why is client autonomy and self-determination violated because the professional disagrees with the decision?

Reamer (1995a) argues that an individual's right to self-determination takes precedence over his or her own right to basic well-being (p. 61). Is self-destructive behavior permissible as long as the individual is truly informed and the actions voluntary? The "greater good" basis of the utilitarian argument begs who decides and how it is decided that a greater good is being served, and that confidentiality be discarded if no utility or benefit is gained from it. However, as Rawls asserts, certain deontological ethics based on the individual's autonomy and right to privacy, such as informed consent and confidentiality, should have "an inviolability founded on justice that even the welfare of society as a whole cannot override" (Selznick, 1996, p. 15).

In any case, the practitioner must make clear to the client *any legal, social, agency, and ethical limitations to confidentiality and the client's privileged communication* in the informed consent process. Some factors that inhibit confidentiality are:

1. Any limits imposed by the theoretical model of intervention, such as involvement of family members.
2. Limits brought about by age and competency of the client.
3. Operating procedures of the agency, such as a "team approach" and supervisory and administrative oversight.
4. Depending on the agency's rules (or funder's rules), whether the information is the property

of the agency and available on the need to know basis and who and how "need to know" is defined and determined.

5. Legal reporting and duty to warn and protect requirements.

Ethics regarding confidentiality are again more rigorous in social research than practice. The American Sociological Association requires that researchers maintain confidentiality *even when the information obtained from respondents enjoys no legal protection or privilege and legal force is applied to extract the information from the researcher* (Bailey, 1996, p. 17).

The Department of Health and Human Services research confidentiality guidelines require that

1. All information on individual participants is kept confidential unless the participant has given written permission to reveal such information.
2. Research should solicit and record only personal information that is necessary for the study to achieve its purposes.
3. All personal information should be secure and available on a need-to-know basis only to researchers.
4. Individual names and identifiers, the ability to link data to a person by name, is limited and used only when absolutely necessary, and is deleted as soon as feasible.
5. Available data, unless in the public domain, should be treated like originally collected data. Data should be destroyed when no longer needed. (Mark, 1996, p. 48)

Part of the issue of revealing confidential communication of clients in practice and subjects in research, according to Bailey (1996, p. 19), involves the power of those doing the harm versus those being harmed, the power of those whose privileged communication is limited or violated and the power of those to whom it is revealed. Research subjects and practice clients need to know the limits to confidentiality and their power prior to giving informed con-

sent, even if the knowledge of their limited privilege in communication keeps them from revealing important information. If subjects and clients are truly informed of the limits to the privilege and to whom the communication will be revealed, and if in that revelation the subject or client might be harmed, it can be reasonably argued that the client has consented, given permission, to breach confidentiality. However, the client has to be truly informed prior to any communication.

• • • • • • • • • • • • • • • • • • • •

*Let us return to Karen, the child welfare worker we discussed in Chapter 2. Respectful of both the professional relationship with Sharra and Sharra's right to privacy, Karen is aware of the many times she has had to testify in court about parental abuse. Accordingly, Karen introduces the concept of confidentiality very early in building the relationship. Informing Sharra that she respects her autonomy and right to privacy, Karen also explains Sharra's responsibility for the welfare of 9-month-old Trish. Karen explains limits to the confidentiality in their discussions (incidents or reports of abuse) and possible consequences of abusing Trish (court hearings, removal of Trish from Sharra's custody, or even termination of Sharra's parental rights). This is not only good practice, enabling quick development of goals to improve parenting, but also illustrates practice that includes informed consent, confidentiality, and duty to protect.*

• • • • • • • • • • • • • • • • • • • •

## Duty to Warn and Protect

Under current ethical and legal restraints, confidentiality in practice is balanced with the duty to protect and warn. The revised *NASW Code of Ethics* (1996) has fairly explicit language on the duty to warn, which is presented first as commitment to clients:

Social workers' primary responsibility is to promote the well-being of clients. In general, clients' interests are primary. However, *social* workers' responsibility to the larger society or specific legal obligations may on limited occasions supersede the loyalty owed clients and clients should be so advised. (Examples include when a social worker is required to report that a client has abused a child or threatened to harm self or others.) [emphasis added] (p. 7, 1.01)

The code follows with self-determination:

Social workers respect and promote the rights of clients to self-determination and assist clients in their efforts to identify and clarify their goals. Social workers may limit clients' right to self-determination when, in their professional judgment, clients' actions or potential actions pose a serious, foreseeable, and imminent risk to themselves or others. (p. 7, 1.02)

Social work practice frequently involves cases of potential harm, including child, spousal, and elder abuse. Case law has protected duty to warn over privileged communication (*Tarasoff v. Regents of the University of California*).

### Guidelines for practice and research

The practicing social worker is then faced with the task of *balancing confidentiality with the duty to warn*. If the social worker leans too far in one direction, there is possible liability for violating a client's right to privacy. But leaning too far in the other direction—of providing confidentiality—may place others at risk, with the social worker liable for violating the ethical codes and legal statutes. We appear to have a dilemma, but Reamer (1994, pp. 41–42; 1995a, p. 159) provides guidance in suggesting that social workers must have evidence of foreseeable, impending, and imminent violence.

In addition to knowing their jurisdiction's specific duty to warn and protect statutes, social workers *must practice within the bounds of the profession's Code of Ethics, be able to defend any assessment and intervention as reasonable and competent, and provide informed consent to clients.* Clients and the public have the right to expect this fiduciary responsibility from professionals. Knowledge of agency and state rules and regulations is essential to ethical practice and research.

· · · · · · · · · · · · · · · · · · · ·

*Continuing with our example of Karen's practice, should she deem Trish at imminent danger, Karen is responsible to immediately obtain court approval and coordinate with local police and other authorities to protect Trish from harm. Likewise, if Elana should consider Sharon in danger from abuse by Bill, her obligation is to warn Sharon. Elana must also attend to the safety of their baby, Matthew, age, 1 year.*

*Informing both Sharon, Bill and Sharra of these principles at the beginning of their professional relationship will not only provide them with informed consent, but will also allow for practice respectful of their privacy.*

· · · · · · · · · · · · · · · · · · · ·

## Evaluation and Research

There are also specific standards in the 1996 Code that address a practitioner's obligations toward research and competency:

(a) Social workers should monitor and evaluate policies, the implementation of programs, and *practice interventions.* [emphasis added]

(b) Social workers should promote and facilitate evaluation and research in order to contribute to the development of knowledge.

(c) Social workers should critically examine and keep current with emerging knowledge relevant to social work and fully use evaluation and research evidence in their professional practice. (pp. 25–26, 5.02)

The remainder of section 5, items (d) through (o), address issues of informed consent, protection of subjects, confidentiality, support services for subjects, accurate reporting while protecting confidentiality, avoiding conflict of interest and dual relationships, and consultation with review boards.

Section (p) states:

> Social workers should educate themselves, their students, and colleagues about responsible research practices.

We presented the domain of professional social work practice in the first two chapters. In the NASW Code, section 2.10, items (a) and (b) require that social workers help colleagues develop appropriate competencies and report those who do not develop the competencies (1996, p. 18). Section 4.01 follows with competence requirements:

> (a) Social workers should accept responsibility or employment only on the basis of existing competencies or the intention to acquire the necessary competence.
>
> (b) Social workers should strive to become and remain proficient in professional practice and the performance of professional functions. Social workers should critically examine and keep current with emerging knowledge relevant to social work. Social workers should routinely review the professional literature and participate in continuing education relevant to social work practice and social work ethics.
>
> (c) Social workers should base practice on recognized knowledge, including empirically based knowledge, relevant to social work and social work ethics. (p. 22)

*Knowledge and research* are an important ethical standard. Social workers are held accountable for possessing the knowledge and competency necessary for correct diagnosis and treatment and for conducting their practice based on appropriate and relevant research.

## Liability and Ethical Behavior

*Ethical behavior is both a moral imperative and a legal obligation.* Ignoring ethical standards can place the social worker in legal jeopardy. Sexual impropriety is one of the most significant taboos of any professional behavior; it is also among the ethical standards most often violated. According

to Reamer's (1995b) data on malpractice claims for social workers insured by the NASW Insurance Trust, of the total dollar amount paid, 41.3% went to sexual impropriety claims, 19.5% to incorrect treatment, and 10.7% to client suicides. No other category accounted for more than 1% of claims paid (p. 598).

Practicing social workers must know the code of ethics and operate within its behavioral standards. Providing informed consent, adhering to the code of ethics, and engaging in competent practice are the basic protections from liability. Interventions should be based on established effectiveness, or the client should be advised about limitations of treatment effectiveness prior to consent. Any potential risks the client faces as a result of the social worker's intervention are the client's choice if informed consent is provided.

While practice should be based on research, practitioners should use caution in adopting the conclusions of a single research study. A single instance of "research" using a sample of convenience, with measurement problems and design weaknesses, may not represent more valid knowledge than practice wisdom and may be just as prone to deductive fallacies and errors of generalization.

An over-emphasis of weak research, endemic to the social sciences, is as ethically problematic as the exclusion of rigor in practice. All practice decisions call for triangulation along with multiple and independent measurements and judgments, cross-checking and verification, and using the breadth of the literature. We fully discuss these requirements in later chapters.

Reamer (1995a) offers a more formal and systematic process for ethical decision making including: identify the conflicts and those affected, consideration of possible courses of action and careful weighing of the reasons for and against each, consultation with colleagues, and documentation and monitoring of the decision (pp. 64–65).

Gibbs and Gambrill (1996) present guidelines for determining if the literature and practice trend is science, or represents fads, quackery, and psuedoscience. They emphasize the importance of close reading for vagueness, quick cures, promotion of dogma or cult worship, and the mixing of bona fide and bogus evidence to support a favored conclusion. (p. 21).

## Ethical Behavior in Research and Practice: The Basics

Schutt (1996) summarizes five basic and related ethical standards for both research and practice including: They should not harm clients, participation should be voluntary (where treatment is mandated clients have the right to refuse treatment and need to know the consequences of this decision), practitioners and researchers should clearly identify themselves, clients need to be aware of the uses of the information they share, and project and practice benefits should outweigh risks. (p. 59)

## Paradoxes in Practice

Many contradictions define professions. A paradox central to social work is its unusual position of seeking to change the very society which provides the sanction to practice. Identified by Porter Lee (1929) as function and cause, the profession struggles to balance protecting the practice of the profession in the larger society to assure social work jobs and continued professional viability, with its cause, as Richmond (1899) states, to "work with forces that make for progress...to forward the advance of the...common people" (p. 151).

With the thrust of social work to create change in the larger society and in the lives of individuals, social workers daily confront another paradox—reconciling the ethic of honoring clients' rights to make their own choices while also upholding the professional mission of change agent. Sanctioned by the larger society to control social problems such as child abuse and neglect, social workers are at the same time obligated to respect client self determination and autonomy.

Numerous public cases indicate problems in adhering equally to both of these commitments.

Consider practice with a client addicted to substances, or one with a suicidal plan, or a homeless person. Though most in the profession would argue that they value clients' freedom to choose, practitioners are also compelled to help these clients end the addiction, contract to not commit suicide, and insist that below a certain temperature the client move off the streets into a shelter (required through legislation in some counties, probably to both protect the individual from freezing as well as residents in the neighborhood from seeing the wrapped bundles lying on heating grates).

The domain of the profession lacks clear boundaries. To achieve its primary values of social justice, freedom from oppression, and opportunities for vulnerable populations requires economic justice and access to resources. The disparity of wealth is increasing in the late 1990's, raising serious concerns about the profession's chances of shaping a good society and achieving its values. These pressures demand knowledge of the profession's values and use of rigorous practice and research methodologies.

## Summary

The mission of social work is an ideal, not something attainable, but a vision to inspire and shape practice goals and interventions. We agree with Bartlett (1958) that ethics and values are not empirically demonstrable, yet they are integral to social work practice. What empirical test could measure the utility of client self-determination or the worth and dignity of each individual? This means that a basic aspect of social work is not understandable by scientific measurements. Rather, other means of analyses are necessary that provide understanding of the relevance and utility of ethics and values in social work practice. Research into social work practice is useless if it ignores the morality and ethics that is basic and inherent to the profession.

Social workers must be aware of their own personal values and those of their chosen profession. It is not unusual for professionals to find themselves facing value dilemmas. Physicians struggle with adhering to their value of restoring health while responding to family and individual requests for assisted suicide. While the 1997 Supreme Court decision seemingly resolved the issue, medical practitioners will continue making judgments for each of their patients. Recent changes place increasing pressure on many professional occupations. Funding sources influence research and determine the populations eligible for treatment. There are limits to truth, if truth exists, and professionals practice with complex human issues and, perhaps, irreconcilable value conflicts.

For social work, values that suffuse the profession's mission include social justice, equality, and self-actualization. In the most recent (1996) NASW Code of Ethics, the primary values are service, social justice, dignity and worth of the person, importance of human relationships, integrity, competence.

Without regular articulation of its value stance, the social work profession risks erosion of its public sanction. Social workers must regularly and openly acknowledge and articulate the profession's values of individual dignity and worth, mutual responsibility, freedom from oppression, interdependence, and social responsibility as its vision for a good society.

Although ethical standards guide behavior, they are often conflictual, requiring human judgment. For a full discussion, see Bisman (1994), where case examples illustrate the complexity of practicing with confidentiality, duty to warn, and informed consent. She juxtaposes the social worker's role as change agent with self-determination while also considering issues of organizational and professional loyalty.

In this chapter we defined and discussed norms, values, and ethics. With morality as the basis for intervening with the social welfare, we reviewed the social work code of ethics and ethical behavior for practice and research.

## Discussion Questions and Exercises

1. Explain the function of values and ethics in professional practice. Draw on examples from your practicum to illustrate practice and research consistent with the ethical principles of informed consent and confidentiality.

2. With the thrust of social work to create change in the larger society and in the lives of individuals, how does the social worker reconcile the ethic of honoring clients' rights to make their own choices and at the same time function as a change agent?

3. Discuss some of the basic paradoxes in the practice of social work. Consider how you will reconcile these contradictions in your professional role.

4. In groups of three, discuss cases from your practicum illustrating how evaluation and research contributes to the development of social work knowledge.

5. How might appropriate ethical behavior require the practice use of research epistemology and methodology?

6. Practice Case:

   *A social worker, Jim, had a client, Diane, age 23, who suffered from bulimia. Based on material Jim read positing a relationship between bulimia and incest, he asked the agency psychiatrist to administer sodium amytal. While under the effects of the bar-*

*biturate, Jim engaged in "memory recovery therapy" and Diane "recalled" sexual abuse from ages 3 until 16. On this basis he advised Diane that she was an incest victim and called the family in for a session, advising them of their need to engage in family treatment.*

a. Was Jim guilty of any ethical or other violations? Please present the areas of possible violation or why you believe Jim was not guilty of violations.

b. How might Jim have reduced any possible violations? Explain, drawing from the NASW Code of Ethics.

# CHAPTER FOUR

# Theory and Case Theory Construction

Social work practice involves developing, using, and testing theories. The core of practice, **case theory,** like all theory, is explanation of phenomena. Building case theory requires practitioner theory building abilities to form concepts, relate concepts into propositions, develop hypotheses, and organize these into a coherent whole.

From case theory's coherent explanation of the problematic situation comes specification of desired outcomes and selection of intervention strategies along with methods to change the condition. Case theory includes support for its explanations along with a foundation for why specific interventions will produce specific outcomes. *Including case background information and relevant professional literature, case theory presents a cogent understanding of the client.*

We know from earlier chapters that professionals need more than understanding to practice effectively. As change agents, they are responsible for altering some phenomena. Physicians diagnose from a range of symptoms to cure or ameliorate illness or reduce pain. Teachers partly base teaching/learning plans on their measures of students' cognitive capacities. Lawyers consult case law to determine strategies for resolution of clients' legal difficulties. *Social workers build case theory to plan and implement change,* whether to create a safe environment for an allegedly abused child, enhance community resources for substance abusers, or facilitate res-

idential treatment for former patients of psychiatric hospitals. In developing the case theory for a potentially abused child, the social worker gathers facts about the allegation. Based on this assessment, the intervention could follow many approaches, from permanent termination of parental rights, to temporary placement outside the home, to finding no abuse and closing the case.

In this chapter we discuss *paradigms* and theory with its relevant components followed by case theory building in social work practice, illustrating the relationship between case theory building and intervention.

## Paradigms

Paradigms are the preeminent level of theory building, the highest and most abstract composition of knowledge. They offer a consistent, though not rigid, means of defining, viewing, and understanding nature. In providing a way of looking at and studying the world, they let us form judgments about phenomena (see Figure 4.1). According to the philosopher of science Kuhn (1970), paradigms direct and organize the development and perception of truth, facts, and knowledge. In directing ways of finding out about nature, rules of particular paradigms limit our view of the world. Paradigms are the basic way we think,

**FIGURE 4.1** The Structure of Knowledge

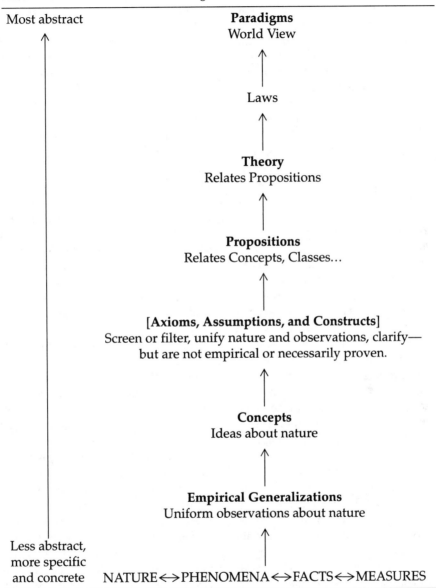

Most abstract

**Paradigms**
World View

Laws

**Theory**
Relates Propositions

**Propositions**
Relates Concepts, Classes…

**[Axioms, Assumptions, and Constructs]**
Screen or filter, unify nature and observations, clarify—
but are not empirical or necessarily proven.

**Concepts**
Ideas about nature

**Empirical Generalizations**
Uniform observations about nature

Less abstract,
more specific
and concrete   NATURE⟷PHENOMENA⟷FACTS⟷MEASURES

value, and do, associated with a specific picture of reality.

It is only when they are viewed through the ideological lens of the paradigm that theories developed by the paradigm's rules appear rea-sonable to the paradigm's adherent scientists, scholars, and other devotees. Paradigms and their resultant theories (including Freudianism, behaviorism, or Einstein's theory of relativity) represent certain idea sets, values, and the way things are and ought to be to their adherents. They may not appear particularly valid or reasonable to observers not following the paradigm's rules and ideology. Often paradigm disciples view other paradigms' research questions, methodologies, and theories as absurd.

An internally consistent set of values that forms a unity and shapes the definer's perception of the social condition, **ideology** goes beyond limited formal political beliefs to reflect a general sense of how the world ought to be. *Paradigms in science, like truth, are transient and evolving.* Paradigm shifts include changes in views of nature from Aristotle to Galileo to Newton to quantum mechanics.

*Paradigms and their inherent methodologies enable disciplines to make sense of and understand realities.* As Kuhn (1970) states, paradigms stand "for the entire constellation of beliefs, values, techniques, and so on shared by the members of a given community" (p. 144) in such a way that "a particular set of shared values interacts with the particular experiences shared by a community of specialists to ensure that most members of the group will ultimately find one set of arguments rather than another decisive" (p. 164). Through paradigms communities of scholars share a set of goals, control membership, and socialize new members with their exemplars for learning about nature.

Different paradigms lead to different questions yielding different facts, beliefs, truths, and views of the world and different answers. While each paradigm represents a unique and perhaps dramatically different view of the world and its phenomena, paradigms suggest particular research procedures and ways of knowing, specific research questions and methodologies, and the observations about nature used to develop theories.

As we discussed in the first two chapters, the social sciences and consequently social work, especially its academic arm, is engaged in a debate on an appropriate paradigm to view and understand nature. The two competing paradigms are *positivism* and *naturalism*. Positivism is also la-beled rational positivism, empiricism, objective-positivism, and logical positivism, among others. Other designations for naturalism are postpositivism, postmodernism, poststructuralism, heuristics, hermeneutics and humanism.

When positivists declared that social work entered a paradigm shift (Fischer, 1981), they were referring to a research method—namely, single subject design. Kuhn (1970), however, distinguished puzzle-solutions from rules and methods. The former, he said, are critical in providing exemplars for the community, especially important in the socialization of new members, and we believe it is here, in Kuhn's distinction, that some of the confusion evolved among social work academics. In his 1970 postscript, Kuhn discusses the controversies after his 1962 publication, clarifying that the search for rules is more difficult than agreement on a paradigm. He presses for dialogue among community members, especially important when entering any paradigm revolution.

But instead, there was a communication breakdown in social work requiring, according to Kuhn, that "participants...recognize each other as members of different language communities and then become translators...each will have learned to translate the other's theory and its consequences into his own language and simultaneously to describe in his language the world to which that theory applies" (Kuhn, p. 166).

In this book we function as those necessary translators, presenting some of the rules posed by the positivists within the social work paradigm of person-and-environment intervention, guided by the social work values of social justice and self-determination. In Chapter 2 we indicated that social workers, like other professionals, often do not share a similar method in the way of chemists or physicists, whose "communication is relatively full and professional judgment relatively unanimous" (Kuhn, p. 146), but they do adhere to a shared code of ethics and a set of values. Rather than continuing the debate about particular rules or methods, throughout this book we offer a translation of some of the positivist research tools into language understandable to practitioners. As we saw in Chapter 2, practitioners probably recognize themselves more readily as members of the naturalist tradition.

For the remainder of this chapter we focus on theory, the importance of practitioners' understanding of their role as knowledge builders, and their need to use theory for accurate practice interventions.

# Theory

Theory provides orderly explanations of the confusions in life experiences. In drawing patterns from observations to explain phenomena, different persons may explain the same events with a range of theories. The theory itself is not real but is rather the individual's attempt to explain real things.

Available technologies and contemporary ideologies influence theories. Contrast Hypocrites' description of the human body as containing humors of blood, phlegm, and bile to contemporary presentations of DNA, genes, and hormones. Or compare theories about depression from the 1970s with those in the 1990s. Freudianism dominated the 1970s, explaining depression as a primarily psychological phenomenon. In the 1990s, pharmacology is the mode and theorists view depression as a biochemical imbalance, while gene research offers new ways to understand and explain the etiology of what was once considered solely a "mental" disorder. We may expect more rapid shifts with increasing advances in technological knowledge. Our understanding of ulcers have changed in etiology from stress effects (again a mental explanation), to bacterial, to the more recent bodily susceptibility caused by stress-induced changes in body chemistry.

As constructions by individuals to order events, *theories offer logical conclusions based on presented relationships* (as we have said, Blumer [1969] has influenced our thinking about theory and theory construction). Other than final

proofs of logic and mathematics, which stem from stated premises and are not from or about the empirical world, theories do not offer universal laws but rather present different levels of abstractness. Yet some believe that even abstract mathematical concepts are based on human experience [Lakoff & Nunez, 1997]), and that mathematics is inseparable from culture (Rothstein, 1997).

*Grand theories* are not locked in time or place and explain many phenomena. Such theories include the Marxist theory of the evolution of economies and the state, and Max Weber's theory of bureaucracy. At the other end of the scale are *concrete case theories*. These are very specific to time and place and event, such as explanations for the case from Chapter 2 of Bill's abuse of his spouse, Sharon. *Middle-range theories* explain certain phenomena related to specific times and places.

Reflecting varying perspectives on the functions and types of knowledge that we discussed in Chapter 2, there are many definitions of theory. Barnum (1990) offers one of the least restrictive: "a statement that purports to account for or characterize some phenomenon" (p. 1). One of the more restrictive is Kerlinger's (1986): "a set of interrelated constructs (concepts), definitions, and propositions that present a systematic view of phenomenon by specifying relations among

## Levels of Theories

**Concrete case theories** explain one person's behavior at a particular time and place: *A practitioner's case theory explains Bill's abuse of his spouse, Sharon, today in their home.*

**Middle-range theories** explain a specific set of events, cases, and phenomena: *These theories explain behavior of alcoholic men who are unemployed and abuse their spouses.*

**Grand theories** explain all sets of events, cases, and phenomena: *Power theories, for example, are grand theories that explain abusive and exploitative behavior of superordinates over subordinates.*

variables, with the purpose of explaining and predicting the phenomena" (p. 9). Perhaps one of the more elegant definitions is by Karl Popper (1982) when he refers to "theories as human inventions—nets designed by us to catch the world" (p. 42) and admonishes us that "there is no absolute measure for the degree of approximation achieved—for the coarseness or fineness of the net" (p. 47).

We define **theory** here as *a set of propositions that explain and/or predict phenomena.* Theories are not inherently "real" or "hypothetical" but are constructions; their usefulness increases the more they can explain and predict. They are generally used to accomplish three goals, in order of complexity: (1) classification of things, as in typologies and taxonomies (what things go together; this level is generally necessary for the following two); (2) explanation to understand things (why things go together, or their relationships; and how they go together, or the nature of their relationships); and (3) prediction, influence, and control (what are the effects of one thing on another and how to use these effects to influence the second thing).

While this order of complexity is *hierarchical,* it is not *sequential.* Prediction is possible without explanation or much depth of understanding, though prediction possibilities increase with enhanced understanding. Even though social workers have traditionally sought understanding, they have much need for theories that offer prediction. Engaged as they are in intervention efforts aimed at change, the theories social workers utilize are most useful if they predict some outcome based on particular treatments.

As we discussed in Chapter 1, however, *prediction is extremely difficult for professionals.* Lacking universal truths, generalizations about groups of persons will not necessarily apply to a specific individual. Dubin (1978) posits the paradoxes of *precision* and *power* to frame the difficulties social scientists and professionals face. A theory narrow in scope can offer high precision, while broad theories are higher in explanatory power but lack ability to predict outcomes. Grand theo-

ries such as those that explain poverty or abuse are more abstract—we have lots of information, for example, explaining the risk factors of abuse, but we cannot precisely predict when or whether Bill will abuse Sharon. On the other hand, we have success applying certain techniques with persons experiencing panic disorders without understanding how or why.

In the practice of social work, moving from explanation to prediction requires moving from theorist to researcher, where testing determines accuracy of explanations. Those social workers who practice rarely see themselves as researchers. Yet it is this very combination that we advocate. *Research as practice allows social workers to establish theories for their practice, with greater opportunities for reliable explanation and prediction.*

## Propositions

Defined as statements about attributes of elements or relationships among elements and concepts of a theoretical model, the fundamental purpose of propositions is to enhance understanding about that theory's concepts. Theories are composed of propositions that can be laws, axioms, statements, definitions, or hypotheses. Propositions can relate two or more concepts, or traits or variables of two or more concepts, or traits or variables of a single concept. Implicit or explicit, their intent is the same—to explain the phenomena, or some aspect of relationships within the phenomena addressed by the theory. According to Reynolds (1971), propositions alone do not constitute a theory but must relate to the specific model from which they derive or which they explain.

Central to building and reviewing theory is clarity about its propositions. We formulate propositions from experience, empirical generalizations, impressions, and the literature.[1]

---

[1] The literature—scientific, professional, or otherwise—reflects its authors' ideas, impressions, and experiences.

An **existence proposition** simply states the existence of a phenomenon. Using social support as an example, an existence proposition is "There is a phenomenon of social support." **Definitional propositions** describe a phenomenon's characteristics. Again, examples about social support include "Social support involves a wide range of social interactions," or "resources provided by people with members of the support network providing tangible support and acceptance" (Cohen and Syme, 1985).

### Relational propositions

Relational propositions assert the association between concepts and may also indicate a causal connection, expressed by *if*/*then* statements. The *if* part of the statements are necessary for the *then* parts, and each proposition is logically related to the preceding proposition. Acceptance of the *if* part establishes the reasonableness of the *then* clause. Continuing with our concept of social support, the following is a statement of association: "Women who are abused by their spouses have low social support." In contrast, the following statement—"Extensive social supports by women decreases the likelihood of abuse by their spouses"—posits that one concept (social support) causes a change in the other (spousal abuse).

### Axioms and assumptions

Axioms and assumptions are propositions within theories that are *not verified and validated but are accepted without validation.* Serving a similar purpose, they are basic beliefs accepted without testing, used to fill empirical gaps, that give direction for the methodology and testing of the theory.

### Laws

Laws (Achienstein, 1971) are also propositions that generally are *not tested but accepted as fact.* Unlike other types of propositions laws are universal, inviolate truths, at least under specified conditions. Laws express regularities and uniformity, in a precise manner, with completeness, and with simplicity that allows quantification in concepts and relationships.

An example of a law is Newton's law of gravity, that bodies attract one another with a force directly proportional to their masses and indirectly proportional to the square of the distance between them. The social sciences have few, if any, laws, and some scientists believe the same is true for certain natural sciences. As the biologist Gould (1983) states: "'Fact' does not mean 'absolute certainty.' The final proofs of logic and mathematics flow deductively from stated premises and achieve certainty only because they are *not* about the empirical world" (p. 254). The domain of social work, like that of biology, is organisms, living and changing in the real world. These highly complex interactions will likely never lend themselves to laws.

### Empirical generalizations

Empirical generalizations are propositions about a class of units that describe the uniform occurrence and recurrence of two or more factors or facts about these units. Because they are empirical, they describe something that is constant and uniform about the phenomena and units but not why the uniformity occurs. The following statement is an empirical generalization: "Crime is higher in urban areas with lower per capita incomes than in those with higher per capita incomes." It states a regularity in the phenomenon but not why the regularity occurs. Along with an assertive generalization about empirical phenomena, we need additional propositions formed into a theory to explain the regularity.

### Hypotheses

Hypotheses are propositions derived from theory that are *capable of empirical testing but as yet are untested.* One function of research is to test and establish the validity of hypothetical propositions. It is possible to deduce hypotheses from theory or induce them from empirical generalizations and experiences. Their purpose is to extend the explanatory and / or predictive capacity of theory or to explain empirical generalizations and experiences. Once tested, if it is verified, the hypothetical proposition is incorporated into the body of the theory and becomes another theoretical proposition that expands the theory. If it is not verified, the hypothesis is rejected. *Practitioners base case plans on the hypothesis that their understanding of the case is accurate and that their selected interventions will produce a positive and predicted change.*

**Deduction.**   Either deduction or induction can be used to develop hypotheses from theory. Deduction is explanation from a general theory's propositions to a more specific application or case.

The reasonableness of the hypothesis, the deduction, depends on (1) the validity, or truthfulness, of the general theoretical propositions from which the hypothesis was deduced; (2) whether the specific case falls within the class of cases covered by the theoretical propositions; and (3) its capacity to guide the intervention hypothesis for this specific case. For the examples in the table—Do biological theories and social isolation explain depression? Does Mia Hanes have a genetic family history of depression and is she socially isolated?—if the answer is no, then the hypothesis that "Mia Hanes's depression is explained by and treated with medication and social supports" is neither logically deduced nor empirically supported.

**Induction.**   Induction, on the other hand, is development of general propositions or theory from a series of specific observations by finding patterns, general rules, or propositions common among those cases. For example: (1) While examining a representative sample of socially isolated persons, we also notice a genetic family history of depression, observing patterns of relationships between depression and social support and genetic family history. (2) We then further explore whether increased social support and medication results in reduction of depression for these persons. If the pattern indicates that there is a reduction, then we can formulate the induction "Medication and social support help reduce depression." In induction, observations lead to analyses of patterns out of which emerge propositions to explain those patterns. For the foregoing situations we are ready for the *if/then* proposition.

## Deduction

**General:**  (*If*) all men are mortal
**Specific:**  (*If*) Socrates is a man
[*then*] Socrates is a mortal.

**General:**  (*If*) biological factors such as genetic family history and social factors such as social isolation contribute to depression
**Specific:**  (*If*) individuals such as Mia Hanes have a genetic family history of depression and are socially isolated
(*then*) Mia Hanes's depression may be explained by and treated through physical and social factors such as medication and increased social support.

## Induction

1. Examine all men (or a random sample of men).
2. Over time, observe that each individual man dies and hence is mortal (a series of specific observations).
3. **Induction:**  Then all men are mortal (a general proposition or common pattern).

**Specific:**  (*If*) examination of specific cases of persons with depression indicate factors other than depression such as social isolation and genetic family history, and (*if*) persons without depression do not share these factors
**General:**  (*then*) the factors of social isolation and genetic family history are associated with depression (a general proposition or common pattern).

The reasonableness of the general proposition from the induction depends on (1) representativeness of the sample of depressed and nondepressed persons, and (2) presence of and observations of the shared factors within the sample. Do these persons share genetic family history and social isolation? Do other persons in the population who are not depressed share these factors? If the answer to either question is no, then the hypothesis that social isolation and genetic family history are associated with depression is not empirically supported.

Research and practice theory building and hypothesis development move between induction and deduction.

*Deductive and inductive fallacies.* In practice, there is always the danger of making deductive and inductive *fallacies* or errors in logic. Called

### Induction and Deduction Together

1. Examine all men (or a random sample of men).
2. Over time, observe that each individual man dies and hence is mortal (a series of specific observations).
3. **Induction:** *Then* all men are mortal (a general proposition or common pattern).
**Deduction:** 1. Establish that Socrates is a man.
2. Deduce or hypothesize that *if* Socrates is a man, *then* he is mortal.

1. Examine a sample of persons who share the factors of depression and social isolation and genetic family history.
2. Observe that increase in social support and use of medications reduces depression.
3. **Induction:** Social support and medication enables people to reduce depression (a general proposition or common pattern).
**Deduction:** Establish that Mia Hanes is suffering from depression. Deduce or hypothesize that if Mia Hanes is suffering from depression, she will reduce her depression with greater social support and medication.

"ecological fallacies" by Rubin and Babbie (1993), these flawed conclusions result when practitioners deduce from general propositions to a specific case and induce general propositions from limited experience in research and practice. Most social science theories and propositions describe characteristics of the general case or group; rarely are the propositions laws. They describe the class of cases, or group as a whole, and not necessarily all cases, a particular case, or even any case, within the class or group. A **deductive fallacy** occurs when the attribute of a group or class described by a general theory is assigned to a specific case within the class and the case does not contain or possess the attribute.

Let us consider a practice situation.

. . . . . . . . . . . . . . . . . . . .

*Research indicates that adults who were abused as children are more likely to abuse children than are adults who were not. In considering this information, if Karen, the child welfare worker from the earlier chapters, obtains family background on the parents of the children in her caseload and then assumes that parents who were abused as children are now abusing their children, she will likely commit a deductive fallacy.*

*Based on the trait of the group—adults who were abused as children—the specific client in all likelihood is not an abuser. A group trait may describe 50%, 60%, or even 70% to 90%, but it rarely describes 100% of the group. Not a conclusion, the group trait is merely a beginning point for information gathering in assessment.*

*As we learned about Sharra in Chapter 2, the family background information that she was abused as a child does not, nor should it, provide information about whether she is abusing her daughter, Trish.*

. . . . . . . . . . . . . . . . . . . .

Related to the deductive fallacy is the statistically significant fallacy. **Statistical significance** provides the probability level of whether differences between two groups is chance or a true descriptor of meaningful difference. A **statistical significance fallacy** occurs when a trait is shared almost proportionally similarly between two groups, although with a difference that is statistically significant. The child abuse case is an example. *Although there is a statistically significant difference between adults who were abused as children and adults who were not abused as children in subsequent abusive behavior, adults in either group are unlikely to abuse. The most accurate statement is most adults in each group do not abuse.*

Statistical significance fallacies are **compounded** when they are combined with deductive fallacies.

· · · · · · · · · · · · · · · · · · · · · ·

*If the social worker Karen assumes from her experience in child welfare that a trait of adults who were abused as children is to abuse children and that a particular client who was abused as a child is abusing his or her children, she commits both fallacies.*

· · · · · · · · · · · · · · · · · · · · · ·

Statistical significance is a function of the sizes of the differences between groups and the sizes of the groups or samples compared. It may or may not be meaningful. In any case, however, the practitioner needs to look beyond statistical significance for practice relevance and significance. The deductive fallacy and statistical significance fallacy are frequently errors of the positivist and quantitative approaches.

An **inductive fallacy** occurs when we assume that the trait of an individual case within a group applies to the individual case's general group or population. Here the fallacy occurs in moving *from a specific case to a general proposition.* This is more likely to happen in qualitative research and research with limited samples of convenience; it is also common in practice.

· · · · · · · · · · · · · · · · · · · · · ·

*Consider Tiffany, a social worker in a family service agency who sees four clients with the problem of bulimia. In the case assessments, Tiffany learns that each was the victim of incest as a child and she concludes that bulimia is caused by incest. Tiffany gives a trait (incest victim) to a group (people who have bulimia). She commits an inductive fallacy by*

*generalizing from the four specific cases to a larger group. Incest is not a trait of all those who have bulimia, nor do most incest victims get bulimia. Social workers who overly rely on practice wisdom and limited case experience are likely to commit inductive fallacies because a few cases will not completely represent the larger group.*

· · · · · · · · · · · · · · · · · · · · · ·

## Concepts

Concepts are fundamental units of propositions and hence of theory. Forming the structure of propositions, concepts are their basic elements or building blocks. To understand theory and the world that theory explains, one must understand the theory's concepts and the concept of *concepts.* Mental constructions or images represented by a label, a word or a set of words, concepts symbolize ideas, things, events, or behaviors. *Concepts represent a mental construction of reality, not reality itself.* The domain of the concept refers to what falls within and what lies outside the construction or idea of the reality (events, things, etc.).

### Conceptualization

Conceptualization is the *process* of assigning words to ideas and abstractions and developing constructions of empirical reality that have empirical references.

*Nominal definitions* are the mental construction of the idea which is an abstraction. *Operational definitions* are the procedures and operations in measuring and determining existence of the idea in the empirical world. They should be inferred in the nominal definition, and the operational definition should reflect the meaning and domain of the nominal definition. Both nominal and operational definitions are not locked in time and place, although nominal definitions are more abstract than operational definitions.

To determine the *empirical phenomenon itself* the operational definition is applied to determine if a particular piece of reality and empirical phenomenon falls within or outside the nominal definition.

The following proposition

> **Poverty** is the **inadequate consumption** of **goods** and **services** below a **socially defined level**

is a *nominal definition* of the concept of poverty. An operational definition of poverty using this nominal definition requires meaning and measurement of the bold face concepts. Yes, you use some concepts in defining other concepts. For those you use, you will require both nominal and operational definitions.

As we discussed earlier in developing an operational definition of social support, the most useful operational definitions are very specific and clearly measurable. Here is an operational definition of poverty:

> **Inadequate consumption,** socially defined, is **consumption** at an **income level** below half the median income of the **community.**

For this operational definition the italicized concepts need greater specificity: What is consumption and how is it measured? What is income and how is it measured? What is the community and its composition?

A concrete application of the operational definition to some part of the empirical world determines whether it is within or beyond the concept's nominal definition and the extent to which it reflects the concept's empirical referents:

> The majority of Karen's families in child welfare have **income that is one-eighth** the median income of the city population, when they do not have food stamps they **spend one-tenth of the median on food.**

*Operational definitions* offer observable data with specifics about how to measure or judge a phenomenon or manipulate its dimensions. Necessary for either quantitative or qualitative research, these propositions link concepts to the real world by stating how to observe and measure them (Fawcett & Downs, 1992).

For example, an operational definition of social support provides specificity of the degree and quality for a particular client. An operational definition could state that a client has good social support "when interacting with at least twelve varied social systems as shown on an ecomap, and over half with positive energy flow." Specific examples of the energy flow present the quality. Hartman (1983) first developed ecomaps, paper-and-pencil constructions to depict a family's relationships with its environment. In understanding Sharra from Chapter 2, the social worker Karen could provide narrative to accompany the ecomap explaining the types of interaction among Sharra and her friends, relatives, colleagues, Karen, and members of her religious affiliation.

Home (1997) used another approach by adapting a scale from Koeske and Koeske (1989) that examined perceptions of emotional, informational, and tangible supports from two sources. Her operational definition includes a specific score on the scale.

Our understanding of the concept shapes the definition and means of measurement. Cobb and Jones (1984) point to interchangeable usage of different concepts for defining social support including the support network, the individual's feelings of support, and the actual behavior of others to that individual. House and Kahn (1985) add that they "are unable to find a single measure that is so well validated and cost effective that it is to be preferred above others; various measures may be appropriate for various purposes" (p. 94). Often in social work practice we see the same word used to describe very different phenomena. *Operational definitions provide the clarity necessary for agreement among different persons that they are describing the same event.*

### Summative concepts

According to Dubin (1978), summative concepts are global and represent "an entire complex thing" (p. 66). Organizing and arranging a series of other concepts under one label, summative concepts are usually about important phenomena that are not clearly defined. Yet it is the *interaction* of these phenomena that comprise the summative concept. Examples in social work are the underclass, family life cycle, borderline personality disorder, bureaucracy, and culture of poverty.

Frequently used in the behavioral and social sciences, these concepts are not particularly useful in theory building because they are too vague and complex. Generating propositions and empirical referents from them is difficult and in most cases not even possible. Summative concepts are useful, however, as a socializing device into a discipline through development of a comprehensive view of the field. Concepts such as ecosystemic practice, dysfunctional family processes, and interpersonal helping offer beginning social workers a context within which to understand the nature of their profession's domain.

## Variables and Attributes

An attribute is the quality of a thing, what specifically gives it its *thingness*, with empirical referents that one can sense and measure, such as height, weight, volume, and density. Variables are changeable factors, usually measurable by their existence, frequency, intensity, and duration. Not all attributes are necessarily variables; some are constant and do not change for the unit. *Because of the practice focus on change, practitioners are primarily concerned with variables.* Variance is necessary for an attribute to relate to other attributes of the same or other concepts.

## Constructs

Concepts that lack empirical referents in the real world are known as constructs. They are abstractions that allow development of ideas, propositions, and theories. Constructs fill empirical gaps and are useful in their ability to promote concept generation. They are untestable but are nevertheless capable of generating concepts with empirical referents. Good examples are psychoanalytic theory's constructs of id, ego, and superego.

Highly abstract, these constructs are not verifiable, but they generate such empirical concepts as cognition or emotions, measurable by brain activity. Assuming the construct is also real, known as **reification,** is a greater risk with constructs than concepts because of their lack of empirical referents.

The same term can be either a construct or concept. Consider the word *intelligence,* an abstract term referring to conceptual ability or to how someone thinks. Since universities believe intelligence is relevant to college performance, the College Board developed a series of standardized tests on which many colleges rely for admission decisions. Initially, these tests emphasized verbal and math abilities through multiple choice questions, thereby making intelligence a concept with empirical referents. Responding to complaints, however, that performance on these tests was an inadequate explanation of intelligence, in the 1990s the College Board added essay questions. These narratives pleased some who believed that they provided information more relevant to conceptual ability and were therefore a better means of testing an individual's ability to think. The debate is still not resolved. Opinions differ about which referents are important—the narratives or the multiple choice test scores. At the same time that these tests correlate with college performance, they measure only very specific features of thinking and reasoning, which was our initial construct of intelligence.

## Dangers in Conceptualization

Dangers or problems in conceptualization include (1) reification of the concept or constructs by assuming that the idea is real or the only authentic construction of reality; (2) use of summative concepts without conceptualizing the component concepts; (3) failure to adequately develop the nominal definition and domain of the concept to allow differentiation of empirical referents that fall within the idea from those that are not empirical referents of the idea; and (4) inadequate formulation of operational definitions that capture the idea.

Consider the concept self-esteem. Beginning in the 1980s some school districts began to increasingly emphasize self-esteem in students over the learning of specific subject areas. Though the intention of educators was to enhance student learning, the concept of self-esteem became a substitute for mastery of content such as English and history. Yet in the 1990s it is becoming clear that this concept refers to many different aspects of a person's behavior, and even if better defined, may not be directly connected to school achievement. The concept was reified with inadequate development of its referents and operational definitions. Yet it became the basis for educational policy decisions.

## The Phenomenon

The phenomenon under study is nature. In social work practice, nature equals the case, its ecology, and the interventions. The case is the **unit of analysis,** the subject for research. It can be an individual, group, family, community, policy, or service delivery.

### Facts

Facts are data and measurements of things. Gibbs and Gambrill (1996) contend that facts are "beliefs that have been critically evaluated and/or tested" (p. 17). As referents of concepts, facts are not the same as ideas but generally depend on our ways of sensing and measuring the referents.

*Facts are not necessarily information.* **Information** is data organized in a format that provides clarity and coherence so that they are usable. As Gould (1983) explains, "facts and theories are different things, not rungs in a hierarchy of increasing certainty. Facts are the world's data. Theories are structures of ideas that explain and interpret facts" (p. 254).

*Organizing facts into information* is central to formulation of accurate theories of the case for social work assessments, the heart of social work practice. We next discuss case theory within the framework of theory just covered and provide

an example illustrating the inherent relationship of case theory to intervention.

## Building Case Theory

Building case theory demands knowledge and skill in concept formation and the linking of concepts into a coherent whole to explain and/or predict factors in the life of a client system. We earlier defined theory as a *set of systematically related propositions that explain and/or predict phenomena.* The phenomena or "something to be explained" in case theory includes *what is happening with the case at this point in time and what needs changing.*

Case theory provides a framework to understand and treat the symptoms or problems in the functioning of a specific client. If successful, a case theory accounts for the phenomena of one case, but it does not prove the general theory for classes of persons.

Whether practice theory, case theory, or disciplinary scientific theory, well-constructed theory rests on the clarity of ideas to produce shared agreement in understanding the ideas' meaning. The ultimate test of theory is its ability to explain the phenomenon of concern. Is it empirical—does it relate to the real world? Can it explain and account for the phenomenon? Does case theory explain the case and predict interventions that accomplish case objectives and treatment impacts on the case?

When interventions are attempted, there are always implicit, if not explicit, hypotheses that the interventions proposed for this case will lead to achieving the case objectives and produce positive changes. Some in the profession argue that practice may be unethical, if not just a waste of time, unless it is directly related to and prescriptive of treatment (Gambrill, 1968). Yet most practitioners would probably agree that while they can rely on current theories for explanation, they place little confidence in the theories' predictive capacities.

Practitioners acquire knowledge about the past to better understand the present in order to change the client's future (Bisman, 1994). A case theory to explain bruises on a child incorporates information about this child's development over time, along with current parenting and social interactions. In addition to providing understanding of why the child has bruises, the case theory also establishes the basis for an intervention to prevent further bruises.

Practitioners evaluate and organize assessment data into a case theory shaped by their ideologies of choice and personal practice model. A *personal practice model* (Mullen, 1983) is a social worker's explicit, self-conscious conceptual scheme which expresses that individual's view of practice and gives orderly direction to the work with specific clients. Like the theory of the case, it is developed from a range of experiences and sources: practice wisdom from practice and life experience, professional and personal ethics and values, formal theories, agency policies and guidelines, and professional colleagues, among other sources. Socialization in graduate social work programs often influences adherence to certain paradigms that, in turn, shape these personal practice models.

## Concept Formation

Case theory building requires *specification and development of concepts*. We said earlier that concepts are ideas in the mind using words or labels to symbolize the external things that the ideas represent. Not reality, concepts represent a mental construction of reality.

Understanding *concept* in developing case theories starts with three components illustrated in the table:

1. The idea or mental image and construction
2. The words or labels symbolizing the idea
3. The external thing, phenomenon, and empirical referents in the world represented by the labels

It is critical that practitioners not reify the concept by assuming that the idea is real or the only construction of reality. Rather, they need to develop the nominal definition and domain of the concept to distinguish empirical referents that fall within the idea from those that do not. *Operational definitions that capture the idea are prerequisite to concepts that are usable in case theory.*

When practitioners rely on diagnostic categories to describe the client's condition, they can easily become trapped into reifying the diagnosis. Consider the term *depression*, which may refer to a range of behaviors, etiologies, and treatments. Yet it is also a term used frequently among laypersons, and we are not clear what meaning each of us attaches to this concept. Specifying the behaviors and symptoms, however, will increase our ability to share understanding when we use the term *depression* to describe a client.

The mental and empirical processes of developing and operationalizing concepts and relating the concepts to explain and predict things is **theory building.** Practitioners must relate concepts in case theory to each other. If the case theory building is faulty, interventions based on the theory are not likely to produce the intended results and may result in harm.

The Three Components of a Concept

| The Idea | The Label | The Referent |
|---|---|---|
| The mental picture and construction of some part of the world | The word or words representing the idea, for example:  child abuse | The thing in the world captured by the idea, for example:  excessive crying, bruises, behavior or mood swings, sleep or eating disturbance |

*For example, a social worker, Nancy, formulates a concise theory of the case explaining that lack of school performance for 7-year-old Tani is related to early separation from an attachment figure. But if the child's difficulties are neurological rather than psychological (or at least a mixture of the two) and related to the mother's drug use during her pregnancy, focusing efforts solely on addressing the absence of a mother figure will ignore possible serious physiological deficits.*

Understanding assessment as case theory building enables practitioners to formulate their own case understanding. Only then can they articulate in ordinary language what is happening with this client and appropriately intervene. When practitioners rely solely on diagnostic categories or concepts such as depression or alcoholic, they falsely assume universal understanding of these phenomena. But as we discussed earlier, these concepts are not real but refer rather to empirical events.

## General Theories

Social, psychological, and behavioral theories—including systems and exchange theory as well as psychodynamic, operant, social learning, and cognitive theories—inform case theories but are quite different from them. These conceptual models are **nomothetic**—that is, they provide generalizations that apply to groups of persons. As Anderson and Carter (1984) advise us, the systems model is a metaphor, a way of looking at and organizing reality, and is useful to guide, construct, and understand the complexities of reality.

Case theories, in contrast, are **idiographic,** offering specifics of person, time, and place. As Bisman (1994) states, "By definition, if the case theory fits this individual case, it will totally fit no other client situation (p. 117). A central feature of case theories is their reliance on nomo-

thetic theories, which provide support from a general body of work. In their assessments, social workers must consider and confront both the social context and the individual content of behavior. Accordingly, they rely on *bio-psycho-social models* in which behavior is a function of the individual client's biological and psychological content and the social context. These models differ from (1) the *bio-psycho-medical models* of human behavior that present behavior as the result of the individual's biological and intrapsychic content, whether the result of genetic content or early socialization, (2) the *educational models* that view behavior and management of social relations and the social environment as learned or conditioned, and (3) the *psycho-social models* that interpret behavior as a function of the individual's psychological content in interaction with the social context.

For fully developed and valid social work case theories, social workers need to use bio-psycho-social models. This broad focus includes: *biological* information of genetic content and physical attributes; *psychological* data covering the intrapsychic and personality factors; and *social* information about range and type of community and social supports and resources, with their availability to the client.

Knowledge of specific circumstances is necessary to understand each client's depression or substance abuse in order to plan an intervention that relates to the client's real life circumstances. This is particularly important because many general theories explain concepts such as depression and child abuse. *Case theory shapes decisions about which general theories or professional literature to choose, with very different implications for intervention.*

We offer two examples illustrating the impact of case theory on intervention. In this model for constructing case theory we advocate incorporating the general theoretical frameworks directly into the case theory. Adherence to such an approach specifies the general theories utilized, clarifying their relationship with the case theory.

## Case Theory Based on Bio-Psycho-Social Models

A concept commonly used in social work practice is depression. In this practice case, note that the social worker draws from bio-psycho-social models, resulting in a broad-based case theory and intervention focused on several variables.

• • • • • • • • • • • • • • • • • • • •

### PRACTICE CASE A BROAD-BASED CASE THEORY

*Based at an urban community mental health center which provides services to any community residents, the social worker, Ingrid, meets with Rosie, a 45-year-old Latina woman. Currently unemployed, Rosie completed tenth grade and has held various jobs, usually as a sales clerk. She lives with her 25- year-old daughter, has little interaction with her family and very few friends. Rosie came into the session complaining that she feels sad and has little energy.*

*When Ingrid pushes for specificity, she learns that Rosie often sits around the house all day doing nothing, sleeps about 12–14 hours, watches TV about 6–8 hours, and is losing weight because she does not eat very much. Ingrid asks how long she has felt this way and learns that Rosie has had these bad feelings on and off since her early teens, when she used to think of killing herself. These low periods often alternated with great bursts of energy when Rosie felt wonderful. Asking how it is that she is now asking for help, she learns Rosie feels worse since testing positive for HIV three months ago.*

*Ingrid formulates the following case theory: Rosie's recent HIV diagnosis is exacerbating her long-term social isolation and possible clinical depression. She learns from Goldstein (1995) and Jue (1994) that stigma from AIDS often socially isolates these patients, while Mancoske (1996) points to their greater risk of suicide. Individuals need an active energy exchange with others, as Greene (1991) explains in her discussion of systems theory, and for a long time Rosie has had no person with whom she can talk openly. Her long*

*history of severe mood swings suggests bipolar disorder. Sperry (1995) supports a biological basis for treatment of depression, whereas Jensen (1994) points to a psychosocial perspective combined with the biological. Cohan (1997) stresses the importance of narrative in constructing a story to explain the illness.*

*As we stressed earlier, Ingrid must identify the **empirical indicators** relevant for her client. This is especially critical when we use a label such as depression, because it describes so many different conditions. These empirical indicators for Rosie's functioning include the following specific behaviors: sleeping an average of 13 hours per day, decrease in appetite, severe mood swings, and extensive sitting around and watching television.*

***Propositions** in Ingrid's case theory pose a relationship between "social isolation, illness, biology" and "depression." Her **hypothesis** is a deduction that Rosie's symptoms are explained by her biology, social isolation, and fear of AIDS. Correspondingly, Ingrid refers to general theories of systems, biological and psychological and social explanations for understanding depression, and psychosocial effects of HIV and AIDS diagnoses.*

*Emerging from this case theory, Ingrid's **intervention** will include both increasing social supports and a medical consult to consider pharmacology for the possible bipolar disorder. Ingrid also recognizes the importance of attending to Rosie's belief system and considering whether natural healers might be of interest to Rosie (Blundo, Greene & Gallant, 1994). While her own family arrived in the Midwest hundreds of years ago from Sweden, Ingrid is sensitive to Rosie's Puerto Rican heritage and her relatively recent arrival in this region (about 15 years ago). Ingrid finds it useful to read Hess's (1997) comments about the additional burden of shame and guilt for Latino families suffering from AIDS, who often lack adequate social supports. Adhering to the social work value of empowerment, Ingrid wants to increase Rosie's feelings and capacities for independence and autonomy.*

• • • • • • • • • • • • • • • • • • • •

Focus on just the HIV, or the social isolation, or the clinical depression ignores important variables, and such a narrow intervention would be harmful to Rosie. The range of these general theories, however, offers Ingrid broad-based information about research and practice with clients who have HIV, pharmacological treatment of depression, and social isolation.

## Case Theory Based on Psychological Models

In this second example we return to Nancy and her client Tani. Here the social worker relies solely on psychological models.

. . . . . . . . . . . . . . . . . . . .

### PRACTICE CASE A NARROW CASE THEORY

*Nancy, a social worker with a county partial hospitalization program for children ages 5 to 12, has recently had Tani transferred to her. The youngest in the household, Tani is 7 years old, in second grade, and resides with her maternal aunt, five cousins (three male and two female), and 12-year-old sister.*

*In treatment for two years since her mother was incarcerated on voluntary manslaughter charges for killing an abusive boyfriend, Tani's diagnosis is depression. Tani cries and bedwets, has little interaction with members of her household or persons at school, and does not complete assignments. Records show that during her pregnancy with Tani, her mother abused drugs and was abused by a number of men. Tani does not know her father, who is also incarcerated.*

*Nancy's case theory: Adapted to an unstable environment that consisted of pathological parenting and unwilling separation from an attachment figure, Tani's depression resulted from failure to develop a stable sense of self. Attachment theory (Bowlby, 1977) presents that discontinuities of parenting can result in depression, and object relations (Winnicott, 1989) offers that Tani's split between good and bad was not resolved before she*

*reached one year old, resulting in antisocial relations with others. Low self-esteem (Winnicott, 1989), can result from lack of a supportive caregiver during infancy.*

*In this case theory the **empirical indicators** for the concept of depression include lack of interpersonal interaction, crying and bedwetting, and uninvolvement in school work.*

*Nancy's **propositions** posit a relationship between "pathological parenting, lack of internalized object relations, low self-esteem" and "depression." Her hypothesis is a deduction that Tani's symptoms are explained by her early parenting, self-esteem, and poor object relations.*

*Accordingly, Nancy refers to **general theories** of attachment and object relations, with her **intervention** focusing on play and supportive group therapy.*

. . . . . . . . . . . . . . . . . . . .

This inadequate case theory relies on the single concept of depression, neglecting in its construction other hypotheses to explain Tani's behavior, including possible biological problems caused by drug use of Tani's mother during her pregnancy or current abuse and neglect in the home. Lacking the breadth of the *social* perspective and ignoring the *biological* dimension, Nancy's case theory results in a narrow use of general theories using concepts about object relations and attachment. This in turn results in only a psychologically oriented treatment.

Furthermore, Nancy commits a *deductive fallacy* by assuming that because early discontinuities in parenting may explain depression in children, parenting of Tani explains her symptoms. She assigns the attribute "discontinuities of parenting" discussed in attachment theory to her client, Tani. The parenting of Tani, however, may not fit that description. Based on limited reading of attachment theory, Nancy constructs the concept of pathological parenting to explain Tani's upbringing, but she lacks information to operationalize this concept or even document Tani's early years. Once she has decided on this hypothesis, Nancy then neglects information about the current home environment, including interactions between Tani and her male cousins. Yet if Tani is currently being abused in her home, Nancy is not responsibly assessing or intervening to prevent imminent risk.

A comparison of these cases illustrates the important relationship among the concept's empirical referents, propositions and hypotheses of the case theory, general theories and intervention, and problems from fallacies in the social worker's thinking. Inclusion of the general theoretical frameworks that inform the case theory provide greater specificity about the theoretical grounding of the case theory. We understand the strong bias to psychological explanation when we know that Nancy draws from attachment theory and object relations. Similarly, we can appreciate the social and biological perspectives of Ingrid's case theory through her identification of systems theory and the biological components of depression. *Broadly based case theories incorporate multiple hypotheses, which then draw from a range of general theories resulting in a plan of intervention that includes a focus on biological, psychological, and social factors—the social work domain.*

## Summary

Beginning with paradigms, we discussed their relevance in the contemporary debates about knowledge and research in social work. We offer case theory building in this chapter, and our following methodology chapters, as a translation to incorporate language from the two dominant social work paradigms, positivism and heuristics.

We define theory as *a set of propositions that explain and/or predict phenomena.* Theories are not inherently "real" or "hypothetical"; they are constructions, used to classify, explain, and predict. Theory building is development of more accurate descriptions of phenomena with better means of predicting events, not a search for real or absolute truth.

Theories are developed from our observations of nature and also from the paradigms used to guide the observations. They are models of reality. Some theories describe aspects of nature, human behavior, and interaction, while others are prescriptive and lay out what should be and what should be done by the social worker. They are abstractions, simplifications— sometimes oversimplifications—of empirical reality. Models are ideas that try to capture empirical referents, but they are not the empirical referents themselves. If they are good models, they contain the essential elements and structure of reality to enable the model's user to gain a better understanding of reality.

Presenting the basic components of theory, we emphasized propositions, conceptualization, and hypothesis formulation. To formulate the social work assessment, practitioners must have theory building knowledge and skills because practice is theory building.

Case theory, like all theory, provides a map and explains phenomena. To base interventions on valid understandings of clients, we need maps and models of the world to simplify, not mimic, in guiding practice decisions. Case theory is idiographic: it applies only to a specific case and is distinct from social and behavioral theories, which are *nomothetic* and apply generally to groups of persons.

In case theory, social workers present their understanding, developed from data collection and observations, of the problematic condition for a unique client at a specific point in time. From case theory's coherent explanation of the empirical referents and reference to general theories and knowledge come selection of intervention strategies with methods to change the presenting problems.

Addressing specific phenomena, the test of the case theory is the extent to which it explains the unique client, accounts for the phenomena, and guides a successful intervention. Examples illustrate how very different case theories used to explain the concept of depression result in divergent general theories and plans of intervention.

Reliance on erroneous general theories or inadequate case theories is ineffectual and harmful to clients.

We leave with a proposition: *if* practice is case theory building and testing, *then* practice requires knowledge of theory construction and skills to build and test case theories.

## Discussion Questions and Exercises

1. Argue for whether or not social work has a paradigm. On what do you base your argument? Why do you think this is such a contentious issue among social work academics?

2. Assessment Exercise: The J Family

> *Ms. J, a 30-year-old white female, came to a family services agency (FSA) seeking emergency help with her current family situation. Dropping out of high school in her sophomore year when she was pregnant with her first child, Ms. J did not return to school or obtain a high school equivalency diploma.*
>
> *The child, John, is now 14 years old. Mr. J is not John's father, and they do not get along. John is habitually absent from school, a member of a loosely formed gang of antisocial white youth who identify themselves as "skinheads." Ms. J complains she has lost control of John and worries that her second child, Susan, age 10, (Mr. J's daughter) is picking up John's "wild ways."*
>
> *The family moved to a warm-weather community from another state about six months ago, relocating so that Mr. J could obtain more consistent employment. Since their move he has been working regularly on construction projects and financially supports the family. John's father provides no financial support, nor does he have any contact with John.*
>
> *Ms. J wants to find a job so that she and John will be less financially dependent on Mr. J. Her desire for a job is a source of some friction between her and her husband. He believes that it is his responsibility to be the family's breadwinner and that Ms. J is responsible for the children's upbringing. He tells her she is not doing a good job raising the children since both children are "going bad," so how does she expect to work outside the home and properly raise them? He does, however, want John to get a job since John is not devoting his full attention to school.*
>
> *Ms. J has not worked outside the home since her marriage. Before that, she worked for about three years as a waitress when her mother babysat John. Ms. J met Mr. J at her waitress job and she has had no other paid employment experience. She has no close friends or relatives in the new community, is far from her family, and feels socially isolated.*
>
> *Ms. J came to the FSA on a referral from an emergency room doctor. Ms. J told the emergency room doctor that she fell. The doctor urged her to go to FSA in any case because the indications were that her injuries were from abuse. John has also been treated for bruises that he claimed he received in tussles at school. No police referrals were made since Ms. J and John were adamant that they were not abused by Mr. J.*
>
> *She did, however, tell the FSA intake social worker that she would like to figure out a way to leave the home with her children. John has threatened to leave home because of Mr. J's strict rules in the house. For now, Ms. J feels at a loss to do anything, because*

*she has neither close friends nor family in this community, a place to go, money of her own, nor a source of income other than Mr. J.*

*Mr. J. refuses to meet with the FSA social worker, telling Ms. J he does not trust outsiders, he knows what is best for his family, and while he would like them to straighten out John, he does not want Ms. J or Susan going to the agency.*

    a. What are the major sources of information necessary to complete the assessment and case theory?

    b. Comment on the initial hypotheses you are formulating in understanding this client situation. What behaviors are you seeking to explain?

    c. What literature will you turn to in further development of your case theory?

    d. What are the concepts and variables, the "things," you will need to measure?

    e. Describe the relationships among events.

    f. What are the potential deductive and inductive fallacies you wish to avoid?

3. Conceptualization Exercise: Racism

Allow 15 minutes in groups of three:

    a. Develop awareness of the concept. What is your mental construction of racism?

    b. List three or more empirical indicators that fall within the nominal definition's domain.

    c. Develop an operational definition of racism, including the procedures and operations for measuring its presence.

    d. Use the concept in a theoretical proposition.

    e. Objectively determine the class instructor's race.

# CHAPTER FIVE

# A Model for Using Research Methodologies in Practice

As we have discussed in the preceding chapters, practitioners and academics in the social work profession often view research and practice as separate, distinct, and perhaps dichotomous activities requiring different ways of thinking, different methodologies, and different skills. *Methodical investigation to uncover data, theories, and applications,* however, describes the work of both practice and research. In this conceptualization, research methodologies are considered practice skills.

Nonetheless, challenges to systematically incorporate research epistemologies and methodologies into practice use are immense. Research and practice each use a different language. Practitioners and researchers have distinct referent groups and self-perceptions. They do not see themselves sharing common ground.

Though it is our position that good practitioners conduct research in their practice, we recognize that many do not perceive research as part of their practice repertoire. The criticism of practitioners' "unscientific thinking" by academic researchers probably reflects a yearning to make social work a science as much as an effective profession. Yet social work cannot be both a science and a profession. As we examined in the first chapter, sciences inherently differ from professions even though they often pursue questions of interest to professions.

Although professions are not sciences, they use scientific knowledge and methods to create change, build knowledge, and answer practice questions. Moreover, a profession's knowledge and truths extend beyond the transitory scientific knowledge, truths, and facts to beliefs rooted in its values, ethics, and client preferences.

In this chapter we highlight the divisions between practice and research in social work and introduce a model for bridging the divide by using research methods as practice skills.

## Social Work Practice/ Research Divisions

Social work practitioners generally view research as something apart from them, impractical, an imposition when done, and largely incompatible with practice. At the same time, researchers, especially academicians, advocate closer links between research and practice, with some arguing that social workers should be practitioner-scientists and practitioner-researchers (Briar, 1973; Hudson, 1982). Other academicians believe that the two arenas of the profession are not only separate but antithetical and advocate maintaining the distinctions between practice and research (Saleebey, 1979).

Many contend that practitioners acquire and use research skills as part and parcel of practice skills. The appeal of this cohort, however, is sadly lost in their division along ideological and methodological lines regarding the basis of knowledge and how it is acquired and verified. One group argues for a positivist construction of knowledge and a quantified approach to its development (Blythe, Tripodi, & Briar, 1994; Fischer, 1993; Hudson, 1982; Ivanoff, Blythe, & Tripodi, 1994; Thyer, 1986 & 1990), while the other group contends that knowledge is a social construction and is best developed for practitioners and by practitioners using qualitative and naturalistic methodologies (Heineman, 1981 & Heineman-Pieper, 1989, Goldstein, 1986; Rodwell, 1987; Tyson, 1992 & 1994).

A third camp of the "research skills as practice" bloc are more pragmatic, pushing for a synthesis of naturalism and positivism as a dialectic contribution to practice (Berlin & Marsh, 1993; Berlin, 1990; Blythe & Tripodi, 1989; Gibbs & Gambrill, 1996; Peile, 1988; Zimmerman, 1989). This is our position. We hold that social work is a profession concerned with helping people achieve better social lives through interventions targeted to large social systems and individual persons. Accordingly, *the profession should embrace scientific research discipline in thinking and theory building along with any research methodologies from all the paradigms that will contribute to more effective practice and service.* Practitioners can then incorporate this knowledge into their repertoire of skills. *Social work practitioners need critical thinking and skills in the appropriate use of research methodologies not to become a hyphenated scientist or research/ practitioner but to be better, more complete practitioners.* At the same time, researchers should focus on work that contributes to the profession's mission of service rather than placing an emphasis solely on any narrow definition of science.

There are real challenges to incorporating research methodologies into practice methodologies, such as time constraints and compatibility between the rigors and discipline of the methodologies and the art of helping. These are pseudo-issues when presented as a dialectic between research skills and practice art. Good art requires both rigor and discipline. A competent and ethical practitioner must assess and make judgments while possessing clarity about the

goals, methodologies, and limitations of interventions. Truly informed consent by clients is not possible if practitioners cannot define, proceduralize, measure, and evaluate their practice behavior and communicate in ways that clients can understand.

Nonetheless, practitioners are still not researchers, nor is science their objective. We agree with Staudt's (1997) contention that

> practice evaluation is not research—rather, students are learning a part of practice, akin to learning assessment and intervention. For example, operationalizing the target behavior is part of assessment; thus students should learn how to operationalize target behaviors in practice. (p. 105)

## Use of Research Epistemologies and Methodologies as Practice Thinking and Skills

The social work profession should take its epistemologies and methodologies from *both* the positivist and naturalist research paradigms as well as other sources of knowledge. These two major paradigms are useful to social work practitioners for effective day-to-day practice. All available tools that contribute to our professional knowledge building and skills development must be incorporated into a nondichotomous approach to practice. The issue, as Franklin (1995) asserts, is relevance for practitioners. We approach our model of research skills as part and parcel of practitioners' development of their individual knowledge and skills as practitioners without regard for paradigmatic ideological boundaries.

## Assumptions of the Model

Conceptualizing research as practice is predicated on several assumptions:

1. The purpose of social work research epistemology and research methodologies is to develop knowledge and skill for the profession.

2. As science is only one source of knowledge and social science is both underdeveloped and strongly ideological, social work's epistemologies and methodologies should not be restricted to a single or simple science paradigm, or even exclusively to science.

3. If the purpose of social work research epistemology and research methodologies is to develop the profession's knowledge and skills, then the profession and professional should use any and all available tools and resources that contribute to this end.

4. Research epistemology and methodologies are critical in practice.

5. The teaching of research in a meaningful way for practitioners is difficult and problematic and must be taught as useful and essential practice epistemology and methodology rather than as a separate discipline. Research epistemologies and methodologies are not limited to research projects and should be mastered as professional practice skills.

A fundamental premise of this model is that social work practitioners require the ability to develop case theory, measure, formulate judgments, and control interventions. In other words, they require skills of research. Social work intervention is a prediction derived from a case theory that a set of behaviors by the practitioner, the client, and other components of an action system will produce desired effects and result in a positive difference for the client. Practitioners intervene and accomplish change through constructing useful theory, called the case theory of the assessment (Bisman, 1994). Including hypotheses to explain the problem situation, case theory directs treatment goals and objectives. In research, the assessment activity is also called *theory development*, including problem and hypothesis formulation. Practice requires the discipline of research epistemologies and methodologies.

The table that follows on pages 68 and 69 presents some of the applications of research as social work practice. Although they appear linear, neither practice or research are linear processes,

nor does any single research component or methodology apply only to a single practice component. While these practice and research components merge, for purposes of clarity and understanding of the model we consider them as parallel processes.

Although readers may not be familiar with the practice components and concepts or the research epistemologies and methodologies introduced in this table, they should have acquired this knowledge after completing the text. During the remaining chapters, readers may find it useful to refer back to this table. (See Bisman [1994] for elaboration of direct practice components and Hardcastle, Wenocur, and Powers [1997] for macro practice.)

## Research and Practice Terminology

In order to use research epistemology and methodologies, the practitioner often needs to translate the rather esoteric language of research into the equally cryptic jargon of practice. Conversely, researchers who want to address practice concerns and questions have to convert their findings into language appropriate to practice. There is no assumption in the conversions that one language is superior to the other, just as there is no need to assume that because one might translate German into Spanish that Spanish is superior to German.

The different labels or words used by each of the languages often refer to similar features of empirical reality. Lacking understanding of the concepts, however, users may assume that the labels refer to different phenomena. Moreover, occasionally true differences exist in the realities constructed by the two languages beyond the labels used. Recognition by practitioners and researchers of these differences in construction may produce a richer, more robust shared construction of reality by both. *In our discussion of Kuhn (Chapter 4), we explain that our purpose is to translate research and practice into a language usable by both, and in the following chapters we elaborate these translations.*

Using a shared language when possible, we offer translations when one is not available. We believe that understanding research language enables social workers to better develop, enact, and evaluate their practice. A major objective of this text is for readers to embrace the translations and accept research tools as practice tools rather than viewing them as part of a separate esoteric discipline.

Accompanying the table is a summary translation of some of the major concepts. We clarify practice components and tasks listed in the table on pp. 68–69, while in the remaining chapters we fully define and illustrate the research epistemologies and methodologies. Readers should make sure they understand both languages and can translate the meanings between the two languages as they progress through the book.

## Relationship

Social work began with the "friendly visitors" who sought to provide "not alms but a friend" through "expert personal services." Though the Charity Organization Societies (COS) offered charity to individuals and families, and the Settlement House workers attended to reforms needed for immigrant acculteration into new communities, both sets of social workers utilized relationship with clients in creating their desired changes.

This professional helping relationship is the vehicle of social work practice. It is through the formation of human contact with clients that social workers enact their practice. Bisman (1994) defines relationship as a belief bonding

> through which the client develops self-worth and trust in the competence of the social worker and establishes belief that the social worker can help initiate change in the client's circumstances. The social work relationship has as its purpose to achieve specific ends.... *Each relationship is unique...reflecting the function of the social work agency.* [emphasis added] (p. 77)

Although it was initially viewed as central to practice, the emphasis on making social work more scientific decreased the importance of relationship. Perceived as "soft," relationship received less attention in many social work texts. At the same time, other disciplines such as psychiatry, psychology, and counseling continued to address relationship in their training programs, also called the *helping alliance* (Luborsky, 1993). Physicians and teachers acknowledge the powerful impact of relationship on patient healing and student learning, while successful businesspeople point to their capacity to develop trust and bond with customers. In all of these fields a **belief bonding** is influential in achieving goals and outcomes. As Bisman (1994) states, "Forming the crux of most professional relationships, this bonding is a necessary, though not sufficient condition for the accomplishment of the client's goals and objectives" (p. 79).

In addition to relationships with clients, it is in their **relationships with supervisors** that practitioners receive ongoing evaluation and feedback about their effectiveness. Inherent in the apprenticeship model still dominant in social work education, supervisory relationships instill practitioners with confidence in their ability to practice. Some have called this a *parallel process,* referring to the importance of social workers addressing with their supervisors the similar issues they confront in relating both as supervisees and as workers (Martin, 1989).

Moreover, with the concurrent model of education in which students have client responsibilities at the same time that they are still in classes, relationships with supervisors and colleagues are critical in providing practical knowledge, support, and advice in social work practice. Just as the *peer review process* provides valuable outside input about the nature and quality of the research project, supervisors, team members, and colleagues offer practitioners the validation necessary to present themselves as competent to help the client.

**Member checking** allows practitioners not only to form relationships with others significant to the client, but also to gain a range of perspectives from different colleagues to clarify or support their interpretation of events presented by the client. In **respondent validation,** a form of member checking, practitioners confirm directly with the client whether they each share the same explanation for events.

Essential in building the bonding and forming the relationship are the ethical principles (discussed in Chapter 3) of **self-determination, duty to warn, informed consent,** and **confidentiality.** To form trust with and respect for the social worker and to retain self-respect, clients need knowledge about the treatment, agency services, and worker competence. It is in the relationship that they develop a **shared conceptualization** with the worker about the reality of their situation along with the possibilities for change.

· · · · · · · · · · · · · · · · · · · ·

*In establishing the relationship with Bill and Sharon, for example, Elana presents herself as a competent social worker who has the expertise to help them. Respectful of both Bill and Sharon, she knows it is important that they in turn view her with respect and believe that she is able to help them change their situation.*

*Respondent validation can be awkward in cases with violent behaviors. Yet it is crucial that Elana confirm directly with Bill and Sharon that they all share the same interpretation for their work together. Without shared conceptualization, there is no clarity about the violence or why they are meeting together and the belief bonding will not occur. Member checking with her colleagues and supervisor about signs to observe for confirmation of abusive relationships offers Elana support to conceptualize these behaviors as abuse by Sharon of Bill. She draws from a number of informants to support or refute her interpretation of events. This couple was referred by a hospital social worker after several emergency room visits by Sharon for unexplained bruises. With the permission of Bill and Sharon, Elana talks with the hospital social worker.*

· · · · · · · · · · · · · · · · · · · ·

## Communication

Lacking the high-powered devices available to physicians, such as electrocardiograms or electroencephalograms, social workers rely on communication as a major measurement technology. Through interviewing and a range of methods and skills, practitioners **exchange information with clients, colleagues, and others related to the client system.**

The Kadushins (1997) define the **interview** as "the context through which social workers offer and implement most human services" (p. 3). They present a comprehensive guide to the steps and skills of interviewing, including special problems and cross-cultural interactions.

Bisman (1994) presents the major methods of communication used by social workers, including:

**exploration**—further and enhance the client's elaboration through open-ended questions.

**reflection**—paraphrase, interpret, and reframe back to the client for clarification and feedback on what they have heard.

**validation**—accept and empower the client by attention to the client's overt and covert cues, accompanied by respectful and supportive behavior.

**confrontation**—point out discrepancies in words and behavior through questions, statements and feedback. (pp. 184–199)

Communication skills discussed in Bisman (1994) include:

**provision of information**—through statements and responses to questions about treatment, the agency, and the worker.

**sustaining dialogue**—maintenance of the interview flow through comments and questions.

**use of silence**—control amount of practitioner talking to encourage client verbalization.

**focusing**—center and highlight the most essential information relevant to the client situation.

**summarize**—review and "pull together" what was covered. (pp. 182–184)

Parallels of Research and Practice

| *Practice Component and Tasks* | *Research Epistemologies and Methodologies* |
| --- | --- |
| **RELATIONSHIP** | |
| **Clients** | |
| Has purpose, shaped by agency function; belief bonding: confidence in worker's competence to create change, client's capacity to change, worthiness of client; informed consent; client self-determination; duty to warn; confidentiality | Shared conceptualization of reality by practitioner and client; respondent validation; informed consent; confidentiality |
| **Supervisors and Colleagues** | |
| Request and receive feedback; identify areas for professional development; engage in relationships with supervisor and others | Member checking for bias and reflexivity reduction; expert validity; peer review process |
| **COMMUNICATION** | |
| Verbal and nonverbal methods and skills: confrontation, reflection, validation, exploration, give and receive information, sustain dialogue, summarize, use silence, focus; interviewing; observation | Sampling; data collection; instrument construction; participant observation and other measurement approaches, interviews, member checking and respondent validation, triangulation; shared constructions of reality |
| **PRACTITIONER OBSERVATION** | |
| Self-awareness; use of self; clinical impressions; articulation of values, feelings, and biases; client self-determination; attention to cultural difference; transference and countertransference | Measurement; objectivity; member checking; participant observation, guard against bias and reflexivity, triangulation, shared constructions of reality |
| **ASSESSMENT AND CASE THEORY** | |
| Construct hypotheses to explain client and problem situation; gather information from a range of sources; observation; interviews; selection of relevant literature and research; develop cognitive map to organize the practice; link client's past with present and future; joint activity with client | Theory building involving joint conceptualization, deduction and induction from the information collected; measurement, observation, interviews (structured, unstructured, and focused), questionnaires; establish reliability and validity; member checking and respondent validation to guard against bias and reflexivity; triangulation; content analysis of narratives and available data; sampling |

| *Practice Component and Tasks* | *Research Epistemologies and Methodologies* |
|---|---|
| **INTERVENTION** | |
| **Case Practice Plan** | |
| Problem statement; goals formulation; indicators of change; design or selection of intervention plan; informed consent with client in contracting and establishing goals; plan strategy; client's capacity to exercise self-determination; practitioner observation; relevance to agency mission and professional ethics; use of relevant literature | Single case and case study designs; recognition of design and external validity limitations; problem and hypothesis formulation of the case goals, objectives and proposed intervention; triangulation; shared perception of client's improved social functioning; proceduralization |
| **Implementation** | |
| Strategies and tactics of change; monitor and control treatment to maintain integrity and reliability, prevent drift, monitor shifts; informed consent; duty to warn; accountability | Design, application and control of treatment or independent variables; intervention measurement; triangulation; internal and external design validity determination; prevent reflexivity; member checking |
| **EVALUATION** | |
| Impressions and judgments of indicators of client change and achievement of case objectives by intervention process and case theory significance; informed consent; accountability | Sampling; analysis of information measured and collected; ethnographic, nomothetic, and group data analytical models appropriate to case design; charting and other visual analysis; descriptive and inferential statistics; statistical significance |
| **Reporting and Reassessment** | |
| Reassessment of the case theory; report progress toward goals to the client and other components of the action and change system; establish new goals; recontract with the client; clinical and case significance; accountability | Construct shared reality with member checking for case study reporting; knowledge conversion, publication, and diffusion |

It is important to remember that practice is not linear; it is an interactive process. These methods and skills are basic to communication, but they are neither exhaustive nor exclusive. A statement can provide validation and confrontation at the same time. Focus usually sustains the dialogue and provides information.

Zuger (1998) reports on a study of 200 doctor patient-relationships in which both increased satisfaction with the session simply by the physicians asking patients at the beginning of each visit, "What would you like me to do for you?" This type of question is a good means of data collection for constructing the case theory and strengthens the relationship.

The purpose of communication as measurement is to **collect data for decisions, develop a shared construction of reality** with the client, and **validate** the information **through member checking, triangulation, and observation** of the client's situation.

Since we concur with Blumer (1969, pp. 4–5) that meaning arises in the interaction between people and that the use of meaning involves an interpretive process, practitioners need to carefully consider data they gather. Clarifying judgments with a number of informants and significant others—member checking—strengthens the interpretation or meaning of the observed events. Use of *multiple sources of information* on phenomena is triangulation.

Lacking hard data of heartbeat measurements or brainwave information, verbal and nonverbal communication is subject to each individual's biases and the meanings attached to the words and body language.

• • • • • • • • • • • • • • • • • • • • • •

*We discussed in Chapter 2 Elana's concern with the meaning of violence to Bill, his expectations of women in general, of Sharon and even of Elana. To obtain **more information**, Elana asks **exploratory questions** while also **confronting** when she observes discrepancies.*

***Triangulation**, by considering several information sources such as the extent of Sharon's social isolation (her contacts with friends and*

*family), employment, and autonomy around financial and house management decisions, helps Elana **validate** the information she collects and determine the extent of Sharon's abuse.*

• • • • • • • • • • • • • • • • • • • • • •

## Practitioner Observation

The subjective nature of practice requires that social workers observe and critique themselves before, during, and after practice interactions. Bisman (1994) refers to this practice component as practitioner observation, pointing to the historical importance of self-awareness and use of self in social work practice and education. *Transference* and *countertransference* are labels widely used in psychotherapy to refer to these same concepts.

Concerned as they are with the very intimate details of the lives of others, social workers cannot escape confrontation with their own highly personal experiences. In order to assure focus on clients and their self-determination, and to avoid attempting to shape clients' lives into the practitioners' image, it is necessary for social workers to develop awareness of their own feelings and biases. Functioning as measurement instruments when they observe and interview, practitioners need to be self-aware.

In Chapter 3 we discussed the impact of morals and values on professional practice, emphasizing that practice cannot be value free. Rather, social workers must develop awareness of and means to articulate their personal reactions and biases. Engagement in this process allows for **objectivity** and **shared constructions of reality** with clients. Use of **member checking** and **triangulation** assists in **accurate measurement** and **guards against bias and reflexivity**. In **reflexivity** the measurement process changes the thing under measurement, while in **bias** the measurement process provides misinformation.

• • • • • • • • • • • • • • • • • • • • • •

*Elana, for example, feels discomfort, sometimes bordering on fear, when she works with families* *where violence is present. Though she herself has not been in an abusive relationship, her close friend is regularly beaten by her husband, leaving Elana feeling helpless, furious, and sad. She knows it is very important that in practice with clients she **acknowledge her feelings** to herself and to her supervisor and distinguish concerns for her friend from those about Sharon. Elana attends to whether she or the client is at risk and separates her wishes from Sharon's expectations for her own life with Bill.*

*As always in social work practice, Elana must remain **attentive to cultural differences.** Her Puerto Rican background emphasized male power and control of the family. Rebellion against this domination over women influenced her choice of social work as a career, with a special interest in women's issues. Elana always needs to be careful that her desires for empowerment of women do not **bias** her observations and constructions of the interactions between Bill and Sharon.*

*When Elana meets with Sharon and Bill, she acknowledges that a social acquiescence **bias** may occur—that is, in acquiescence to the situation, Bill may not honestly respond to questions about whether he hits Sharon. At the same time, in acquiescing to Bill's presence, Sharon may not honestly report Bill's abuse.*

*Elana must also recognize that the act of her involvement with Bill and Sharon may stop the violence. Talking with them and observing their behavior, whether in the home or office, may result in **reflexivity.** Elana needs to plan with them about possible reappearance of the violence when they are not in the process of monitoring it.*

• • • • • • • • • • • • • • • • • • • •

## Assessment

As we discussed in Chapter 4, assessment involves generating a set of **hypotheses** to explain the case—individual clients, families, groups, the organization, or community—and why this case is as it is. Through **observation, interviews,** and other measurement approaches, practitioners **gather information** to develop a

**cognitive map** for organizing the practice. They select relevant literature and research to validate their theory of the case, which, if accurate, will fit only one client at a particular point of time. *Practitioners should not constrain the case to fit the theory, but rather construct case theory that fits the case.*

Assessment is the meaning or construct attached by the social worker to the client's narrative and other gathered information. Not a search for absolute truth or the ultimate explanation for problems, assessment is intended to determine the *nature of the current problem at a particular point in time.*

Without theory, we would be overwhelmed by the phenomenon under study. Theory often moves beyond the "what is" to address the "hows," "whens," and "whys." In practice we are concerned with developing case theory that explains and also predicts. Otherwise interventions will be random, with one intervention as good as another, lacking direct connection to the client situation.

Theories are useful only as long as they explain with **reliability** (consistency) and **validity** (accuracy) and incorporate the **deductions** and **inductions** from the information collected and analyzed. As in the previous practice components, **member checking** along with **respondent validation** and **triangulation** are central to validity and an accurate theory of the case and help prevent **bias** and **reflexivity.**

The most important ingredient of good research and good practice is **measurement,** how we obtain information for judgment. Practitioners use a variety of measurement devices, including observation, whether or not they call it measurement. Concern is always with the information's reliability and truthfulness. **Reliability** refers to the **consistency** of the information yielded by a measurement when applied to the same and similar phenomena. When two or more practitioners look at the same situation, the same client, and the same problem with the same assessment processes, they should reach the same assessment if their judgments are reliable. When practitioners look at different clients in the same situation, with the same assessment processes, the assessment should be similar.

Truthfulness is *validity,* the extent to which the measurement processes used actually measure what the practitioner intended to measure, and not something else. **Validity** refers to whether the measure, the theory, model, or concept **describes reality with a good fit.**

· · · · · · · · · · · · · · · · · · · ·

*In constructing the case theory to explain Sharra and her mothering of Trish, our social worker Karen must present a risk assessment for both mother and daughter. Illustrating the enormous complexity of social work practice, the child welfare agency became active with Sharra because of sexual abuse by her stepfather, resulting in her pregnancy with Trish.*

*Karen's case theory must explain Sharra's **specific situation,** not just present general theories about group behavior patterns of teen mothers.*

*Karen draws from literature on substance abuse and homeless mothers (Lee and Nisivoccia, 1997), incest (Strand, 1997), and empowerment for women of color (Gutierrez, 1990).*

*Through **member checking** with staff at the facility where Sharra and Trish reside, Karen verifies that Sharra gives loving attention to Trish, and no one has seen her strike Trish. The drug counselors believe that Sharra remains drug free. Karen also uses **respondent validation** by regularly checking in directly with Sharra about any parenting concerns and pressures to return to drugs.*

*To guard against **reflexivity, triangulation** is important in developing a valid case theory (Sharra knew Karen was observing her closely to assess her parenting and would therefore tend to be on best behavior). Accordingly, Karen uses **multiple measures** including examining the cleanliness of Sharra's room and general care of Trish, specifically looking Trish over for bruises or signs of abuse (**trace measures**). Karen also attends to whether Trish gains weight appropriately for her age with close attention to how her clothing fits for*

*any signs of possible mal-nourishment (**indirect measures**). Acutely aware of horrible outcomes for some of the children active with child welfare, Karen knows that in many of the cases that aroused public attention the workers did not **triangulate** or recognize the importance of **measurement.** She works to assure she never has a child in her caseload found emaciated from starvation, beaten to death, or sexually abused over a period of years. To construct a valid case theory Karen knows she may appear intrusive in order to gather accurate information.*

*Karen's case theory is that "due to the sexual abuse of Sharra by her stepfather, accompanied by denial and fury with Sharra by her mother, Sharra has little trust in or support by her family and little knowledge about parenting. On a variety of drugs since the age of 15, she was drug free for the last three months of her pregnancy. Angry, mistrustful, and overwhelmed with mothering, Sharra is at risk of abusing Trish and relapsing on drugs, but she is currently providing good parental care, is not abusing, and has the potential to support and care for Trish. Her severe mood swings, with spells of uncontrolled crying, are probably reflective of the uncertainties and risks in her current situation."*

· · · · · · · · · · · · · · · · · · · ·

## Intervention: Case Practice Plan and Implementation

Though we argue that assessment and theory construction is the most critical practice component because it shapes all of practice, we fail in our professional function unless we build intervention on the assessment. Our task is not merely to understand clients and explain their behaviors. Rather, we must use conceptualization to do *specific things that result in changes* for individuals, families, communities, organizations, and policies.

In the early 1900s, social workers turned to diagnosis for increasing the scientific aspect of social work and aiding development of their profession (Richmond, 1917). Although it was a very important development, emphasis on diagnosis overshadowed treatment, placing the thrust of practice on understanding the case. Paradoxically, renewed pressures in the 1980s to make social work more scientific have continued to confuse diagnosis and treatment. The stress on quantification encourages use of scales and increasing reliance on categorization. This trend is exacerbated by managed care, which insists on diagnoses for billing purposes, although over use of diagnostic categories preceded managed care in efforts to define normality.

An overly simplistic example illustrates the problem. Using the *Diagnostic and Statistical Manual of Mental Disorders,* 4th ed. (*DSM–IV*), a social worker may diagnose the client's problem as *depression.* This social worker might also have the client complete the Beck inventory, finding that the score supports the depression diagnosis. After a specified period of time, the social worker again administers the Beck and reports the change in the scale score as a successful social work intervention.

But effective social work practice requires behavioral changes—actual improvements in social functioning, not mere changes on a scale score. We fear that we have reified the diagnostic categories, substituting them for clear problem statements that explain individual client difficulties in functioning. Lacking specificity of the problematic behaviors, we then rely on test scores changes as evidence of client change. Classification, however, is not treatment, nor is change in scale scores.

As professionals, our primary responsibility is service to our clients. In social work this means improving social functioning by intervening with individuals and societies. To accomplish these changes, it is necessary to develop clarity about specific problems in functioning.

Categorization is only a useful beginning. For any category, you must identify the actual problematic behaviors in social functioning.

Using **triangulation** by obtaining different indicators for depression helps specify goals formulation. Such indicators might include changes in eating and sleeping patterns, severe mood swings, lack of social interactions, problems with school or job performance, or changes in energy level.

Effective practice impacts on and ameliorates these identified problems. When using diagnostic categories, practitioners must first identify behavioral problems experienced by the client stated in ordinary language in order to target them for change. Gergen agrees that the increasing use of jargon over ordinary language obfuscates meaning (Maranto, 1998). To create change on specific issues in the client's life, social workers must clearly identify these problems in the case theory and include them in the problem statement and intervention plan.

While brief treatment and payment through managed care have resulted in greater specificity for some agencies, effective social work practice has never been possible without the specificity of a problem statement. As Bisman states (1994), "the **problem statement** provides focus to the intervention and identifies for the social worker and the client the substance of what the intervention is to address" (p. 249).

While most agencies ask for presenting problems, a **case practice plan,** including the **problem statement, goals, strategy,** and **relevant literature** provides a broader conception. By placing the range of presenting problems into this framework, the social worker identifies the specific problematic behaviors and the strategy to achieve the goals of intervention.

**Implementation** includes the actual tactics of change, with means to **monitor shifts,** and control the intervention to **prevent drifting** away from the established goals. Practitioners intervene using **single case** and **case study designs,** but they usually find it very difficult to control treatment and the independent variables, essential for determination of validity. **Member checking, triangulation,** and **prevention of reflexivity**

all assist in achieving **validity** and **control of treatment.**

• • • • • • • • • • • • • • • • • • • •

*In our example, Karen's problem statement is that "Sharra and her daughter, Trish, are at risk because of Sharra's drug use, Sharra's young age and lack of familial support, and a home environment that may not be conducive to raising Trish in safety." Because Sharra was removed from her home at 17 when she was six months pregnant,* **goals** *are safety, staying drug free, high school graduation, good parenting of Trish (her daughter), employment, independence, and safety of Trish. The* **strategy** *includes placement in a facility, to provide a safe shelter, support to end her drug addiction, and opportunity to take classes.*

*Karen* **implements** *this strategy through* **controlling treatment** *by regularly scheduled meetings with Sharra and Trish,* **member checking** *with shelter and drug counseling and high school tutoring staff to assure that all share the* **treatment goals** *and* **prevent drift.** *Karen monitors any* **shifts** *she plans, such as length and frequency of visits. Sharra participates in parenting classes, group therapy sessions, and daily group meetings with the drug counselors. Her monthly meetings with the shelter psychiatrist confirm Karen's case theory and no drugs are prescribed for the mood swings.*

*Through* **triangulation,** *Karen checks on Sharra's school grades, the clothing and care of Trish, and the urine analysis results to measure the variables relevant to their treatment goals.*

*It is very difficult to prevent* **reflexivity** *in this intensive treatment approach—urine testing for drug abuse while the client is residing in a protected environment usually results in negative testing. The measurement process of urine testing itself impacts on the drug taking.*

• • • • • • • • • • • • • • • • • • • •

## Evaluation and Reassessment

Accountable and responsible practice requires **judgments** about client change and **achievement**

**of case objectives.** As Bisman (1994) explains "Knowledge of the variables responsible for the change is particularly important in replicating the process, if successful, or modifying it, if the desired results have not been achieved" (p. 251).

Though practitioners may place evaluation at the end of the practice, it is not possible to evaluate without identifying early on the **mode of evaluation,** including specific steps for measuring changes and attaining goals. We must remember that practice is not linear. Practitioners identify means of charting and recording changes while engaged in building relationship, constructing case theory, communicating, observing their reactions, and intervening. Adherence to the ethic of **informed consent** obligates practitioners to inform clients about measurement approaches along with making periodic reassessments.

Depending on the agency mission and typical length of treatment, practitioners need to reconsider the initial set of presenting problems and case theory at regular intervals. **Reassessment** and **recontracting** should probably occur after no more than 12 sessions or three months of treatment.

Appropriate **analysis** and **use of statistics** and other findings provide valuable feedback for the practitioner in planning ongoing treatment with this client. Moreover, though it is not directly applicable to a similar client, this information should help guide future treatment and evaluation approaches.

**Reporting** by practitioners to clients supports informed consent. Reporting also allows clients to utilize the knowledge in their future behaviors. Other practitioners gain from reporting the development of professional knowledge.

• • • • • • • • • • • • • • • • • • • •

*Sharra seems attached to and loving of Trish, expressing the desire to "protect Trish and provide her a decent home."* **Recontracting** *at three-month intervals enables regular* **feedback** *and* **reporting progress** *to Sharra by Karen. To be useful in guiding Karen's future treatment of Sharra and other clients with similar problems, Karen must* *try to **analyze** the distinct intervention effects, including the daily meetings with drug counselors, the group sessions, individual therapy with the psychiatrist, parenting classes, and overall climate of the shelter.*

*Karen acknowledges the importance of prompt removal of adolescents from their abusive situations with placement in a protected environment. She positively evaluates placement in this shelter and the firm but caring approach used by staff and drug counselors. Unlike many such facilities, this center provides in-house high school tutoring, expecting residents to achieve their high school equivalency. Parenting classes, a requirement of residing in the shelter, are a valuable aspect of the treatment. The combination of services addresses the complexity of Sharra's needs, including parenting, drug use, and protection from violence.*

· · · · · · · · · · · · · · · · · · · ·

## Summary

Social workers continually attend to outcomes and linkages among case theory, intervention, and all the other practice components. At the same time, they measure, analyze, and evaluate their utilization of each practice component. Social work practice is a complex undertaking, comprised of a multitude of behaviors by social workers and clients within context of a continually changing set of events. Each component contributes to the overall practice. Understanding and using research knowledge and skills is necessary for practicing social work and adds to development of the profession's knowledge base.

We discussed the professional helping relationship as a belief bonding with clients, possessing purpose and shaped by agency function. The profession's ethical principles of informed consent, confidentiality, and duty to warn establish social work values for protection of clients, the larger society and the profession. At the same time, relationships with supervisors and colleagues along with a process of peer review provide collateral information to reduce bias and unplanned changes.

Practitioners communicate with clients using a range of methods and skills, engage in data collection, and construct instruments for measurement to obtain valid information. The subject matter of practice is often very intimate, requiring practitioner observation to guard against bias and ensure shared constructions of reality with clients.

Constructing the theory of the case through which to organize the practice utilizes a range of measurement approaches, establishment of validity and reliability, and a shared understanding of the nature of the client's situation.

Intervention consists of a case practice plan with a problem statement, goals and objectives and a case study design. Application and control of treatment, intervention measurement, monitoring shifts, and prevention of drift results in accountable practice. Reassessing the case theory and goals and reporting with the client and others in the action system establish new goals or termination.

Serving as translators between researchers and practitioners, we provide a model that juxtaposes research methodologies with each major component of practice. Readers may refer back to the table on pp. 68–69 in this chapter as they engage with the remaining methodology chapters.

## Discussion Questions and Exercises

1. For class discussion: Why is it necessary to translate research terminology into terms relevant for practitioners?

2. Discuss the importance of a joint conceptualization by practitioners and clients to the helping relationship, communication, case theory, intervention, and evaluation.

3. Consider the necessity of reassessing progress toward goals and the theory of the case.

4. Break into small groups and have each define and discuss one of the major practice components: relationship, communication, practitioner observation, assessment, intervention, evaluation.

5. Follow up with a larger class discussion relating use of research methodologies with each of these components.

# CHAPTER SIX

# Measurement: The Core of Practice

Measurement is fundamental to social work practice. Practitioners constantly measure whether their clients are individuals, families, groups, organizations, or communities. Practice rests on judgments that are based on impressions or measurements by practitioners, clients, and other case stakeholders. Intake and determining eligibility, assessment and developing case theory, implementing and monitoring intervention plans, and the final evaluation of the intervention's effects on progress toward case objectives, all involve a continual process of *measurements, impressions,* and *judgments.* Without measurement in some form, judgments of changes, accountability, and informed consent are not possible. Assessment requires gathering and integrating measurements as information about the client and the client's social context from a variety of sources. There is no doubt that practitioners measure and use measurements; the practice task is to measure well and with clarity.

This chapter reviews the logic, components, and construction of measurement as a process. We will focus on general measurement issues and explore reliability, validity, reflexivity, sensitivity and precision, and practicality for practice relevance. In Chapter 7 we will analyze more specific data collection approaches, such as paper-and-pencil questionnaires and interviews.

## Measurement Defined

Measurement is the process and methodology of collecting information, data, facts, and impressions. Along with data collection, the purpose of measurement is to get the information needed

Parallels of Practice and Research

| Research Epistemology and Methodologies | Practice Component and Tasks |
|---|---|
| Measurement | Selecting and using indicators for assessment of client situation, changes in the client's situation, and appropriate intervention and its implementation |
| Data collection | Processes used to gather information for assessing client situation, changes, and progress toward the intervention goals and appropriate intervention and its implementation |

for judgments. Developing and applying specific measurements means constructing shared realties. The measurement's *operational construction* is the way of constructing the reality shared by practitioners, clients, and other stakeholders. Specifying what we want to know, the construction of reality used, and means for sharing that construction, measurements capture the empirical domains specified in the case theory, hypothesis, research questions, and practice plan. Blythe and Tripodi (1989) assert that "measurement is a basic process that can contribute to gathering and analyzing information pertaining to each phase of practice" (p. 23). Hudson (1982a, p. 254) portrays measurement as assigning symbols to properties of objects according to rules. The rules allow sharing between people a construction of reality developed from the measurements.

Siegel (1984, p. 329) infers that measurement is inherent in empirically based practice. If all practice deals with the reality of the client or case, then all practice is inherently empirical (see Figure 6.1). Practice is empirical in that it addresses things that are not solely the practitioner's mental constructions. The measures are the indicators, the different aspects, of a variable of a common core concept. The concepts and variables relate to the client's or case's behavior and ecology and the interventions. Variables are the traits and indicators of the concept and unit of analysis. We will discuss variables and unit of analysis in greater detail later in this chapter.

## Measurement, Practice, and Data Collection

Measurement and measurement processes are operationally inseparable from data collection processes that practitioners use in assessing and monitoring the case. Measurement in practice is real, and measurement error has severe ramifications. Newspapers (Bernstein, 1995; Parent, 1995; Sexton, 1996) are replete with reports of faulty practitioner assessments rooted in fallacious measurements when child protective services workers fail to recognize and accurately measure child abuse indicators and traits. *Measurement, and data collection flaws and errors cannot be corrected by sophisticated research design, practice plans, or statistical analytical approaches.*

The practitioner does not have to cling to the perspective of Dr. David H. Barlow, a SUNY-Albany psychologist, to appreciate the need for measurement. In the introduction to Fischer and Corcoran's (1994) sourcebook on clinical practice measurement tools, Dr. Barlow predicted that future historians will ridicule the lack of extrinsic behavioral measurement by social work practitioners and their reliance on simply asking the client how he or she feels as an informal way of measuring. Effective practice requires appropriate measurement and data collection. Good measurement is not limited to any single approach.

Historians will point out wryly that this practice would be analogous to physicians periodically

**FIGURE 6.1**  Relationship Among Concepts, Measurement Referents, and Perceived Reality

---

Concepts as ideals and mental constructions in the mind of the client, practitioner, or other stakeholders

Concept operationalized in traits or referents— whether client trait, situational trait, or intervention trait—that can be measured

Developing and selecting specific measurement tools and approaches to capture and serve as proxies for the construction of the referents

Perceived and empirical reality containing the referents

---

asking patients with blood infections or fractures "how are you feeling" without bothering to analyze blood samples or take X rays. "How could this have been?" they will ask. In searching for answers they will examine records of clinical practice in the late twentieth century and find that the most usual response from clinicians was that they were simply too busy to evaluate what they were doing. But the real reason, astute historians will note, is they never had learned how. (p. xxxviii)

Dr. Barlow coyly ignores that physicians also measure by asking "How do you feel?" and "What hurts?" as a part of their measurement approach. And as we discuss in Chapter 7, the paper-and-pencil measures advocated by Fischer and Corcoran amount largely to "How do you feel?" in that they ask respondents or clients to evaluate and self-report attitudes, opinions, feelings, and observations.

## Measurement Approaches: Quantitative or Qualitative

The process of measurement, according to Bernard (1994, p. 8), is deciding which value to record for something out of the range of possible values for meaning. There are two general approaches to measurement—*quantitative* and *qualitative*. While they are often viewed as dichotomous and distinct, most social work practice measurement processes generally require both. In social work, measurement requires specification of the problems, interventions, and outcomes with referents that are concrete, observable, and capable of judgment, hopefully, by clients, practitioners, and other case participants.

### Measures as Proxies

Measurement is a process of assigning numbers or symbols to ideas. The tools and approaches used for assigning represent proxies for the idea or concepts. *Measurements are proxies because they substitute for the ideas and the referents.* As we discussed in Chapter 4, concepts as ideas are the user's constructions to understand the world, but they are not the world itself. If we mistake our ideas and mental constructions for the world itself, we are guilty of *reification*, or making the mental constructions real (Blumer, 1969, p. 150). Measurements are the user's construction of the idea or its referent and are not synonymous with the world itself. To confuse them with the world is to be doubly guilty of reification. In Chapter 4, we saw that scores on IQ tests are intelligence only if we designate intelligence as scores on IQ tests. Scores on depression inventories and self-rating scales are not a person's depression; they are a proxy measure for a person's depression. Depression is a mood disorder and specific behavior accompanying the mood occurring in a context that we can measure by duration and intensity through self-reports and observations by others.

The measurement's strength of linkage to empirical indicators, referents, and variables of the ideas moves the concepts and resultant theories from metaphysical mental constructions, logic, and philosophy into the empirical realm (Blumer, 1969, pp. 164–165). The measurement methodologies used in "looking at the world" should be self-evident proxies and not mystified in imperceptive mentalism or extreme scientism, statistical quantification, and mathematical rationalism. Reification of concepts or measurements risks losing social meaning, resulting in irrelevant knowledge without real-world consequence. **Measures should capture phenomena rather than requiring phenomena to be pushed and contorted to fit within their parameters.**

### Quantitative Approaches

Numbers are used in quantitative measurements to indicate relationships of intensity, magnitude, severity, duration, and frequency. Nugent and Hankins (1989) hold that "measurement is concerned with the methods used to provide quantitative descriptions of the extent to which individuals manifest or possess specified characteristics" (p. 449). We are using quantitative indicators when we measure a client's income by counting the number of dollars the client receives in wages and other sources. We use quantitative measures when we indicate a client's depression level by the score on a depression inventory, the unintentional 5% or more weight gain or loss in a month, and the number of days the client sleeps excessively, with excessive denoted as over 8 to 10 hours on a regular basis.

## Qualitative Approaches

Symbols, usually descriptive words (Sherman & Reid, 1994), are used in qualitative measurement approaches. Social work practitioners cannot rely only on quantitative measurements; like ethnographers, they need "to explain human behavior in terms of meaning" (Spradley, 1980, p. 8). The social world does not exist in an obdurate and whole form apart from the observer's measurement and social construction. Though the parts exist, the construction and meaning of the whole is a social expression and dependent for definition on the observers and the social context. Understanding and measurement, then, must consider both *content* and *context* (Blumer, 1969; Berger & Luckmann, 1966; Spradley, 1980).

*Social work practitioners look at and understand social behavior and phenomena in the world in all its complexity rather than as a laboratory simplification. Coupling qualitative approaches featuring meaning with the greater reliability of quantified approaches has great practice relevance.*

## Measurement Tasks

Measurement involves construction of a theory about reality along with decisions on ways to assess the existence of reality in order to test the theory.

## Operationalizing Ideas into Measurements

Taking the ideas used to reflect the world and applying them to a construction of the world, the measurement process, is called **operationalization.** Measurement as a tool in the construction of reality for practice depends on operational definitions of the concepts of the case theory, practice hypothesis and objectives, and the intervention. The things measured are a concept's *empirical referents.* Operationalization involves defining concepts by their empirical indicators, traits, and attributes. These referents are usually called *variables* because they can have different values across different units and under different conditions.

Steps in Operationalizing the Variables

| 1. Case Theory → | 2. Variables → | 3. Measurement → | 4. Measurement's Usefulness |
|---|---|---|---|
| Case theory, outcomes, and interventions concepts (ideas) and their domains. → | Indicators and empirical referents of the concepts' domains. What are the variables and indicators of each concept? → | How will the existence, intensity, magnitude, and duration of each relevant indicator be determined? → | Establish the reliability, validity, reflexivity, precision, and practicality of each measurement and select the stronger on all criteria. |

| | |
|---|---|
| Conceptual definitions | Words, ideas, and mental pictures that cannot be directly measured, clear conceptual definitions must be transformed into *operational definitions*. |
| Operational definitions | In measuring a conceptually defined variable (Bernard, 1994, p. 26), the operational definition must indicate the variable, its values, and *how to measure* and record the values. |

Operational definitions or measurements become the proxy for the concept and are necessary for intersubjectivity or agreement between people about what exists and its meaning. Links between the concept and referent should be direct and not obscure, tenuous, or cryptic. Agreement on operationalizing and measuring indicators of concepts allows different observers to "talk the same language."

Decisions on the measurements and processes to use in practice judgments involve operationalizing case theory and outcomes along with the intervention concepts and the variables.

1. *Develop the case theory, outcomes, and intervention concepts with their nominal definitions, ideas, and domains.* What is each concept's domain? What lies within and outside the domains of these ideas? This is constructing reality with the client and other stakeholders. If the case involves child abuse, what behavior is abusive and what behavior lies outside the domain and boundary of abuse? What is different about the two types of behavior?

2. *Determine and specify each concept's empirical referents and traits.* Traits are indicators, while variables are dimensions of the concept that fall within the concept's domain, demonstrating its existence and boundaries. Whether the indicators can vary by intensity, duration, and magnitude needs to be established. Can abuse vary in intensity, magnitude, or duration? The indica-

tors and idea should correspond in their characteristics.

3. *Judge the existence, intensity, magnitude, and duration of the indicators.* This task involves defining the data necessary to obtain from the measurement processes: (a) whether it is possible to directly measure the trait, indicator, or variable; and (b) whether the best measurement approach is quantitative, qualitative, or both. The processes and tools should distinguish between what lies within and ouside the domains. Be sensitive to differences in the indicators or variables and avoid false positives and false negative judgments.

4. *Decide whether existing or new measurement instruments are needed and who will measure.* Review available tools for their reliability, validity, reflexivity, and practicality for current practice uses with the relevant population and conditions.

5. *If there are no available tools and processes they will have to be developed and pretested and piloted to establish reliability, validity, reflexivity, and practicality.* Generally, a minimum of ten cases should be used to establish reliability.

Compare alternative methods of measuring and obtaining information for judgments according to the preceding criteria. Select the stronger tools; the weaker the tools, the more the need for triangulation and use of multiple measurement tools and approaches.

A good operationalization results in a measurement process that yields information for judgments with, as Bernard (1994) indicated, a low "probability of and amount of error" (p. 24).

## Operationalization and Information Needs

Measurement operationalization is a necessary element in responding to and satisfying assessment and case theory information needs. Operationalization, when completed, addresses the questions of *who, what, when, where,* and *how* (Jayaratne & Levy, 1979, pp. 46–66).

On **whom** is information needed?
**What** information is needed?
**What** are the indicators?
**What** other information is needed?
**How** is the information to be gathered?
**When** is the information to be gathered?
**Where** is the information to be gathered?

## *Who—The unit of analysis*

Who is being measured? In operationalizing concepts and variables, we need to distinguish between the variable or trait being measured and the unit or entity being measured. The latter is the unit of analysis, the entity described by the variable of which the variable is a trait, and to which we apply the measures and whose characteristics and behavior we want to understand, explain or predict. Typically in social work practice, the unit of analysis is an individual, group, family organization, program, community, or some other social entity.

The unit of analysis, like the client in family therapy, group therapy or social action, is not always self-evident. If we are concerned with the effects of marital therapy on marital stability and divorce, the unit of analysis is the couple in marital therapy, the marriage partners as a unit and not as individuals. The trait or variable of the unit of analysis is marital stability and divorce.

*It is necessary to define the unit of analysis with boundaries that distinguish it from other units.* Yin (1984) advocates in a case study:

> If the unit of analysis is a small group, for instance, the persons to be included within the group…must be distinguished from those outside it…. Finally… specific time boundaries are needed to define the beginning and end of the case. All of these types of questions need to be considered and answered to define the unit of analysis and thereby to determine the limits of the data collection and analysis. (p. 33)

Measurement, analysis, and assessment are tools to help us understand the unit of analysis.

## *What—The variable or trait measured*

What are the variables being measured? They consist of the concept's empirical traits as characteristics of the unit. These indicators can be measured by one or more of the four measurement levels: nominal, ordinal, equal interval, or ratio. The most appropriate measurement level best fits the concept's construction. And, as Bernard (1994) admonishes us,

> Remember this rule: Always measure things at the highest level of measurement possible. Don't measure things at the ordinal level if you can measure them intervally. If you want to know the price that farmers paid for the land, then ask the price. (p. 35)

Do not ask if the price is between $100 and $200 if you can ask the specific price. Do not ask if the price is low, medium, or high if you can determine the precise dollars, or unless you are seeking its meaning to the respondent and not its level. Measurements of the client outcome variables and the interventions, if possible, should move to higher and richer measurement systems than the nominal (such as to ordinal, interval, and ratio) to allow for more use. Using measurement systems for the intervention that corresponds to those used for the outcome variables allows for more direct comparisons in relating the two sets of measures and the data. Does greater intensity, magnitude, and duration of the outcomes correlate with greater magnitude, intensity, and duration of treatment and intervention? Quantification's strength over qualitative measures is that quantitative data allow for more precision. Low-order measurements weaken the subsequent data and the theory developed from the data. We know less about the case or unit.

There are four levels of measurement: nominal, ordinal, interval, and ratio.

***Nominal measures.*** The lowest order of measures, nominal measures, yield the least precise and sensitive information of the four measurement levels. They measure the existence of something and essentially are limited to classifying traits into mutually exclusive categories, such as male and female in gender. Nominal measures classify or name something only and do not measure intensity, weight, quality or quantity other than a 0 indicating the value is not present or a 1 indicating the value is present. The measure cannot place an object or phenomenon into more than one classification. Under the prevalent contemporary gender conceptualization, a person cannot be classified as both male and female simultaneously.

The numbers used in nominal measures are *proxy labels* for names and classifications. They have no intrinsic or relational value. Assigning a 1 to males and 2 to females does not indicate that females have greater gender weighting, nor are males first in a rank order. Females can validly be assigned a 1 and males a 2 as long as the assignment is consistent. Numbers are used for ease of recording and analyzing, especially in this computer data processing era.

*Ordinal measures.* Remembering Bernard's admonition, we want to use a higher measurement level than nominal when possible. Mattaini and Kirk (1993) illustrate the practice importance:

Measurement Scales for Indicators of Conditions

| Indicator of Condition | Type of Measurement | Example |
|---|---|---|
| Existence of condition | Nominal and qualitative | Presence of male gender, absence of female gender |
| Magnitude, intensity, or severity | Ordinal | Depression scale rating depression severity level on a 1 to 10 scale |
| Duration | Interval | Length of time condition exists; as days, weeks, etc. |
| Frequency | Ratio | Number of times a condition or behavior occurs within a specific time interval |

It may occasionally be useful for practitioners to know a client's categorical religious affiliation. For assessing these matters, approaches that provide "scalar" measures will be more

Characteristics of the Four Levels of Measure

| | | | Characteristic of Measure | |
|---|---|---|---|---|
| Measurement | Mutually Exclusive | Fixed Order | Equal Spacing Between Indicators in Ordering | A True Zero Point Determined (complete absence of) |
| Nominal | Yes | No | No | No |
| Ordinal | Yes | Yes | No | No |
| Interval | Yes | Yes | Yes | No |
| Ratio | Yes | Yes | Yes | Yes |

Adapted from *Social Research: A Tool for the Human Services*, 2nd Edition, by D. R. Monette, T. J. Sullivan, and C. R. DeJong, p. 111. Copyright © 1995 Holt Rinehart & Winston, Inc. Reprinted by permission.

informative than simply indicating (i.e. by nominal categories) that a person is Protestant, Catholic, or Jewish…purpose is primary. (p. 231)

* * * * * * * * * * * * * * * * * * * *

*For most practice purposes [i.e., if Karen had been practicing with Sharra early in her pregnancy], the social worker would be much more interested in, say, the extent to which Sharra is involved in religious organizations, the amount of social supports she receives from people in her religious community, the priority that specific religious values have for her, and the relationship among all of these.*

* * * * * * * * * * * * * * * * * * * *

**Ordinal measures** allow an examination of a variable in a *scalar* or "greater than or less than" *sequence* or order. Ordinal measurement allows greater understanding of the variable than the nominal measure does. We can now examine the internal ordering of the variable and changes in the variable's conditions not possible with a nominal measure.

Useful in judgments of change on client behavior or social conditions over time, ordinal measures *do not allow* precise judgment on how much "greater or less" the change is. Comparing the meaning of two different measures on the same ordinal scale, one a measure of 5 and the other a 2 on the same variable by the same scale or measure, the measures only indicate that the 5 is greater than the 2 measure on the variable or trait. It does not indicate distance between the measurement points or the anchoring of the points. The distance between a 1 and 2 on the measure may not be the same as the distance between 4 and 5, nor may it indicate whether a score of 5 is 150% greater than the measure of 2. The ordinal measures are more useful for comparing change within a case than between cases. One client's 5 on the scale need not be the same as another client's 5.

The *Family-of-Origin Scale* (*FOS*) developed by Hovestadt, Anderson, Piercy, Cochran, and Fine (Fischer & Corcoran, 1994, pp. 303–307) is an example of an ordinal scale.

* * * * * * * * * * * * * * * * * * * *

*Back to our earlier case, Elana could have the couple Bill and Sharon judge the value of each item on a 1 to 5 weighting and then sum scores of each item to give a total ordinal score. The responses are Bill and Sharon's perception, recall, and reporting of their family's interaction or intimacy, if these questions capture an idea of intimacy. The scale, like all ordinal measures, gives "ordinality" or the ability to judge "greater than–less than."* Strongly Agree *is greater than* Agree, *and* Agree *is greater than* Disagree *in the ordering on the weight of agreement with the statement. However, no judgments can be made regarding the distance between or the relationships of the weights other than ordering. While* Strongly Agree *is coded a 5 and* Agree *a 4, these numbers represent order, not distance. Don't assume that the distance between* Strongly Agree *and* Agree *is the same as the distance between* Agree *and* Neutral *or the distance between* Neutral *and* Strongly Agree *is the same as between* Disagree *and* Agree. *Do assume that the ordering is fixed. Ordinal scales allow ordering and indication of change on the dimension of the ordering, but not precision in judging the amount of change. The*

---

**Question Examples**

In my family, it was normal to show both positive and negative feelings.

   5 (SA)   4 (A)   3 (N)   2 (D)   1 (SD)

In my family, I expressed just about every feeling I had.

   5 (SA)   4 (A)   3 (N)   2 (D)   1 (SD)

In my family, certain feelings were not allowed to be expressed.

   5 (SA)   4 (A)   3 (N)   2 (D)   1 (SD)

My family had an unwritten rule: Don't express your feelings.

   5 (SA)   4 (A)   3 (N)   2 (D)   1 (SD)

Strongly Agree *by Sharon may not have the same strength of Bill's* Strongly Agree.

. . . . . . . . . . . . . . . . . . . . . .

A more complex use of ordinality is offered by the *Depression Self-Rating Scale (DSRS)* (Corcoran & Fischer, 1994, pp. 464–465) developed by Peter Birlson to measure the extent and severity of depression in children.

. . . . . . . . . . . . . . . . . . . . . .

*The social worker, Nancy, who we discussed in Chapter 4, could administer this scale to Tani, age 7. Nancy's assessment and case theory construction is not possible without measurement.*

. . . . . . . . . . . . . . . . . . . . . .

The range of possible scores is 0–36, with positive items scored 0 to 2 and negative items -2 to 0. Lower scores indicate higher depression.

Each item is given a score that can be *0 to 2* with a positive or negative weighting similar to the *Strongly Agree* to *Strongly Disagree*. But the items should not be considered equal depression indicators. Although both are negative indicators, "I think that life isn't worth living" does not appear equal to "I feel very bored." If they are not equal, then weighting of the strength of agreement of the statements cannot be treated as equal, nor can comparisons between respondents be treated as equal. Equality comparisons require higher levels of measurement than ordinal measurements.

*Ordinal measures are limited and suspect in making comparisons between clients unless a shared anchoring of meaning of the different scale items and ordinal points can be established.* Do different clients mean the same thing when they say *Strongly Agree, Agree, Neutral, Disagree,* or *Strongly Disagree* to the statement:

My family had an unwritten rule: Don't express your feelings.

Do different clients mean the same thing when they say: *Most of the Time, Sometimes,* and *Never* to the statement:

I don't look forward to things as much as I used to.

. . . . . . . . . . . . . . . . . . . . . .

*Use of these measures by the social worker Elana with the family, Bill and Sharon, can assist Elana in better understanding the meaning of the violent interactions in their marriage.*

. . . . . . . . . . . . . . . . . . . . . .

If not, then comparisons among clients of magnitude, intensity, and severity cannot reasonably be made. Nevertheless, comparisons of change for the same client are reasonably made.

***Equal interval measures.*** When the phenomenon can be divided into units or points with equal distance or differences between the units,

---

Most of the Time (Coding: If positive item = 2, if negative = 0)

Sometimes (Coding: If positive item = 1, if negative = 1)

Never (Coding: If positive item = 0, if negative = 2)

1. I look forward to things as much as I used to. (+)
2. I sleep very well. (+)
3. I feel like crying. (–)
4. I like to go out and play. (+)
5. I feel like running away. (–)
6. I get tummy aches. (–)
7. I have a lot of energy. (+)
8. I enjoy my food. (+)
9. I can stick up for my self. (+)
10. I think that life isn't worth living. (–)
11. I am very good at the things I do. (+)
12. I enjoy the things I do as much as I used to. (+)
13. I like talking about my family. (+)
14. I have horrible dreams. (–)
15. I feel very lonely. (–)
16. I am easily cheered up. (+)
17. I feel so sad I can hardly stand it. (–)
18. I feel very bored. (–)

we speak of equal interval measurement. The distance or change between any two sequential points on the measurement is equal. The distance or change between a 1 and 2 is the same as the distance between a 199 and a 200. With equal interval measures, the intervals can be aggregated and still be comparable as long as the number of points aggregated is the same. The distance between 2 and 6 is the same as the distance between 102 and 106.

Equal interval measures do not assume an absolute zero or the total absence of the phenomenon. An example of equal interval measurement use with physical phenomena is the Fahrenheit thermometer for the measurement of temperature.[1] This measurement assumes the difference between a unit of heat is the same at 32 degrees and 33 degrees as between 99 and 100 degrees. Zero on the measure, however, does not indicate the absence of heat or freezing. Freezing occurs at 32 degrees.

In the social sciences it is difficult to find examples of equal interval measures of purely social things, although they often treat ordinal measures as equal interval measures. The interval between a 3 and 4 and 1 and 2 is equal in an equal interval scale but not in an ordinal scale. Intelligence or IQ tests are often presented as equal interval measures, although it is difficult to assume that the social meaning and social functioning of an IQ scale distance of 30 units is the same between any set of consecutive 30 points on the scale. It does not appear the same functional distance between 80 and 110 as between 50 and 80.

**Ratio measures.**   Ratio measures share all the strengths of ordinal and equal interval measures plus the additional strength of an *absolute zero*

*point that connotes the complete absence of the unit.* Ratio measures are the most powerful level of measurement because they produce the best understanding of a phenomenon. If we can conceptualize and measure a phenomenon in ratio measures, we enrich our understanding with greater precision and specificity than with other measures. We no longer have to describe in terms of closer or farther but can use exact distances. *Ratio measures can classify, order, determine the distance between points and compare them.* Ratio measures allow the use of the full range of analytical tools in analysis. Examples are dollar systems with income measures in dollars, physical weight with troy weights, physical distance with the metric or other systems, and time measures in seconds and minutes.

In dealing with purely social phenomena and social interactions, we should recognize the difficulty in developing measures of meaning that have equal interval and absolute zeros across people and clients. While we can measure an amount of money with ratio measures—the distance between $10,000 and $20,000 is the same as the distance between $1,990,000 and $2,000,000—their social meanings are different. The loss of $10,000 to working-class persons halving their income is not the same as the loss of $10,000 to an affluent person. With social phenomena, the social meaning is often as important as the phenomenon itself.

### When—The times to measure

In operationalizing a measurement process, the researcher or practitioner has to decide on *optimal times* to measure something in order to best capture the information and empirical indicators for judgment. The most optimal time to measure something is when it is occurring. This is usually not possible, however, and measurement is generally indirect. We measure the results, effects, and traces of things, not the events or behaviors directly. We examine trauma and question victims, the results of abuse, rather than measuring the abusive behavior itself. We will discuss guide-

---

[1]Note that temperature is the unit of measurement and not the phenomenon. A temperature of 32 degrees on a Fahrenheit thermometer only indicates the temperature that water freezes at sea level; it is not water freezing.

lines for selecting the measurement in the chapters on design and practice plans and sampling.

### Where—The places for measurement

When we operationalize a measurement process, we need to determine the *context* most appropriate to the meaning. *Where* relates to determining the most appropriate context—locations and situations—to reflect the indicators and where the measurement tools and processes can be most appropriately used. Behavior will vary by context. Direct measures are applied where the behavior is actually occurring. Indirect measures can be applied in other contexts.

### How—The measurement tools

How to determine the empirical indicators' values? The *how* in operationalizing is concerned with *selecting the appropriate measurement tools, instruments, and processes to collect the information used in the judgments.* The tools and processes can range from questionnaires and paper-and-pencil scales through observations.

Relationship of Directness and Intrusiveness

|          | Obtrusive                    | Unobtrusive            |
|----------|------------------------------|------------------------|
| Indirect | Least favorable measures     |                        |
| Direct   |                              | Most favorable measures |

*Direct measures.* Measurement tools, instruments, and processes vary on directness and intrusiveness. Generally, *direct measures are preferred over indirect measures and unobtrusive measures over obtrusive measures.* Direct measures include direct observations, sensing, and recording of the phenomenon. Although instruments may be used to record the measure, the measurement is applied directly to the phenomenon, such as (1) directly observing behavior by visual observation or the use of video cameras, and (2) directly measuring physiological conditions, such as measuring blood pressure and pulse rates. *Direct measures are generally stronger because they are closer to the phenomenon than are indirect measures.*

There are many challenges connected with the use of direct measures. Though they are the stronger forms of measurement, they are also more intrusive because they are applied directly to the unit or client. When the measures are known to and intrude on the client, there can be a reaction to the measurement, an altering of the client's behavior by the very act of measuring. *Direct measures' intrusiveness can produce social desirability and social acquiescence effects, especially when used in practice. Further, direct measures can only be used if the phenomenon is accessible to direct measurement and if it is happening when the measurements can be applied.* Much behavior, such as child or spouse abuse, is not always readily available for direct measurement. Finally, direct measures are often costly, especially in the time required for observation or measurement of infrequently occurring events.

*Indirect measures.* When direct measurement is not possible, we must use indirect measures, which are at least one step removed from the phenomenon. Here, we do not directly observe the behavior but rely on reports or, as Bernard (1994) advises, trace indicators. **Trace indicators** and **trace studies** measure the "evidence" left by the behavior, such as the traces of drugs left in urine samples to infer drug use. Investigations of civil disasters such as airplane wrecks often rely on indirect and trace measures. Indirect measures and trace measures are the only measurement methods available to explore historical events—those that occurred in the past and that we did not measure at the time of occurrence.

Indirect measures tend to be less intrusive on the phenomenon than direct measures, although they may be intrusive on the respondent. Urine analysis does not intrude on the prior drug use behavior measured, but it may intrude on subsequent behavior. Unobtrusive measurements do not intrude on or manipulate the phenomenon. Deception is more possible, however, with unobtrusive measurements, especially if informed consent is not obtained.

Paper-and-pencil tests such as attitude scales and reports such as a depression inventory and client logs are examples of indirect measures. They are indirect in that they ask for reports on behavior in the past, albeit on the patient's own behavior. Measures and the measurement processes vary on their degree of obtrusiveness and directness. Practitioners have to judge the degree to which the obtrusiveness alters the variable or the indirectness loses the meaning. *We advocate triangulation or use of multiple information sources, measurements, and composite indicators to overcome the biases and limitations of any single approach.* It is important to use multiple measures and data collection processes that do not share the same methodological weaknesses and biases (Singleton, Strait, & Strait, 1993, p. 526). Triangulation is fully discussed in the section on validity.

## Practice Ethics and Measurement

Hudson's (1978) advocacy of explicit measurement elevates it from a pragmatic necessity to an ethical requirement of good practice.

> The necessity for obtaining measurement of the client's problem...arises from the implicit or explicit contract created by the therapist's agreement to provide professional service.... The contract carries with it the obligation to demonstrate to the client, oneself, one's superiors, and the professional community that treatment is effective or to refer the client to some other resource. Anything short of adherence to this commitment represents a *flaw in one's professional ethics.* [emphasis added] (p. 65)

Hudson then offers two supporting axioms that reify the measurements as reality:

> If you can't measure the client's problem, it does not exist.

> If you cannot measure the client's problem, you cannot treat it. (p. 65)

The axioms exaggerate, while emphasizing measurement's importance. Whether practitioners are able or willing to measure clients' problems, the problems still exist for clients and others but the meaning and relationships of the problems, interventions, and any changes in either cannot be known without measurement. Practitioners can treat without measuring, but they will know neither the effects nor whether clients receive the treatments.

The ethical and practical demands that practitioners use appropriate measurements are these: the need to determine if they address the client's problems, whether they use appropriate treatment, and consideration of any results. The ethical logic is that problems, objectives, *and* interventions must be stated in measurable terms. The constructions must allow information for judgments to be collected, used, and communicated. If practitioners continue treatment without knowing if it helps, harms, or does nothing, they are arguably acting unethically.

Hudson's axioms might reasonably be modified to satisfy a broader measurement perspective.

1. If you cannot measure and make judgments about a client's problems, *you won't know their existence, extent, frequency, intensity, magnitude, and duration.* Nor will you have any capacity to judge changes in these problems.
2. If you cannot measure and make judgments about a client's problems, *effective intervention to alter the problem's existence, extent, frequency, intensity, magnitude, duration becomes difficult.*
3. If you cannot measure and make judgments about a client's strengths and resources, *you won't know their existence, extent, frequency, intensity, magnitude, and duration.* Nor will you have the capacity to use them.
4. If you cannot measure an intervention, *you won't know if you are administering the appropriate intervention, how it is being administered, or what interventions, in fact, you implement.*

## Measurement and Informed Consent

Over and above measurement's capacity to provide knowledge of the problem and intervention, lend precision and clarity on what is being changed, improve objectivity in judgments of treatment and change, and determine what was done in treatment—all necessary for accountable practice—*measurement is also necessary for the ethical imperative of informed consent.* Dependent on clients' understanding of what they are consenting to, they need information on the problem's scope, appropriate interventions and their administration, and any resultant changes.

## Arguments against Measurement

There are arguments against practice measurement. The most telling is that certain quantified measurement processes, especially paper-and-pencil measurements, often result in *oversimplifying problems and treatments to fit available measurement tools.* Practice and problem conception are configured into a rigid "research" format that ignores the qualitative and subjective complexities of problem definitions, outcome conceptions, and treatments (Saleebey, 1974; Tripodi, 1994, pp. 27–28; Tyson, 1992). "Research" interests supersede "practice" interests, and practice becomes the servant of science rather than science and research the servants and tools of practice. The fear that practice will be subservant to research is based on the advocacy by researchers to conduct research on practice in agencies (Aronson & Sherwood, 1967; Blythe, Tripodi, & Briar, 1994; Briar, 1973; Rosenblatt, 1968; Wodarski, 1997).

The arguments against measurement on analysis appear to rest on a pseudoissue (Staudt, 1997). Practitioners constantly make judgments unless they are practicing randomly or rely solely on intuition. Practitioners use information for judgments. The practice concern is whether the judgments construct the complexities of the situation or are simplistic and naive constructions of reality. All data and measurements involve explicit or implicit theoretical assumptions or the thing would not be examined.

Judgments are part of the practice relationship. The intent of practice is to alter the case situation in some way that would not occur if the practitioner were not involved. To argue otherwise is to argue for meaningless practice. Measurement need not adhere to a rigid, limited, or naive process to provide information for judgments. Measurement can and should be quantitative and qualitative. Both approaches have value; they can be used independently and in combination. The challenge is to use the most appropriate, reliable, truthful, and practical means to obtain information.

. . . . . . . . . . . . . . . . . . . . .

### PRACTICE CASE DRUG USE AND SELF-ESTEEM

#### THE UNIT OF ANALYSIS (WHO)

*A 14-year-old middle-class white male, Tad, was referred to a social worker, Mr. Noble, for drug counseling. Tad says that he is only a "recreational user." He is a low B average student in high school. He presented no other significant behavioral problems. Tad's parents, both employed and in the home, are high achievers. He has an older sister, presently a sophomore at a prestigious university on an academic scholarship, who was an honor student in high school. Tad was assessed by his teachers as demonstrating "low self-esteem." The parents and school officials referred Tad for counseling hoping that early intervention might prevent later problems. Mr. Noble selected counseling as the intervention of choice to raise Tad's self-esteem.*

#### CASE THEORY PROPOSITIONS

*(1) Tad's drug use is at least partially the result of low self-esteem (Griffin-Shelley, Sandler, & Lees, 1990; Kinnier, Metha, Okey, & Keim, 1994; Richter, Brown, & Mott, 1991). (2) Increased self-esteem will decrease Tad's drug use. (3) Mr. Noble's model of counseling will enhance self-esteem. These propositions remain tentative until empirically established. There are several possible relationships*

and outcomes among self-esteem, drug use, and counseling. The case theory propositions of relationships between self-esteem and drug use indicated by cells 2 and 3 will "explain" this unit of analysis' behavior. Tad falls into cell 3 prior to counseling and into cell 2 after counseling. His actual placement is unknown without measuring his self-esteem and drug use. The youth might fall into any one of the four cells.

|              |      | Drug Use |      |
|--------------|------|----------|------|
|              |      | High     | Low  |
| Self-esteem  | High | 1        | 2    |
|              | Low  | 3        | 4    |

The relationship between self-esteem and drug use for this case may not be inverse. It can be direct or curvilinear with marginally increasing self-esteem accompanied by increased drug use, or no relationship may exist for this case. Counseling may have no effect on self-esteem with Tad, raise it, or lower it. There can be three variants on two possible conditions: (1) the intervention was delivered as designed, or (2) the intervention was not delivered as designed, with (a) self-esteem increased, (b) self-esteem decreased, (c) self-esteem unchanged. The logical sequence of the theoretical chain of the effects of, or relationship of, self-esteem to drug use can have variants of three possible relationships: (1) drug use can increase, with a direct relationship between self-esteem and drug use;

(2) drug use can remain unchanged and there is no relationship; or (3) drug use can decline and there is an inverse relationship between self-esteem and use. In all, 18 possible relationships are possible in the implied theoretical propositions among intervention, self-esteem, and drug use behavior.

The case theory is not supported unless Mr. Noble conducts appropriate intervention, improves Tad's self-esteem, and lowers his drug use with any improved self-esteem. The case theory's hypothetical propositions are not valid or true until Mr. Noble establishes their empirical validity and truthfulness in this practice situation, which requires measurement. Mr. Noble must measure to determine (1) if he administered the counseling as intended, (2) Tad's pre- and postprogram self-esteem levels, and (3) Tad's pre- and postprogram drug use. Measurement is required of all the components, because changes in one do not indicate either the existence of or changes in the other two. Changes in Tad's drug use behavior do not necessarily mean that Mr. Noble intervened as designed, any more than measuring the intervention and determining that it was delivered as designed means Tad changed his drug use behavior. All need measurement.

## THE INDICATORS OF SELF-ESTEEM, DRUG USE, AND COUNSELING (WHAT)

Before selecting measurement tools and processes, Mr. Noble needs to select appropriate indicators of the concepts of self-esteem, drug use, and counseling for this case. The indicators are the things he will measure with the tools and processes.

| Counseling Conducted | Self-Esteem | Drug Use |          |          |
|----------------------|-------------|----------|----------|----------|
| Appropriately        | Increase    | Increase | Unchange | Decrease |
|                      | Unchange    | Increase | Unchange | Decrease |
|                      | Decrease    | Increase | Unchange | Decrease |
| Inappropriately      | Increase    | Increase | Unchange | Decrease |
|                      | Unchange    | Increase | Unchange | Decrease |
|                      | Decrease    | Increase | Unchange | Decrease |

## Self-Esteem

*Self esteem is generally taken to mean self-image evaluation or feelings about oneself, described in either positive or negative terms, and overall worthiness (Gurney, 1988; Hudson, 1982b; Pope, McHale, & Craighead, 1988; Rosenberg, 1979). Self-esteem is generally held to be important in adolescents (Chubb, Fertman, & Ross, 1997; Juhasz, 1985; Keefe & Berndt, 1996; Nielsen & Metha, 1994). [In developing case theory, practitioners need to be clear on whether a variable is causative, an effect, or only a correlate. Based on California research, self-esteem itself may not be a significant contributing factor to many social and personal problems, contrary to what is often assumed and included from cross-sectional research designs. It may be a result and by-product of, or a correlate of, personal problems and social behavior. The California Task Force on Self-Esteem and Personal and Social Responsibility's (Mecca, Smelser, & Vasconcellos, 1989, pp. 15–17) research arm concluded that "the association between self-esteem and its expected consequences are mixed, insignificant, or absent.... the association between self-esteem and behavior...is weak; even less can be said of a causal relationship between the two." The Task Force (Toward a State of Esteem, 1990) discounted the empirical findings in their research team. The Task Force's belief that low self-esteem causes personal problems and behavior such as school failure and other problems, and a belief in improved self-esteem as a social panacea, was unshaken by the counterintuitive evidence.] The case theory holds that it is an important factor in Tad's drug use.*

## Drug Use

*The drug use's most direct indicators are the ingestion, inhalation, or injection of a substance classified as a drug. There are a series of less direct behavioral indicators derived from the theory of drug use's impact on behavior. Accompanying reported decreases in drug use should be improvements in grades, changes in friendship patterns and school activities, and other behavior. This es-*

*tablishes predictive validity. Mr. Noble can track Tad's peer friendship patterns, school activities, and grades.*

## THE TIMES TO MEASURE (WHEN)[2]

*Self-esteem and drug use needs measuring prior to the intervention to establish Tad's problematic baseline levels. Measurements also are needed after intervention to assess change and objectives achievement. As we said earlier, the most suitable time to measure something is when it is occurring. However, with Tad's drug use, this may not be possible. Judgments of drug use will probably be based on information obtained from indirect measurements. The use of indirect measures — reports and traces of past events — depends on the duration of the events' effects and how the indicator is conceptualized. If self-esteem is conceptualized as a fairly stable trait, measurement can be less situationally temporal. Tad's drug use and self-esteem prior to, during, and after the counseling will need assessing.*

## LOCATION OF THE BEHAVIORS AND CHANGES (WHERE)[3]

*The ideal place to measure all sets of indicators is where, as well as when, they occur: drug use in the places where the youth is most likely to use drugs, self-esteem continuously, and counseling where it occurs. We are not merely concerned with self-esteem in Mr. Noble's office but in the school, home, and places where Tad may use drugs — the places where the interaction between self-esteem and drug use is important. Unfortunately, this is not practical. Mr. Noble will need to select other locations where the indicators or traces may be present. If self-esteem is conceptualized as a fairly stable trait (Bachman & O'Malley, 1977), self-esteem measurements taken at more convenient*

---

[2]See Chapters 8, 9, and 11 on design, case planning, and sampling for issues in selecting the appropriate times for measuring.

[3]See the sampling in Chapter 11 for issues in selecting the appropriate places to measure.

*places may suffice. If, however, it is conceptualized as situational, measurement will need to reflect the situational configuration.*

*Conceptualization, theory, and the sampling strategy should lend insight into the measurement of any specific trait or variable indicators.*

## THE MEASUREMENT TOOLS AND PROCESSES (HOW)

*Once indicators are determined, Mr. Noble can address the question of specific measurement tools to use. He needs to determine and apply any combination of approaches that capture the traits and any changes. This usually involves a combination or triangulation of observations, interviews for self-reports by the clients and others, and paper-and-pencil and other measurements.*

### Self-Esteem

*Self-esteem as conceptualized can only be measured by Tad's self-reports. The self-reports might be obtained through interviews for self-assessment of self-esteem accompanied by the use of one or more of the various self-esteem paper and pencil instruments. **Triangulation** by interviews and the paper-and-pencil instruments enhances reliability and validity.*

---

### Self-Esteem Measurement Instruments

*Coopersmith Self-Esteem Inventory* (Coopersmith, 1959; Gurney, 1988)

*How I See Myself* (Juhasz, 1985)

*Index of Self-Esteem* (Hudson, 1982b)

*Rosenberg Self-Esteem Scale* (Nielsen & Metha, 1994; Rosenberg, 1979)

---

*To measure Tad's drug use, Mr. Noble might use interviews or the boy's self-reports and reports of others' observations as well as Mr. Noble's observations of behaviors associated with drug use. However, self-reports by drug users tend to be unreliable (Maisto, McKay, & Connors, 1990), and observations by others difficult if the youth doesn't use the drugs in the observers' presence. Observers are limited to observing behaviors associated with*

*drug use. Random urinanalysis or blood analysis of drug traces in the blood or urine may be more appropriate, especially as a criterion measurement. The frequency needed and the times for random tests for drug metabolites will vary with drug types used, dose, duration of use, time lapse since use, and Tad's metabolic rate and recreational use pattern. Other behavioral indicators of drug use changes might be measured by additional observations, interviews, and available data.*

*Any specific combination of measurement tools and approaches with Tad must be practical and feasible for the time and place and must also capture the indicators.*

• • • • • • • • • • • • • • • • • • • •

• • • • • • • • • • • • • • • • • • • •

## PRACTICE CASE CHILD ABUSE AND MULTIPLE MEASURES

*A second case confirms the imperative of measurement. Child protective services require accurate measurement in potentially life-threatening situations. Protective services also require a precise determination of the **unit of analysis** to apply in the measurement processes. In child abuse the unit of analysis consists of both the abuser and the child victim. The trait of abuse is a trait of the interaction between the abuser and victim.*

*Whether a child remains in a home or is permanently or temporarily removed is often a matter of a protective service worker's measurement, judgments, assessment, and case theory. While a judge may make the final decision, a protective services worker (such as Karen, whom we discussed in earlier chapters), measures, assesses, and recommends, providing information to the judge or hearing officer. Karen uses measurement processes of observations, interviewing, available data and trace indicators, a variety of information sources and measurements of other professionals, and in some cases risk assessment scales (Camasso & Jagannathan, 1995). She uses measurements and risk assessment scales to measure the indicators of abuse, assess its existence, and develop a case theory to predict future parental abusive behavior.*

Risk assessment scales include The **Child Well-Being Scale** (Magura & Moses, 1986) and **Conflict Tactics Scale** (Straus & Gelles, 1990).

Karen is concerned with assessing a threshold where the behavior is judged severe enough to pose a threat to the child's (Trish) well-being and requires removal of Trish from the mother Sharra's care. Any single measurement approach is precarious and the decision important enough to argue for more than a single measurement process, especially if the processes are indirect and obtrusive. The scales are self-reports of risk behaviors, and conditions need supplementation by observations and interviews, not merely other scales. **The use of multiple measures, or triangulation, should be the routine practice protocol.**

Serious repercussions occur from assessments made on faulty measurements. If Karen judges that the parental care is good and it is not (a **false positive** assessment), Trish remains in or is returned to her mother and faces serious risk of abuse. However, a judgment called a **false negative** will mean that Trish is kept away from her parent home with no serious risk of abuse. **Errors of measurements and judgments expose children to high potential for abuse or keep them from their parents' homes with a low potential for abuse.**

False positive judgments (a home is safe when it is not) result in severe and often fatal trauma for children. One example, among too many, is the case of Elisa Izquierdo in New York City. Elisa, a 6-year-old, was chronically abused by her mother since and perhaps even prior to her birth, as she was born cocaine addicted. The mother eventually killed Elisa. Several different child protective workers had seen Elisa and her mother in the home many times over the years and had collateral information from other sources. Based on their assessments, child protective workers consistently recommended that Elisa remain with her mother. While the "system" is overloaded and workers are under pressure not to open new cases and to close old cases, the fault here appears to lie in the workers' measurements and assessment skills. They were in the home and engaged in observations and interviews, used available data and trace indica-

tors, and had a variety of information sources and measurements of other professionals. Yet they did not adequately conceptualize, operationalize, and apply measurements to assess and build a case theory. More disturbing alternative conclusions are (1) that the workers accurately measured and assessed but intentionally did not report their assessment of a true risk situation, or (2) that the agency ignored the assessments and intentionally left the child in a high-risk environment. For elaboration of the case, see the long running series of articles, editorials, and op-ed pieces in the **New York Times,** November and December 1995, such as Bernstein (December 2, 1995, pp. 1, 26), Parent (November 28, 1995, p. A23), and "What Happened to Elisa?" (November 28, 1995, p. A22).

· · · · · · · · · · · · · · · · · · ·

## Useful Characteristics of the Practice Measurement Process

"Sound diagnostic and treatment formulations are dependent upon information that accurately portrays the client's situation" (Tripodi & Epstein, 1983, p. 13). It does practitioners no good and may do clients and others harm if information used for practice judgments is inconsistent, erratic, and not relevant to the things under judgment. There are several useful characteristics of good practice measurements:

1. Reliability of the measurements with capacity for consistency when repeatedly applied by the same and different practitioner, clients and other stakeholders.

2. Validity or truthfulness of the measure to the intended conditions under measurement in ways relevant to and understandable by the practitioner, client and other stake-holders.

3. Knowledge of the measurement process's effects or reflexivity on the things measured.

4. Specificity and precision or the ability of the measure to produce information that allows for necessary judgments in this case.

5. Practicality and feasibility or the extent that it is possible to use the measurement's processes and techniques within the practice situation.

In practice, "the tool or instrument to gather data should be understandable, relatively easy to use, and not too costly in terms of time involved to gather information as well as costs for protocols, equipment, forms, scoring, and data processing" (Blythe & Tripodi, 1989, p. 42).

## Reliability

Reliability is the consistency of the measurements and measurement processes in response to the stimulus of a phenomenon or variable. The classic illustration is a bathroom scale that indicates the same weight for an object whenever it is placed on the scale and the same weight for similar objects that, in fact, have the same weight. The weights indicated may not be the real weight, but the scale is consistent in the weights, real or not, indicated. *A reliable measurement process yields the same information or measures when receiving the same stimulus and different information when receiving different stimuli.* A reliable measurement is when a practitioner makes the same judgment after observing the same behavior and a different judgment when observing different behaviors. Two or more social workers are reliable in their observations if, when observing the same case, they obtain approximately the same information.

Reliability of the measurement tools and processes can be enhanced by:

1. **Test-retest** of the same measurements and measurement processes by repeated application to the same thing. *If reliable, the same results should be obtained with each retest or reapplication on the same specific phenomenon.* For example, the application of an assessment process should generally obtain the same or very similar information when applied to similar clients with similar conditions under similar circumstances. If so, the measurements and processes are reliable. If not,

either the measurement is unreliable, the conditions of application have changed, or the phenomenon, the case, has changed. Test-retest can be used with paper-and-pencil instruments, mechanical and electronic measurements, or observations and interviews. The tasks in establishing reliability is to repeatedly apply and adjust the measurement processes until they yield consistent results when applied to the same stimulus and differ in their results as the stimuli differ. The task is to train observers by having them repeatedly observe and code stimuli until they yield consistent observations when observing the same stimulus and different observations as the stimuli differ.

2. **Parallel form** or **parallel equivalency** involves the *use of different measurement processes for the same variable under the same conditions.* Generally one of the measures has known reliability and serves as a criterion. When the information yielded by the measurement device or process with unknown reliability correlates with the information furnished by the process with known reliability, the first measurement process has established reliability. A paper-and-pencil inventory such as the *Beck Depression Inventory* and an independent clinician observation of the same client at the same time can be used to establish reliability. If the measurements are consistent with each other in their assessment of depression, they are reliable. When independent observations of a client by two clinical observers or raters is consistent, then interobserver or rater reliability is present.

3. **Internal consistency methods** of determining reliability *use similar measurement items that vary in form within an overall measurement.* Paper-and-pencil measurements such as scales enhance reliability by splitting the scale into halves and examining whether the results of one half of the measurement instrument compares to the results of the other half. The two halves are adjusted until they correlate. Correlational matrix approaches compare each item's responses to other item responses. If reliable, the

halves yield similar results and the items correlate. If not, items are discarded and added until a consistency is obtained. A similar internal consistency is sought in an observer's ratings. Internal consistency approaches require the measurement subparts to measure components of the same variables. If they are measuring the same variable, all items for that variable should indicate similar scores.

Reverse order questions and alternative forms of the same question or measurement in questionnaires with preset response categories and interviews also help to establish reliability. A **reverse order question** is a question in which the pattern of the preset responses is altered. Two questionnaire items from the *Family-of-Origin Scale* (cited in Fischer & Corcoran, 1994, pp. 303–307) illustrate the reverse order question.

In my family, I expressed just about every feeling I had.

    5 (SA)   4 (A)   3 (N)   2 (D)   1 (SD)

In my family, certain feelings were not allowed to be expressed.

    5 (SA)   4 (A)   3 (N)   2 (D)   1 (SD)

The FOS is a 40-item Likert-type instrument designed to measure one's perception of the "health" of the family of origin. The two key concepts are autonomy and intimacy. Stronger intimacy in the family of origin is indicated by *SA* (5) on first items and *SD* (1) on the second of the two items. The items have a reverse order in that a *SD* response direction on one item should accompany a *SA* response direction on the other item. The questions were interspersed among the 36 other scale questions. In the analysis for meaning, the response scores for question 2 are reversed. *Reverse order questions mitigate against respondents establishing response patterns and require independent consideration of each item.* A reverse order question is most effective in preventing a response pattern if it occurs early in the questionnaire and periodically thereafter.

**Alternative form** items or questions are questions with *different forms that seek exactly the same information.* Consistent answers indicate reliability. Clients or respondents asked their age and, in a different part of the instrument or interview, their birthyear demonstrate consistency when the age and birthyear correlate.

How old are you?_____.

What year were you born?_____.

### *Establishing reliability in practice: training practitioners, observers, and other participant-observers*

Reliable information for practice decisions is critical for social workers to reasonably assess clients and develop case theories, determine intervention effectiveness and practice consistently and fairly in eligibility determination. Practitioners can enhance the reliability of information they use in the following ways.

1. Consistently employ the same conceptual definitions and develop a shared understanding of meaning and of operational measurement procedures by all case stakeholders.

2. Consistently use the same kinds of information processes in judgments. All relevant participants in measuring and information collection—workers, clients, and others—need training in the same conceptual meanings and operational procedures.

3. Demonstrate how the information will help the client and other stakeholders and informants. Doing this helps establish trust and rapport, making informants more likely to provide reliable and valid information. The process is circular and self-reinforcing. Trust and rapport are enhanced when informants and clients believe the information provided will be used to help them, and the information will more likely help them when they provide reliable and valid information (Fine & Glasser, 1996; Loneck & Way, 1997; Schilling, 1990, p. 256).

Social workers, clients, and other case participants are observers of the processes in the client's situation and life as well as the intervention. As such, they become measurement devices when used to make and report on observations. They are observers and participant-observers. If social workers, clients, or other observers are looking at the same phenomenon repeatedly, establishing reliability is similar to the test-retest and parallel forms used with electronic, mechanical, and paper-and-pencil measurement processes. The observers are exposed to a phenomenon and asked to independently judge or rate it. Then the ratings are reviewed and compared to the conceptual definitions and to one another (or each rater's independent reviews to the previous reviews) until consistency is obtained across reviews and reviewers. Reliability is established when they yield similar and consistent results in separately repeated observations and across observers.

Establishing consistency of practice observations is enhanced with training of practitioner observers in the conceptual definitions and procedures of measurement so they all share the same meanings and use the same conceptual anchors and indicators. Users of logs and other recording devices need to recognize the indicators of a variable and record them in the same way. They must use the same operational definition of frequency (number of different times an indicator occurs or is present), duration of indicators (length of time the indicator is present), and intensity or magnitude of the indicator (the strength at least at an ordinal level). If there is not consistency within the observer, it is like a clock that runs erratically fast and then slow, and if there is not consistency in observations and recording across observers, the different clocks will not give the same time. Time has a different meaning for each clock. Which is the appropriate clock to use?

Training of observers is intended to secure consistency with the anchor points or indicators of the conceptual definition. Training usually has the observers independently observe and re-

spond to the same phenomenon with repeated iterations: the observers rate or measure the same level of phenomena until there is a consistency among observers; observers rate different levels of phenomena until there is a consistency in the differences in behaviors or phenomena similar for all observers and they reach agreement that a certain level of behavior is demonstrated. The agreements can be with a preestablished normative standard or between observers. The latter is interrater reliability.

**Reliability alone does not establish good measurement processes.** It is a necessary but not sufficient condition for good practice measurement. Practitioners must have true measurements, measuring what they want to measure. Reliability, while a necessary prerequisite for truthfulness, does not give a solid basis for assuming truthfulness (Hammersley & Atkinson, 1983, pp. 184–186).

## Validity

Measurement validity, or truthfulness, is crucial for practice decisions. Does the measurement process truthfully provide the information that it is intended to provide? Does a "depression inventory," when responded to by a client, measure the client's depression? Do inventory score changes over time—say, before and after treatment—measure changes in client depression levels? Or is this a rather naive construction of the reality of depression by the practitioner or researcher? Blythe and Tripodi (1989) interpret measurement validity as "the degree of correspondence between the concept being measured and the variable used to represent the concept" (p. 35). Nugent and Hankins (1989) interpret measurement validity as the extent to which the measurement instrument, methods, and processes do what they are supposed to do in indicating the presence, absence and degree of the trait and indicators (p. 450).

Measurement validity is *not* an abstraction; it decides reality. Measurement validity in naturalistic inquiry is conceived of as truthworthiness:

**Measuring the Caseworker Recruits**

The February 17, 1996 *New York Times* (Sexton, p. 25) printed a sampling of test questions given to Child Welfare Administration caseworker recruits. The questions are intended to assess the recruits' knowledge of and ability to detect child abuse.

1. A 10-year-old child's injury requires a thorough assessment to determine if it is accidental or nonaccidental. Which of the following is MOST LIKELY to be an indicator of nonaccidental abuse?*
   a. a patch of scaly red skin on the hand.
   b. Bruises on both sides of the face.
   c. Fracture of a wrist.
   d. Black and blue marks on both knees and shins.

2. A family that has recently experienced a sexual-abuse incident may typically exhibit the following EXCEPT**
   a. Denial behavior.
   b. Disintegration of the family system.
   c. Feelings of shame or guilt.
   d. The perpetrator acknowledging and accepting responsibility for the act.

These and the test's other questions are intended to measure a caseworker recruit's ability to detect child abuse. The test's measurement validity is whether the test accurately assesses the recruit's ability to detect child abuse. If the measurement tool's content corresponds to the knowledge necessary to detect abuse, the test has content validity. It has empirical validity when the tool actually measures the empirical phenomenon—when recruits' abuse detection ability and recruits' higher scores demonstrate their greater ability to detect child *abuse than do recruits with lower scores.*

*The correct answer indicated is b.

**The correct answer is d.

whether you can trust the measurement processes and information (Lincoln & Guba, 1985, pp. 289–331). Gummesson indicates concern that the ideas and their measurements should capture the elements of reality and holds that measurements, as well as theories and concepts, are valid when they describe "reality with a good fit, just like a good map properly describes Earth.... If the map did not reflect the terrain, most people would trust the terrain and abandon the map" (1991, p. 81). Without measurement validity, the balance of practice lacks trustworthiness.

Variables, as discussed in the first part of this chapter, are the traits and indicators of the concept and unit of analysis. Most measurement tools are proxies for the traits, substituting referents for ideas or referents that cannot easily be measured directly. Valid measures are the proxies or indicators directly representative of the referent with identifiable and clear links to the object, behavior, or attitudes we want to measure (Alter & Evens, 1990, pp. 41–43). If a test purports to measure self-esteem, it must yield a higher score for those individuals who appear very self-confident than for those who appear less self-confident.

### Challenges to measurement validity

A measurement's validity, or truthfulness, is affected by errors in the choice, development, and use of the measurements. These can result from selecting indicators inappropriate to the concept or variable, observer biases, and instrument and observer fatigue. **Testing effects, or the reflexivity** *of the instrument and measurement processes on the thing being measured, limit validity.* If the measurement changes a thing to something different when not under measurement, the measurement process is not giving a true picture of the phenomenon in an unmeasured situation. The phenomenon may exist as it is measured only as long as it is being measured. (Reflexivity is discussed in greater detail later.)

Other errors can come from social acquiescence or deference and desirability biases. **Social** acquiescence bias *occurs when the respondent gives the answer the respondent thinks is wanted because the respondent is afraid of the consequences imposed for a true answer.*

A child protective services worker interviews a father who abuses his child by asking: "Do you abuse your child?" Father responds: "No." The father's response may reflect social acquiescence bias because he is afraid of what the protective services worker will do to him for a truthful answer.

Social desirability bias, *similar to the acquiescence bias, occurs when a respondent gives answers that are socially desirable.* Social desirability bias is one reason why pre-election polls taken in predominantly white areas generally indicate higher preferences for ethnic minority candidates than votes tallied. The abusing father may say no because he thinks this is what the worker wants to hear and is how he wants to present himself.

Distortion biases also exist that allow for seeing what you want to see even when it is not there, and the converse distortion effect of not seeing what you don't want to see even when it is there. If we think that no set of parents could really abuse a child, we may have distortion biases. These, and the challenges just cited are all critical errors when they occur in practice. The practice component of practitioner-observation, discussed in Chapter 5, is critical to reduce distortion bias.

### Measurement validity and practice

Measurement validity is essential to mitigate against practitioner false positive and negative judgments. A measurement has validity if it detects and accurately represents true positives and true negatives and can distinguish these from false positives and negatives. Otherwise a measurement is invalid. Denotations of true and false relate to the measurement's ability to measure accurately what you seek to measure.

A true positive occurs when the measurement measures what exists in the way that it actually does. The measure is sensitive to the phenomenon. True positive measures for child abuse will indicate the existence of child abuse when there is child abuse. A false positive occurs when the measurement engenders a measure of a phenomenon when the phenomenon does not exist in the way that the measurement indicates. The measurement is not sensitive to the phenomenon. Assessment based on child abuse measures that yield false positives will indicate child abuse when there is no child abuse present.

A true negative occurs when the phenomenon does not exist and the measurement does not indicate its existence. The measure is sensitive to the phenomenon. An example of a true negative is when child abuse measures indicate no child abuse when no child abuse exists. A false negative occurs when the phenomenon exists but the measurement does not measure it. The measure is not sensitive to the phenomenon. Child abuse measures that yield false negatives, for example, will lead to missed assessments of child abuse when child abuse exists.

### Establishing measurement validity

A measurement's validity has two different facets: (1) *construct and content validity,* or the truthfulness of the lines of inference running between ideas of the measurements of the indicators and the concepts or the ideas that the measurement

Relationship of Phenomenon and Measurements

|  | Measurement Yields a Measure of the Phenomenon | Measurement Doesn't Yield a Measure of the Phenomenon |
|---|---|---|
| Phenomenon exists | True positive | False negative |
| Phenomenon doesn't exist | False positive | True negative |

indicators represent, and (2) *empirical validity,* or "the empirical verifications of predictions that are logical if the variable provides a measure of the concept" (Blythe & Tripodi, 1989, p. 37).

*Content and construct validity.* With content *and construct validity, the inferences from the idea and variables are clearly indicated in the measurement.* The measurement should cover the variable's range of variation and values as well as the range of meanings and values to the respondents and should not force the variable or respondent to one side or the other of the range because the tool has cut off the extremes. Content and construct validity is enhanced by a clear specification of objectives, case theory, and the intervention with fully developed concepts and their indicators and variables. These factors guide the operationalization of the concepts.

**Expert and panel validity** *uses a nominal expert or group of nominal experts, a panel, to review and assess the measurement tools and process.* The expert or panel judge whether the measurements and process will yield the information desired. An expert is someone knowledgeable about the given phenomenon. Experts can be clients, co-workers, supervisors, and social scientists. The panel should make their judgment independently and then compare these for correspondence. If there is none, then the instrument and processes should be reworked with the panel's goal to obtain correspondence of the independent judgments.

Hammersley and Atkinson (1983) advocate a form of expert validity called **respondent validation,** achieved when "the actors whose beliefs and behaviour they (i.e., the measurement processes) purport to describe recognize the validity (i.e., truthfulness) of the accounts" (p. 195). There is correspondence between the measurement or observer's and the subject's view of the reality. Respondent validation is part of naturalistic inquiry's **member checking** (Lincoln & Guba, 1985,

pp. 236, 314–315; Spradley, 1980; Stakes, 1995, p. 115), which *is taking the data and interpretations to the respondents providing the information: the clients, case representatives and other stakeholders, key informants, and experts to determine if the information and interpretations capture and reflect their meanings.* Meaning, or construct validity, is the intent of member checking and respondent validation. Their use does not necessarily mean the observer "believes" the respondent's construction, just that the measures are an accurate reflection of the respondent's construction of reality. Member checking does not preclude using additional approaches to validation. Member checking and respondent validation with clients are essential if social workers are to understand the clients' construction of reality and "to start where the client is."

Construct and content validity are the most basic form of measurement validity. They are necessary, but not sufficient, for establishing measurement validity. Beyond content and construct validity, the measurement should have a strong correlation to the measurement of similar constructs and weak or no correlation to the measurement of dissimilar constructs.

*Empirical validity.* Empirical validity moves beyond the logic of the measurement's construction to inspecting how the measurement fits the empirical phenomenon it purports to measure. Establishing a measurement process's empirical validity can be done by using the three approaches of concurrent validity, criterion validity, and productive validity.

**Concurrent validity** *approaches examine the correspondence of different, independent measures of the same variable.* Concurrent validity is established when paper-and-pencil scales, observations of expert observers, and self-reports correspond or match. It is also established when client logs, observer logs, and other measures of client behavior agree. Each measurement tool's application needs to be independent from the other measurement tools.

### *Triangulation*

Empirical measurement validity, especially concurrent validity, is most readily established in practice by *triangulation* using multiple measures. Jayaratne and Levy (1979, p. 48) argue for multiple measures, triangulation, and "multifactorial measures" because "it would be presumptuous to expect a single measure to tap all the different areas of change (i.e., of the same variable), particularly where the intervention concerns multiple target problems. Hence each area should be measured specifically." Hammersley and Atkinson (1983, p. 198) argue that different types of data have different types of error built into them. *Triangulation taps different indicators of the same idea or concept or different facets of the same indicator.* Since any measurement tool is subject to error, the use of different measurement tools on the same variable allows for a greater possibility of discovering the error and locating the true measure.

*Triangulation's logic is that it locates a concept or variable's empirical domain and meaning by independent multiple observers, observations, measurement tools and processes, and reference points.* Triangulation reduces the likelihood of false judgments, whether false positives or negatives, and improves assessments and judgments of conditions, strengths, problems, outcomes, and interventions. If different measurement approaches yield similar findings, greater confidence can be placed in the findings than if they were produced by a single approach. The numbers of different measurements necessary depends on the type of social phenomenon and the strength, validity, and confidence in each measurement tool. The stronger the confidence in a single measurement process, the less the need for continuous triangulation.

**Client validation** is a particular form of triangulation and establishes the client's meaning for the concept and its operationalization. Client validation is a starting point in triangulation. If social desirability and acquiescence biases can be avoided, we can heed Cowger's (1994) assertion that there is no evidence that "people needing social work services tell untruths more than anyone else" (p. 265).

**Criterion validity,** a special form of concurrent validity, is established when measurement tools and process correspond to a known valid measure of the variable. Criteria do not often indicate false positives or negatives. The pretesting of instruments, measurements tools, and processes often serve a criterion function. The pretest applies a series of measures and compares other criterion measures or asks in-depth follow-up questions to determine if respondents' answers to an instrument item was what they really meant, or compares data yielded by an instrument with observations of actual behavior. Comparing drug use self-reports with random urine analysis (the criterion), is a criterion approach.

A reasonable question regarding criterion validity is: Why do it? If a known criterion measure exists that can check another measurement's va-

| Data (Measurement) Situation | Triangulation Need |
|---|---|
| Uncontested and strong measurements with established validity | Low need |
| Dubious and contested description by measurement tools without established validity | High need |
| Critical data to assessment, case theory, and intervention judgments | High need |
| Data subject to various interpretation and possible false positives and negatives | High need |
| Data viewed as observer or respondent opinion only | Low need |

Based on Stakes (1995, p. 112).

lidity, why not use the valid criterion measure alone and avoid the cost and effort of the second measure? A second measurement process may be wanted because of ease or practicality, or because it may not always be possible to use the criterion measurement process. Establishing the correspondence of this measurement with the criterion measurement process allows it to stand in as a proxy for the criterion process. It is easier and more practical to use a paper-and-pencil test or an interview schedule than to observe behavior in its natural community setting, or to use self-reports of drug use with the criterion measure of random drug tests than to conduct daily drug tests.

**Predictive validity** is the strongest form of measurement validity for theoretical concepts and is established when the measurements enable prediction of other measurements. Predictive validity measures the indicators of one variable and predicts future behaviors of that variable or another variable based on the theory. The variables are then followed up to see if the prediction indeed actually occurs. Do people with high index scores on child abuse potential scales or depression scales exhibit the behaviors associated with high child abuse or depression? They do if the scales have predictive validity.

*Predictive validity depends on the truthfulness of the theoretical relationships assumed to exist between the variables or indicators as well as the ability of the measurement tools to capture the indicators.* But if the theoretical relationships between the variables do not exist, they will not be found regardless of the capacity of the measurement tool to honestly measure each variable separately.

## Ways to Enhance Validity

In addition to triangulation, measurement errors and bias are reduced and truthfulness improved by *pretesting the measurement tools and processes*. The pretest is part of measurement de-velopment of reliable and valid ways of measuring and judging the phenomenon. In pretesting, we want to examine whether the tools and processes capture the true phenomenon and avoid errors in a consistent direction. Systematic errors include social acquiescence bias and social desirability bias. Observer training is "pretesting" of observers.

Good practice requires both reliable and valid measurements. We need to be clear that these are two separate, though related, features of a measurement. The reliability or consistency of a measurement is a necessary prerequisite for validity but does not ensure validity. A measurement tool can be consistently off, an informant can consistently exaggerate in a certain direction, and the consistency represents reliability. Any given measurement process can be: neither reliable nor valid, reliable only, or both reliable and valid. *A measurement can never be valid and not reliable,* measurements can be valid only if they are reliable.

Once reliability is established, at a minimum there should be agreement on the content validity of the measurement process and verification through concurrent validity or triangulation. Like the carpenter, measure and remeasure before you saw.

### *Reflexivity*

Reflexivity and ecological validity are other measurement concerns for practitioners. Reflexivity, *as discussed earlier, occurs when the measurement processes alter and change the phenomenon being measured. Reflexivity is generally inverse to the intrusiveness of the measurements and the measurement processes.* Unobtrusive measurements and processes reduce reflexivity. All measurements are potentially reflexive and can change practice and the practice relationship. Who asks a question may change the response elicited (Bachman & O'Malley, 1984; Cotter, Cohen, & Coulter, 1982; Hammersley & Atkinson, 1983, pp. 14–15). Tyson (1992) illustrates the practice dangers of reflexivity.

An illustration of that distortion occurred when…members of a family spent the beginning of their first session discussing the questionnaire they had filled out, which asked them to count the frequency of their child's swearing. Without the use of the questionnaire, the content of the first session would have been entirely different. Accordingly, such objective measures are not "unbiased" but produce data that are biased in a different way. For example, the precategorizing of client responses through measurement procedures is biased against the complexity that inheres naturally in the casework process.

Even more important, practitioners recognize that such "objective" measures are in themselves interventions because they alter the nature of the casework relationship process.… [that] questionnaires are a more legitimate source of information than the client's self-determined self-description. (p. 550)

Measurement approaches are reflexive when they establish expectations and limitations in communication and measurement of the problems, case objectives, and intervention in ways that fit preordained measurements. Reflexivity is different from bias. **Bias** *is erroneous information produced by the measurement process, whereas reflexivity is a change caused by the measurement process.* The question to any parent "Do you abuse your children?" may yield a socially desirable and biased response of "No, I do not" without altering any behavior. The question is biasing but not reflexive. Observing parent-child interactions of an abusing parent is reflexive if the parent ceases the abusive behavior because he or she is aware of the observation. It has changed the thing being measured.

*Reflexive measures lack validity if the intent is to capture a situation as it exists when it is not being measured.* If a person's blood pressure goes up when the blood pressure cuff is applied at the doctor's office, the measurement process is reflexive. While it is a true measure of the person's blood pressure in the doctor's office with the cuff on the arm, it is not a true measure of the person's blood pressure when it is not under measurement. If the intent is to measure the person's usual blood pressure, the limited reflexive measure at the office is invalid. If a smoker in a smoking secession program is asked to keep a log of the number of cigarettes smoked each hour and accurately keeps the log with the number going down as long as the log is kept, this is also reflexivity. The log and smoker may accurately measure the number of cigarettes smoked when the log is kept, but if this is not the number smoked when the log is not kept, the measurement process has altered the smoking behavior.

Part of the case situation once assessment begins, practioners shape the information that affects the case. Methods of gathering information, whether paper-and-pencil measurements, client logs, participant-observer or observer measurements, affect the unit of analysis if they intrude on it. A practice task, then, is to ascertain the amount and effects of the measurements' reflexivity and the ecological validity of measures. If reflexivity occurs and is intended, measurement is part of intervention. If the reflexivity of measurement processes is unintended and the amount unknown, then its intervention effects are partially unintended and unknown. In this case reflexivity either may supplement or hinder the intended intervention.

### Sensitivity and specificity

Practitioners need measurements and data collection procedures that are *sensitive* and *specific* to the information necessary for assessment, intervention, and reassessment judgments. Blythe and Tripodi (1989) describe sensitivity as "the number of values of a variable that can reliably be discriminated" (p. 42). **Sensitive measurements** *accurately detect the existence of the phenomenon and differences in its intensity, magnitude, and duration.* Sensitive measures enable the practitioner to better discriminate true positives and negatives from false positives and negatives.

**Specificity** *is the measurement's focus on what it is intended to measure and not on other things.* The likelihood of false positives and false negatives can be altered by the threshold level and cutoff point—the specificity—used to conceptualize and measure a condition.

Specificity is affected by whether the phenomenon's trait is conceptualized as a continuous or an inherently dichotomous variable. A **continuous variable** is something that can exist to a greater or lesser degree. A **dichotomous variable** is when something either is present or not present. Determining true positives and negatives in practice becomes a complex task for continuous variables. Like the question: "How far is far?" when does behavior cross over the line and become abusive? Extremes are easily recognized, but the specificity of the crossover point where near becomes far and acceptable behavior enters the area of abuse is more complex. Sensitivity is especially required with continuous variables.

Specificity is needed for dichotomous variables, especially at the cut-point between its existence or nonexistence. You can decrease false negatives by lowering the threshold or cutoff level to ensure measurement of all true events. This may, however, increase the likelihood of false positives due to measuring nonevents or conditions as events, unless the measurement processes are highly sensitive and specific. In child welfare policy and practice, the threshold for classifying a specific set of behaviors as constituting abusive behaviors can be raised or lowered. Generally social policy is often more willing to risk false positives than false negatives if the condition is potentially highly traumatic. In the criminal justice system we are more willing, in protecting the rights of the accused, to risk a false negative, letting the guilty free, than a false positive, convicting the innocent to avoid arbitrary restriction of a person's liberty.

A measurement's sensitivity and specificity determines its **precision,** *that is, how specifically the measurements measure and their sensitivity to nu-*ances of the condition. As measurement tools and processes move up the number system from nominal through ordinal and equal interval to ratio, their precision is increased. If two measurement approaches are similarly practical, use the highest measurement level available because it provides more information. Higher measurement levels, in terms of the variable's conception and the number system that underlies the measurement, allow greater specificity, precision, and ability to use higher order mathematics for analysis of the relationships.

### *Practicality*

In addition to the other criteria, it is necessary to have tools and processes that are practical. The measurement instruments and processes must be understandable and usable, both in the available time and with relative ease by the practitioner, the client, and any other participants. If training is necessary to use them, it must be possible within the time, cost, and energy constraints. They should not be so costly to prohibit their use. Impractical measurement tools are usually not used regardless of their reliability, validity, and precision.

## Using Available Measurements

Available measurements tools can reduce time, costs, and efforts of measurement. There is no need to reinvent the wheel if an adequate wheel exists and is available for use. However, existing measurement instruments, tools, and processes need to be adequate for and available to do the job. If an available measurement device adequately fits your needs, is reliable and valid for your uses, and is practical, then use it. Often available measurement tools are standardized and have established reliability and validity, which aids in comparisons between clients and comparisons to normative standards. Again, *use them if they fit the purpose and yield the needed valid informa-*

*tion in making judgments. Simply because something exists and has been used several times, however, does not mean you should use it. Prior use and popularity does not ensure a good instrument.*

Base decisions to use particular measurement tools and processes on the following issues.

1. Do the tools and processes capture the variable and range of variation needed for adequate judgment? Look for the instrument's fit with your needs and case theory, and its ease of use in the practice situation.

2. Do the tools and processes fit your unit of measurement (your clients) and situation?

3. Are the tools and processes reliable, and how was their reliability established? If reported, assess the reliability level and whether it will be transferred and maintained for practice uses. Was reliability established for the client's population base? The reliability of measurement tools and processes is needed for each new client population that does not fall within the parameters of prior groups used to establish reliability.

If the review of the literature or contacts with the instrument's developer reveals no reliability level and tests are reported but reliability cannot be established, then use caution until reliability for practice uses is established. Be conservative in using information produced by instruments with unknown reliability.

4. What is the validity, how was it established, and what types of validity tests were used? At the least, confirm construct validity for current uses. Does the validity fit your client and use? Was it "normed" or standardized with a population in which the client fits or belongs? Are the norms and norming procedures available? What are the norms? If the norms are not available, why not? What reflexive effects will the instruments and processes have? Again, be conservative in using information produced by tools and processes with unknown validity because the resulting judgments may be false positives or negatives.

5. What are the availability and costs for practice uses of the tools and processes to practitioners, agency, and clients? Is the instrument copyright protected, and does its use require permission and purchase? In the use of available instruments, the legal control of intellectual property rights must be respected. Can the instruments, techniques, and processes readily provide information for judgments? Use availability includes access to using, coding, and scoring the information provided by the instruments and processes. If the data must be interpreted by specialists not readily available, the instrument may not be usable for day to day practice.

Unfortunately, as Tripodi and Epstein (1983) conclude, "this kind of thoroughness can rarely be afforded in a practice context" (p. 43) and, we might add, is not often achieved in a research context. If adequate and available instruments or measurement devices that meet the tests do not exist, the practitioner is faced with the responsibility of developing instruments and devices and testing them.

## Locating Available Instruments

To locate available instruments, *practitioners need to first determine variables to measure, whether they need qualitative, quantitative, or both types of data, and any case limitations applicable to using instruments.* Paper-and-pencil measurement tools requiring literacy cannot be used with cases not literate in the language of the tool. The literature in the field, especially resources containing compilations of instruments such as those cited at the end of this chapter, is a valuable information source. Authors of research or practice articles not containing instruments and sufficient details of measurement process may be able to provide the information. This task is made easier by computerized indexes and abstracting services on the Internet and through the use of e-mail with the authors. College and university libraries are a valuable resource for measurement tools and compilations such as those indicated here. Colleagues also can be a fruitful source of information on available instruments. Again, be mindful always of intellectual property rights.

The following references contain measurements for clinical practice outcomes and are a partial list of available resources.

Corcoran, K., & Fischer, J. (1994). *Measures for clinical practice: A sourcebook*, vols. 1, 2 (2nd ed.). New York: The Free Press.

Corcoran, K., & Fischer, J. (1987). *The clinical measurement package: A field handbook*. Chicago: Dorsey Press.

Dunst, C., Trivette, C., & Deal, A. (1988). *Enabling and empowering families*. Cambridge, MA: Brookline.

Hudson, W. W. (1982). *The clinical measurement package: A field manual*. Homewood, IL: Dorsey Press.

Magura, S., & Moses, B. S. (1986). *Outcome measures for child welfare services: Theory and application*. Washington, DC: Child Welfare League of America.

Magura, S., Moses, B. S., & Jones, M. S. (1986). *Assessing risk and measuring change in families*. Washington, DC: Child Welfare League of America.

McCubbin, H. I., & Thompson, A. I. (Eds.). (1987). *Family assessment inventories for research and practice*. Madison: University of Wisconsin Press.

## Summary

A continual process through every phase of practice, measurement is the most essential skill required of practitioners. Without good measurement skills, practitioners cannot determine what information they need, use what they collect, or plan intervention. Client informed consent is superfluous because there is no information. Practitioners cannot assess or judge changes; interventions are random. Case plans and practice become a mental construction unrelated to the client, the case, or the empirical world. *Measurement, however, is best viewed broadly as a process of collecting information for judgment rather than as a single narrow methodology.* In social work practice, measurement's truthworthiness is enhanced by a use of multiple sources of information, direct and indirect measures, qualitative and quantitative approaches, and operationalization.

We discussed the relationship between reliability and validity. Good practice requires both in the information used for practitioner judgements. We have offered several examples to illustrate reliability and validity in practice measures. Reduction of bias and unintended reflexivity, and attention to sensitivity, specificity, and practicality increases the value of measurements and the resultant judgements. Measurement tools and processes provide the information necessary for a shared construction by a practitioner, client, and other stakeholders to understand the reality of the case. The challenge is to select and use the measurements that best capture the realities in the case constructions.

## Discussion Questions and Exercises

1. Select a client or some unit of analysis from a case and specify the *outcome* or *impact variable* to change.

2. Present the conceptual definition of the outcome or dependent variable. Be sure that the meaning of the dependent variable is understandable by the unit of analysis.

3. Select or develop at least two, preferably three, operational measures for each outcome variable. The operational measures must capture the variable's empirical

indicators and allow judgment regarding changes. *Make sure that at least one measure for each variable is behavioral.* If triangulation is not used, defend the use of a single measurement by the triangulation criteria and *the strength of the single measurement's validity.*

4. Determine the *reliability* and *validity* of each measurement tool. For new tools, present the stepwise plans and protocols for establishing each measurement's reliability and validity. For available measurement tools, what is the reliability and validity and how were they established? How does the instrument fit the unit of analysis?

5. Estimate each measurement tool's reflexivity and whether the reflexivity supports or detracts from the intervention and case objectives.

6. Describe the practicality of the measurements and measurement process in the practice situation.

## Resources for Measurement in Practice

In addition to the compilations of clinical outcome measurements on p. 94, the following references elaborate the importance of measurement and its use in practice with discussion of the measurement processes.

Bloom, M., Fischer, J., & Orme, J. G. (1995). *Evaluating practice: Guidelines for the accountable professional* (2nd ed.). Needham Heights, MA: Allyn and Bacon. Includes software disks for Computer Assisted Social Services and Mystat for practice evaluations.

Blythe, B. J., & Tripodi, T. (1989). *Measurement in direct social work practice.* Newbury Park, CA: Sage.

Mullen, E. J., & Magnabosco. (Eds.). (1997). *Outcome measurement in the human services: Cross-cutting issues and methods.* Annapolis Junction, MD: NASW Press.

Tripodi, T., & Epstein, I. (1983). *Research techniques for clinical social workers.* New York: Columbia University Press.

Tripodi, T. (1994). *A primer on single subject design for clinical social workers.* Annapolis Junction, MD: NASW.

# CHAPTER SEVEN

# Data Collection: Gathering Information for Decision Making

Data collection covers the actual processes used to get information from clients, other informants, or research subjects using the measurement methodologies. Data are used here in their common, lay and dictionary meaning as material or information that provides the basis for reasoning or decision (*Webster's Seventh New Collegiate Dictionary*, 1993, p. 210; Hawkins & Allen, 1991, p. 367). Social workers collect data to answer questions and make decisions on client eligibility, case assessments, intervention effectiveness, and research questions and hypotheses. This chapter reviews and critiques for practice application the major forms of data collection and presents a methodology to assess readability of written data collection approaches. We begin with a review of ethical considerations.

Data collection and measurement processes are operationally inseparable. Application of measurement tools and processes is the first step in data collection. Data's integrity is dependent first on the measurement's integrity. No measurement tool will provide valid information if improperly used. No amount of application care and precision will provide authentic information if the basic measurement tool or process is faulty or inappropriate to the measurement task. No appropriate judgment can be derived from fallacious measurements and inept data collection.

The case plan or research design determines data collection strategies. Data collection, whether for practice or research, requires a plan specifying *what* information is needed, from *whom, when* it is needed, and *how* and in *what* form. The tools, instruments, and protocols used should be understandable by the users, whether clients or practitioners, relatively easy to use by those who have to use them, and not too costly in time and money for application protocols, scoring, processing, analysis, and storage.

## Ethics and Data Collection

While ethics are more fully discussed in Chapter 3, the review here focuses on ethics of data collection. A dominant and continuing data collection concern is establishing and maintaining the integrity of the data collection and storage system. The system should ensure that information is not altered or lost in collection and storage. Prudent researchers and practitioners always look for the lurking gremlins of "Murphy's Law" or "what can go wrong, will" and constantly monitor collection and storage processes and protocols to avoid the gremlins.

## Privacy, Privileged Communication, and Confidentiality

Data collection and storage protocols need to protect the privacy, privilege, and confidentiality of clients and other informants. Informants, whether clients, research subjects, or others, should be advised of the uses and limits to their privacy when they provide information, and access to the data should be limited.

The ethical code for social work practice is somewhat looser than the generally used research ethical standards for privacy and confidentiality. The American Sociological Association requires that researchers maintain confidentiality *even when the information obtained from respondents enjoys no legal protection or privilege and legal force is applied to extract the information from the researcher* (Bailey, 1996, p. 17).

The Department of Health and Human Services research confidentiality guidelines (Mark, 1996, p. 48), applicable to practice, require only collection and recoding of personal information necessary for the study to achieve its purposes: that all information on individual participants be secure and confidential unless written permission is given to reveal it, and even within the research project available only on a need-to-know basis; and that the ability to link data to a specific person by name is limited and used only when absolutely necessary. Identifiers are deleted as soon as feasible. Data is destroyed when no longer needed. Available data, unless in the public domain, is treated similar to originally collected data.

The National Association of Social Worker's 1996 revised Code of Ethics, standards 1.07 addressing confidentiality and privacy and 1.08 dealing with access to records (pp. 10–12), indicate that social workers should limit data collection and records to essential information only and respect the client's right to privacy. Available data, trace studies, and observational data collection, as well as the other forms of data collection discussed in the next sections, are not exempt from the ethical imperatives. Privacy rights are respected unless the information is truly in the public domain. A client may release the claim to privacy by a valid release consent, or the practitioner or agency may abridge the privacy for compelling professional reasons, such as a duty to warn or when other public laws require it. For social workers who act as agents for employers,

the code recognizes that the information is often the property of the employing agency and available to others on a need-to-know basis. In no circumstance is the information to be fodder for casual conversations or amusement.

Clients, research subjects, and other informants have a right to *informed consent.* This includes limits to their privacy, confidentiality, who has access to the information, and its uses by researchers, practitioners, agencies, and others, even if this knowledge inhibits them from revealing important information. If subjects and clients are truly informed of the limits to the privilege and to whom the communication will be revealed, and if in that revelation the subject or client might be harmed, one can reasonably argue that the client has consented or given permission, to a breach of confidentiality. Even accused criminals have the right to know that information they provide can be used against them. Clients deserve the same right to be truly informed prior to communicating with researchers and practitioners.

## Data Collection Guidelines

1. What decisions and judgments are necessary?
2. What information do you need to make the decisions?
3. Where are the best sources of information?
4. When are the most appropriate times to obtain information?
5. What are the most appropriate measures and measurement processes (rather than necessarily the most convenient) to obtain the information for practice decisions?
6. What is the reliability, validity, sensitivity, precision, and practicality of the measurements and measurement processes?
7. Based on the response to question 6, do you need multiple measurements and triangulation to obtain the information for practice decisions?

8. Have you obtained and respected informed consents from informants?

9. How can you ensure the integrity of the data collection process to maintain information integrity and protect informants' privacy rights?

## Data Collection Approaches

The following are some major data collection approaches with a practice application. Some research texts present data collection approaches in measurement chapters. As already indicated, measurement and data collection are functionally inseparable and text divisions reflect organizing preferences only.

Data collection on the ecology and community resources include community surveys such as "walking and driving surveys," available data from resources such as census and other demographic sources, resource directories, key informants, and original data from focus groups and community assessment, since community and social forces influence behavior and resources.

### Available Data

Available data is an imprecise term but usually refers to previously collected and recorded information for purposes other than contemporary uses. As such, the original measurement tools and processes require assessment for relevance to current needs. General sources include government documents and reports such as birth certificates and marriage certificates, vital statistics, and census reports; agency case records; agency records and archives; research reports; family documents such as diaries, photo albums, and Bibles; telephone books; social agency directories; news media files; electronic networks; social science literature; and local colleges and universities' social science and professional school departments for relevant community studies and research reports.

Recall from informants, including clients, of events occurring in the past, narratives, and life and other oral histories are considered a form of available data because the informants originally "collected the information" for purposes other than its current use. The researcher or practitioner has to rely on the available recall because they cannot collect direct data on past events. The information customarily is collected from informants through some type of written or oral history processes. These processes involve

Advantages and Disadvantages of Previously Recorded Available Data Sources[a]

| Advantages | Disadvantages |
|---|---|
| Relatively inexpensive compared to other forms of data collection | Data may be incomplete or dated for current uses and direct control of measurement process not possible. |
| Generally the only way to collect historical data | Definitions, measurement categories, and data aggregations may not fit current needs, resulting in possible validity concerns. |
| Previously recorded data are protected from respondent social acquiescence and desirability biases as well as reflexivity for current uses. | Original data collection methodologies, reliability, and validity are often unknown, suspect, or can't be established. |
| Generally unobtrusive in the current use and hence low reflexivity | Integrity and ethics of the data collection system may be unknown or suspect. |

[a]Advantages and disadvantages are applicable to interviews and questionnaires dealing with recall of events and behavior.

questionnaires and structured interviews, or semistructured interviews recorded by tape recorder, transcribed, and then analyzed by a content analysis approach. Interviews and structured questionnaires such as recall are explored later in this chapter.

Strengths of available data are weighed against their limitations in the specific practice situation. The data's compatibility with current needs is paramount if they are to provide appropriate decisional information. Ascertain their reliability, validity, integrity, biases, and norming for current uses. If unknown, be conservative and suspect the data's reliability and validity. Triangulation is a good idea with any data collection approach and is especially critical when using suspect available data.

**Trace studies,** *used as available data collections can examine historical events, although the practitioner may have to collect original data of the trace effects.* Trace measures or studies present the effects or "traces" of a prior event or behavior. Examples are traces of a drug in the system of a drug user, indicated by urine analysis assumed to indicate prior use; the physical trauma, bruises, and scars resulting from prior physical abuse; "garbage studies" examining consumption behavior; and wear and tear on furniture and floors to assess varying use and traffic flow.

. . . . . . . . . . . . . . . . . . . .

*Consider Trish from our earlier chapters. Trace measures of abuse on Trish include bruises, scabs, scratches, burn marks, and signs of malnourishment. Since it is unlikely that the social worker Karen will see Sharra directly abusing Trish, Karen has to rely on these trace measures.*

. . . . . . . . . . . . . . . . . . . .

## Observation and Participant/ Practitioner Observation

*Observation* and *participant observation* are fertile information-gathering methodologies for practitioners. Observation is involved in almost all the data collection methodologies. Trained to observe and assess behaviors and events, practitioners are participant observers when they observe the behaviors of clients, other participants and events in the case's ecology, and practitioner observers when they observe their own practice behaviors. Practitioners observe when they witness family interactions in family therapy or parent-and-child interactions to gather information on allegations of abuse. Observation is a less intrusive data collection approach than some alternatives because the practitioner is already a participant in the intervention. However, it requires disciplined observation to reduce practitioner bias, as we discussed in Chapter 5.

Observation and participant observation for information-gathering uses ethnographic techniques (Hammersley & Atkinson, 1983; Spradley, 1980). *Ethnographic observation* focuses on the person's behavioral content and the context to provide a backdrop for understanding the behavior's meaning. As Spradley points out:

> Every social situation can be identified by three primary elements; *a place, actors,* and *activities* [emphasis original]. In doing participant observation you will locate yourself in some place, you will watch actors of one sort or another and become involved with them; you will participate in activities. (pp. 39–40)

Observational data collection approaches generally have two components: (1) observation, and (2) recording of observational data. In practitioner and participant observation, *the observer is the principal measurement instrument.* Technology such as electronic and mechanical recording devices, can aid and supplement but the observer remains the principle measurement instrument. Videos and audio recorders reduce observer distractions and more accurately record the event for analysis. Recording is in narrative format or by previously constructed and encoded charts, questionnaires, checklists, and scales. Narrative content in the analysis phase is usually reduced to checklists and scales. Narrative content analysis is explored in greater detail in the analysis chapter.

Behavior  ← Observation →  Recording
and event     by observer        and
                                            encoding

### Unsystematic and systematic participant observation

Observations fall along a continuum of *unsystematic* to *systematic* observations depending upon the conceptual and methodological structure guiding them. **Unsystematic observation** is a potluck approach to data collection, where observations are made broadly with the observer scrutinizing whatever behavior occurs at the observation times. Times, events, and behaviors observed and recorded are not necessarily selected for case theoretical reasons, and may not represent either more general or specific behavior patterns. The use of haphazardly scheduled home visits for child protective services or adoption investigations to take advantage of the practitioner's work hours convenience move toward the unsystematic end of the observation continuum because the observation methodology is not guided by the theory of the phenomenon of concern—behaviors of parents or potential parents interacting with children.

**Systematic observations** generally are preferred to unsystematic observations because they enhance reliability. While Tripodi (1994)

## Advantages and Disadvantages of Observations

| Advantages | Disadvantages |
|---|---|
| A direct form of information collection in which behavior or events of concern are directly observed. | Time and resource intensive, requiring observer presence at times of events and behaviors, so generally limited to relatively frequently recurring events. |
| Provides information about individuals who are unwilling or unable to provide self-reports (e.g., infant, illiterate with written reports) | Restricted to visible events that occur at the time of observation. Information on invisible and hidden events, such as feelings and thoughts, are precluded. |
| Validity can be high if events or behaviors are observed in a natural environment as they occur. | Vulnerable to extraneous influences and distractions by and of observers. Observation process can create reflexivity and damage validity. |
| If observed person is ignorant of observation or can adjust to and disregard the observer's presence, observations are unobtrusive and have little biasing effect. | Highly dependent on observer's observational and recording skills for reliability and validity. Use limited by observer's capacity in observing and recording complex events. |
| Observers can (and must) be trained for a high reliability level. | Observers subject to fatigue with resultant observations and recording errors. |
|  | Observers tend to mix and confuse inference and interpretation with description. |
|  | Observers with complete and total immersion in participation, no detachment, can lose objectivity and "go native." Observers with too little involvement may lose subject's meaning. |

limits systematic observation to "quantitative data collection that involves one or more observers, observing events or behaviors as they occur, and reliably recording their observations in...previously structured numerical categories" (p. 54), our conception is broader. **Systematic observations** *are observations of behaviors and events made according to a combination of preset time sample frames, observation protocols, and recording and coding protocols.* The observations must be recorded and capable of reduction to numerical ratings only if anticipating quantitative analysis. Dimensions of systematic observations to capture both content and context are (Hammersley & Atkinson, 1983; Spradley, 1980):(1) *space,* the physical place or places; (2) *actors,* the people involved; (3) *activity,* the actors' behaviors; (4) *objects,* the physical things present; (5) *act,* the single component of behavior that people do; (6) *event,* a set of related activities that people carry out; (7) *time,* the sequencing of acts and events; (8) *goal,* inferences of what people are trying to accomplish by activities; and (9) *feeling,* the visible and expressed acts of emotions.

. . . . . . . . . . . . . . . . . . . .

*Consider the social worker Karen from our earlier chapters. In order to follow systematic observation Karen must be clear about abuse indicators and observe Sharra and Trish when these indicators would most likely be present. Abuse is a result of interaction, so Karen must observe Sharra and Trish together in the space they live, as well as observe Trish alone in her room. It is most crucial for Karen to directly and systematically observe Trish. This may involve watching Trish play with her toys and watching her play with other children. Karen can also play with Trish observing her manner of interaction and communication. Karen should schedule visits at varying times to assure a range of opportunities for systematic observation of Sharra and Trisha.*

. . . . . . . . . . . . . . . . . . . .

When using systematic observation, practitioners need to follow the guidance of the *why, who, what, when,* and *how* of information needs.

### Recording observations

Observations as information, however, generally require recording and often coding. Systematic observations provide some degree of coding and content analysis in the recording instrument's construction, while unsystematic recordings or narratives require later content analysis. Recording instruments and protocols require accuracy, reliability, validity, sensitivity, and practicality. Categories for recording observations need to be exhaustive, one-dimensional, exclusive response categories, well defined and easily understood.

Observers also need to understand and be able to easily use the instruments. Complicated recording categories and unbalanced scales are likely to produce spurious precision and lead to recording errors. Observers using complex, overly elaborate instruments often seek the middle-range categories regardless of the behavior observed. Clarity in training, written instructions, and pretesting is critical for "understandability." When recording is completed as close to the time of observation as feasible, errors are likely to decrease. Similar rules, principles and guidelines as described in Chapter 6 apply to observational recording instruments, including the use of available instruments.

Observer training is necessary to enable observers to separate observations of the actual behavior from inferences, global interpretations, premature conclusions, and summaries of conditions and events. Information is lost if the leap is made too quickly from observation to inference. The leap itself may be a deductive fallacy: "For example, a client may be described as communicating in monosyllables and avoiding eye contact, behavior interpreted by one practitioner as hostile and by another practitioner as anxious" (Berlin & Marsh, 1993, p. 106). In fact, such an inference may be fallacious for both practitioners. Following the disaggregation principle, it is more productive in dealing with qualitative information to describe behavior rather than leaping prematurely to recording inferences. If the inference or conclusion of either "hostile" or "anxious"

# ITP HIGHER EDUCATION
DISTRIBUTION CENTER
7625 EMPIRE DRIVE
FLORENCE, KY 41042

The enclosed materials are sent to you for your review by
RON HARRIS 208 664-3380

## SALES SUPPORT

| Date | Account | Contact |
|------|---------|---------|
| 11/30/98 | 694035 | 16 |

SHIP TO: Robert O Rich
E WA U CPSW
Social Work Department
Cheney WA 990040000

## WAREHOUSE INSTRUCTIONS

SLA: 7    BOX: Staple

| LOCATION | QTY | ISBN | AUTHOR/TITLE |
|----------|-----|------|--------------|
| K-19D-007-27 | 1 | 0-534-36215-X | BISMAN/HARDCASTLE INTEGR RESCH INTO PRACT:MODEL1 |

INV# 141654759750
PO#
DATE: / /
CARTON: 1 of 1
ID# 9478069

PRIME-INDUCT
-SLSB

VIA: UP

PAGE 1 OF 1

BATCH: 0671452
018/019

## Basic Questions in Data Collection

1. **Why** are observations made? **Why** is this methodology selected?

Determine the observation's purpose and information needed for decisions.

2. **Who** are the actors to observe? **Who** is the unit of analysis?

In practice this is generally the client, although it can be collateral people or actors in the action or target systems.

3. **What** are the acts, activities, and events to observe?

The acts, activities, and events guide the selection of information sources or actors, and are the *indicators* of the concept. In observing for depression, the practitioner will look for at least five of the following areas of indicators, acts, and events that connote depression (Zimmerman, 1994):

- *Mood:* For most or nearly every day, the person looks unhappy, sad, and down in the dumps and exhibits a decreased interest in pleasure without bereavement within two months, other major medical disorder, or clinically important substance use. The indicators are reduced work role performance, withdrawal or discord in social life, disruption or disinterest in sex.
- *Interests:* For most or nearly every day, the person displays marked decreased interest or pleasure in nearly all activities.
- *Eating* or *weight:* Person eats less or more than prior amounts.
- *Sleep:* For most or nearly every day, the person sleeps excessively or not enough.
- *Observable psychomotor activity:* For most or nearly every day, the person's activity is speeded up or slowed down.
- *Fatigue:* For most or nearly every day, person displays a tiredness or loss of energy.
- *Concentration:* For most or nearly every day, person is indecisive or has trouble thinking or concentrating.

- *Death:* Patient has made a suicide attempt. (pp. 34–37)

The mood disorder can be measured by duration; minimum of two weeks, and severity from mild (barely meets criteria, little interference) to severe with psychotic features that interfere with social functioning. *The assessment task is to gather information for judgment to classify the condition or behavior as depression or something else.* The time period or duration, the indicators, and the severity must be observed by the practitioner, patient, or others. A depression scale is an inherent self-report of a self-observation.

4. **When** are observations made?

The nature and frequency of acts, activities, and events guide the selection of times and frequency of observations. The depression indicators listed under item 3 require a time duration of at least two weeks to assess. In determining frequency of observations, time sampling of times the relevant events or actions are likely to occur is the most optimal method for determining when to observe. Practitioners need to avoid limiting observations to "time samples of convenience," or times most convenient to the observer. Sampling theory for times and events sampling that hold the best mix of economy and feasibility is discussed more thoroughly in Chapter 11.

5. **How** are observations made and recorded? **How** is the observer to relate to the observed?

Systematic observation moves toward operationally defining the variables by how to measure and record them. The recordings can be by logs or diaries with preset time and response categories or scales.

6. Test the observation processes and tools for reliability and validity. There are two parts to reliability and validity: the observer and the recording of the observation.

Inter-Rater Reliability Coefficient (Percentage Agreement = $100 \times O1/O2$; with O being the raters, rating, observer, or observation.

behavior is recorded, the behavior cannot be re-analyzed for other interpretations. If the behavior is simply recorded, the information can be triangulated or compared with other information to arrive at a conclusion. Observer training is part of the practice skill discussed in Chapter 5 of practitioner observation, or a practitioner's self-assessment in the practice relationship.

### Intra- and interrater reliability

Observation recording and rating devices are subject to the same concerns present for all structured instruments, especially inter- and intraobserver reliability, when observers, practitioners, clients, and others are themselves measurement instruments. Observers require training to establish observer and interobserver reliability. Reliable observers share common conceptual grounding or anchoring in observing and recording. Common ground is achieved by providing observers with shared conceptual and operational definitions of variables and then exposing them to and having them record similar and different events. Although a high percentage of agreement is always good, the percentage of agreement necessary is dictated by the ramifications of false positives and negatives made by the observer. *When clients do self-rating and keep diaries, logs, and journals, they are systematically observing their own behavior, and the guidelines for establishing reliability and validity are applied.*

Interobserver and interrater or recorder reliability for *how* and *what* to observe and record and *when* inferences, summaries, and conclusions should be made is crucial for all classifications and comparisons. **Remember that observers are measurement instruments.** For observation and participant observation, the test-retest process involves establishing (1) observer reliability or intrarater consistency over time in observing and recording similar and different events, actors, and activities, and (2) interrater and observer reliability of different observers in viewing and recording similar and different events, actors, and actions.

Observer Agreements

|  | Observation Agreement | Observation Disagreement |
| --- | --- | --- |
| Observers agree on recording | [+,+] High reliability and probable validity | [+,–] Low reliability and probable validity |
| Observers disagree on recording | [–,+] Low reliability and probable validity | [–,–] Low reliability and probable validity |

Only the [+,+] box represents acceptable interobserver reliability in the observational data collection process.

### Informed consent and reflexivity

Reflexivity and social acquiescence and desirability biases can significantly affect observational data. Clients or other informants may alter their behavior once they are aware that they are or may be observed. Reflexivity and bias, of course, can be reduced by covert observation. As with research, however, covert observations and deception can present ethical issues. Bailey's (1996) assertion for field research is relevant for practitioners: "Because researchers expect those in the setting to be honest with them, the reciprocal nature of the relationship is harmed if the researcher engages in deception" (p. 13). Clandestine observations are generally permissible only within the constraints of informed consent—that is, the client or subject agrees to being observed but is ignorant of when and where exactly the observations occur. Public behavior—behavior occurring in public that is exposed to any observer—is generally exempted from the informed consent requirement.

Deception in qualitative data collection is limited by the need to member-check that meanings intended by the client or subject are the same meanings imputed to the observed behavior by the observer. *Check out information and inferences of meaning with clients or other informants for accu-*

*racy.* Observing conditions such as homelessness or even experiencing it for a time-limited period is a poor approximation of the meaning of homelessness for the homeless. The researcher or practitioner-observer can pack up and go home if things get too rough on the streets. The fatalism and other helpless feelings of the homeless and the meaning of the experience to the homeless can not be obtained merely by observation. Observation should be triangulated with other data collection methodologies.

# Interviews

*Interviews,* a basic social work tool, are the most common form of information gathering in social work practice. Information-gathering interviews are distinct from the range of treatment communications. Interviews generally obtain supplemental observational data to be obtained from the respondent or interviewee's body language and, if in the field, from the respondent's physical and social environment.

Kadushin and Kadushin (1997, pp. 15–16) distinguish two types of data collection interviews: (1) information gathering, and (2) social study. Both are necessary data collection approaches. The information-gathering interview "is to obtain a focused account of the individual, group, or community in terms of social functioning" (p. 15). The social study interview "is the selective gathering of a client's life history as it relates to social function" (p. 15). The former is information gathering *qua* information while the latter is a more intensive information-gathering process guided by the need to complete a particular case theory. Its purpose is not just data, but understanding the respondent's meaning.

*Interviewing's special strength over other forms of information gathering is its interactional potential to clarify information and meaning with the respondents.* Interviews can socialize respondents to the data collection needs and processes (Kadushin & Kadushin, 1997, pp. 235–237). The interviewer can establish empathy with the respondent necessary to sharing meaning that probably is not as

possible with other less interactive forms of data collection. Empathy is critical to understanding the respondent's construction and meaning of reality (Reinharz, 1992, pp. 27–30). A workable definition of empathy provided by Donner and Sessions (1995) demonstrates its importance for discovering meaning.

> the ability to see the world through another's eyes…the vehicle into the subjective world of another.… In order to approximate empathetic understanding to another's subjective world, the interviewer must listen…to what a client has to say.… (p. 101)

Empathy does not require a loss of objectivity or "going native." Empathy is not the same as adopting the respondent's world construction, but it does compel an understanding of the construction. Empathy is a component of **belief bonding,** the belief shared by both client and practitioner in the helping nature of the relationship.

## Unstructured and Structured Interviews

Interviews can range on a continuum from highly unstructured and unfocused to highly structured and focused. Unstructured interviews are free form and flowing, without a preset question order but with questioning that follows clues from the respondent about order, direction, and content. Structured interviews have greater direction and construction. The structure generally relates to the wording and sequence of questions. Highly structured interviews can limit response options available to the respondent and are basically oral preset response questionnaires. The range of structures is somewhat analogous to the continuum of examinations from essay through open-ended questions to multiple choice examinations.

The principles for interviewing as an information collection tool follow the *why, who, what, when,* and *how* imperatives common to the other information tools.

1. *Why are interviews conducted? Why select this methodology?*

Determine the interview's purpose and information needed for decisions. The interview might be to gather information or to establish the reliability and validity of another information-gathering process (triangulation). Interviews, rather than observations, appear to be more optimal in gathering information on hidden phenomena such as attitudes, emotions, and feelings. Purpose or information need will guide the selection of an unfocused or a highly structured interview. The question frame consists of the general questions related to the information sought.

2. *Who are the interview respondents? Who has the necessary information?*

Are respondents capable of responding to questions? What interview structure do they need?

3. *What are the acts, activities, and events on which respondents can provide information?*

The acts, activities, and events guide the selection sources of information or respondents. A practitioner using interviewing to gather information from a client about the client's depression will need questions concerning the areas reviewed earlier. Use and structure of the interviews is guided by the information needs and the respondent's capacity.

4. *When are the interviews conducted and for how long?*

The nature and frequency of the interviews will depend on the respondent's capacity to recall events, acts, and feelings. Both interviewer and respondent fatigue affect the data. Tired respondents and interviewers are more concerned with completing interviews than with giving and receiving accurate information. As the interviewer is literally a measurement instrument for data collection and the client an information source, fatigue can greatly inhibit reliability and validity.

5. *How are interviews structured?*

The practitioner decides whether to use a funnel or inverted funnel approach to the interview.

The **funnel approach** goes from more general questions to specific questions, from unfocused to focused, from unstandardized to standardized. The **inverted funnel** approach goes from specific to more general questions. With sensitive questions, a funnel approach that progresses from more general and less sensitive questions to more specific and sensitive questions may be appropriate if the interviewer is able to establish empathy, trust, and bonding with the respondent. Some authorities (Kadushin & Kadushin, 1997, pp. 238–243; Tripodi & Epstein, 1983, p. 29; Merton, Fiske, & Kendall, 1952, 1956) believe that semistructured, open-ended questions are better for eliciting expressions of emotion, personal need, and answers to questions in areas where there is little previous knowledge about the client or the content area.

In addition to the specific questions, there are concerns for flexibility in the ordering and structure. In deciding on structure, the interviewer needs to determine the thresholds or depths of information sought and choose between an umbrella approach covering all dimensions exhaustively or a more focused approach seeking only specific information.

An interview schedule with closed response categories, such as checklists and preset closed response categories, needs careful construction. In their effort to enhance reliability, they lose some strength of the open-ended question to elaborate meaning. Response categories need to be exhaustive and cover the range of potential responses, mutually exclusive and with recognition of the upper and lower thresholds. Avoid, if possible, the noncommittal option of "undecided."[1] The strength of interviewing in data collection is its capacity for feedback and clarification of meaning for both questions and responses. This strength contributes to potential

---

[1]Questionnaire construction will be discussed in greater detail later. The principals are similar regardless of whether the questions are provided to the respondent in an oral or written format.

validity, and it should be maintained and not discarded for potential reliability and analysis efficiency.

### 6. *Where are the interviews conducted and recorded?*

The interview environment and context should be conducive to communication; context does affect content. Children suspected of being abused by their parents will provide different information depending on whether they are interviewed in private or in the presence of their parents. As we discussed earlier the social worker Karen should interview Trish with her mother, Sharra, and also interview Trish alone. Interview time and location scheduling should take into account the capacity of the respondent to fully engage in the interview. Home interviews need to allow the respondent to focus on the interview rather than the myriad of other responsibilities and distractions present in the home. Depending on the purpose of the interview and information sought, the interview environment should be conducive to confidentiality and privacy.

### 7. *Test interview processes and schedules for reliability and validity.*

Interviews are an information approach very amenable to social work practice if their reliability and validity concerns can be resolved.

### Reliability and validity

Interviews as data collection mechanisms are more complex than observations in their reliability and validity. Because interviews generally

place another person between the interviewer and the behavior or phenomenon, the experience or phenomenon is not experienced directly but through reports—albeit often reports of self-observations and experiences of the interviewee or respondent. *Respondent and interviewer need to share the same meanings or constructions.*

There are four parts to the data collection's reliability and validity: (1) the interviewee's observations, including self-observations or practitioner observation; (2) the interviewee's encoding and reports; (3) the interviewer's questioning; and (4) the encoding and recording of the interview. Problems with reliability and validity can occur with any of these parts and the fits between them. With unstructured interviews and open-ended questions, the interviewer becomes a greater part of the data collection process in formulating questions and recording and responses. Reliability is affected at this end of the continuum in all areas: the interview itself, recording, and subsequent content analysis for coding. The interviewer must ask the questions, interpret and clarify with the respondent, and decide when to elicit and what to record as appropriate information. These tasks provide an opportunity for interviewer bias reducing reliability and subsequent validity.

A potential weakness of interviews is inadequate reliability across interviewers and with the same interviewer at different times with different respondents. The interview's information often reflects more the skills, attitudes, opinions, and inconsistencies of the interviewer than differences in or changes in the respondents.

### Interviewing Information Flow

| Empirical behavior or phenomenon or attitude, feeling, or belief $\rightarrow$ | ← Respondent observations, including self-observations and assessments $\rightarrow$ | ← Encoding by observer-respondent of observations $\rightarrow$ | ← Interviewer questioning of observer-respondent $\rightarrow$ | ← Observer-respondent recodes observations to respond to interviewer's questions $\rightarrow$ | ← Interviewer records and encodes (unless response categories are previously coded) |
|---|---|---|---|---|---|

Interviews are intrusive, can be reflexive, subject to social acquiescence and desirability bias, and very reflective of interviewer skills. Even a skilled interviewer can accurately report interviews, but the reports will not be valid if the information provided is not valid.

*Interviewer reliability can be enhanced with training and role-play by interviewers to increase interviewer consistency and skills.* The observers also can be trained to observe, including self-observation. Case scenarios can be used in training to simulate real information-gathering events. Audio and videotaping of training interviews, role-play, and the actual interviews can promote reliability.

Open-ended interview questions and loose question frames and interview schedules require more skilled interviewers with more training than do tightly constructed interview schedules and closed response category questions. At the highly structured end of the interviewing continuum the interviewer's responsibilities are essentially to read the questions and record the response selected.

Interviewer intrusiveness can be mitigated, if not eliminated, by seeking ways to be nonintrusive and inoffensive to the respondent in language, demeanor, and dress. In information-gathering interviews, the interviewer should not "make a statement" to the client other than setting the interview's purpose, nor should the interviewer attempt to intervene with the client but rather allow the client or respondent to make the statement. Ethnicity (Bachman & O'Malley, 1984; Cotter, Cohen & Coulter, 1982), age, and gender (Kadushin & Kadushin, 1997, pp. 321–354; Reinharz, 1992, pp. 23–26) matches of interviewers and respondent should be examined prior to the interview to determine their potential positive and negative impact on the interview. As we discussed in Chapter 5 on practitioner observation, interviewers need awareness of their own emotions and sensitivities. We all have them, and they will affect the communication and information obtained. Member checking with informants is a safe guard against interviewer bias.

It is critical to *pretest* interview schedules and question frames for understandability by the target respondents and for sequencing questions. The pretests should address concerns for reliability, validity, and reflexivity. Pretests are done with role-play and simulation, with client groupings serving as advisory and focus groups, and with SMOG approaches, discussed later. Interview schedules and the information obtained are subject to adaptations of reliability and validity tests discussed in the measurement chapter.

Record interviews as soon as feasible after the interview. If notes or audio recordings cannot be made during the interview, Tripodi and Epstein (1983) recommend that "interviewers should write down the information *immediately* after termination of the interview" (p. 29). Delays mean that interviewers must rely on the infallibility of their memory and their discipline to not let their own values color recall.

*Audio* and *video interview recording* can enhance reliability and accuracy of data recording, although the information, like a narrative, must generally be coded through content analysis. Subsequent codings can be compared to the actual information provided by the respondent on audio or videotapes, which is not possible with an interviewer-written narrative. Any biases or misinformation in the narrative can be accurately reflected in coding, but it remains misinformation. Audio and videotapes can also be used to monitor the interviewers for enhancement of reliability. Random sampling of time points in the taped interview can be used for efficiency. If interviews are taped, respondents need to provide informed consent and the logistics of the taping must be arranged to minimize interviewer intrusiveness and the disruption of notetaking.

. . . . . . . . . . . . . . . . . . .

*Back to our earlier case—Karen must ask Sharra and Trish specific and general questions. She needs to **interview Trish separately from Sharra to reduce social acquiescence and desirability*** *bias. Beginning with general questions regarding relationship and interaction with Sharra, as Karen establishes closer bonding with Trish she can* **move to more specific and sensitive questions** *about Trish's interaction with her mother, Sharra, and the care she receives from her. To* **establish reliability Karen must ask questions in different ways seeking the same information**— *whether Trish is abused. Karen tries to audio record her interviews with Sharra and Trish, although does not always have the time to listen to them. When she has concerns she tries to play the recordings for her supervisor or in team meetings. Social workers are ethically bound to uphold the values and knowledge of the profession (1996,*

*Code of Ethics, Section 5.01). If Karen feels pressured to handle too many cases and is not able to adequately collect data she is prepared to confront her supervisor, or the agency director.*

. . . . . . . . . . . . . . . . . . . .

## Telephone Interviews

Telephone interviews capture some of the same advantages and disadvantages as direct, face-to-face interviews, but they also offer some additional advantages and disadvantages. While telephone interviews allow for some clarification of meaning they are limited to audio

Advantages and Disadvantages of Interviews

| *Advantages* | *Disadvantages* |
| --- | --- |
| Allows for immediate clarity, feedback, and member checking; has the capacity to deal directly and in depth with subtle, complex, and emotional information and attend to meaning for enhanced respondent validity. | Interviewer's and respondent's verbal skills and respondent's observational skills can bias the information's reliability, completeness, accuracy, validity, and sensitivity. |
| Can obtain information from nonliterate clients and respondents. | Highly intrusive and easily subjected to social acquiescence and desirability biases. |
| Of all data collection approaches, provides individual respondent with the most freedom and opportunity to shape responses and information. | Limited to information sources possessing the capacity and willingness to engage in verbal interaction. |
| Can be easily combined with observations of affect, body language, visual cues, and other contextual conditions for triangulation and improved validity. | Can place the interviewer at physical risk from irate respondents or hostile social environments. |
| Response rates are generally higher than with more indirect forms of data collection, such as mailed questionnaires. | More costly in time and efforts to construct, conduct, record, and analyze than are respondent-completed precoded questionnaires. |
| Required skills are a part of the competent social work practitioner's practice technology. | Reliability easily influenced by the interviewer and interview's physical and social context. |
| A data collection approach suitable for "hidden" client attributes such as feelings, attitudes, beliefs. | Tendency for task confusion; social workers may drift from information collection to intervention prematurely. |

sources. Providing a relatively safe environment for the interviewer and some social as well as physical distance between interviewer and respondent, telephone interviews are less costly than face-to-face interviews in time, energy, and fiscal resources. Reflexivity is reduced because the effects of the interviewer's physical appearance, gender, age, and ethnicity are mitigated, although some research (Cotter, Cohen, & Coulter, 1982) indicates that they are not eliminated. It is easier to monitor these interviews for reliability.

Telephone interviews limit information gathering to respondents with telephones. The advent of the answering machine allows respondents to more easily control whether they engage in the interview. When a telephone interview becomes too intrusive, the respondent can terminate it by hanging up the phone without having to engage in other social interactions. The respondent's social context and any of its biasing effects are more difficult to ascertain with telephone than with face-to-face interviews. Sometimes the respondent's identity cannot be established with certainty. And with the surge in telemarketing there is a growing reluctance to reveal information over the telephone to a faceless, nameless person on the other end. Some prior relationship between the interviewer and respondent is helpful. Early in the interview process, the interviewer should provide the respondent a call-back number the respondent can use to verify the interviewer's credentials and credibility.

## Written Questionnaires, Scales, and Logs

Questionnaires, scales, and logs are generally paper-and-pencil recording devices (although their computerization is increasing) that ask respondents to record their reaction to the questions or stimuli of the questionnaire or scale. Clients or respondents assess and record their current or prior behavior, feelings, attitude, or knowledge according to the questions asked and, with pre-coded questionnaires, answers provided. The in-

struments, contrary to the claims of some (Fischer & Corcoran, 1994, p. xxxviiii), do not directly measure the phenomenon. The paper-and-pencil measures are largely recall coding or coding devices asking respondents to evaluate and report their perceptions (often self-perceptions), attitudes, opinions, and feelings. This data collection methodology embraces a range of instruments, including intelligence tests, attitude and behavioral inventories, and opinionnaires.

Basic principles applicable to selecting observations and interviews as data collection processes apply to the selection and use of standardized and specific paper-and-pencil approaches. The principles for using standardized questionnaires as information collection tools follow the *why, who, what, when,* and *how* imperatives common to the other information tools.

1. *Why is the information needed? Why is this methodology selected?*

First, determine the purpose of the information and its contributions to the decisions that have to be made. This purpose will guide whether to use an unstructured or highly structured device.

2. *Who has the information? Who will complete the device? Are the respondents capable of answering written questions?*

Written devices require literate respondents.

3. *What are the acts, activities, and events that respondents can provide information about through the written device? What is the appropriate structure for the device?*

The acts, activities, and events and respondent capacities guide the selection of information-gathering processes. Using depression inventories to assess a client's depression level requires a client who is literate and capable of responding to written stimuli.

The practitioner needs to be attentive to the considerations discussed earlier for an interview structure with written devices. These considerations involve (1) selecting a funnel or inverted funnel approach on semistructured, open-ended, and fixed or preset response questions, (2) flexibility in the ordering and structure, and (3) available tools or develop new tools. Available standardized measurement tools, discussed in Chapter 6, can reduce the time, cost, and efforts of measurement and data collection if they serve current information needs. If standardized, they are more likely to allow for comparison and may have norms established. They should be used *if they fit the purpose and yield the needed valid information that is usable in making judgments.*

4. *When are the devices best used and how frequently?*

Frequency of use depends on the respondent's capacity and recall of events, acts, and feelings. Overly long and complex devices can fatigue a respondent and affect the data. Tired respondents are more concerned with completing the ordeal than in providing accurate information.

5. *Where are the devices to be used?*

The use environment and context needs to be conducive to completing written communication. Context considers the capacity of a respondent to engage fully in the process of responding to the instrument.

6. *Establish the processes' and instruments' reliability and validity for the particular client or respondent in the specific context.*

The environment and social conditions of application and client characteristics can affect the ability of a measurement device and process to yield valid information. Reliability and validity generally are established in a specific or limited number of social and physical settings with a restricted set of people. The practitioner concerned with the information's truthfulness obtained in the practice application of the device needs to establish its validity in its specific application processes with the particular group of clients.

## Questionnaires

The questionnaire format has wide application. Service eligibility forms, civil service and professional licensure examinations, and depression inventories as information-gathering tools all

## Advantages and Disadvantages of Standardized Instruments

| Standardized Measures | |
| --- | --- |
| *Advantages* | *Disadvantages* |
| Relatively inexpensive, expedient, and easy to use compared to specifically developed instruments, observations, and interviews. | May have been developed and standardized for a population or a group the client does not fit into. |
| Often has established reliability and validity. | Limited number of viable instruments to fit the range of information needs (content validity concerns). |
| Can allow for normative comparisons with other clients or the normative standards. | Information on reliability and validity often is not readily available or is suspect. |
| Promotes reliability with written, consistent, and standardized questions and possible response categories. | Preset response categories may not fit current needs and threaten validity. |
| Can be readily triangulated with other measurements and data collection approaches. | |

fall into this category. Questionnaires are sets of questions that can be open ended, in which the respondent chooses the response wording or preset "forced-choice" with response categories provided.

Either choice is a function of the questionnaire designer's and practitioner's knowledge of the respondents. *Preset response category questions provide the respondent with preset responses to the questions.* The respondent is "forced" to select one of the preset responses. These questions are useful when the range of potential response categories and thresholds of the variable are known and preselected. They also are easier to tabulate, code, and analyze than open-ended questions.

**Open-ended questions** that leave the response narratives open are useful (1) when the possible response range is not known making it impossible to establish preset response categories; (2) for respondent "ventilation," allowing release of frustrations and statements important to the respondent; (3) in providing information requiring so large a number of preset categories as to be cumbersome, such as interval categories for age and income; and (4) when a contextual flavor is needed from the respondent. The disaggregated data of open-ended questions provide analysis flexibility. The *other (describe)* response category in preset response categories addresses the first three reasons.

Used sparingly with preset categories, open-ended questions can be coded through computer and statistical analysis and reduced to quantitative and set categories similar to preset category questions. This is done a priori with preset response categories. Open-ended questions are more vulnerable to recording and systematic and random coding errors affecting their reliability and validity. If they are not analyzed, they are "throw-aways" with little purpose other than respondent ventilation.

Think ahead about how to analyze the information, because open-ended questions add to time and cost. They lengthen the instrument and add to the respondent's time, effort, and degree of complexity experienced in completing the questionnaire. The need for open-ended questions is reduced by (1) reviewing the literature to develop fuller knowledge and conceptualization for establishing preset responses, (2) drawing from experiences of other researchers and practitioners in measuring the phenomenon, (3) pilot studies of respondents and phenomenon using a grounded and naturalistic approach to develop response categories, and (4) pretesting instruments. Tripodi (1994) recommends the use of "mostly force-choice and only a few open-ended questions so that the social worker can tabulate the responses more easily" (p. 35). The guiding criteria, however, are whether forced-choice and preset response questions can best—or better—measure the nuances of what is important and significant in intervention with the respondent condition than alterative open-ended questions can. *Open-ended questions are preferred when the full range of a client's perspective is not known.*

### Reliability and validity

Written response instruments involve observation and translating the observation into a narrative or preset response categories. As measurement and data collection processes, their reliability and validity rests on five components: (1) the variable, behavior, attitude, or phenomenon; (2) the respondent's observations, including self-observations and assessments; (3) the respondent's personal coding; (4) the respondent's recoding according to the structure and stimuli of the questionnaires, scales, and logs, and (5) the instrument's structure and construction of reality. The reliability and validity of the measurement and data collection process entails a fit among all components.

Paper-and-pencil tests, self-administered, make gains in reliability over interviews. Respondents read the question, select and record responses from the preset response categories or by open-ended narrative, reducing error possibilities in reading and recording by a second person. Biasing effects of a second reader's voice tones, inflection, and other cues on question and subse-

## Information Flow of Written Instruments

| Empirical behavior or phenomenon or attitude, feeling, or belief ⟶ | ← Respondent observations, including self-observations and assessments ⟶ | ← Encoding by observer-respondent of observations ⟶ | ← Observer-respondent recodes observations to respond to instrument's categories or presents uncoded narrative ⟶ | ← Narratives recoded by instrument coder and previously coded response categories recorded |
|---|---|---|---|---|

quent responses are less likely. Written questions remain the same with repeated application. They will not, however, record information on respondent body language, voice tone, inflection, or whether respondents appear nervous. The preset and limited nature of these items offer increased reliability over the open-ended questionnaire and loosely focused interview.

Preset items can be challenged, however, on the more important criteria of construct and empirical validity. While they report on something, is the report an account of the actual behavior? If the measurement concerns are largely "How do you feel?" and "How have you behaved?" the validity concerns relate to the respondent's sharing the same constructions for these concepts as the questionnaire response categories. The questions are made finite and precise to promote consistency in the construction of reality, but its accuracy will depend on similar constructions of meaning between response categories and respondent. Without a shared mental construction, the accuracy of any behavior reports beyond "motion" reports is conceptually suspect.

The *Family-of-Origin Scale* (*FOS*) (Fischer & Corcoran, 1994, pp. 303–307) referred to in Chapter 6 requests responses to a series of 40 self-assessment items. The two key concepts measured by the scale and on which data are collected are autonomy and intimacy in the respondent's family of origin.

The responses, however, are the respondent's perception, recall, and reporting of the family's interaction by the questionnaire's construction of autonomy and intimacy. Norming of the scale was done with college students and did not empirically measure family interaction in other ways. To assume that the questions in fact measure the interaction is reification.

---

**Sample of the 40 FOS Items**

In my family, it was normal to show both positive and negative feelings.

  5 (SA)  4 (A)  3 (N)  2 (D)  1 (SD)

In my family, I expressed just about every feeling I had.

  5 (SA)  4 (A)  3 (N)  2 (D)  1 (SD)

In my family, certain feelings were not allowed to be expressed.

  5 (SA)  4 (A)  3 (N)  2 (D)  1 (SD)

My family had an unwritten rule: Don't express your feelings.

  5 (SA)  4 (A)  3 (N)  2 (D)  1 (SD)

---

The *Depression Self-Rating Scale* (*DSRS*) (Fischer & Corcoran, 1994, pp. 464–465) is used to measure and collect information on the extent and severity of depression in children. It reported concurrent validity with another scale, *Children's Depression Inventory.*

1. I look forward to things as much as I used to. (+)
2. I sleep very well. (+)

3. I feel like crying. (–)
4. I like to go out and play. (+)
5. I feel like running away. (–)
6. I get tummy aches. (–)
7. I have a lot of energy. (+)
8. I enjoy my food. (+)
9. I can stick up for my self. (+)
10. I think that life isn't worth living. (–)
11. I am very good at the things I do. (+)
12. I enjoy the things I do as much as I used to. (+)
13. I like talking about my family. (+)
14. I have horrible dreams. (–)
15. I feel very lonely. (–)
16. I am easily cheered up. (+)
17. I feel so sad I can hardly stand it. (–)
18. I feel very bored. (–)

Again, the scale is a self-report or self-observation and reporting tool. It is inherently subjective in its concern for feelings more than behavior. Its construct validity in practice is dependent on the practitioner and client sharing similar meanings for such labels and terms as "lot of energy," "enjoy," "horrible dreams" as well as accepting these labels as indicators of depression. Its empirical validity, the central practice concern, depends on whether the reported perceptions correspond to actual feelings and behaviors. The scale's most appropriate use, as with most social and behavior sciences scales, appears to be gauging movement or changes for a single client rather than for comparing clients.

*The arguments are not that written questionnaires and preset response categories are not useful, should not be used, or make no contribution to measurement and data collection. They do measure, are useful, and should be used in data collection. But their practice limitations need to be recognized.* They generally were developed and their reliability and validity established with specific groups. However, neither are a perfect "1.0" correlation and the scales rarely describe accurately all individuals within the norming group's reliability or validity. The emphasis on scales, especially attitude scales, was an effort by the social science positivists

from the 1920s onward to emulate their view of the natural sciences. These reduction measurements, are often oversold. "The opinion survey or questionnaire assumed a reified, unitary, and simple construct that could be abstracted out of context" (Ross, 1991, p. 433). Instead, we should recognize them as one imperfect approach and use in triangulation with the other imperfect approaches.

### Enhancing reliability

The following are several useful criteria applicable to assessing reliability in available instruments or to guide development of new measurement tools.

**Reduce complexity.** Instruments, scales, questionnaires, or diaries need to be simple and direct as possible within the constraints of information needs. Avoid unnecessary work for the respondent in questionnaire and question design and construction, complexity, length, and format. Users need to understand the instrument, its purpose, and the logic of its construction, but not be led to specific answers or responses. The *face sheet,* or introduction to the instrument, generally instructs users in the easy use of the instrument. Instruments that are too complex or involve too much work encourage respondents to reduce their effort, resulting in measurement and recording errors.

**Avoid fatigue.** The instrument's design should consider and minimize user fatigue effects of bias and reflexivity. Long, complex instruments might better be broken down into multiple shorter time span applications. Instrument fatigue—tiring and losing accuracy and consistency—is always a measurement concern, whether the instrument is electronic, mechanical, or human. *Remember that the respondent to a questionnaire is a part of the measurement process.*

**Reconsider contingency questions.** Contingency questions are those that instruct the respondent to go to other parts of the questionnaire based on the answer to the contingency question. Complex, busy instruments with many contingency questions are likely to induce fatigue and produce errors:

> If the question is answered "yes," go to question X, If answered "No," go to question Y, If answered "Don't Know," go to question "Z" …

While these questions shorten a questionnaire carefully consider using them, since they add complexity and possible confusion. It is often difficult to detect when a respondent makes a mistake following the contingency instructions.

*Eliminate double-barreled questions.* Questions that ask for responses to two areas at once are *double-barreled*. Avoid them. An example is (1) "Do you sometimes feel anxious or depressed?" An affirmative answer will not provide information about whether respondents feel depressed or anxious, only that they feel one of these conditions. A negative response will not eliminate the respondent who "sometimes feels anxious and depressed." The question is double-barreled if the intent is to measure the two conditions as distinct. The question is also different from (2) "Do you sometimes feel anxious *and* depressed?" which covers the presence of both conditions. Neither question is double-barreled if the intent is to measure either of the conditions as one condition in (1), or both conditions as one condition in (2).

*Follow the disaggregation principle.* In the questions above, the *disaggregation principle* applies. Measurement and data collection that is disaggregated is preferred over aggregated measurement and collection. In other words, ask as separate questions:

> Do you sometimes feel anxious?
> Do you sometimes feel depressed?

These will provide information on each condition separately and also enable combination of the conditions in analysis. You can always com-bine disaggregated data, but cannot separate information collected in an aggregate. Categories can always be collapsed, but you cannot later expand if begun as collapsed categories. If you ask age in five-year bands, you cannot determine where a respondent falls within a selected age band. A better approach—better in the specificity of information provided—is to ask the age in years or, even better yet, the birthdate. Birthdate information lends itself to a variety of analyses.

If interested in the lower end of the income range, and respondents indicate their yearly income in bands of $5000, such as:

| | |
|---|---|
| $5000 or under | $15,001–$20,000 |
| $5001–$10,000 | $20,001–$25,000 |
| $10,001–$15,000 | $25,001 and above |

we can analyze the information only in these bands. We will not know if a homeless respondent selecting the first band has no income or a $5000 income, or when a respondent indicates the second band if the yearly income is a $5000 or $10,000 income, or if the difference in income between the homeless respondent and the second respondent is $1.00 or $10,000, and we can never know based on the information provided. Disaggregated information is more precise and informative.

The degree of disaggregation depends on the sensitivity of the question and response and the precision needed. But recalling Bernard's (1994, p. 35) admonition discussed in Chapter 6, always measure things at the highest level of measurement possible. Higher levels of measurement can safely be reduced to lower levels, equal interval data treated as ordinal data, but nominal data cannot safely be treated as ordinal data nor ordinal data as equal interval data. Do not ask if something is between x and y or between y and z, if you can ask the specific value. Aggregate data questions weaken subsequent analysis.

*Use simple and nonjudgmental language.* Language should be neutral, nonjudgmental, and direct to avoid social acquiescence and social desirability response biases. Use language that is understandable, and do not play up or down to the respondent. Be careful in the use of jargon and slang in an effort to bond. Jargon is often quickly outdated or inappropriately used.

***Understand the question frame.*** Location and sequencing of questions is important. Start with the least sensitive, and move to more sensitive questions after the occurrence of some respondent bonding and investment. Most sensitive questions are better placed in the middle or toward the end of the questionnaire. Knowledge of respondents and their cultural sensitivities is obtained though experience, discussion with other experts, review of the literature, pretesting, and observation of respondents.

***Determine appropriate preset response ranges.*** When developing response categories for preset response questions cover the full range of interest in the variable. For example, if the questionnaire designer's interest is in establishing the self-identified ethnicity of the respondent, the questions can be:

> Ethnicity: Please indicate which of the following ethnic groups you most identify with (Check only one):
>
> African-American ☐
> Asian American ☐
> Hispanic ☐
> American Indian ☐
> White, Not Hispanic ☐
> Other (describe)_____

The response categories indicate interest only in the response categories provided. It is exhaustive with the use of the *Other* response. Without the *Other* response, the full potential range is not covered. And without the *Other* response, ethnic identifications are limited to those provided by the instrument.

***Use mutually exclusive preset response categories.*** Preset response categories should be mutually exclusive with a response capable of falling into only one response category. A questionnaire using the following response categories for age is neither exhaustive, nor are response categories mutually exclusive.

> Please indicate the number of members of the household with ages:
>
> 5–10 (  )
> 10–15 (  )
> 15–20 (  )
> 20–25 (  )
> 25 and above (  )

Given the upper threshold, we might conclude that the questioner's interest is limited to certain age clusters of children and young adults in the household. However, the response categories are neither exhaustive nor appropriate. Although the over 25-year-olds are provided a response category, the under 5-year-olds are not. All categories overlap. Respondents aged 10, 15, 20, and 25 years can fall into two categories. The respondent does not know the appropriate response to indicate or whether both responses should be checked. The information user will be similarly confused. *Response categories should cover the range of responses and be mutually exclusive. A response should not fall within two categories simultaneously.*

***Establish reliability and validity.*** Always pretest for reliability, validity, reflexivity, and readability as discussed in the measurement chapter. Use pretesting to assess ways for improving the instrument. Reliability and validity of instruments as measurement and data collection devices exist only if users use them appropriately. They are standardized for general use or created for the specific use of a particular client.

## Mailed Questionnaires

Mailed information-gathering tools require greater adherence to the construction and pre-testing procedures just described than do questionnaires administered directly to respondents. Mailed questionnaires do not allow for clarification through immediate respondent feedback while completing the questionnaire. Instructions must be clear and readable. The cover letter and informed consent agreements, unless previously obtained, need to detail how and for what purpose the information will be used, how it will be treated, and how privacy and confidentiality will be maintained with any limits to confidentiality. Mailed questionnaires, of course, can only be used with literate respondents. The questionnaire's literacy level and language must be assessed for its fit with the target respondents. And with mailed questionnaires, there is never absolute certainty about who completes the questionnaire. Their great advantage, often overriding the drawbacks, is their low administrative costs.

## Self-Anchoring Movement Scales

Self-anchoring movement scales are special forms of questionnaires that have self-anchoring or respondent-anchoring features, in which the respondent determines the anchoring or weights of the response categories. They are used to rate a dimension of a variable chosen by the client and the social worker. Self-anchoring movement scales provide measurements of changes in behavior, attitudes, or other variables in their frequency, intensity, magnitude, or duration. The scale's range should cover the continuum from the lowest possible level of interest, the lowest relevant threshold for the client, and the highest possible level of interest or relevant upper threshold for the client. Surgical patients use self-anchoring scales to rate their pain on a 1 to 10 scale, with 1 representing no pain and 10 the most pain imaginable. Tripodi (1994) recommends generally between 5 to 9 rating points, such as the response categories of *1. Strongly dis-*

*agree, 2. Disagree, 3. Neutral, 4. Agree,* and *5. Strongly agree.* The condition and the need for precision guides the number of points used. A lower range and number of points lacks precision; a greater number of points may present a false precision. True discrimination is often more difficult with scales that have too many points because they confuse the respondent.

Self-anchoring movement scales best measure a client's perception of movement over time. Self-rating scales are routinely administered several times, at least prior to and after intervention, to assess change. Self-anchoring movement scales are less useful in comparing movement between clients because the anchoring or meaning of the indicators may not be the same for different clients. Each person's 5 or *Strongly agree* on the scale is not the same as 5 or *Strongly agree* for everyone.

The tasks in using self-anchoring movement scales are to

1. Prepare the client by explaining the scale's purpose, how to use it, and establish its high and low points.

2. With the client, select the extremes of the scales and the number of scale points within the extremes.

3. With the client, establish the intervals between the points, using equal intervals. The client should regard the distance between adjacent numbers as equal intervals.

4. Use one dimension for each item, with the item or question referring to only one attitude, variable, behavior or mood to reduce ambiguity.

Tripodi (1994, pp. 19–20) recommends against using scales that presents opposite dichotomous dimensions such as intelligent–stupid, rigid–flexible, and so forth because these are often confusing to respondents. Dichotomies often might be better presented as dual continuums requiring two-item responses rather than as dichotomies of a single continuum. Dual items for the dichotomies aids in establishing reliability because they can be compared. A high score on one dimension should be accompanied by a low score on the companion dimension. However, dichotomous scales are widely used.

5. Anchor the scale points by *determining and establishing the dimension's and points' meaning for the client.*
6. Decide when, where, and how often to administer the scale. *Note the need for consistency of administrative conditions of and for guidance by the case theory in selecting times of administration.*
7. Use as repeated measures for trend analysis and to assess movement and change, but be aware of the potential reflexivity and reactivity effects of repeated administrations.

Movement scales can also be used without self-anchoring by including specific behaviors such as job-seeking behavior to gauge change:

---

Numbers of times applied for employment in

Week 1 (   )

Week 2 (   ) or—numbers of incidents for a given time     _____

                   Intervention
                   _____

Week 10 (    )

---

Client anchoring is unnecessary when the movement involves counting specific behaviors or events. Again as discussed earlier, the highest order of measurement possible and disaggregated data are appropriate whenever movement is assessed. Nominal response categories such as *Applied for a Job Last Week: Yes (   ), No (   ),* or ordinal response categories, even with efforts to anchor them and make them equal interval, such as: *Applied for a Job Last Week: Never (   ), Seldom (   ), Occasionally (   ), Frequently (   ), and Very Frequently (   ),* will yield less information than the ratio measurements of the number of times the client actually applied for a job: *Enter the Number of Jobs Applied for Last Week* _____. Regardless of the response categories used and the need for anchoring, the meaning of *Applied for a Job* will have to be shared between practitioner and client.

## Client Logs and Diaries

Client self-reports in logs and diaries are fertile information sources. Clients can use them to record a range of behaviors, events, emotions, and attitudes, and to develop client life stories and narratives and assess behavior changes. *Logs and diaries can be combined with other self-report measures such as the questionnaires, scales, and interviews discussed earlier for easy triangulation.* The logs and diaries can ask preset response questions as well as open-ended questions. These are the recording tools and the client is operationally the measurement instrument. The practitioner and client must develop similar conceptual and operational definitions and meanings for the behaviors, events, emotions, and attitudes recorded.

•  •  •  •  •  •  •  •  •  •  •  •  •  •  •  •  •  •

*The following is a partial diary facsimile for Mary, a mother in constant conflict with her 8-year-old son, Johnny. Mary uses the diary to record her angry interactions with Johnny, rate the intensity of her anger on a self-anchoring movement scale, and a description of the circumstances of the interaction.*

*Mary and the social worker, Amy, need mutual constructions of the meanings of "angry interactions," ratings of the anger's intensity, and the critical attributes of the circumstances. Mary must be trained as a participant-observer in what to observe and how to record it and in the protocols for the self-anchored components. This member checking and training is critical for reliability and for respondent and content validity. Empirical validity can be heightened by triangulation with other trained observers, with Johnny, and with Amy; by observing logging; and by rating interactions. If similar constructions are used, similar loggings and ratings should occur.*

•  •  •  •  •  •  •  •  •  •  •  •  •  •  •  •  •  •

Validity is enhanced by triangulation. If the case theory indicates angry interactions are associated with other attitudes or conditions, measurement and changes in these conditions should correspond with the client's logs. For example, if depression is associated with specific behaviors and feelings, respondent behavior recorded in logs should correspond to changes in client scores on depression inventories. If there is no correspondence, we don't know *prima facie* which measure is invalid unless there is an a priori established criterion validity. The lack of correspondence does tell us to reexamine our measurement processes. Without validity, we are prone to making false positive and negative judgments and to acting on these judgements.

Using logs and diaries presents the challenge of developing a tool that captures the desired information in a format conducive to practical use. The log facsimile reproduced earlier could ask that all interactions be recorded. While doing this might reduce the inherent social desirability bias and reduce a possible acquiescence bias if this is a child abuse case, it would be impractical for the client to record, rate, and describe the circumstances of all interactions in the day.

Logs and diaries as self-monitoring mechanisms are highly vulnerable to reflexivity. In observing, evaluating, and recording their own behaviors, log keepers may alter the behaviors. Johnny's mother in keeping the log (p. 130) may reduce her angry interactions by virtue of observing, rating, and recording her angry interactions. Without the observation and tracking,

## Advantages and Disadvantages of Client Logs and Diaries

| Advantages | Disadvantages | Advantages | Disadvantages |
|---|---|---|---|
| Obtain idiosyncratic information about events that cannot be observed, felt, or experienced by other than the client. | Vulnerable to a range of social desirability and acquiescence biases related to client's desire to minimize or exaggerate a problem or condition. | Structured with standard format, anchoring, instruction, and training to enhance reliability and uniformity across measurement circumstances. | Requires triangulation to enhance reliability and validity for other than attitudes and opinion. |
| Emphasize client perspective and meaning. | Potentially high reflexivity that may make isolation of other treatment effects difficult. | Easily triangulated with other measurement and data collection processes. | Except for audio recordings, requires literate clients with capacity and discipline to keep the log or diary. |
| Private character of measurement and data collection process may foster client candidness. | | Reflexivity may reinforce other interventions and can be used as an economical intervention. | |
| | | Efficient, requires minimum investment of time by practitioner and client if appropriately designed. | |

Diary of Daily Angry Interactions with Johnny

Date _____

| Time | Number Rating | Describe Circumstances |
|---|---|---|
| 1:01–6:00 A.M. | | |
| 6:01–8:00 A.M. | | |
| 8:01–12:00 | | |
| 12:01–2:00 P.M. | | |
| Continue for balance of day | | |

**Instructions:**

1. Column 2: Enter the number of angry interactions with Johnny occurring during the time span of column 1.

2. Column 3: How angry were you at each interaction? 1 = Not Very Angry and 7 = Uncontrollable Anger.

3. Column 4: Describe the circumstances of each angry interaction with Johnny.

there might be more angry interactions. The measurement processes become part of the treatment and have an effect on the client. Amy, the practitioner needs to assess what part of client change is a result of self-monitoring and what part of the change ensues from the other intervention components. If there is a reflexive effect, a major treatment task for the client is to continue the self-monitoring after conclusion of the formal treatment and measurements.

## Observer Rating Scales

Similar to self-report scales, observer rating scales are scales used by others, such as the practitioner or others knowledgeable of the client, to rate the client. If the same scales are used for self-reports and by other observers, all users observing the same behavior need to use common anchoring.

## Assessing the Readability of the Written and Oral Questions

Written and verbal communications, questionnaires, and interview schedules need to be understood by the client or other respondents if the information yielded is to have respondent validity. The communication's ability to impart an intended meaning to the respondents can be assessed in several ways. Perhaps the best approach is to pilot field-test the material or messages with a representative sample of its target audience. A second and less expensive method is to test the communication with a focused group or member-checking panel composed of the target population. Interviews allow adjustments to obtain clarity of meaning. Both of these methods suffer from the expense of developing an inventory of the target population, constructing the sample or recruiting the focused group, field-testing the messages with the sample, and reiterating the process until the appropriate message level is developed.

Less costly in time and effort are the variety of computer software programs available that assess the readability of messages and education levels required to understand the messages. They are easily used, though require entering the message into an appropriate software file.

A less expensive, quick method, though with suspect validity, is the SMOG Readability Formula (Office of Cancer Communication, 1992, p. 77; Hardcastle, Wenocur, & Powers, 1997, pp. 336–338). This uses a logic similar to the various computer software programs based on the structure and complexity of the message words. The SMOG Readability Formula is used to calculate the reading grade level necessary for comprehension of the written material. For written messages of 30 sentences or more:

1. Take the beginning 10, approximate middle 10, and last 10 sentences or phrases of the written material message for a total of thirty sentences. A phrase is considered a sentence when the string of words ends in a period, question mark, or exclamation mark even

though it may not be a grammatically complete sentence. The intent is to obtain a representation of the total message. Random sampling of all the sentences could obtain the 30 sentences, although this is spurious precision for a rather imprecise procedure.

2. Count the number of polysyllabic words, words of three or more syllables, in the 30 sentences or phrases. Numbers, whether written as *one hundred fifty* or numeric as *150*, abbreviations such as *etc.*, and hyphenated words have the same number of syllables as when spoken (*150* has five syllables and *etc.* has four syllables). Hyphenated words and numbers count as one word.

3. Compute the square root of the number of polysyllabic words in the 30 sentences to the nearest whole square root. For example, if the 30 sentences have 200 polysyllabic words, the square root is 14.14 and the nearest whole square root is 14.

4. Add the constant 3 to the square root and the sum is the approximate educational level required to read the message. As the level is approximate, a plus or minus of 1.5 grades is added, with the level assumed to lie within this range. The plus or minus of 1.5 grade levels is the estimated error range.

If a selected thirty sentences in a document contain 70 polysyllabic words, the computation is:

| Readability Test Calculation Steps | |
| --- | --- |
| Total number of polysyllabic words | 70 |
| Square root | 8.37 |
| Nearest whole square root | 8 |
| Addition of constant | 3 |
| Approximate grade level | 11 |
| Approximate grade level range (11 + or – 1.5) | 9.5 to 12.5 |

The message should be appropriate for an 11th grade reading level, although the error range indicates that it might be readable as low as a 9.5 reading level or require 12.5 years and high school graduation to comprehend. If clients or targeted subjects for the above 9.5–12.5 reading level message have a general reading level of 10 years, given the error range the researcher or practitioner probably should lower the readability level. They fall within the range, but there is risk it will miss the target audience if it generally requires 12th grade capacity.

Lower the message level by altering its structure and complexity. Change the number and ratio of polysyllabic words per sentence by using fewer complex words and increasing use of short declarative sentences. Ten long, complex sentences are likely to contain more polysyllabic words than are ten short declarative sentences. Rework messages with upper-range scores above the audience's minimum education level even though the score lacks precision and people with the same education level have different reading and comprehension capacities.

Documents and messages with less than 30 sentences use the following adjustment formula

> Total number of polysyllabic words in the communication/total number of sentences in the communication × 30 = Adjusted total number of polysyllabic words

to convert them into a format appropriate to SMOG. Enter the adjusted total number of polysyllabic words into the box above and complete the remaining steps. For example, if a communication has 20 polysyllabic words in nine sentences, the readability level is: Total number of polysyllabic words Used = 20/9 = 2.22 × 30 = 66.67 adjusted polysyllabic words.

This is the probable number of polysyllabic words the message would contain if elaborated to 30 sentences with the structure and complexity remaining the same.

SMOG's advantages over the other methods are that it requires comparatively little time and expense. No representative sample or focus group from the target audience is needed, nor is field testing, computers, software or computer expertise required. The message does not have to be entered into the appropriate software file. Skills and costs for this communication assessment method are the ability to recognize sentences and polysyllabic words, the costs of a calculator to compute the square roots (less than $10.00), possibly the cost of a dictionary to look up words to determine their syllables, and time needed to count sentences and polysyllabic words and do the computation.

SMOG's major disadvantage is inherent in its virtue. It is "quick and dirty," providing only a crude approximation of the readability grade level. SMOG does not directly deal with the message complexities beyond the mathematical relationships of individual words and sentences. SMOG provides no feedback to develop an appropriate massage other than to reduce the complexity. Development of appropriate communication of meaning requires member checking and field testing with the target respondents.

## Summary

Data collection applied in practice situations is the process of getting the assessment information on the case from the most relevant information sources. Integrity and validity of the data are paramount. They depend on the integrity of the measures and the processes used to obtain the information. Integrity requires that data are not altered or lost because of a faulty data collection system.

The social worker in the assessment phase gathers information on the presenting condition and problem to develop case theory and provide

the basis for an intervention plan. The case is periodically reassessed. Information gathering includes accumulating information and data on the problem itself; the case system, including strengths and potential resources useful for intervention; the strengths and limitations of resources and potential support systems; and possible constraints to any change effort from the targets for change. Community- and socially based practice models devote more attention in assessment to social ecology, the environment and the social systems, than do psychologically centered problem-solving strategies, though these are necessary components in all social work assessments.

Data collection, whether in practice or research, requires a plan for gathering information specifying what information is needed, when it is needed, and how it will be gathered. The tool and instrument to gather data should be understandable, relatively easy to use, and practical—in cost, in time involved in gathering information, in scoring or coding, and in data processing.

A major data source in assessment is the case (Bisman, 1994, pp. 111–176; Lukus, 1993). Client systems should tell the story in their own words, responding to unstructured and structured interviews as well as to preset response approaches. Social workers should let participants know that the story is understood by member-checking. Data collection approaches that supplement interviews include use of measurement tactics such as questionnaires and scales, observation, and participant observation and mechanical, electronic, and physical measurement methods. Available data such as case records, other retrospective data, and data from other observers and sources are also used. Literature on human and social behavior is often valuable in case theory building guiding data collection.

## Discussion Questions and Exercises

1. How might you use available data, observations, interviews, and paper-and-pencil scales to assess the level and changes in such things as child abuse, depression, and income for a client in practice?

2. Of the conditions of child abuse, depression, and income, which is most likely to require triangulation? In considering the measurement approaches of available data, observations, interviews, and paper-and-pencil scales for the preceding conditions, which measurement approach is most likely to need triangulation? Why?

3. How does member checking contribute to truthfulness of the information? How can you use member checking in practice?

4. Unobtrusive measurements and data collection processes have less reflexivity. How can you use unobtrusive measurements and data collection processes without engaging in covert practice?

# CHAPTER EIGHT

# Designs and Practice Plans

**Research designs** are plans specifying procedures and protocols for gathering the information necessary to answer research questions and to test hypotheses. *Research designs perform similar functions in the conduct of research as practice case plans do in the practice problem-solving process. A case practice plan is a blueprint setting forth the components, sequencing, application, and timing of the intervention tasks to effect change in the case's outcome objectives.* Bisman (1994) holds that a practice plan, a plan for intervening with a case, contains "a problem statement, the established objectives, the specifics of the contract including the frequency and length of sessions and the modal-

ity of treatment, as well as the evaluation process and guiding knowledge and theories" (p. 4).

This chapter examines research designs, especially the classic experimental design, for the guidance they provide in developing and implementing case practice plans.

Both research designs and case plans address the following issues, although the labels used in the plan or design may differ:

1. What changes in the case(s) are sought on outcomes and dependent variables?

2. What will produce the changes; intervention and independent variables?

## Parallels of Practice and Research

| *Practice Components and Tasks* | *Research Epistemologies and Methodologies* |
| --- | --- |
| **Case practice plan** | **Research designs (including single subject design and case study designs)** |
| Goals formulation and contracting; | |
| determining how and when the judgments of change on outcome condition are made; | Determining how and when the judgments of change on the dependent variables are made; |
| design or selection of intervention plan, how to implement, control and measure; | design or selection of independent variables and how and when to measure; |
| client's informed consent in contracting and establishing goals and objectives: exercise of self-determination; | research subject informed consent, recognition of design causal or internal and external validity limitations; |
| practitioner observation, and self-awareness; | use of literature to support design |
| use of literature to support case plan and relevance to agency's mission and profession's ethics | |

3. If the hypothesis predicts a causal relationship between variables, when are independent or intervention variables introduced?

4. How to control and monitor independent variables or interventions.

5. What other conditions need controlling and/or influencing; ecological and community conditions or control and covariables?

6. How and when do all these variables need measurement or assessment?

7. How to eliminate or control alternative explanations to the independent variable or intervention producing the change.

8. Are the results applicable, and under what conditions, to other cases or situations?

**Alternative explanations** are reasonable and plausible statements that something other than the independent variables or intervention produced the changes in the dependent variable or outcome. They are alternative explanations. Alternative explanations threaten the capacity of the design to provide truthful information about the relationships between the independent and dependent variables, or between interventions and outcomes. A design's foremost task is to eliminate alternative explanations so that the changes in the dependent variables can be attributed to changes in the independent variable. In case plans, a task is to be able to reasonably infer that changes in the outcomes result, at least in part, from the intervention.

## Design Models

Research designs and case plans come in all shapes and types. *The research question or hypothesis to be addressed, the theory to be tested, and the predicted relationship between variables determine the appropriateness of a particular research design.* A case practice plan's appropriateness depends on having a case theory that sets forth the predicted relationship among the case resources, intervention, and case objectives. Selection and construction of a design or case plan provide a framework

Basic Design Concepts

| | |
|---|---|
| Independent variable | Variable's relationship with another variable that acts on the other variable to produce change in the other variable, such as the intervention on an outcome variable. |
| Dependent variable | Variable's relationship with another variable and whose change is the result of the other variable affecting it, such as a client's condition changing as a result of intervention. |
| Internal and causal validity | Whether the changes occurring in the dependent variable truly result from the effects of the independent variables or interventions. |
| External validity | Whether a particular relationship between dependent and independent variables or intervention in a particular unit or set of units can be generalized to a larger population of units. |
| Treatment group | Group that receives the intervention, usually referred to as the *treatment* or *independent variable,* in a research design. |
| Control or contrast group | Group that does not receive the treatment or intervention of concern that serves as a basis of comparison to determine the relationship between the independent variables on the dependent variables. |
| Control and covariables | Variables other than the independent variable that may influence the dependent variable and may need controlling or their effects assessed. |

Brief Review of Major Research Designs
and Purposes

| | |
|---|---|
| Exploratory designs | Used to gather preliminary information on subjects or research units that determine characteristics and variables and examine the relationship between variables. |
| Descriptive designs | Used to gather information describing and delineating variables and relationships between variables of research subjects or units. |
| Survey and cross-sectional designs | Used to gather information from a large number of respondents or subjects at a particular time point. |
| Longitudinal and panel designs | Used to gather information from subjects by measuring their variables over several time points. |
| Experimental and quasi-experimental designs | Used to gather information on the relationship between independent and dependent variables by manipulating the independent variable and examining its effects on the dependent variable over time. |
| Case study designs | Used to gather information limited to a single case that can have the characteristics of a quasi-experimental design. |

for manipulating variables and obtaining information on the variables' relationships to answer the research questions, reject the null and confirm the hypothesis, and construct and test a model of reality.

A particular research design can combine elements of several design types, depending on the design's purpose. A design seeking to determine factors related to people's opinions about a particular presidential candidate at a specific point in time will combine features of an exploratory-descriptive and survey design. If the panel of people is followed over time, the design takes on the characteristics of a longitudinal and panel design. Only research designs with a longitudinal component can assess changes in dependent variables. The longitudinal component is a necessary feature for assessing intervention effectiveness.

## Practice Plans and Research Designs

We examine in detail only the experimental design in this chapter and single case study designs in Chapter 9. Experimental designs are rarely used, or even usable, in most social work practice situations and are only occasionally used in social research. Nor are they generally politically feasible, even when operationally feasible. This does not make social work's knowledge base unique among the professions or sciences. It is arguable that proportionally only a little of the world's knowledge was developed by classic experimental research. Most knowledge is developed by research and experience in the natural world, although pieces of theory have been developed by experimentation. Social work intervention plans can be likened to what Bernard (1994, pp. 56–57) calls "natural experiments." Natural experiments, like quasi-experimental designs, evaluate occurring phenomena and try to make things happen, but their design cannot control all natural conditions as possible with a true experimental design. The single subject or single case design, examined in detail in Chapter 9, is a quasi-experimental design easily adaptable to and highly beneficial in shaping meaningful case practice plans.

**Case practice and intervention plans** *are single case designs with longitudinal components.* Survey designs are frequently used in community planning and community assessment. Practitioners using community surveys should review their methodologies. Descriptions are generally available in texts such as Bloom, Fischer, and

Orme (1995), Rubin and Babbie (1997), and Grinnell (1997).

The experimental design forms the standard of comparison for assessing other designs' causal or internal validity. Case practice plans are quasi-experimental natural research designs and practice blueprints. Comparison of the case practice plan to the experimental design provides the practitioner with a standard for inferences regarding change and reducing fallacies in deductions pertaining to the intervention's causal validity. **Causal validity** *in practice plans is the truthfulness that the intervention causes all or some part of the desired objectives to be achieved.* Knowledge of causal validity challenges limits confidence that the intervention effected achievement of case objectives, even when valid measurements indicate change. Knowledge of challenges to external or generalization validity limits the overgeneralizations of inductive fallacies to populations for inappropriate interventions, although the interventions might be appropriate to some population.

## The Classic Experimental Design

Classic experimental designs allow the researcher to ascertain the causal nature and magnitude of the relationship under controlled conditions between the sets of independent and dependent variables. They assess changes and their causes in dependent variables. Experimental designs have equivalent groups that allow for the isolation and manipulation of an independent variable, a treatment, in one group to determine its effects on the dependent variables. Equivalent comparison groups receive no treatment or independent variable, allowing comparison of changes on the dependent variable between the two groups. Group differences are attributed to the treatment or independent variable if comparability has otherwise been maintained. Empirical examination of causal relationships between variables are determined with the greatest confidence in designs that allow comparison of equivalent groups over

time. A causal relationship cannot empirically be examined by a single set of observations of a single group. Although it is rarely used in practice situations, understanding the definitive experimental design is important because practitioners are concerned with establishing and using *causal relationships* between interventions and outcomes. Social work practice focuses on change, and experimental designs are best able to assess change. *Experimental designs are the gold standard to compare with other designs for impurities in their capacity to infer causal validity.* If alternative explanations for changes can be ruled out, then the predicted relationship between the independent and dependent variables can be isolated and the independent variable's effects is the most reasonable explanation for changes. Without recognizing, eliminating, or identifying alternative explanations, the practitioner is prone to draw false conclusions about practice effectiveness and to create erroneous practice wisdom. Experimental design's value is its relevance as a model for examining the causal validity limitations of the designs and practice plans used.

Experimental designs have the following features. They:

1. Use equivalent treatment and contrast groups.
2. Randomly assign subjects to equivalent groups.
3. Measure dependent variables before and after treatment and in at least one contrast group.
4. Apply, monitor, and measure treatment or independent variables in the treatment group only.

The prototypical experimental design requires random assignment of subjects to a treatment group and one, preferably two or more, equivalent contrast groups. *Random assignment of subjects promotes the necessary equivalency between groups on all important traits at the preintervention or treatment phase.* The treatment group then receives intervention or treatment while the contrast group receives none, providing a contrast to the treatment group and allowing the isolation

Classic Experimental Design Model

| Sample | Groups | Baseline ($T^1$) | Treatment | Follow-up ($T^2$) |
|---|---|---|---|---|
| Randomly assign each subject to one of the three groups | Treatment group | Measure dependent and other control variables; no treatment during baseline | Treatment introduced, monitored, and measured; other variables may be monitored and measured | Measure dependent and other control variables; Cease treatment during follow-up |
| | Control or contrast group 1 | Measure dependent and other control variables | No treatment; other variables may be monitored and measured. | Measure dependent and other control variables |
| | Control or contrast group 2 | No measurements | No treatment or measurements | Measure dependent and other control variables |

and assessment of the treatment's effects on the treatment group. The conditions for all groups are very similar prior to and during the experiment except for the treatment provided to the treatment group.

## Dependent and Independent Variable Measurement

Measurements of the treatment group and a control group are taken on the relevant dependent and control variables during the preintervention or baseline phase. No baseline measurement is done on a second control group, if one is used, allowing judgment of any reflexivity effects from measurement processes. During the intervention phase, intervention or treatment introduced to the treatment group is measured and monitored. No treatment is introduced to either control group. The three groups are kept *as equivalent as possible during the entire experiment except for the intervention or treatment introduced, measured, and monitored in the treatment group.* All groups are measured on the dependent variables during the post-intervention follow-up phase

*Any differences between the groups during follow-up can reasonably be attributed to the treatment if the groups are kept equivalent at baseline and during the treatment phase except for the treatment to the treatment group.* Baseline equivalency beginning with random assignment of subjects between the groups is checked by measurements of baseline dependent variables from the treatment and one of the contrast groups. The two contrast groups should have essentially the same values on the dependent and other control variables at the post treatment measurement phase, unless the baseline measurements themselves produce change.

If time$_1$ and time$_2$ measurements of a contrast group or between contrast groups on the dependent variables at the different measurement phases do not equal zero, something other than treatment is effecting changes. These other things are challenges to the causal validity of the treatment and may also be changing the treatment group's measures on the dependent variables between baseline and follow-up. They need to be considered before attributing all the dependent variable's changes to the treatment..

## PRACTICE CASE TESTING AN EMPLOYMENT ORIENTATION PROGRAM

*A public assistance agency in an urban county is faced with implementing the 1996 federal welfare reform. It has to prepare the mothers receiving support under its program funded by the Personal Responsibility and Work Opportunity Reconciliation Act of 1996 for employment within two years. The agency decides to use a new employment orientation program to increase mothers' knowledge of the local job market. However, before the agency commits to a long-term investment in the orientation program, which is costly, it wants to test the program's effectiveness. The agency randomly assigns 200 mothers to each of three groups: a treatment group and two contrast groups. The agency uses a paper-and-pencil job market knowledge examination to measure the mothers' local job market knowledge. The examination scores can range from 0 to 100. Below is the summary and analysis of the relationship between the employment orientation program (independent variable or treatment) and the mothers' local job market knowledge (dependent variable) measured by scores on the paper-and-pencil job market knowledge examination.*

| Groups | $T_1$ Dependent Variable GroupMean Average Score | $T_2$ Dependent Variable Group Mean Average Score | $T_2 - T_1$ Dependent Variable Group Mean Average Score Difference |
|---|---|---|---|
| Treatment | 33 | 67 | 34 |
| Contrast 1 | 34 | 36 | 2 |
| Contrast 2 | No measurements | 35 | $35 - 34 = 1$ |

*Differences on the dependent variable attributable to the treatment (the contribution of the em-*

*ployment orientation program to increasing the mother's knowledge) are:*

*34 points – 1 to 2 points = 32 to 33 points*

*One to two points are possible effects of the measurements on the subjects or are the result of unknown factors. The agency decided the causal change was sufficient to purchase the program on a continuing basis.*

# Quasi-Experimental Designs

Quasi-experimental designs are used to gather information on the relationship between independent and dependent variables by manipulating the independent variable and examining its effects on the dependent variable over time.

### Steps in Analysis of Experimental Designs

1. Treatment (TG) time$_2$ measures on the dependent variables – Treatment group time$_1$ measures on dependent variables = treatment group differences on dependent variables

2. Control group 1 time$_2$ measures on dependent variables – (control group 1 time$_1$ measures on dependent variables – control group 2 time$_2$ measures on dependent variables) = contrast group differences measures on dependent variables

Any dependent variable differences here are due to factors other than the treatment and these effects must be considered before all the dependent variable changes in the treatment groups (step 1) can be attributed to the treatment

3. Treatment group differences on dependent variables – contrast group differences on dependent variables = treatment effects on dependent variables

Sharing the intent of an experimental design, these designs are generally longitudinal, and often have many but not all components of the true experimental design. They lack a truly equivalent contrast group. Quasi-experimental designs suffer from a greater inability than experimental designs to eliminate causal validity challenges. Much of evaluation research and demonstration projects use quasi-experimental rather than true experimental designs. They usually do not have treatment and contrast groups constructed by random assignment, but are used because they are feasible. Classic experimental designs generally are neither feasible nor practical. *Although generally it is not possible to shape practice to fit the rigors of an experimental design, it is ethical and necessary to recognize the causal validity challenges and limit conclusions accordingly.*

## Causal Validity Challenges

Causal validity challenges, also called internal validity or internal design validity challenges, relate to factors usually occurring within the research design. They confound the design's ability to attribute causality to relationships discovered between independent and dependent variables or treatment effects on outcomes. Causal validity challenges represent classes of variables extraneous to treatment variables that *may be* present; *if* present and *if* not controlled, they *may* produce effects that confound and confuse the experimental or treatment effects on the dependent variable. Rather than the treatment, they *may* produce the dependent variable's change and provide an alternative explanation to treatment for any apparent changes in dependent variables. In social work practice, any change in the case objectives, achievements, improvements, or deterioration of the case's conditions, may result from one or more classes of the design's internal causal validity challenges rather than from treatment and intervention. Designs other than experi-

mental will not control for nor eliminate causal validity challenges.

## Measurement Validity, Causal Validity, and External Validity

Causal validity challenges need to be conceptually separated from measurement validity. Measurement validity is a necessary precondition for causal validity. If the measurements are faulty, any changes indicated by the measurements may be spurious. If change can not be determined, causes are not relevant. However, measurement validity is not sufficient. Causal validity's challenge is to determine what produces the changes in valid measurement scores.

Causal validity is a necessary precondition for external or generalization validity, or the ability to go beyond the treatment subjects or clients and infer that similar results would be obtained if the treatment were applied to a larger population of clients or subjects not yet treated. If the apparently causal relationship between the variables for the subjects or clients is not true, there is nothing to generalize.

Types of Validity

| | |
|---|---|
| Measurement validity | Truthfulness of a measurement and measurement process in measuring what it intends to measure. |
| Causal or internal design validity | Truthfulness of an assertion that changes in the independent variable caused changes in dependent variable. |
| External or generalization validity | Truthfulness of generalizations about the results of the research, demonstration, or practice intervention to a population not treated. |

Causal validity challenges can be classified into four broad categories (Schutt, 1996):

1. **Selection bias** occurs when basic characteristics of the treatment and contrast groups differ and the groups are not equivalent at the baseline.
2. **Endogenous change** is change that occurs in the subjects that is not a result of the treatment and affects the outcomes.
3. **Exogenous change** occurs when members of the group are exposed to things that change them during the experiment but that are not part of the treatment and this affects the outcomes.
4. **Contamination** occurs when members of the treatment or contrast groups are aware of the other group and the outcomes are influenced by this awareness. (pp. 242–249)

Each causal validity challenge provides an *alternative explanation* to the treatment for any differences between the treatment and contrast groups on the posttreatment measurements. These challenges confound the capacity to attribute causality to independent variables or treatments. The relevance of each class of design validity challenges is determined by the research questions, the predicted relation between variables, design feasibility, and inferences made. In any case, the limitations of a particular design or practice plan used need to be recognized in the analysis, inferences, and generalizations (Campbell & Stanley, 1966; Cook & Campbell, 1979).

## Selection Bias

*Differential selection* occurs when different assignment criteria are used to assign subjects to either the treatment or contrast groups.

Differential selection is akin to the common social program phenomenon of "creaming," or assigning subjects most likely to respond to the program's treatment group and subjects less likely to respond or demonstrate change to contrast groups. Differences between the two groups

on the dependent variables and outcomes is as much a result of assignments as treatment. *The basic control for differential selection effects is to randomly assign subjects to the groups.*

Differential selection can occur in surveys with response biases. The actual respondents to the survey constitute its subjects, with the units providing the information and not the original sample to whom the measurement instruments were mailed or given. There is a differential selection effect if respondents' participation is less than 100%. Respondents self-select themselves in or out of the sample by either responding or not. Respondents and nonrespondents are not likely to have the same characteristics. Survey respondents probably are more interested in the survey, more responsive to questions, and more personally organized than are nonrespondents. *If a survey is used to determine the prevalence of a condition, and prevalence is based on responses only, there is a response rate bias analogous to differential selection.*

Here is an example of this effect. If a survey's results, indicated in the following table, are interpreted to indicate that the sample and population prevalence value on the variable is 75%, these generalization *must* assume that the actual respondents to the survey, only 40% of the original random probability sample, replicate the random probability sample without any response bias and differential self-selection. If there is differential self-selection in the original sample, the instrument's content could be more critical to the 400 self-selected respondents returning the questionnaire than to the 600 nonrespondents. The 300 people responding positively to the item could contain most, if not all, of the original 1000-subject sample who would respond positively to the variable's measurement. Then prevalence will not be 75% of the original sample but more like 30%.

The usable population sample consists of people who returned questionnaires rather than the 1000 people receiving questionnaires. Whether results of the survey can be generalized to the original sample's population is dependent on the self-selected respondents' representativeness to the original sample and population and not the original sample's representativeness. If subjects respond who believe they have a bigger stake in the survey, a self-selection response bias, then no assumption can be made that the prevalence is 75%. We must move toward the 30% prevalence level for the population. In order to move toward the 75% level, we have to establish a lack of response bias—that the 400 actual respondents represent the original random probability sample and the population.

> **Experimental mortality** represents the losses or attrition of subjects in the treatment and control groups or from the single group in a quasi-experimental design between the pre- and postintervention measurement phases.

The differences on the dependent variable group scores between the groups or within a single group between measurement phases may be a function of a loss of dropout scores rather than the treatment's effects. Control for experimental mortality cannot be done by random assignment, although this may randomly distribute respondents with a predisposition to experimental

mortality. You can control follow-up efforts to keep subjects in the research project, tracking individual group member scores, and analyzing the lost respondents on pretreatment measures that may affect the posttreatment group scores and adjust the scores accordingly.

Here is an example of this effect. Treatment and contrast groups have equal sizes, total scores, and average scores in the pretreatment phase but indicate a difference in the posttreatment phase scores. The treatment group accumulates 40 more points for an average gain of eight points per member over the contrast group. Looking at the two groups and their pre- and post-intervention scores, you conclude that the intervention makes a difference. On examination, however, you find these differences to not reflect any individual score changes by remaining members of either the treatment or contrast groups. The differences are generated exclusively by the loss in each group of a single member with the extreme scores. The differences are solely the result of experimental mortality.

## Endogenous Changes

Endogenous changes are those that occur in the subjects not as a result of the treatment, but by maturation, testing, and regression.

> **Maturation** includes conditions internal to the subjects changing with the passage of time, such as the aging process and fatigue, that affect dependent variables and outcomes.

Practice is replete with examples of maturation producing changes. An example is the maturation process's influence on youth and the reduction of deviant behavior as adolescents grow into adults. For youth involved in youth programs aimed at reducing deviant behavior, consider effects of maturation in assessing the program's impact in reducing deviancy.

Maturation is controlled by randomly assigning subjects to the treatment and contrast groups so that any differences and effects of maturation

Survey Distributed to 1000 Randomly Sampled Potential Respondents

| Factor | Number of People |
| --- | --- |
| Number of questionnaires mailed to a random probability sample of a population | 1000 |
| Response rate of questionnaires returned from the random probability sample | 40% or 400 |
| Prevalence (percent of respondents responding positively to a question) | 75% or 300 |
| Prevalence and generalization to original random sample and population | 750 (75%) or 300 (30%)? |

## Experimental Mortality and Attrition Effects

| Preintervention Scores: | | Postintervention Scores: | |
|---|---|---|---|
| *Treatment Group Subject Scores* | *Contrast Group Subject Scores* | *Treatment Group Subject Scores* | *Contrast Group Subject Scores* |
| 100 | 100 | 100 | Lost respondent |
| 90 | 90 | 90 | 90 |
| 80 | 80 | 80 | 80 |
| 70 | 70 | 70 | 70 |
| 70 | 70 | 70 | 70 |
| 60 | 60 | Lost respondent | 60 |
| Total = 470 | Total = 470 | Total = 410 | Total = 370 |
| Average score for a group member = 78.33 | Average score for a group member = 78.33 | Average score for a group member = 82 | Average score for a group member = 74 |

will have similar probability of appearing equally in all the groups.

> **Testing effects** are effects of the first set of tests, measurements, or observations of dependent and outcome variables on subsequent measurements, tests, and observations of the dependent variable. They can result from the measurement's reflexivity or biasing in alerting the respondent to appropriate responses.

When the first measurement application sensitizes the subject to, or effects changes on, the dependent variable that are reflected in the subsequent measurements, some part of the changes are a result of testing and not treatment. High school students generally find their SAT test scores improve if they take the test several times. Clients who modify their behavior in response to eligibility questions and log or diary questions demonstrate a testing effect.

Testing and measurement effects are revealed in the experimental design by *using a second contrast group*. Members in contrast group 2 are not measured during the preintervention baseline phase, so there is no testing effect or sensitizing to measurements used during the postintervention phrase. The treatment group, and both contrast groups, are measured during the postintervention phase. These measurement scores of the different contrast groups are similar if history and maturation are controlled by random assignment. If they are not similar, the differences may be a result of testing effects. Testing effects are weighed in comparing the treatment and contrast groups scores and in pre- and posttreatment scores.

Unobtrusive measurements, different forms of measurements, and triangulation also reduce or isolate possible testing effects. If subjects are unaware of the measures, do not know when they are measured, or are unfamiliar with the measures, it is more difficult for them to anticipate and react to the measures and measurement processes.

> **Statistical regression effect** is present when measurement scores fluctuate because of measurement error. Generally any measurement score is only an approximation of the true score.

As any single measurement of a variable is only an approximation of the variable's true score, there will be a tendency for high and low scores to "regress" or move to the "true" score with repeated measurements. Any single measurement may be a true score, above a true score, or below a true score. If the first measurement is higher than the true score and a subsequent measurement is lower than the true score, the change in the variable indicated by the subsequent measurement from the prior measurement may be the result of a regression effect. For example, if subjects are assigned to a treatment group based on a high score on a variable to be changed, by the treatment, "those most in need of treatment," and other subjects assigned to a contrast group based on a single low score on the variable, "those not in the most need of treatment," the treatment group subjects' score may regress with subsequent measures, and the low score subjects' scores may increase with subsequent measures. If the subsequent measures are taken during the postintervention phase, the scores indicate that the treatment group improved and the contrast group got worse without treatment. However, the conclusion that the treatment influences the variable may not be true. The changes in the two group scores may represent merely a regression effect.

*As with differential selection, random assignment of subjects rather than the assignment of subjects by scores or other indicators to treatment and control groups guards against regression effects.* Random assignment randomly distributes any regression effects between the groups. Repeated measurements to obtain a stable baseline and follow-up measures and then using the average score of the repeated measures reduces regression effect, although it possibly contributes to testing effects. *Triangulation using different measures of the same variable also can mitigate against regression.*

Regressionlike effects commonly occur in social work practice. People tend to seek help and intake usually occurs when their problems are most acute or severe. If the conditions or problems are cyclical and fluctuate up and down, baseline measures will be taken when the problem's measures are highest. Later measures as the condition fluctuates downward can indicate improvement. This is a regression toward the true mean or level of the problem or condition over a long time period. Subsequent measures taken after treatment may lead to the possibly erroneous conclusion that changes in the problem's severity and magnitude are because of the treatment when, in fact, they result from the condition's natural fluctuations or life cycle.

Regression effects in practice are addressed by using repeated measurements, including retrospective data, to obtain a stable baseline and

understanding of the variable's shape or life cycle and fluctuations, especially for the particular client. The length of baseline, follow-up, and number of measurement points needed to determine stability are guided by the case theory on the variable's shape, stability, and life cycle.

Without random assignment of subjects between treatment and contrast groups, a variety of possible assignment biases is possible. Differential selection and assignment interact with maturation, testing, and regression to produce differential changes and confound the effects of treatment. An example is placing subjects by age in either the treatment or control groups or alternative treatment groups and then comparing their performance. If elderly subjects are placed in one group only and not randomly distributed between groups, maturation and fatigue rather than the alternative treatment may account for any group performance differences.

The control for interaction effects is to randomly assign subjects to the groups rather than assignment based on any trait.

## Exogenous Changes

A series of external factors can also produce change in subjects' scores and confuse the determination of any independent variable's causal validity on a dependent variable.

**History** is specific events occurring over time, such as between baseline and follow-up, other than the treatment, that happen to the subjects.

These things, the history, rather than the independent variable, treatment, may explain any changes in the dependent variable. History in practice are the things and experiences other than the intervention happening to clients that might cause or influence changes in the outcomes. History can include such events as a death in the client's family, winning the lottery, reactions to a political election, and loss of a job. Changes in the client's social ecology may explain any changes or variations on outcome variable. They, rather than the intervention, have the causal relationship.

History cannot be assessed in one-shot survey designs when subjects and variables are measured only once. No causal relationship can be empirically examined by a single set of observations. History is always a factor with a single panel design, a design lacking contrast groups, even when subjects are measured over time. The effects of history cannot be determined without equivalent treatment and contrast groups measured over time and with similar conditions for all groups other than the treatment given to the treatment group.

> **Instrumentation** consists of changes in a measurement instrument's calibration or in an observer's scores that occur from repeated use or fatigue and produce changes in the measurement processes between the measurement phases, between the applications to different subjects, or between the treatment and the contrast groups.

An example of instrumentation effect is when observers measure (observe and record) a treatment group in the morning when the observers are rested, and a contrast group in the late afternoon when the observers are tired and hurrying to end the workday. Fatigue might affect diligence and sensitivity in observation and recording in the late afternoon. In observations, the observer is the measurement instrument. Instrumentation is possible when clients are observers of their own behavior. Mechanical scales may also lose their consistency with continued use.

Instrumentation effects are addressed by taking similar measurements under similar conditions and by randomizing the measurement times and processes between treatment and contrast groups. Continued attention to establishing and maintaining the reliability of the measurements and the measurement processes is important.

## Contamination

Contaminations are intrusions from one experimental group to another.

These are additional threats to causal validity that cannot be handled by random assignment. Especially prevalent in program evaluation and field research on social programs, they are generally addressed in the design's structure to limit participants' knowledge and awareness of the experiment's design and what is happening to the other groups.

> **Ambiguity about the direction of causal inference** is lack of clarity about which variable is causing change in other variables.

This is a most common error in surveys and correlational and cross-sectional designs with only one observation or measurement phase and two or more correlated variables. Variables appear together in the same relationship across subjects. Causal direction cannot be determined from a cross-sectional design. Without manipulating variables or observing the relationship between variables over time, there is confusion about which variable is the independent variable that causes variation in the other variable, labeled the dependent variable.

Here any attribution of causal relationship is based on theory rather than empirical evidence and remains hypothetical. If a survey of people with varying degrees of employment and self-esteem indicates a direct correlation between employment and self-esteem—low self-esteem correlates with low employment levels and high self-esteem correlates with high employment levels—questions of causation direction remain. Does high self-esteem positively affect the ability to obtain and maintain employment, and do people with low self-esteem lack the ability to get and maintain employment? Or do people with good employment develop higher self-esteem and people without employment lose self-esteem? Is the correlation between self-esteem and employment levels caused by a third unmeasured variable? Direction of causality can only be inferred by examining the changes and relationship of the variables over time or by certain multivariant analytical models that can isolate the relationship of the independent and dependent variables from the effects of other variables.

**Diffusion or limitation of treatment** occurs when the treatment permeates the contrast group.

This happens when the treatment and control groups are not isolated from each other. Contrast group members interact or have knowledge of what is happening to the treatment group. Subjects in the treatment group may share some of the treatment with those in the control group when interacting with them. For example, when students in a special education demonstration program share their experiences with other students serving as a contrast group, thus allowing the contrast group to receive some of the benefits, the true, or causal, validity of the special education on student performance will be confused.

Control for treatment diffusion is accomplished by socially and physically isolating the two groups to prevent interaction and possible diffusion. Control is facilitated by *blind experiments,* where subjects are unaware or "blind" about who receives the experimental treatment variables and the nature of the experimental treatment variables. Blind social experiments, however, are difficult given the political reactions that usually accompany their initiation. Blind practice interventions are more difficult if practitioners satisfy the ethical imperative of client informed consent.

**Compensatory equalization of treatment** occurs when control group members receive extra effort from the control group service providers to compensate for the lack of experimental treatment.

Compensatory equalization may take place under the ethical guise of not denying service to anyone. It may occur when the experiment is to test a new or innovative model and compare it to a preexisting treatment approach. Treatment personnel for the preexisting treatment group who know of the application of an innovative intervention giving experimental group respondents additional benefits may work harder to compensate their clients. The treatment the contrast group actually receives is different and more intensive than the treatment they would receive if not compensated.

Control for compensatory equalization of treatment is accomplished by carefully monitoring treatments of all groups to maintain treatment models and by comparing posttreatment scores for contrast groups with preexperiment treatment effectiveness for other respondents receiving similar treatments. Control is facilitated by blind and double blind experiments where neither subjects nor treatment personnel know which is the experiment or control group.

**Compensatory rivalry by respondents and service providers receiving less desirable treatment** occurs when the contrast group of service providers and subjects tries harder to achieve the specific outcomes and perform better on outcome measures than does the treatment group.

Another label for compensatory rivalry is the *John Henry effect.* A railroad spike driver, John Henry set the rails on the cross ties. The steel-driving man of the folk ballad, a hero to Luddites everywhere, challenged the steam powered spike-driving machine to a contest. The railroad companies anticipated that the machine would replace the human spike driver. While John Henry won the contest in the legend, he overcompensated and worked himself to death.

In like manner, projects demonstrating new interventive methodologies and programs often evoke a response in the contrast group service providers that improves their service performance outcomes. Public school teachers may perform better when compared to demonstrations of privatized public education or staff social workers to contract and contingent employees. The contrast group's performance level is altered because of the competition, rivalry, and possibility of replacement by the innovative program. The contrast group's performance does not provide a valid comparison.

Control for compensatory rivalry can be expedited by some combination of blind and double blind experiments and demonstrations using the predemonstration baseline as the comparison, or by conducting the demonstration over a sufficient time span where it is difficult for the contrast group to maintain compensatory rivalry.

**Resentful demoralization of service providers or respondents receiving less desirable treatment** happens when the contrast group believes its treatment is less desirable and the group loses interest in the treatment process, drops out, and increases experimental mortality effects, or they or their service providers reduce performance below its predemonstration level.

This challenge to causal validity is the converse of compensatory rivalry. Here the contrast group subjects are resentful of not being included in the treatment group and they quit. Similarly, the service providers may also give up because they believe the demonstration's conclusions are politically preordained, with the innovative treatment receiving the most favorable consideration. In this era of privatization, cutbacks and downsizing, and "out-siding" to contract and contingent employees in health care and public social services, this effect may become more frequent. Unfortunately, the results confound the ability to determine true differences between treatment and contrast groups.

Like the causal validity challenges inherent in treatment diffusion and compensatory equalization and rivalry, control of compensatory demoralization can be promoted by blind and double blind experiments and demonstrations and by using the predemonstration baseline as the comparison. Social and physical isolation of the groups is helpful.

## External or Generalization Validity

External or generalization validity concerns the truthfulness of generalizations about the results of the research, demonstration, or practice intervention effects from the research, demonstration, and practice to a population not treated. Challenges to external validity limit the ability to take the research or project's findings and prac-

tice experience beyond the specific experimental subjects, project participants, and practice clients. Tasks in improving external validity are to ensure that the subjects represent the population that the research, demonstration, and practice is to generalize. If a particular intervention is found successful in achieving change with a particular group of clients, its replication depends on whether the treatment is effective in producing a similar change in other people. To whom can the processes and results be generalized? Generalization is limited by the treatment sample's critical traits, these affect the treatment's capacity to produce change on traits that also are present in the population, and the population's lack of any inhibiting traits. Generalization is limited to the actual intervention processes used (Campbell & Stanley, 1966: Cook & Campbell, 1979).

*The primary tools in promoting external validity are random probability sampling methodologies and random assignment within the research and demonstration's design.* Samples need to represent any population that the research is describing and to have applicable generalizations. If random probability sampling is not practical or possible—and often it is not—the sample's profile of characteristics needs to be determined and any generalizations cautiously limited to populations or sample frames with this profile.

Some special classes of external or generalization validity challenges are not readily addressable by simple random sampling and assignment. These occur when the traits relate to prior treatment experience of subjects or the conditions under which the research or program is conducted (Cook & Campbell, 1979, pp. 73–74). They are intimately related to the causal validity challenges.

**Reactive or interactive effects of testing** occurs when the testing processes prior to the treatment used in selecting subjects, demonstration program participants and in pretesting increase or decrease the subjects' sensitivity to the treatment.

The effects obtained for a pretested population might not represent the true results of the treatment for an un-tested population from which the experimental or demonstrational sample was selected and the treatment results are to be generalized. *The experimental population now is a special or different population. It is altered by the testing process.* Any treatment generalization will need to include pretesting as part of treatment. The outcome is a function of pretesting and treatment, not of treatment alone.

The control of reactive or interactive effects of testing is inherent in causal design validity. If you cannot eliminate the testing effects, incorporate the testing processes as part of any treatment generalization.

**Interaction effects of selected biases plus treatment** occur when results are a function of treatment and any biases in selection and assignment of the sample to treatment or contrast groups and not the treatment alone.

Generalizations of the treatment's effects can safely be made only to populations with the same characteristics as the experiment's or project's biased treatment and contrast groups. Control by random probability sampling and assignment promotes group equivalency. Careful definition of the population and sample frame are necessary for random probability sampling. Generalizations are prudently limited to clients with similar traits as the sample's.

**Reactive effects of experimental arrangement** occurs when subjects may be reacting to the environment and conditions of the treatment and not to the treatment itself.

The reactive effects are the *halo* or *Hawthorne effects* often resulting from the attention subjects receive as subjects rather than from specific treatments. The effects can be of two types: (1) effects that enhance treatment group scores, and (2) effects that detract from treatment group scores because of improved contrast group scores resulting from the attention. Reactive effects become a treatment diffusion in the second type. The first type is more common. Examples are readily found in demonstrational programs

conducted with optimal and "hothouse" environments more positive than those in normal program operating conditions. Results are often fragile and not replicable except under similar hothouse conditions. Internal causal effects on dependent variables are a function of treatment and the treatment's optimum environment, not of treatment alone. Any generalizations for replication must include both the treatment and the treatment's environment. Control is best obtained under conditions that replicate the field environment of the population and treatment conditions of the anticipated application rather than those that produce a sterile hothouse environment.

**Multiple treatment interference** occurs when subjects have been exposed to multiple treatments, either sequentially or concurrently, so that conclusions and generalizations about a single, specific treatment effect cannot be made because the other preceding treatments effects intrude.

Multiple treatment interference is common in projects involving long-term recipients of services. Because they receive the current service or intervention plus a number of prior interventions, any effects may be predicated on having received the prior services. This often occurs when subjects "recycle" through various programs, as is common with public assistance recipients and institutionalized mental patients. Conclusions attributing all changes to the most recent treatment are likely to be erroneous. Changes in performance may be the result of the current intervention plus the accumulated effects of all prior interventions. Any results are generalizable only to a population sharing the sample's total programmatic intervention history.

Control is promoted by knowing the profiles of participants and either physically randomly assigning or matching histories of participants between treatment and contrast groups or analytically isolating various treatment histories and limiting generalizations to similar histories.

## Ethics and Experimentation

*We do not hold that experimental designs are unethical in developing new interventions and knowledge because they involve denying services to people in a contrast group.* The contrast group can be given the preexisting treatment rather than denied any treatment. If we assume that the experiment is conducted because effects of the experimental treatment are unknown, then contrast group members are only denied an unknown and possibly nonexistent, even harmful, benefit. Denial then becomes an ethical good. It is only a real benefit if the hypothesis is confirmed. The experiment's purpose is to test the hypothesis. If it is a known and assured benefit, then there is no need or justification for the experiment. The ethical issue when benefits are known involves conducting an unneeded experiment as well as denying services to the contrast group.

Ethics also require informed consent. Informed consent does not require that subjects choose to belong to a treatment or a contrast group but that they be informed of assignment protocols, the full range of benefits and risks, any compensations for risk, protections and limits to privacy, and time requirements of membership in either a treatment or contrast group (Baily, 1996, p. 11; Mark, 1996, p. 41).

## Summary

This chapter has reviewed research design and its application to practice. Special attention was devoted to the classic experimental design, although probably it is one of the least used designs in social work practice and research. Experimental designs provide a standard for examining the challenges to inferences of causal validity made by other designs. These challenges are important to the causal validity inferences of practice plans.

Inherently quasi-experimental longitudinal designs, practice plans lay out case objectives and conditions that are to be achieved by the intervention. These plans require design decisions on what and when to measure. They are natural quasi-experiments when done well and suffer from the causal validity weakness of all quasi-experimental designs. Conscientious practitioners recognize and account for these weaknesses. When a case plan is poorly done, causal validity inferences (inferences that the intervention contributed to achieving case objectives) are most probably only mental constructions. Without the guidance of a reasonable design or case plan, any movement toward case objectives can as easily be the result of all the other things happening to the client and case as to an intervention effect.

Knowledge of design and experimental design assists practitioners in evaluating research reports and the strength and limitations of their findings in contributing to practice knowledge. Being an "informed consumer" is more than a marketing slogan; it is a necessity if practitioners are to adequately use knowledge generated by social work and social science research in building case theory.

## Discussion Questions and Exercises

1. What are the similarities and differences in the concepts of measurement validity, causal or internal design validity, and external or generalization validity? Is it possible to have any one of the three types of validity without the other two?

2. *A social worker treated the Bickersons, a squabbling and hostile married couple on the verge of divorce, with marital therapy for a year. The couple wanted to develop a more*

*intimate, satisfying relationship and avoid divorce. At the end of the year, the couple reported an intimate and satisfying relationship.*

Can the social worker attribute this change to the intervention? Why or why not?

3. Design Exercise: Hustle Mental Health Agency had 50 clients in treatment for depression for one year without psycho-pharmacological drugs. After the year of treatment, 30 of the 50 clients (60%) reported their depression reduced to a degree that allowed them normal functioning. Hustle's director concluded that the treatment was effective in reducing the depression in 60% of the clients. Never one to miss an opportunity, the director used the finding in a radio advertisement for the agency that stated: "Hustle is successful in the social treatment of depression in a majority of cases of depression."

The conclusion was based on an inferred design involving 50 clients making a self-judgment and report of depression levels at $time_1$ or baseline, intervention for one year of a therapy session a week, and client self-reports of social functioning at the end of the year. The $time_2$ or posttreatment follow-up measurements indicated an improvement over the baseline measures.

a. Can the director legitimately make the assertion in the radio advertisement? Defend or challenge the statement in terms of measurement validity and the design's causal and generalization validity.

b. What alternative explanations to the demonstration program might account for the differences in the measures after the year of treatment?

c. How might the director improve his knowledge base regarding the agency's treatment?

d. In addition to design considerations, what other things might be done to strengthen the causal and generalization validity?

# CHAPTER NINE

# Single Case Designs and Practice Case Plans

Single subject design (SSD), single system design, and single case design (SCD) are very amenable to and usable in practice. Both SSD and SCD are labels that refer to the same design model. We prefer the label *single case design* because of its inferred broader inclusion of cases other than an individual client as a subject. It can evaluate intervention and situations other than individual therapies, such as supervisory and management technologies (Harkness & Hensley, 1991). This chapter reviews the development, practice applications, and limitations of single case designs. Compared to other research designs, SCDs have a relatively straightforward application to case plans. Single case designs

> focus on *specific interactions* between a *specific practitioner* and a *specific client or client system*. The practitioner gathers a large sample of behavior of a single system...It is the best means...that practitioners can use to study their own practice effectiveness. (Alter & Evens, 1990, p. 17, emphasis added)

SCD requires operational measurements from both sides of the interaction: client or case effects of the intervention and the practitioner's behavior or intervention. Intervention is the interaction, or what is actually done to and with the client even if it is not what was intended to be done. **Single case designs** are longitudinal quasi-experimental designs involving only one unit of analysis or case. The case can be an individual, family, group or some other collective.

Case plans are derived from the early case assessment and theory and are revised by continuing assessment. They guide the reassessment; specify case objectives and changes sought with a client in behaviors, attitudes, and emotional state, health, and/or social conditions; develop and implement an intervention plan to effect the changes; and assess the intervention's effects on the case objectives. As Tripodi (1994, p. 5) observes, with single case studies the research case questions are the practice case questions. Conversely, practice case questions are amenable to the use of research methodologies in seeking answers. SCD occurs inherently in a practice plan that involves assessment, intervention, and reassessment. Its components are intrinsic in, and required of, effective and ethical practice. SCD's purpose is to guide, control, and evaluate the intervention process to assess and relate changes in the dependent variables (the case objectives) to application and variation of the intervention processes.

As with all designs, SCD addresses the *who, what, how, when, where,* and *why* questions. SCD's critical tasks, whether used in practice or solely for research purposes, are to define or determine:

1. case problems and objectives and their operational measurements
2. reliability, validity, practicality, and reflexivity of the operational measurements
3. treatment or intervention to use
4. means to measure, monitor, and control the treatment for maintenance of treatment

## Parallels of Practice and Research

| Practice Components and Tasks | Research Epistemologies and Methodologies |
| --- | --- |
| Assessment and developing case theory | Constructing theory |
| Contracting with client, establishing case plan goals and objectives and intervention hypothesis | Formulating hypotheses |
| Determining indicators of client change, changes in the client's situation, and judgments of change | Selecting and/or developing measurements |
| Clinical impressions and other measurements to make judgments of changes in client situation and progress toward goals | Applying measures and collecting data |
| Implementing, measuring, and controlling treatment and intervention | Selecting and/or developing and applying measurements and controlling independent variable |
| Assessing and evaluating progress toward goals with client and other components of the action and change system | Data analysis and inferences of causal and external validity |
| Reporting, assessment, and reassessment of progress toward goals and establishing new goals or terminating with client and other components of action and change system | Reporting to relevant publics |

integrity, and to reduce any treatment drift and monitor treatment shift

5. reliability, validity, and practicality of the treatment's operational measurements
6. changes of the outcome variables, directions of changes, and whether changes are significant in the various forms of significance
7. if the changes can be attributed to the interventions and whether the interventions can be used with others to produce similar outcomes

The conscious application of single case design to the case plan's problem-solving strategy is similar to the logic modeling required in critical thinking (Alter & Egan, 1997). It adds rigor to practice.

## Measurement in Group Comparison and Single Case Designs

The single subject of a single case design is likened to one of the subjects in a group comparison design. However, because a single case design's measurements are limited to a single subject, other subjects cannot be used to establish measurement correspondence. Lacking comparison groups or multiple subjects, it is vital that a practitioner exercise care in the applications of measurement processes, including observation and self-observation, for consistency and accuracy in recording. Measurement reliability and validity can be addressed by using standardized instruments with preestablished reliability and validity for populations that fit the case or client. Reliability also is enhanced with repeated measurement applications under consistent conditions. Measurement triangulation in SCD provides a form of concurrent validity to the measures.

## Single Case Design Phases

Single case design, like a case plan, has three phases: (1) baseline or the preintervention phase (A), (2) intervention (B), and (3) withdrawal of intervention, repeat of the baseline measures or the follow-up phase (A).

Single Case Design $(A - B - A)$

where

A = Baseline observations and assessment on outcome variables;

B = intervention phase; and

A = follow-up observations and reassessment on outcome variables.

## The Baseline Phase (A)

The preintervention baseline phase consists of developing case theory and objectives, assessment, developing measurements for the case objectives, and measuring variables. This is the first phase of the linear or time series design that measures and follows outcome variables. You will also follow and measure them during and after the intervention phase. The baseline phase addresses the first three of the five general practice problem-solving strategy's components (Alter & Egan, 1997, p. 88; Hardcastle, Wenocur, & Powers, 1997):

1. Recognition of a problem and establishment of the need for change.

2. Information gathering on the case and problem.

3. Assessment and the development of a case theory and plan for change.

4. Intervention and the change effort.

5. Evaluation of and termination of the change effort. (pp. 10–20)

The fourth component is the design's intervention or B phase, and the follow-up or second A phase of the single case design addresses the fifth phase.

The baseline phase assesses and develops case theory in locating and identifying the extent of the client's problem and resources, strengths and weaknesses, and opportunities and limits of ecology to guide the intervention. Baseline information is needed and gathered prior to intervention. It is important for comparisons with the posttreatment phase to determine changes by obtaining information on the severity, magnitude, intensity, and duration of the case conditions on which change is sought and to guide selection of the intervention. As a fundamental task in reassessment is to assess change, the *baseline phase measurement tasks are not limited solely to the preintervention phase.* The baseline phase measurements are part of assessment and reassessment at the follow-up phase. If you cannot directly measure the baseline conditions, substitute retrospective available data collection and baseline reconstruction. *"Intake" and eligibility information and judgments are baseline measures.*

### Baseline assessment practice tasks

Baseline assessment requires a wide-ranging use of measurements to confront the pivotal questions inherent in developing:

1. the problems and goals and outcomes in operational terms

2. the operational model of the intervention with assigned responsibilities

3. selecting, and using operational measures and, if possible, establishing their reliability, validity, reflexivity, and practicality

4. the measurement and data collection to construct baseline conditions

Selection of measurement tools and processes is aided if practitioners develop SMARRT objectives (Hardcastle, Wenocur & Powers, 1997, p. 395). The SMARRT format requires goals and objectives specified according to an interrelated set of criteria calling for objectives that are

Baseline Measurements

- Collect information for assessment, develop case theory and intervention hypothesis.

- Compare baseline measurements during the pretreatment, treatment, and posttreatment phases to monitor change.

- Compare case measurements to normative standards.

specific, measurable, acceptable, realistic, results-oriented, and time specific.

### Length of baseline and follow-up phases

The preintervention as well as postintervention phases **should last until stability of the indicators' measurements is achieved.** Stable does not necessarily mean consistency of measurement re-

sults but rather that the baseline measurements capture the shape (magnitude, frequency, intensity, duration) of the phenomenon's pattern of behavior. If not constant, then a longer time frame is needed to capture the pattern. At least three observations (measurement points) are generally considered minimally required. Bloom, Fischer, and Orme (1995, p. 9) argue for 10 measurement points if practical and ethical, or for at

### SMARRT Criteria

- **Specific:** Goals and objectives and the words, ideas, and concepts used to describe them are precise and not vague or stated in generic language such as to "improve the condition of." Specific criteria indicating the operational meanings of "improvement" are used. They reflect the meaning for the client. While the mission and eligibility criteria of the agency constrain goals and objectives, the client can be asked to give indicators of "improvement."

- **Measurable:** Goals and objectives need to contain operational measurement criteria usable to indicate change and achievement. Clients and other stakeholders need to understand the objectives, the measurements to be used, and how they both relate to their condition and indicators. Measurement can be quantitative *and* qualitative; the SMARRT objective statement lends itself to triangulation.

- **Acceptable:** Goals and objectives need to be acceptable to the client and, ultimately, to other resource providers and stakeholders whose cooperation is needed. The case plan requires informed consent.

- **Realistic:** Goals and objectives potentially are accomplishable within the limits of the available time frame, resources, and intervention methodologies available in the practitioner's, client's, and other stakeholders' best judgements. The objectives are accomplishable but not so mundane that accomplishment is meaningless. The practitioner's fiduciary responsibility to the client requires the practitioner to operate within realistic time and resources boundaries and advise the client of these limits and probabilities of success.

- **Results Oriented:** The final goals and all objectives are expressed as outcomes, events, and accomplishments by the client or the ecology in relation to the client rather than as services provided or processes. Statements of service provision are interventions, the plan's "B" phase, and not outcomes or objectives. The criterion requires specificity about the results of the service—what the service is to accomplish and how it will benefit the client.

- **Time specific:** A specific time frame for accomplishing the goals and objectives is projected. A practice plan is not accountable without a time frame. The promise that an intervention can improve, a treatment can cure, or an investment can make the investor a billionaire is meaningless and can never be established as true or false without a time frame. The time frame and limits are inherent in determining realism, acceptability, and accountability. The time limits are the projected reasonable time needed to achieve the goals and objectives, based on case theory, intervention's strength and certainty, and resources.

least a one week measurement time span if 10 separate measurement time points are not possible. If there is high variability, a longer phase and more measurement points are required.

Although it is better to establish a stable baseline from direct measurements, including observations over time, *often the nature and severity of the case condition precludes establishing a stable baseline.* When this is the situation, retrospective baselines are established by the use of the client's and others' reconstruction of the baseline or other available historical data sources, such as hospital or school records.

Basically, the length of the baseline and how much of it is retrospective is a judgment balancing:

1. How rapidly intervention is necessary because of risks to the client if intervention is delayed.
2. The phenomenon's potential shape, frequency of occurrence, and variability based on theory, conceptualization, and knowledge of the phenomenon.
3. When the phenomenon occurs and its context.
4. Duration of the phenomenon; how long it lasts and the time intervals between incidences.
5. Magnitude of the phenomenon and the ability to measure it over time.
6. Stability of the measurements indicating stability of the condition.
7. Reliability and validity of any post hoc measurements for a retrospective baseline from available information.

Conditions that might occur relatively infrequently in a context difficult to measure but with severe ramifications and requiring immediate intervention, such as child abuse, cannot afford the time to establish prospective stable baselines. Retrospective baselines using available data are the practice alternative.

## The Intervention Phase (B)

Assessment and case theory gives direction to the intervention. Indeed, the interventions, the "B" phase, are to satisfy hypotheses derived from the case theory. Mattaini and Kirk (1993) rather strongly assert that "if assessment is not directly related to and prescriptive of treatment, it is, at best, a waste of client and practitioner time and, at worst, unethical" (p. 231).

The intervention phase occurs when one or more interventions are implemented, measured, and monitored. Interventions are planned behaviors and activities to produce effects on targeted change variables (outcomes) or to maintain a stable condition. Intervention can be simple verbal exchanges, psychotherapies, advice giving, developing and manipulating social support systems, and other environmental and ecological changes. Interventions involve prescriptions, proscriptions, and descriptions of both practitioner and client behaviors. This can include modeling of client behavior and client behavior protocols or things clients are to do. Interventions include the subtleties of bonding, rapport, and the other contextual variables. Interventions are guided not only by case theory but also the agency and other *extratheoretical* constraints as national, state and local social policies and professional ethics. Location and context of the practice venue will affect and constrain the intervention.

Implementing, measuring, and monitoring of intervention is the additional task during the intervention phase.

> **Monitoring** is the process by which judgments are made about the extent to which the client is actually receiving the prescribed treatment in a manner which is consistent with prior planning, agency and professional standards, and the contractual agreement between client and social worker. (Tripodi & Epstein, 1983, p. 95)

Outcome measures are not ignored during the intervention phase. They are measured to assess progress. However, the measurement of the *intervention variables* needs distinction from measurement of the *hypothesized effects of the intervention.* Measuring and monitoring the intervention first involves developing and specifying the interventive model by tasks, sequence of tasks, and timing of tasks, establishing thresholds for each, and then determining and developing operational measures for the tasks reflecting the thresholds. This requires *operationalizing,* called *proceduralization,* of the intervention model's concepts and variables. This model anchors the intervention. Proceduralizing, monitoring, and measurements in intervention are discussed more fully in Chapter 10.

## Outcomes Follow-up, or the Second Phase (A)

The practice problem-solving strategy's component involving *evaluation of and termination of the change effort* is the second A phase and the third phase of the single case design. The follow-up phase is indicated as an A phase because dependent variables, objectives, and outcomes specified in the assessment and baseline phase are measured during the follow-up. The A essentially refers to a nontreatment phase and consists of evaluating the problem-solving efforts, the intervention's effectiveness in achieving case objectives. It is the follow-up phase of the design and is necessary to assess any changes after intervention or a particular intervention for an outcome is completed and withdrawn.

Occasionally, additional dependent variables and case objective measures are added or deleted during the intervention or follow-up phases to reflect changes in objectives and goals or externally imposed changes, such as by an employing agency or funding source. Depending on the level of achievement, the stability of the change, and client, practitioner, or agency interests, one or more of several outcomes can follow from the evaluation. The case may be terminated or the process repeated to enhance effectiveness. A new plan may be implemented with new objectives and the same or different interventions. If the evaluation does not indicate intervention effectiveness, a case plan may be tried with alternative interventions used with the current or alternative objectives. The case can

be referred to additional service resources. While the evaluation phase is presented as the termination phase of practice or the research effort, in practice and case research it is a continuous effort and part of all phases.

When, how often, and for how long to measure during the follow-up phase are questions directed by the same considerations as for the baseline phase. Ideally, the length of the preintervention and postintervention phases, as indicated, are until measurements are stable. The decisions about when to begin and how long to continue the follow-up measure of the behaviors and intervention effects are guided by the case theory's prediction of when effects will occur. Repeated measurements are important to determine patterns of variations on the variables within and between each phase. If the pattern reflected by the measures is inconsistent, then a longer follow-up time is needed to capture the pattern. As discussed previously, at least three observations (measurement points) are necessary for minimal adequacy. If there is high variability, a longer follow-up phase and more measurement points are required. Certain phenomena such as abuse, although not allowing for long preintervention baselines, compel long-term follow-up. Without the baseline and follow-up measurements, determination and comparison of changes are not possible.

At the end of this chapter we discuss other variations of the basic single case design, such as the multiple and interrupted treatment designs.

. . . . . . . . . . . . . . . . . . . . . .

*Referring back to Tad and his social worker, Mr. Noble, from Chapter 6, the practice plan basically follows a single case design. Tad, a 14-year-old middle class white male, was referred to Mr. Noble for drug counseling. Tad was assessed as having "low self-esteem." The case theory is that Tad's drug use is at least partially a result of low self-esteem (Griffin-Shelley, Sandler, & Lees, 1990; Kinnier, Metha, Okey, & Keim, 1994; Richter, Brown, & Mott, 1991), and an increase in self-esteem will decrease his drug use. The intervention hypothesis* is that Mr. Noble's model of counseling will enhance self-esteem.

The single case design, A-B-A, rests on taking baseline measures of Tad's pre and post-program self-esteem levels and drug use, and "B" or intervention phase measures of a proceduralized intervention (see Chapter 10). Mr. Noble must measure the intervention to determine if he administered the counseling as intended. Measurement, as indicated in Chapter 6, is required of all the components because changes in one variable do not necessarily indicate changes in the others. Changes in Tad's drug use behavior or self-esteem do not necessarily mean that the intervention was administered as intended or caused the change.

## THE "A" MEASURES

During the baseline and follow-up phases, Mr. Noble triangulated his measures of self-esteem by a combination of observations, interviews for self-reports by Tad of his feelings about himself, his school performance, and paper-and-pencil measurements such as the Coopersmith Self-Esteem Inventory (Coopersmith, 1959; Gurney, 1988), How I See Myself (Juhasz, 1985), Index of Self-Esteem (Hudson, 1982b), or the Rosenberg Self-Esteem Scale (Nielsen & Metha, 1994; Rosenberg, 1979). Drug use was measured by a cluster of triangulated measures: interviews or the boy's self-reports and reports of others' observations of behavior for drug use indicators, Mr. Noble's observations of behaviors associated with drug use, and random urinalysis.

## THE TIMES TO MEASURE

Mr. Noble will probably rely heavily on a reconstruction from self reports and available data for baseline measures of self-esteem and drug use. He

Relationship of Clinical Practice Decisions and Information Provided by Single Subject Design Methodology Phases

| Clinical Social Work Practice | Assessment and Treatment Planning | Treatment Implementation and Monitoring | Treatment Evaluation, Termination and Follow-Up |
|---|---|---|---|
| Decisions | Is the designated problem severe and persistent; is treatment required? | Has the social worker implemented the appropriate treatment plan, and has the severity and nature of the client's problem changed? | Should the social worker withdraw treatment? Will the treatment objectives be successfully accomplished and maintained after treatment? |
| Single-Subject Design Methodology | Baseline | Intervention or Treatment | Follow-Up |
| Information | Specification of treatment objectives into measurable statements. Measurement of nature, severity, and persistence of problem prior to intervention. | Measurement of changes in nature and severity of problem over time. Inferences about attainment of objectives. Observations of treatment implementation. | Measurement of maintenance of change. Provision of descriptive, correlational, and approximation to causal knowledge. Observation for emergence of any new problems. |

*takes two to three concurrent measures using the paper-and-pencil tests and random urinalysis. The outcome measures are continued during the "B" or intervention phase and in a follow-up phase of longer duration. Follow-up measurements are needed after intervention to assess change and objectives achievement.*

## The "B" Measures

*The "B" or intervention phase is when Mr. Noble is counseling Tad. The case theory guides Mr. Noble's selection of the intervention. Mr. Noble proceduralized, developing a model of the counseling by specifying its indicators. He measured the indicators to determine if the counseling was conducted as intended. The outcome indicators are measured during this phase to monitor change. If drug use increases or self-esteem decreases Mr. Noble will reassess continuing the intervention.*

· · · · · · · · · · · · · · · · · · · ·

# Single Case Designs, Causal Validity, and External Validity

Single case designs, as well as single group panel designs and other quasi-experimental designs, suffer from a *low capacity to definitely rule out causal validity challenges because of their lack of equivalent control or comparison groups.* They cannot rule out the possibility that factors other than the treatment produce the change. Relevant variables of change are difficult to isolate in the complex social situation of practice, limiting ability to replicate them in other complex social situations. This is why it is critical to collect baseline information for providing a comparison to assess change. Case assessment, including the case's ecology beyond the outcome variables, is crucial for the analytical assessment of the possible effects of history, maturation, and other alternative explanations challenging causal validity.

Validity issues confront all research. Though the magnitude may be different, the issues are not. SCD shares its limitations with designs using samples of convenience, panel designs with no contrast group, designs with a single "pre" or $T_1$ measurement point, and designs using "group measures" of central tendencies that both lose the individual scores within the group and are severely affected by extreme scores and attrition. A group comparison design that indicates 70% of participants have changes after an intervention may not reveal if the intervention is effective for any particular subject. True experimental designs can provide information to make judgments about the treatment's causal validity for the group, but not for any single individual in the group, unless the analytical elements of a single case design are incorporated into the experimental design (Nugent, 1987, 1991). Generalized information about patterns is very helpful in developing theories of patterns as a start for case theory development and interventions directed at populations. It is not as helpful, however, with individual predictions and practitioners evaluating individual practice because the information is about the pattern and not the specific individual.

## Addressing Causal Validity

Below are some approaches to addressing causal validity challenges in Single-Case Design.

1. History and maturation are problematic, especially for long-term interventions. They are addressed by baseline measures over time, comparisons to normative population standards, analysis of the social ecology, and replication with subjects who share similar maturation and social ecologies.

2. Testing effects are problematic because of repeated baseline measurements, the subject's repeated use of the measurements, and use of measurements as part of treatment when the subject logs behaviors. Measurements become a treatment, as when self-monitoring of behavior influences behavior. Although triangulation, such as measurement by someone or something other than the subject, is critical for measurement reliability and validity, it can add to reflexivity if the case is constantly being

measured, unless the measurement process is unobtrusive.

3. Instrumentation effects in SCD face the same concerns and procedures involved in group comparison and experimental designs.

4. Statistical regression is addressed by repeating measurements over time to obtain a stable baseline.

5. Ambiguity about the direction of causal inference is met by the basic longitudinal design. Measurements are taken on the outcome variables before and after treatment.

6. SCDs often exacerbate multiple treatment interference. Good control and measurement of treatments is required. When there are multiple concurrent treatments, internal validity can be inferred only to the complete treatment package.

Experimental mortality and selection-maturation interaction are not particularly relevant. If the case leaves, there is no single case design. Experimental mortality is 100% or zero in SCD. The case is the case, regardless of the selection process.

*Causal validity is improved by repeated applications or clinical trials with similar subjects or clients in similar ecologies.* Use of extended baselines, continuous measurements whether interrupted or not, and baselines prior to the introduction of new treatments in graduated treatment designs all provide some greater capacity for inferring causal validity. But extended baselines do not allow for disregarding most of the challenges to causal validity. Causal validity, the ability to attribute change to the treatment, is best established through *careful replication*, limited to cases essentially similar on all important variables. The more often similar results are found in the repeated applications of the treatment to similar cases under similar circumstances, the greater ability to attribute causal validity.

## Addressing External Validity

External validity, the ability to induce generalized patterns, is weak because *the case, a sample of one,*

*has little power for generalization.* Any generalizations from a single case likely are inductive fallacies. External validity in single case designs, the ability to generalize the treatment effects to cases not yet treated is best established through careful replication and clinical trials with similar subjects or clients in similar ecologies. Tripodi and Epstein (1983) argue: "As a rule of thumb, 3 out of 4 successful replications would indicate that the treatment procedures used are generalizable to a comparable group of clients" (p. 240). This small number of replications appears overly liberal and optimistic. Replications are limited to cases essentially similar on all important variables. The more often similar results are found in the repeated applications of the treatment to similar cases under similar circumstances, the greater confidence in generalizations to a population represented by the aggregate of cases or clients. In the final analysis, however, conclusions and inferences from SCD, and perhaps from all designs, regarding causal and external validity should be prudent, tentative, and limited.

## Alternative Single Case Design Models

There are a range of alternative single case designs, and they generally reflect the introduction

Alternative Single Case Designs

| Design | Explanation |
|---|---|
| ABABA | Introduction, withdrawal, reintroduction of a single coherent intervention |
| ABCA | Introduction and withdrawal of two distinct coherent interventions |
| ABACADA | Introduction and withdrawal of two distinct interventions, reintroduction of one of the interventions with a third distinct coherent intervention, withdrawal of all interventions |

and withdrawal of additional treatments or the introduction, withdrawal, and reintroduction of a single treatment. The A designation in the design symbolizes measurement of the dependent variables and no treatment, B indicates a single coherent treatment phase, and the other letters represent phases that introduce distinct differentiated coherent treatments. The following table presents three examples. Of course there are almost endless sets of designs reflecting the combinations and permutations of interventions and measurement sequences.

For a more extensive review of single case designs and selection criteria, see Bloom, Fischer, and Orme (1995, pp. 367–478).

## Withdrawal-Reversal Designs

Withdrawal-reversal designs, which involve intervention and reintroduction of the problem-

Comparison of Experimental Design and Single Subject Design

| Feature Required | Experimental | Single Case |
|---|---|---|
| Random sampling | Yes | No, the case only |
| Random assignment | Yes | No, the case only |
| $T_1$ baseline DV[a] measures | Yes | Yes |
| $T_2$ follow-up DV measures | Yes | Yes, multiple time points for follow-up |
| Control and measurement of IV,[b] treatment or intervention | Yes | Yes, tight measurement protocols |
| Triangulation | Varies by research intent[c] | Yes, basis for measurement reliability and validity |
| Multiple measurements of DV in baseline and follow-up | Varies by research intent[c] | Yes, basis for stability of change and causal validity |
| External validity | Yes, random sampling and assignment | No, requires replication for cautious external validity |
| Causal validity | Best addresses of all available design types | Single SCD doesn't rule out alternative explanations. Follow-up measures for stability of change. Replication |
| Measurement reliability | Required, correspondence in sample measures[c] | Yes, repeated measures in baseline, pretest measures, triangulation, training |
| Measurement validity | Required, construct or panel at minimum, concurrent | Pretest, construct, and panel triangulation for concurrent criterion; empirical validity of measurements |
| Most likely ecological fallacies | Deductive | Inductive |

[a]Dependent variables.

[b]Independent variables.

[c]Depends on sensitivity of the single measurement. The application of many applications of the same measurement to one subject and triangulation provides some of the function of a single measurement to many subjects.

atic conditions to be altered, have scientific knowledge development value but limited practical practice applications with traumatic clinically or socially significant cases. Reversal designs are operationally not possible with cases addressing community intervention regardless of their ability to contribute greater confidence in causal validity. It is not possible to conceive of how to return a complex system, such as a community, to a "preintervention" state. Reversal designs may be appropriate for limited clinical trials and research addressing low trauma and low-risk situations that are not life threatening. It is perplexing to seriously consider the reintroduction of abuse or the withdrawal and subsequent reintroduction of social supports for an adolescent mother in order to test the efficacy and causal validity of an intervention. When she exhausts her eligibility for assistance under the Personal Responsibility and Work Opportunity Rehabilitation Act of 1996, her survival is a clear worry during this era of limited and severe welfare assistance. Causal validity of the intervention will be better established by repeated application to other clients with the same characteristics, conditions, and case goals rather than the reintroduction of the problem and trauma to clients enjoying successful case outcomes.

Withdrawal-reversal designs in practice situations most often are accidental, unintended, and detrimental to clients, rather than intentional. They are present when clients lose eligibility, abruptly withdraw from the intervention against practitioner advice, or lose the practitioner for a variety of reasons, and later re-enter treatment. Unfortunately, the effects of such withdrawal-reversal conditions are rarely monitored and reported.

## Summary

Practice plans are single case designs. Natural quasi-experimental longitudinal designs manipulate a set of variables called the intervention and examine changes in another set of variables representing case objectives. The research design intent of a practice plan is to ascertain if the intervention has contributed to changes in the case objectives and the direction and magnitude of the changes. Definitive attribution of changes in the case objective variables to the intervention is difficult because of the single quasi-experimental design's deficiencies in eliminating a variety of challenges to its causal validity. Prudent practitioners recognize these challenges in their case plans and limit inferences to fit the design. Causal validity and the advisability of using a particular intervention with other similar cases is enhanced with design replication. Practice plans should, at the least, adhere to a basic single case design model of A-B-A or measurement of case objectives before, during, and after intervention, with measurement of intervention during its implementation. Assessment of any changes and progress toward case objectives requires at least an A-B-A single case design.

## Discussion Questions and Exercises

1. A social worker, Michael, used recovery memory therapy with Florence, an 18 year old woman with bulimia to help her come to grips with past repressed incestuous experiences. Although Florence did not originally recall incestuous experiences, the assessment of repressed memories of incest and the memory recovery therapy as intervention were based on Michael's theoretical propositions that "bulimia is usually caused by incest" and "when there is no memory of incest, it is because the memories of the experience are repressed." Michael developed the theory based on his practice experience with a previous client

who had bulimia and was a prior incest victim and on an article he read. This previous client, after dealing with her feelings about the incest, was able to control her eating disorder.

    a. Was Michael's case theory and intervention reasonable for Florence? Consider the causal and external validity of the first case.

2. Mr. and Mrs. Battle engaged in marital therapy once a week for a year with a social worker. The social worker used an intervention model that he had used successfully with other couples based on confronting and exploring areas of differences between the couple. At the end of the year, the Battles filed for divorce. Does the following statement have causal validity? "Marital therapy caused the divorce."

| Couple Married (Baseline Condition) | → | Couple Receive Marital Therapy (Intervention) | → | Couple Divorced After Marital Therapy (Follow-up Outcome Condition) |
|---|---|---|---|---|

3. Can you better establish causal validity in a single case design by comparing baseline measures with follow-up measures, or by comparing two sets of baseline measures in two single case designs?

4. Measuring the case plan intervention itself is necessary for (*select all that apply and defend selections*):

    a. accountability
    b. any ability to replicate the intervention
    c. determine change in the client or case

5. The length of baseline in single case designs or practice plans are (*select all that apply and defend selections*):

    a. as long as is practically and ethically possible
    b. longer with a high-frequency behavior than with a low-frequency behavior
    c. longer with high-intensity behavior than with low-intensity behavior

6. In deciding what to measure in a single case design or practice plan, it usually is best to (*select all that apply and defend selections*):

    a. pick variables implied by how the clinical goals were operationally defined
    b. use a single measurement
    c. choose a behavior that occurs less frequently to reduce measurement costs

# Interventions and Treatment Plans: The Measurement and Control of Intervention

Intervention begins with the first case contact by the practitioner that alters the situation. However, our conception of intervention is limited here to the more formal planned intervention phase of the case plan. To briefly review our earlier discussion, Bisman (1994) defines intervention as

> the mode[s] of procedure[s] used by the social worker to create change in the life of the client. Emerging from the goals and based on the case theory, a[n intervention] plan of treatment states a problem, outlines a strategy of the specific steps in the social work practice, and includes a means of evaluation. (p. 248)

Bloom, Fischer, and Orme (1995) limit intervention in this phase of the case plan to "planned changes in which practitioners perform certain actions with regard to their clients, to other people, or in situations in order to achieve specific objectives" (p. 8). Blythe, Tripodi, and Briar (1994) describe an intervention as

> a set of activities designed to meet client needs and/or ameliorate client problems.... [they] may be complex, involving a theory of practice and a number of techniques designed to help clients achieve their goals.... [they] may be relatively simple, involving a single procedure. (p. 88)

Interventions, according to all the preceding conceptions, are planned behaviors and activities to produce particular effects on targeted dependent variables or outcomes, or interven-

ing variables that will influence outcomes. Intervention's purpose is to achieve change or maintain a stable condition and can be as simple as a verbal exchange and advice, to complex psychosocial individual and group therapies, referrals linking cases with social supports systems, or social action to produce environmental and ecological changes. These can include monitoring client behavior and developing client behavior protocols of things the client does as part of the intervention. Interventions involve prescriptions, proscriptions, and descriptions of both practitioner and client behaviors and can include the subtleties of bonding, rapport, and other contextual variables. Case theory as well as agency and other "extratheory" constraints such as national, state, and local social policies and professional ethics guide interventions. Location and context of the practice venue also affect and constrain the nature of the intervention.

This chapter reviews intervention as a specific phase in the case plan and discusses the importance of its measurement, monitoring, and control. The chapter examines the ethical necessity and methodologies of specifying and proceduralizing interventions for measurement, monitoring, and control. Proceduralization and measurement are indispensable for informed consent, accountability, and intervention integrity. Proceduralization involves conceptualizing and operationalizing the intervention.

## Case Theory and Intervention Measurement

Choosing an intervention is guided by feasibility, viability, cost, and client and practitioner preferences. An intervention's feasibility and practicality, as Bisman (1994, p. 248) contends, emerges from the case goals and objectives and is based on the case theory developed from the case assessment. Essentially, the intervention of choice derived from case theory is a prediction, a hypothesis, and a theoretical proposition that asserts:

> *If* this treatment or intervention is successfully implemented as planned, *then* the outcomes will be achieved or affected as set forth in the case theory.

The strength of the hypothesis is a function of the case theory's strength, the logic of the hypothesis derivation, and, inherently, the empirical support for the case theory and the intervention when previously used with similar cases. Its effects remain a hypothesis for this case plan until implemented as specified in the case plan and verified by measuring its implementation.

We discussed Tad and Mr. Noble in Chapter 6. If a case theory propositions that Tad's (1) drug use is at least partially the result of low self-esteem (Griffin-Shelley, Sandler, & Lees, 1990; Kinnier, Metha, Okey, & Keim, 1994; Richter, Brown, & Mott, 1991), and (2) increased self-esteem will decrease drug use by Tad, the theory directs the intervention to improve self-esteem. Mr. Noble's model of counseling needs to enhance self-esteem.

## Ethics and Intervention Measurement

Social work's largest professional association's ethical standards (NASW, 1996) require informed consent. **Informed consent** *is at the core of worker accountability and client self-determination and empowerment.* Informed consent obliges the practitioner to provide clients with sufficient information to understand expected outcomes, what is needed from them in achieving outcomes, and what will happen to them in the process of attaining outcomes. In order to determine if what *is* happening to the client is what was intended to happen (the consented intervention) it is necessary to specify the intended intervention, articulate what is happening, or measure the actual intervention as implemented. Tripodi (1994) holds that "[A] social worker cannot adopt an intervention unless she or he knows specifically what is involved in carrying out the intervention. As they become more specific and detailed, interventions are more likely to be adopted" (p. 96). The National Association of Social Worker's Code explicitly mandates in Section 5.02 (a) that "social workers should monitor and evaluate policies, the implementation of programs, and *practice interventions*" [emphasis added].

## Measuring the Intervention

The same concerns pertain to measuring interventions as to measuring the client's condition, ecology, and case objectives. *Measuring the intervention is necessary to determine if the appropriate treatment or intervention is administered.* Intervention measurement's tasks are to determine (1) the treatment's **integrity,** or if the intervention is implemented as prescribed or planned; and (2) the treatment's **procedural reliability,** or if the intervention is being consistently administered by the same practitioner across time and clients and is the same procedure consistently administered by different practitioners (Blythe & Tripodi, 1989, pp. 105–106).

Intervention procedural reliability requires an accounting of intervention shifts and a prevention of intervention drift. **Intervention shift** *is the intentional alteration of treatment demanded by changing case circumstances.* **Intervention drift,** *on the other hand, is when the intervention is* *unintentionally changed due to practitioner inattention, negligence, or ignorance as to what is occurring.*

Inherent in treatment integrity and procedural reliability is **practitioner accountability,** which requires that the practitioner does what is supposed to be done, in the way that it is supposed to be done, and when it is supposed to be done. Lastly, measuring the intervention is indispensable to supporting case theory by ascertaining if any changes in the client's behavior, the client's social ecology, and the achievement of case objectives can be attributed to the intervention. *Intervention replication requires measuring the intervention.* While measurements alone will not satisfy these concerns, they cannot be satisfied without measurement.

Intervention measurement often presents a threat to the practitioner because it *requires measurement of behaviors of the practitioner, others involved in the intervention, and client behaviors to achieve the client's outcome objectives.* Measuring interventions is measuring what practitioners and action systems do to, with, and for client systems to influence and effect outcome objectives. In a design, intervention variables are the independent variables and outcomes are dependent variables. It is important to distin-

| Intervention integrity | The extent an intervention is implemented as planned, modeled, and proceduralized. |
| Intervention procedural reliability | Consistent implementation of a standardized intervention model and procedure by practitioners over repeated applications with different cases. |
| Intervention drift | Unintentional alteration of an intervention in the process of administering it. |
| Intervention shift | Intentional alteration of an intervention in the process of administering it. |

guish between *measurement of the intervention variables themselves* and *measurement of hypothesized effects of intervention,* or what intervention is to accomplish.

## Intervention Proceduralization

Too often social workers so globally conceptualize their interventions as to make measurement irrelevant. This is often true of research studies, which, according to Wodarski (1997, p. 12), tautologically define social work interventions as interventions done by social work degree holders. Global definitions make concerns for informed consent, integrity, reliability, accountability, and replication meaningless. Adequate measuring and monitoring of the intervention to discharge these obligations first involves developing and specifying the interventive model by tasks, sequence of tasks, timing of tasks, and establishing minimum thresholds for each and then determining and developing operational measures for the tasks reflecting the thresholds. Adequate measuring and monitoring an intervention requires operationalizing the intervention model's concepts and variables. This model guides and anchors the practitioner and action system's interventive behavior.

Proceduralization focuses on specific arrangement, steps, activities and behaviors, interactions, and communications that a social worker and others in the action system use and do to implement the intervention. If an intervention's procedures and techniques can be specified, it is more likely that it can and will be implemented. *If the procedures and techniques cannot be specified, it is unlikely that the intervention is being implemented and impossible to determine what, if anything, was done.*

Proceduralization and its reliable and valid measurement are critical for protecting intervention integrity, maintaining procedural reliability, preventing intervention drift, and determining when to make intervention shifts. It is essential for compliance to the intervention protocol by practitioners, clients, and others. Client compliance is when clients adhere to the prescribed behaviors in the intervention protocol. *Measuring compliance prevents intervention drift and can aid in determining when conscious intervention shifts are needed.*

Intervention proceduralization and measurement is intentionally *reflexive* if compliance is obtained, a model for monitoring is provided, and intervention drifts are avoided. Proceduralization intrudes on behavior.

## Proceduralization Protocols

Proceduralization, like the operationalizing of any measurement process, specifies the intervention's components of *who* does *what* to *whom, when, where,* and *why?*

*Who* refers to the person or persons involved in providing the intervention (worker, client, significant others, other professionals and paraprofessionals, support groups) and targets of the intervention.

*What* is the substance and content of the intervention. *What* can be as specific as seating arrangements in a group therapy session, length of meetings, number of meetings, topics, and sequences of activities. *What* includes all the important components.

*Where* is the place of the intervention—where the intervention occurs, but not necessarily where the outcomes occur.

*When* is the implementation timing and timing sequence of the components.

*Why* is the purpose of the intervention and that part of the case theory prescribing the intervention.

While it is difficult or impossible to specify all the content of an intervention, if the intervention is successful, identify the essential components and sequences in as much detail as required to ensure their implementation, accountability, and possible replication with similar cases.

Intervention proceduralization's logic and format is similar to the GANNT Milestone Charting and Critical Path Method (CPM) used in program design and management (Krist-Ashman & Hull, 1997, pp. 232–234, 256–257; Netting, Kettner, & McMurtry, 1993, pp. 240–247, 269–272; Weiner, 1982, pp. 253–285). The procedures contain the necessary prescribed tasks and protocols laid out in a sequence specifying when completed and with and by whom, as guided by case theory and prescriptions of agency or social policy.

Proceduralization requires the capacity to specify:

1. the events necessary to achieve case objectives
2. the intervention activities (tasks) necessary for achieving the events
3. the time requirements for the activities
4. the start and ending indicator for an activity or task
5. the ability to sequence intervention tasks and their indicators from the first to last event for the objective

### Protocol for selecting treatment and interventions techniques

1. Specify and operationally define the problem or condition to change (case objectives).

2. Review relevant literature, theories, and prior experience to build a case theory and intervention hypothesis for the specific case.

3. Develop the case theory, which delineates the problem, assesses resources, explains the relationship between variables and elements of the condition, establishes SMARRT objectives, and provides a basis to derive intervention hypotheses.

4. From the case and intervention theory, specify the essential techniques, traits, characteristics, responsibilities, and timing of the intervention model (*who, what, when, where,* and *why*). This protocol seeks clear specification of the behavior and practice expectations of the client, social worker, and significant others in the action and change agent systems. The intervention's likelihood of success is indicated by (a) empirical and scientific evidence supporting the case the-

ory that the plan will be effective with this class of problem and with this type of client, or (b) empirical and scientific evidence supporting the case theory that this intervention plan is more likely to be more effective for this client and this problem than alternative intervention plans. Time estimates are based on the most likely times required to complete the tasks. This estimate incorporates both optimistic and pessimistic projections.

5. Translate the intervention specifications into specific empirical behaviors and events whose occurrence must take place for a successful intervention. The specifications are stated in specific, understandable, and measurable terms with clear assignments of responsibility.

6. Assemble the intervention specifications and or procedures into a monitoring format ranging from simple checksheets to more complex GANNT Milestone Charts or Critical Path Charts, depending on the specificity and precision needed.

7. Assess the theoretical linkages between the intervention specifications and the relevant outcome measurements on the strength and predictability of the relationship of the case theory's independent-dependent variables. Neutralize barriers to successful implementation within the practice situation or select alternative objectives and intervention proceduralization.

8. Consider and weigh the interventive model by the criteria of feasibility, effectiveness, efficiency, and accountability (that it has been performed as intended, with knowledge of the intervention generated by measurement efforts).

9. Assess the competency and ability of those in the action and change agent system to implement the proceduralized intervention. Those with intervention assignments (client, practitioners, and others) will need to understand and be capable of fulfilling their intervention roles and obligations. If they cannot, it is unlikely that the intervention will be successful. If significant actors of the change agent systems cannot fulfill their interventive roles, the intervention plan and case plan will need revision.

10. If the intervention is changed because of inadequate case theory, ecological barriers, or inability of significant actors to fulfill interventive roles, new case theory guiding formulation of a new case plan and intervention proceduralization will have to be developed and protocols 1 through 9 repeated.

11. When protocols 1 through 9 are adequately satisfied, locate and select or develop and assess the measurements and information sources and a data collection process that will operationally measure the specifications and provide information appropriate for judgments necessary to determine if implementation adheres to the model.

12. Assess reliability and validity for the intervention measurement and data collection processes. Be alert to treatments tested and standardized under hothouse conditions on samples of convenience that may not be applicable or generalizable to the current case and its ecology.

13. Implement procedures in accordance with agency and professional standards, the intervention contract, and with informed consent. Monitor and measure the intervention procedures.

### GANNT milestone and critical path method (CPM) charting

GANNT and CPM serve similar proceduralization functions. They detail proceduralization and allow for closer control of activities according to the projected time schedule. GANNT Milestone Charting is the simpler and quicker of the two approaches. It elaborates a sequential checksheet listing of events or milestones with addition of time and activities required to achieve the events.

### GANNT milestone charting elements

1. An *event*, the **milestone,** is an instantaneous measurable occurrence in time.

2. An **activity** or **task** is the behavior necessary to achieve the event.

3. **Time** is the number of hours, days, weeks or months required to perform the activity. Time

is a linear concept, summated as the total time required from starting event to ending event of a task (such as eight weeks), and the total time to complete all tasks or activities and achieve all events for an intervention's final objective.

GANNT arranges the intervention's events and activities from start to the projected accomplishment of case objectives in a visual and linear time sequence format (see Figure 10.1).

GANNT Milestone Charting's major limitations are that its sequencing is linear only and it does not allow for precision in determining confidence of the time estimations. GANNT Charting is linear because it does not indicate the networked relationship between events and activities. Nor does it give the practitioner capacity to determine a priori confidence in the time projections except in a heuristic fashion based on prior experience or rough estimates. GANNT Charting does not have ability to test estimates prior to implementation. CPM, especially in its more sophisticated PERT model, satisfies these limitations.

***Program evaluation and review technique/ critical path method (PERT/CPM).*** Program Evaluation and Review Technique/Critical Path Method (PERT/CPM) are systematic techniques for projecting and controlling multiple events, tasks, their required times and interrelationships among events, tasks, and time using the probabilistic likelihood of critical or longest time path. PERT and CPM organize all anticipated activities from the first event through the final task necessary for achievement of objectives into an interrelated logical network. This network presents a visual image of the organization of all significant events, tasks, and times for achieving objectives. PERT and CPM are more sophisticated than GANNT Milestone Charting because they present the relationship between events and require establishing probabilities for time estimates.

PERT and CPM's limitations are generally inherent in their strengths. They require SMARRT events, time estimations, and an accurate net-

Required linear time in hours, days, weeks, months, years or calendar time ⟶

TIME UNITS ⟶

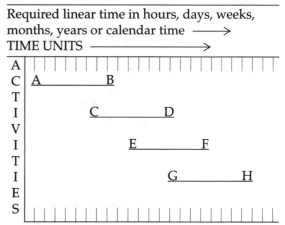

Legend:
- The bars [A]–[B], [C]–[D], and so forth represent the time required for the activity from the start of the activity, as [A], to the completion of the activity, as [B]. The bar contains the amount of time required for the activity from the starting event (the first letter of the bar) for the bar or activity to achievement of the ending event (the second letter of the bar) for the bar or activity. The time is measured in the linear time units indicated at the top of the chart, such as calendar days; November 1, 2, 3…June 30, 1997. This represents the anticipated amount of time needed to complete or the time that can be allowed to complete the intervention and achieve case objectives.
- [A] is the start of the intervention and [H] is the final intervention event and objective.
- The intervention's events and activities are represented by the letters and bars arranged in time sequence from left to right across the chart and from top to bottom of the chart. [A], the first event of the project, is in the upper lefthand corner, and [H], the final event of the project, is in the lower right corner. The relationship between events and activities is represented in a linear fashion: [A] must be achieved before [B], [B] and [C] before [D], and so forth. Activities of the [A]–[B] bar must be nearly completed before the start of [C]–[D] bar activities and completed before the start of [E]–[F] bar activities. This allows for a visual image of the linear time requirements and sequence of activities and events of an intervention from start to finish.

**FIGURE 10.1**  General Form of the GANNT Milestone Chart

work construction. This requires considerable time and knowledge about intervention protocols prior to beginning intervention, as well as some statistical sophistication.

## Intervention Measurement

After proceduralization, you can implement and measure the intervention. Intervention measurements generally are made by a combination of participant observations by practitioners, clients, and others in the action system, and observation by supervisors and colleagues recorded on checksheets, case charts, and case recordings. Emphasis is on the prescribed and significant proceduralized intervention behaviors, questionnaires completed by the participants, and electronic observation by video and audio recording for subsequent content analysis. Some intervention measures are mandated by the agency and its management information system and funding sources including time reports, critical incidence reports, and chartings of medication.

Measurements of the interventions—measuring the procedures set forth in the proceduralization—can, at a minimum, be nominal and recorded on a checklist such as *Yes [], No []* for the occurrence or nonoccurrence of prescribed interventive behaviors and actions of the practitioner and/or client and in the sequence prescribed by the intervention model. If possible, measurements of interventions should move to higher and richer measurement systems than nominal (occurrence and existence). Assess and measure intervention variables according to their existence, magnitude, intensity, frequency, and duration. When they correspond to the systems used for measuring outcome variables, the more powerful ordinal, interval, and ratio measurement systems allow for a more direct comparison of the intervention and outcomes, better testing and refining of case theory, and replications of the intervention. Intervention measurements, at the least, can assess and record time, dates, numbers of contacts, durations of contacts, types of contacts, checkoffs of intended worker-client discussions and behaviors, and possibly intensity of intervention. Time sampling and recordings can be used to capture critical events.

Intervention Measurement Levels

| Measurement System | Intervention Variable |
|---|---|
| Nominal | Occurrence of an intervention, type of intervention |
| Ordinal | Worker's degree of directiveness in counseling |
| Interval | Length of counseling sessions |
| Ratio | Time between counseling sessions |

## Reliability, Validity, and Practicality

The measurement tools used to measure interventions need reliability, validity, and practicality. Tools have reliability when users obtain consistency in their use. Intervention measurements have validity when the practitioner and other observers accurately observe and record interventions that actually occur along with when they occur. Concurrent validity is obtained when two or more independent observers concur that the measurement tools accurately represent what occurred. These observers may be the practitioner, the client, or others, such as colleagues. The reliability and validity procedures discussed in the earlier measurement and data collection chapters can be readily adapted for application to intervention measurements.

Practicality is an important consideration. While reflexivity is often intended if it contributes to accountability, the measurement tools have to be useable within the practice context, and not replace the intervention's content. *Measuring and monitoring the intervention should not be so complex and time consuming that it leaves little time for the intervention.*

### *Checksheets*

The following are two very minimal and preliminary checksheets. The first can be used to monitor an elderly client being discharged from a health care facility to an extended care facility. Measurement processes are the practitioner's "self-observations" encoded and reported on the checksheet.

The "Date Completion Needed" column is established in the proceduralization process and provides a structure for task monitoring. The actual date completed should be entered in the "Date Completed" column when the task is actually completed. It can be compared with the Date Completion Needed column to monitor case progress. The intervention monitoring data across several cases can be compared with client

Checksheet of Practitioner Tasks

| Intervention Task | Date Completion Needed | Date Completed |
|---|---|---|
| 1. Assess with client and client's family client preferred living arrangements. | | |
| 2. Complete community assessment to locate facilities offering preferred living arrangements. | | |
| 3. Complete and submit necessary insurance forms for client expenses. | | |
| 4. Refer and relocate client to preferred living arrangement. | | |
| 5. Follow-up assessment with client and family the client's living arrangements. | | |

and family satisfaction and client well-being measurements to examine whether expedient intervention is related to these outcome measures.

The second checksheet monitors a group session. The group sessions are intended to address adolescent drug use. The sheet specifies important components the group leader is to include in each session: factual information about drugs, a quiz on the factual information, a discussion of the quiz, a role-play for group members to demonstrate the capacity to use the factual information, and the time devoted to each component.

Small Group Intervention Checklist

Group leader _____ Group ID # _____
Group session # _____ Date _____
Attendance _____
_____
_____
_____

Check Whether the Following Occurred:

( ) Factual presentation
Content (Describe)
Estimated time duration ( )

( ) Quiz:
Content (Describe)
Estimated time duration ( )

( ) Quiz discussed
Content (Describe)
Estimated time duration ( )

( ) Role-Play
Content (Describe)
Estimated time duration ( )

( ) Other important group content
Content (Describe)
Estimated time duration ( )

Group session recording date_____

Recorded by _____

Group composition, session number, date, and leader are also measured and recorded. Measurement is observation by the practitioner of the group composition and processes with subsequent encoding and recording.

Intervention data can be compared to group participants' changes in drug knowledge levels, behavioral skills in applying the knowledge, and subsequent drug use

## Summary

Intervention is the set of activities, technologies, procedures, and things used by a social worker to create changes in the life of a client or in a case to achieve case objectives. Measuring these things, especially what a social worker does as part of an intervention, might appear unwarranted to some practitioners. Intervention measurement involves measuring a practitioner's behavior as well as the behaviors of others contributing to the intervention. It also requires measuring any chemical, mechanical, and electronic applications. Intervention measurement measures the intervention and not its effects. While effects, a case objective's variables, are measured in effective practice, these measures do not indicate the presence or character of an intervention. Intervention measurement is essential for reflective, ethical, and accountable practice. Intervention measurement is part of practitioner observation and practitioner self-awareness. Without measurement, informed consent is embarrassing, if even possible at all. An honest social worker is faced with asking the client to consent to an unknown intervention that actually may not be implemented. Intervention becomes a series of random, perhaps spontaneous or intuitive acts that may be more exclusively mentalisms than empirical phenomena. Accountability is moot because there is nothing to hold the practitioner accountable to.

Ethical, accountable, and effective practice requires intervention proceduralization and measurement. Effective practice compels developing, implementing, and measuring intervention models. Intervention integrity is maintained by measurement, and intervention drift is avoided by proceduralization and measurement to assess compliance until any intervention shifts are required. Proceduralization and measurement are a requisite for replication and sharing of practice skills within the profession.

## Discussion Questions and Exercises

Select a case from practicum:

1. Specify and present the conceptual definition for the treatment or intervention (the independent variable[s]) that will produce change(s) on the dependent variable(s) and achieve case objectives. First efforts at proceduralization should select specific, limited, and well-defined case objectives and interventions. Limit the exercise to only one case objective and its intervention, although most cases have multiple case objectives.

2. Present the case theory that supports the prediction or hypothesis that this intervention(s) or the treatment(s) will produce the case objective's sought-after effects. The case theory leads you to predict that this intervention with this client will produce the desired effects on the dependent variables or case objective variable. Be sure to address the ecology of the case in developing the theory of the case. Basically, what leads you to believe that the independent variables, the intervention, will produce the predicted variation in the dependent variables

(that the intervention will change things, behavior, or produce the desired outcome[s] for this client)?

3. Proceduralize the intervention, specifying the important components, their sequence, and the critical indicators of each of the components.

4. Present the operational measures, the actual protocols and tools, for the intervention procedures. What will you do, and when and how will you know that it is done in measuring the intervention? Is triangulation necessary, and, if so, what are the multiple measurements and processes?

5. Present how you will establish (or already established) reliability and validity of each intervention measurement. If the reliability and validity of each measurement has been established, what is the reliability level? Validity? If not yet established, please present in a stepwise fashion your plans and protocols for establishing each measurement's reliability and validity.

6. Are the measurements practical? Can they be used within the context of the intervention without adversely disrupting its content? If they are not practical, select or develop alternative practical measurements and processes.

7. Present how you will maintain treatment integrity and procedural reliability, avoid treatment drift, and monitor treatment shifts.

For purposes of the exercise, it is **not** permissible to assert that measurement is not possible without also advocating that any intervention is as acceptable as any other intervention, informed consent is not needed, and accountability is a myth.

# CHAPTER ELEVEN

# Populations, Samples, and Sampling: Getting the Units

What has sampling to do with the day-to-day activities of a social work practitioner? Social workers rarely obtain clients by systematically sampling a population of potential clients, yet their day is replete with the use of sampling methodologies. This chapter defines samples, populations, and sample frames. It examines sampling theory, approaches to sampling, and sampling strategies and their application and frequent misuse in practice.

## Samples

Whenever a smaller number of units is used to gather information for generalizations or decisions about a larger number of units, the smaller number of units constitute a sample of the larger number of units. A unit in sampling is the thing being examined and on or from which information is gathered. The units of analysis can be people, groups, families, organizations, communities, social artifacts, time, events, behaviors, and social relations. A social artifact can be a particular type of behavior, such as abusive behavior, or a material object, such as a book.

Whenever you as a practitioner make inferences based on experiences with a few cases to other potential cases, the few clients on which the inferences are drawn constitute a sample. Whenever you as a practitioner use observations of a client's specific behaviors at specific times and then generalize to client behaviors not observed or measured, you are sampling social artifacts. An understanding of sampling theory is critical for practitioners whenever generalizing or inferring from a sample about the characteristics of a larger population of people, times, or events.

## Key Concepts in Sampling

Below are the key concepts of sampling theory.

### Sampling

Sampling consists of the processes and protocols used to select some population units to represent all the population units (people, times, events, or other units) from which the sample units are drawn (Grinnell, 1997, p. 237).

When drawing conclusions about a client's behavior from a limited number of observations, sampling theory should guide the conclusions or generalizations. The limited number of observations constitute a sample if generalizations are drawn to behavior not observed. Decisions on what to observe, when to observe, and where to observe require an understanding of sampling theory.

### Population

A population is all the units, elements, or cases of people, times, or events that share some

---

**Population Examples**

- Population of United States—All people living in the United States (population defined by residence or where people live).
- Population of Child Abusers in the United States—All people in the United States who engage in behaviors conceptualized as child abuse (Population defined by geographic area and the behavior trait of child abuse).

---

defining characteristic or trait and to whom generalizations of the theory are applied. The population of some type of unit is all there is of that unit; it is the collection of all the units that contains all the known and unknown elements or traits of concern. For example, the population of the United States, defined by residence or where people live, is all people living in the United States. The population of child abusers in the United States, defined by geographic area and the behavior trait of child abuse, is all people in the United States who engage in behaviors conceptualized as child abuse. A population, therefore, is determined by the definition of elements, traits, and variables to be examined.

## Sample

A sample is a composition of units from a population that is at least one unit less than the composition of total population units:

Population – 1 = sample

Samples are *subsets of populations.* Samples are used in research and in practice when it is impractical or impossible to examine the total population. It is not possible to scrutinize all population units if all units are not inventoried, are not accessible, or do not allow themselves to be examined. In these cases samples are used. A practitioner may use a sample of time intervals to observe events because not all times and events

are available for observation. The sample's pivotal attribute is its representiveness to the population for which it will make generalizations. The following are some examples of samples:

- A subset of the people living in the United States obtained by drawing 1000 people from mailing addresses for each U.S. zip codes (*sample of people living in the United States from the population of people living in the United States*)
- A subset of a client's daily activities by observing the client for 5 hours of the 24 hours in a day for 3 of the 7 days in the week (*time sample of the population of hours in a week*)
- A quality control subset of case records by examining every fifth record from all case records (*sample of case records from a population of all case records*)

## Population and Sample Frames

The sample frame is the inventory of the actual accessible population units available for sampling and examination. It may or may not correspond to the total units in the population. The inventory, mix, and definitions of the critical variables and traits of the population that are sought in the sample are present in the sample frame proportionately equivalent to their distribution in the population, if the sample drawn from the sample frame represents the population of units. Representation is necessary to make reasonable inferences and generalizations from the sample to the population. *If the sample frame's traits are not proportionally representative of the population's traits, sample generalizations will apply only to the sample frame and not the population.* For people, traits include any physical, demographic, behavioral, social, or psychological variable.

## Sample Error

Samples and sample frames rarely, if ever, exactly replicate populations and samples rarely exactly replicate sample frames. Unless they are proportionally identical to the population or sample frame on every variable, samples are not exact

Population Characteristics and Sample Frame Characteristics

| Critical Variables | Population Characteristics | Sample Frame Characteristics Should Be |
|---|---|---|
| Gender | 20% male, 80% female | 20% male, 80% female |
| Ethnicity | 30% white, 70 % nonwhite | 30% white, 70% nonwhite |
| Socioeconomic status | 5% elite, 5% upper middle class, 15% middle class, 30% working class, 45% poor | 5% elite, 5% upper middle class, 15% middle class, 30% working class, 45% poor |
| Employment | 30% regularly employed, 70% irregularly employed | 30% regularly employed, 70% irregularly employed |

replications. Any differences between characteristics of the sample, the population and sample frame are **sample errors.** The larger and more numerous the sample errors, the less a sample represents a population and a sample frame. Of course, the greater a sample's errors, the less any findings from a sample apply to a population.

The amount of sample error to tolerate is a function of the precision needed in the sample's traits to represent the population or sample frame and in the generalizations made from a sample to a larger population. This is the sample's **margin of error.** A margin of error of 5%, for example, means that the true measures in the population may go 5% either way. Some of the difference is by chance and inherent in the sampling processes, it is randomly distributed and referred to as **random sampling error** or unsystematic sampling error (Schutt, 1996, p. 177). Random sampling error may or may not result in sample bias and unrepresentative samples. This form of error can be estimated statistically. Larger random samples reduce random sampling error as the errors or biases are likely to cancel each other out.

If the sample error is caused by consistent biases in the sampling methodology used, the error is **systematic sampling error.** This form of bias, *systematic bias,* is a consistent distortion of a sam-

ple's capacity to represent a population and will reduce its findings applicability to a population. Larger samples increase systematic error as the errors or biases accumulate with increasing sample size. Samples composed of research subjects "most in need" reflect systematic sampling error.

Both random and systematic error reduce a sample's capacity for generalizations to populations, and limit the confidence to place in the sample representing a population. This confidence in the sample traits representing population traits is expressed in a "give-or-take" range and is the sample's confidence level and the confidence interval. Rubin and Babbie (1997, p. 239) define **confidence level** as the level of confidence that a sample statistic or value yielded on the measurement of a sample trait will fall within a specific interval from the population's trait's true value. It is the probability level of how often similar results will be obtained within the give-or-take range if the sampling procedures are repeated with the same population or sample frame. The **confidence interval** is the give-or-take range of values in which the true population trait is expected to fall. Broader confidence intervals have increased confidence levels. You can place more confidence that a sample trait value represents a population's true trait value if the sample trait value lies within a 25% give-or-take range than in a 5% range. A

25% give-or-take range from the sample trait value is more likely to contain a population's true trait value than is a 5% range, although the 25% range lacks precision.

If you know the population's true values on some traits and the sample's values on these traits fall within the confidence interval, you can feel reasonably confident that the other sample traits values represent unknown population trait values. The reasonable confidence is limited to the confidence interval's precision. A 5% confidence interval has more precision than a 25% confidence interval.

## Sampling Strategies

The important questions in any sampling strategy must guide development of a sample representative of the population and allow generalizations from the sample to the population. These questions are:

1. What are the population units (people, objects, times, behaviors, events)? Can the population be inventoried with each unit known and accessible for sampling?

2. What is the sample frame of the critical known variables and traits? Are there possible critical unknown variables and traits of the unit?

3. What sample size and power is needed to capture the critical variance of traits and relationships between traits without bias to allow generalizations from the sample back to its population?

4. What are the sampling protocols that will allow generalization from the sample to the population? How can the sample be obtained?

Comparison of Population and Sample of Social Work MSW Students in Great Deeds College

| Variable | Population or Sample Frame's Distribution of Values | Confidence Interval (+ or − 5%) | Sample's Distribution of Values |
|---|---|---|---|
| Gender | | | |
| Female | 80% | 75–85% | 81% |
| Male | 20% | 15–25% | 19% |
| Ethnicity | | | |
| White | 80% | 75–85% | 82% |
| African American | 15% | 10–20% | 14% |
| Hispanic | 3% | 0–8% | 2% |
| Other | 2% | 0–5% | 2% |
| Age | | | |
| Under 20 | 2% | 0–7% | 2% |
| 21–22 | 5% | 0–10% | 4% |
| 23–24 | 30% | 25–35% | 31% |
| 25–26 | 35% | 30–40% | 33% |
| 27–28 | 20% | 15–25% | 22% |
| 29 and above | 8% | 3–13% | 8% |

## Types of Samples and Sampling

There are two general sampling approaches: (1) probability sampling, and (2) nonprobability sampling. Only probability sampling strategies safely allow for generalizations and inferences from the sample to a population or sample frame based on the sampling strategy. Strategies that best mitigate sampling error rely on random probability sampling. Only probability samples have the capacity to infer a statistical representation of the sample to a larger population.

### *Random probability samples*

A random probability sample requires each population or sample frame unit to have a known probability of being selected. Its probability of

Sample Types

| *Probability Samples* | *Nonprobability Samples* |
|---|---|
| Can generalize to a larger population. Have to know and have access to all population units. | Cannot generalize to a larger population based on sampling procedures. Used when all population units are not known, inaccessible, or some are too expensive to reach. |
| **Simple random:** Strongest form of probability samples. All population units must be known and available to the sample. | **Quota:** Selecting units from the available sample frame based on distribution of selected traits in sample frame. When the sample matches the sample frame on selected traits, sampling ceases. Intent is to improve the sample's precision to the sample frame, but it can only address known traits. |
| | **Purposive:** Intentional selection of units from an available population by some specific trait sought. It samples for specific things, and may over-sample for trait. |
| **Proportionate stratified:** Ensures inclusion of units with traits that constitute a small number of units in the population. | **Snowball:** Purposive and quota samples obtained from referrals of units from the first (entry) population units, usually key informants contacted. |
| **Disproportionate stratified:** Allows for overrepresentation of population's scarce trait units in the sample. | **Samples of convenience:** Also called **available samples.** Use whatever part of the population that is available and convenient. Weakest form of sample for generalization based on sampling methodology. All nonprobability samples have some characteristics of a sample of convenience. |
| **Area sampling:** Application of probability sampling techniques to geographic areas. Used when other probability sampling is not possible. Weakest probability sample and moves toward nonprobability sampling when population is assumed to be people rather than geographic area traits. | Other nonprobability samples are generally based on quota, purposive, and convenience considerations, such as mall and cluster samples. |

selection is a function of the ratio of the desired sample size to the population size.

· · · · · · · · · · · · · · · · · · · · ·

### PRACTICE CASE RANDOM PROBABILITY SAMPLING

*An agency has a client population (caseload) of 1500 clients. The agency's director wants to create a 50-member advisory board that represents all clients. The director does not want to arbitrarily select the board but wants it to "represent" the caseload. Democratic voting by the caseload would be false democracy because the clients in the caseload are not familiar with one another and their privacy rights preclude the director's making relevant information known or campaigning. The director assigns each client an identifier number from 0001 to 1500 and randomly selects a sample of 50 clients to constitute the advisory board. An individual client's probability of selection is 0.0333, or 1 in 30 (sample size/population or sample frame size or 50/1500 = 0.0333). The director can use simple random probability sampling to select the advisory board since each client in the caseload population is known, inventoried, and capable and available for inclusion in the sample to be on the board.*

· · · · · · · · · · · · · · · · · · · · ·

*Simple random probability samples.* If each population or sample frame unit's opportunity for selection is equal and known, no greater or no less, the sample is a simple random probability sample. If each population unit has a known and equal probability of being in the sample, then each unit's traits and characteristics, whether the traits are known or unknown, have an equal and known probability of inclusion in the sample. The sample's probability of representing the population is known. For this to occur, however—for each population unit to have a known and equal probability of selection for the sample—all the population units must be known and available for sampling. If some population units are unknown or unaccessible, as are some homeless in the U.S. population census, they cannot be included in a sample. The

sample that excludes a population's unknown or unaccessible units does not represent that population but is a sample frame of known units.

---

**Selecting a Simple Random Probability Sample of 50 Units from a Population of 1500 Units**

1. Assign each population unit a separate identifying number. (The numbers for a 1500 unit population will range from 0001 to 1500).
2. Determine the needed sample size to represent the population by sample power analysis (see p. 182).
3. If power analysis indicates a needed sample size of 50 units, each population unit has a 1 in 30 chance of selection.
4. Select the 50 population units for the sample by selecting their identifying numbers using a computer program of random numbers or a random numbers table.

---

· · · · · · · · · · · · · · · · · · · · ·

*If the third client randomly selected by the administrator declines to participate on the board in our example, the population now becomes a sample frame of 1499 clients. The probability of selecting any client for one of the remaining 48 board seats is different from the first two clients selected. It has changed from 0.033 to 0.032 unless the client is replaced in the sample frame. But even if the client is replaced for probability purposes, the sample's representiveness of the population has been altered. The unavailable client is no longer a part of the sample frame, although still a population unit. While the selection probability change is trivial in this example, it increases if unavailable population units increase. The sample frame and sample's capacity to represent the population decreases.*

· · · · · · · · · · · · · · · · · · · · ·

The sample is the sample obtained and used. A survey or sample that begins as a simple random probability sample but suffers from differential selection and attrition or mortality, as discussed in Chapter 8, is no longer a simple random probability sample. The remaining respondents constitute the sample, the units providing the information, and not the original sample selected. Generalizations are limited to whatever population the usable sample represents. Unfortunately, this population is generally unknown, and the sample becomes one of convenience.

***Stratified probability sample.*** Stratified probability samples use sampling strategies that divide or stratify the population units according to their values on an identifying trait. The stratification variables can be any population or sample frame variable with a known value distribution for the population and known value for each population unit. Stratification is useful when desiring precise representation of the sample to the population or sample frame with the value distribution of the stratified variable. Stratification allows for greater precision and less sample error in a sample's capacity to represent the stratified traits of a population. Stratification is also useful when critical traits or a specific value of a trait are contained in only a small number of population units, and it is important that the sample includes all the values for this variable or trait. Stratified samples will have less sample error on the variables and traits used for stratification than comparable simple random samples of similar size, although sample errors on other variables can be greater. Any variable can be used for stratifying the population if the value for each population unit is known. Common stratification variables are age, income, ethnicity, and gender.

There are two types of stratified samples: (1) proportionate stratified samples, and (2) disproportionate stratified samples.

*Proportionate stratified sample.* Proportionate stratified samples select sample units from each

## Proportionate Stratified Sampling of Two Population Strata

Population Size or Number of Population Units ($N = 1500$)

Population composition and distribution are by ethnicity trait. Values for ethnicity trait are minority and nonminority. Each unit must be classified as either a minority or a nonminority but not both.

150 Minorities (10% of population)

1350 Nonminorities (90% of population)

Sample size is 50% or 30% of population and is to be proportionately stratified on the trait of ethnicity.

Minority stratum randomly sampled for 10% of sample of 50 or 5 Minorities (30%) from the 150 population Minorities.

Nonminority stratum randomly sampled for 90% of the sample of 50 or 45 Nonminorities (30%) from the 1350 population Nonminorities.

---

stratum of a variable proportionate to the population variable stratum size that the sample represents.

. . . . . . . . . . . . . . . . . . .

*If, using our advisory board example, the client caseload contains only 150 ethnic minorities and the administrator wants to be certain that minority clients are on the board, the administrator might stratify the caseload by ethnicity values and then randomly sample within each ethnicity value stratum. The stratification of the caseload by ethnicity and then sampling within each stratum ensures inclusion of ethnic minorities in the sample (the advisory board) proportionate to their population size. Without stratification and using simple random probability sampling, ethnic minorities might be excluded or fall below their population proportion on the board; alternatively, the board size might be increased to ensure representation.*

. . . . . . . . . . . . . . . . . . . .

Proportionate stratified random sampling does not alter the probability of selection of any individual unit, but only ensures that there will be representation in the sample of all variable value strata. The probability of an individual minority client selection to the board remains 0.0333, whether or not random sampling by ethnicity stratification is used. *Operationally, each stratum in proportionate stratified random sampling is treated as a population and simple random probability sampling is then done within each stratum.*

$$1 / 1500 \times 50 = 0.0333$$

$$1 / 150 \times 5 = 0.0333$$

*Disproportionate stratified sampling.* Disproportionate stratified sampling is used when a population has a relatively small number of population units with a particularly important variable's value stratum needing representation in the sample. With disproportionate stratified sampling, the population is stratified by the variable's values, a value stratum with a relatively low number of population units is *oversampled* and *overrepresented* in the sample compared to its proportion in the population. A value stratum with a comparative high number of population units is *undersampled* and *underrepresented* in the sample. The sampling within each over- and underrepresented stratum is by simple random probability sampling within each stratum according to the proportions desired to allow for subsequent analysis. The over- and underrepresenting value stratum ensures that the units with the more infrequent values are sufficiently present in a smaller sample to permit their analysis. Disproportionate stratified sampling allows for the inclusion of these units in smaller, more manageably sized samples.

The critical criterion of sampling, *the sample's capacity to represent and allow for making valid generalizations to a larger population,* is obtained by mathematically adjusting the sample's values to proportionally fit the original population parameters.

. . . . . . . . . . . . . . . . . . .

*In the advisory board selection example, minority males comprise a third or 50 cases of the total caseload's 150 minority cases, but only 3.33% of the total 1500 caseload.*

    *50/150 = 33.3%*

    *50/1500 = 3.33%*

*The agency's director wants to ensure inclusion of minority male cases on the advisory board in sufficient numbers to allow their opinions to be heard but does not want a board larger than 50 members, believing a larger board will inhibit interaction and be too costly to maintain. With a 50-member board and only 50 minority males out of 1500 cases, the probability of obtaining a minority male board member by simple random sampling is very low, about 0.0333. A 50-member advisory board selected by simple random probability sampling with no sample error will include 1.66 minorities, or rounded to 2 minority males. While sampling error might increase the number, it can also eliminate minority males from selection. Proportionately stratified random sampling, while ensuring inclusion of minorities with little sampling error within the stratum will include the 1.66 or 2 minority males. The director rightly fears sampling error and also believes that 2 out of 50 is an insufficient voice on the advisory board.*

*The minority stratum randomly sampled for 10% of sample of 50, or 5 Minorities (30%) from the 150 population Minorities. Minority males represent 33.3% of the total Minority population units.*

*The director decides to use disproportionate stratified sampling to select the members. The caseload is stratified by the values on ethnicity and gender. Disproportionate stratified sampling will oversample the Minority value stratum's low number of units and oversample the low number of males within the Minority value stratum. Con-*

Disproportionate Stratified Sampling

| Caseload Distribution | Caseload (N) | Sample Frame (%) | Proportional Sample to Caseload (N) | Disproportionate Sample (N) |
|---|---|---|---|---|
| All clients | 1500 | 100% | 50 | 50 |
| Ethnic majority | 1350 | 90% | 45 | 30 |
|    Females | 900 | 60% | 30 | 20 |
|    Males | 450 | 30% | 15 | 10 |
| Ethnic minorities | 150 | 10% | 5 | 20 |
|    Females | 100 | 6.7% | 3 | 12 |
|    Males | 50 | 3.3% | 2 | 8 |

versely, the Nonminority stratum will be under-sampled and represented in proportion to their population size.

Disproportionate sampling ensures that minorities and minority males will be sufficiently represented to allow their opinions to be heard. Instead of five members, minority cases are represented by 20 advisory board members. Minority male cases are represented by 8 rather than 2 members.

When the director wants proportional caseload precision in the board's advisory council, mathe-matical adjustments or weighting of the opinions—the sample's findings—can be made for each value stratum in the sample or board when inferences are made to the population or caseload. The adjustments are according to the degree that each value stratum is disproportionately over- or undersampled from the population.

. . . . . . . . . . . . . . . . . . . .

Population representation is generally best served by simple random probability samples or

| | Majority Females | Majority Males | Minority Females | Minority Males |
|---|---|---|---|---|
| Number of units and % of caseload population | 900, 60% | 450, 30% | 100, 6.7% | 50, 3.3% |
| Number of units and % of disproportionate sample | 20, 40% | 10, 20% | 12, 24% | 8, 16% |
| Sample's % and number (N) over (+) or under (–) value in caseload | –33% (–10) | –33% (–5) | +300% (+8) | +300% (+6) |
| Weighting adjustment (×%)[a] of sample values when generalizing to caseload | (× 150%) | (× 150%) | (× 0.299%) | (× 0.25%) |

[a]Scores or values of the stratum are multiplied by the weighting adjustment to adjust the stratum sample score's weight to the population's weight.

proportionate stratified random samples. Proportionate stratified random probability samples decrease sample error on the stratified variable and provide more sample precision in representing the population or sample frame without requiring a large sample size. *Disproportionate stratified random probability sampling allows a few units in the population with a critical value on a variable or trait assured inclusion in the sample without increasing sample size.*

## Sample Size and Statistical Power Analysis

A nagging question in any research effort, and hopefully frequently in practice, is: How large a sample size is needed to represent the population, to provide sufficient information to answer the questions, and to allow valid generalizations made from the sample to a population or sample frame? For practice this is framed as: Is the sample of events large enough to infer a pattern of client or case behavior? The sample size needed to adequately represent a population and to detect the effects of one set of variables on another set is the sample's **power.** Power is a function of the (1) homogeneity and difference within the population and between its units,[1] (2) the potential effect sizes of the independent variables on the dependent variables, (3) the sample error that can be tolerated, and (4) the alpha or statistical significance level used in any statistical analytical tests. Let's consider each in turn.

### Homogeneity

Homogeneity is the amount of variation or difference between population units on any particular variable or trait's values. If all population units have essentially the same values on all

variables of concern, then one population unit or a few units are as good as any other unit or set of units. A few sample units can represent a lot of population or sample frame units because all the units are very similar. But if the units differ in value, if they are diverse, then more units are required in the sample to capture the population's variance with precision. If a population is homogeneous, a sample of convenience is sufficient.

But the problem with samples of convenience is that most populations are not homogeneous or they have isolated dichotomous variables—many continuous variables interacting with many interaction effects. A few convenient and available units will not capture the range of diversity. This is why some variant of random sampling, when possible, is the most optimal and prudent sampling for representiveness and generalizations. *Larger random probability samples, simply put, have fewer opportunities for sampling error and better odds of representing the population than samples of convenience* (Craft, 1990, pp. 110–112).

In practice, you will rarely obtain truly representative samples for practice generalizations, so be cautious in the scope of practice generalizations to avoid both deductive and inductive fallacies. Always be circumspect in applying conclusions from a *sample of one or a few,* a single or a few cases, to a heterogeneous case population. Remember we discussed Tiffany in Chapter 4 who committed an inductive fallacy by concluding that bulimia is caused by incest on the basis of her four cases!

### Effect Size

Effect size (ES) is the number that represents the strength of the effect or association of a given independent variable on a specified dependent variable. ES is a concern only when an independent-dependent relationship (one variable having effect on another variable) is predicted between variables, such as in practice situations when interventions affect outcomes. The inter-

---

[1]Stratification can improve the sample's precision in representing the population, reducing the needed sample size.

vention's effect size is its contribution to achieving the case objectives. If the ES is 25%, this indicates that the independent variables will produce a 25% change in the dependent variable. The 25% change is the estimated change on the dependent variable between the baseline or pre-intervention phase and the follow-up phase. ES in group comparison designs is the proportion of the treatment group with improved scores compared to the proportion of the contrast group with improved scores in the posttreatment phase compared to the pretreatment phase.

In developing the sample, the estimated size of the intervention effect guides the sample size needed. The literature review, prior experience, and the case theory provide guidance in estimating effect size. *There is an inverse relationship between effect size and sample size.* Large sample sizes are more likely to accurately detect small effects not due to chance. Prudence argues for a conservative approach in projecting ES—it is better to underestimate. While low projections will enlarge a needed sample size, it is better to have a sample larger than required to detect small but real effects than miss real effects because of an inadequately sized sample.

· · · · · · · · · · · · · · · · · · · · · ·

### PRACTICE CASES INTERVENTION EFFECT SIZE

*A caseload or sample of 10 clients exhibit a small (5%) average decrease in depression indicators measured by a series of depression scales after completing six months of cognitive counseling treatment for depression. The decreases range from 2 to 7%. Reasonably and statistically, this small change cannot be attributed to the treatment. However, if 100 or 1000 similar clients consistently demonstrate the same small change of from 2 to 7%, we can more reasonably and by statistical analysis conclude the change is a treatment effect rather than a chance phenomenon.*

*Twenty clients, married couples, with similar levels of marital conflict and dissatisfaction, are randomly assigned to equal-sized treatment and*

*contrast groups. The treatment group receives conjoint marital counseling for six weeks and the contrast group receives no counseling. After the six weeks, seven of the treatment group couples and four of the contrast group couples report a small improvement of their marital satisfaction compared to the pretreatment phase levels. Short of sheer practice boosterism, it is difficult to reasonably or statistically rule out chance or some other challenge to causal validity as producing the positive effects of improved marital satisfaction. While seven treatment group members report improvement, four members of the contrast group exhibit the same change. The between-group difference is only three members. But if the two equivalent groups are 100 members each with the same proportion of members changing in the desired direction, we now have only 40 in the contrast group compared to 70 in the control group demonstrating the desired effects. If the two equivalent groups are increased to 1000 members each and the same proportion report similar changes in each group, then 300 more people report improvement in the treatment group than in the contrast group.* **Given the greater numbers, both logically and statistically, we can be more comfortable with attributing the dependent variable changes and differences between the two groups to conjoint marital therapy's treatment effects.**

· · · · · · · · · · · · · · · · · · · · · ·

In single case designs and case practice plans, you can compute the ES by comparing baseline or pretreatment scores with follow-up or post treatment scores on the outcome variable. The *sample size* is the sampling of the effects, or the sampling of levels of the outcome variable at various times as represented by measurement scores taken at different sampling times. *In single case practice situations with small effect sizes, you must take repeated measurements over time to determine if apparent changes are stable rather than prematurely generalizing from a few measures.* The intervention is repeated with similar cases to functionally increase sample size. Each case becomes a new sample unit, albeit a sample of convenience unit.

## Error Rate Tolerance and Confidence Interval Range

The error rate indicates the probability that a given confidence interval for a given sample size will contain the true values of the variables for the population or sample frame, and the ability to tolerate the error when the sample does not contain the true estimate of the population or sample frame's values. In other words, how well does the sample represent the population or sample frame, and are any sample errors tolerable? *When the population is diverse and sampling errors cannot be tolerated, you need a large sample size.*

Population homogeneity is inversely related to sample error rate. Heterogeneous populations are more likely to produce higher sample error rates. Larger samples are required for heterogeneous populations to capture the population's diversity. The more homogeneous a population, the more likely each unit is like any other unit, and small samples are likely to represent the population with little error.

Similarly, broader acceptable confidence intervals and a higher sample error tolerance can accommodate small samples. Broader confidence intervals indicate either a lack of concern with the sample precision in representing a population or an inability to obtain a representative sample. With a potential high sample error, be cautious and limit generalizations from the sample.

### Alpha level

The alpha level is a probability level used to accept or reject a null hypothesis that asserts the observed relationship between the variables is due to chance. The alpha level holds that the probability of the observed relationships are a chance relationship, at least as strong as the alpha's probability level. It determines the re-

searcher's or practitioner's willingness to accept or reject the relationship found between two variables as a true relationship rather than simply a chance relationship. The alpha level is usually and by tradition expressed in social science research as a significance level of $P < 0.01$, or 0.05. This is the probability that the strength of the relationship between the numbers representing the units' values will be found or exist by chance less than 1 in 100 or 5 in 100 times. Lower, more stringent alpha levels of chance with larger samples or larger effect sizes are more likely to rule out the observed relationship or effect size being a chance occurrence. Small effect sizes with lower alpha levels require larger samples.

## Statistical Power Analysis

Other things equal, larger samples will capture a wider range of heterogeneity, reduce sample er-

Relationship of Sample Size to Population Homogeneity, Effect Size, Sample Error Tolerance, and Alpha Level

|  | Sample Size, Other Things Equal |
| --- | --- |
| Population Homogeneity | |
| High | Smaller |
| Low | Larger |
| Potential Effect Size | |
| Large | Smaller |
| Small | Larger |
| Sample Error Tolerance | |
| High | Smaller |
| Low | Larger |
| Acceptable Alpha Level | |
| High (.01 and higher) | Larger |
| Low (.05 and less) | Smaller |

ror, detect smaller effect sizes, and allow more stringent alpha level use. The procedures used to determine the needed sample size for any given combination of population homogeneity—heterogeneity, effect size, sampling error, and alpha level—is statistical power analysis. Although the needed sample size can be computed without the aid of a computer[2] and sample size tables with the calculations completed for varying combinations exist, computer software programs are readily available that can compute the needed sample size. The programs use an estimation of the number of variables (homogeneity), acceptable sampling error tolerance, alpha level desired, and estimated effect size for the computation. These factors can be varied to allow for different estimates.

But all things are not equal when determining sample size. Practicality must be weighted with needs. Larger sample sizes are more costly, difficult to manage, and vulnerable to attrition than are smaller sample sizes. While statistical power increases and sample error decreases with increasing size, the changes are geometric and not direct. Increasing a small sample has proportionately more impact than increasing a large one. Increasing a sample size from 20 to 30 units decreases the sample error proportionately more than increasing a sample size from 50 to 60 units. The sample error reduction is 18% for an increase from 20 to 30 units. If a 100-unit sample is increased by 10 to 110, the proportionate sample error reduction is only 5%. It takes an increase of 50 units to 150 units for the original 100 unit sample to achieve the 18% reduction achieved by adding 10 to the 20 unit sample (Craft, 1990, p. 111).

Nevertheless, larger samples have fewer errors than smaller samples. A simple random probability sample composed of 100 units has

fewer sample errors than samples using the same sampling strategy composed of 30 units, 50 units, or 99 units.

The formula for computing sample error reduction is:

Proportional reduction in sample error = 1 − square root of [original sample size/new sample size]

## Proportional Sample Error Reduction

| Increasing a Sample Size from 20 to 30 Units | Increasing a Sample Size from 100 to 110 Units | Increasing a Sample Size from 100 to 150 Units |
| --- | --- | --- |
| 1 − square root of [20/30] or | 1 − square root of [100/110] or | 1 − square root of [100/150] or |
| 1 − 0.816 = 0.18 or 18% | 1 − 0.95 = 0.05 or 5% | 1 − 0.816 = 0.18 or 18% |

Remember, in determining power and error, the sample is the sample actually used; the actual units of respondents, times, and events measured and available for analysis. It is the operational sample that will contain the sample error, determine whether the sample is a probability sample, and determine the sample size needed to have sufficient power. Practice assessment sampling client behavior needs to recognize the sample's capacity to capture the behavioral diversity and its potential for sample error. If behavior is diverse and errors are intolerable, a larger sampling of behavior is required. In surveying, the usable sample is the proportion of survey respondents who return completed and usable measurements tools and not the original sample panel. If the return rate is less than 100%, the sample moves away from being a probability sample to become a sample of convenience. It may then be insufficient to represent the population's heterogeneity, detect small effect size, and offer intolerable sample errors. As discussed in Chapter 8, a survey's results from a sample of convenience has suspect and limited generalizability.

---

[2]See Royce and Thyer (1996, p. 242) for formula and computation procedures.

The following are additional references on power analysis with computation procedures:

Borenstein, M., & Cohen, J. (1988). *Statistical power analysis: A computer program.* Hillsdale, NJ: Lawrence Erlbaum.

Cohen, J. (1988). *Statistical power analysis for the behavioral science.* (2nd ed.) Hillsdale, NJ: Lawrence Erlbaum.

Kraemer, H. C., & Thiemann, S. (1987). *How many subjects? Statistical power analysis in research.* Stanford, CA: Stanford University Press, 1987.

Orme, J. G., & Combs-Orme, T. D. (1986). Statistical power and type II errors in social work research. *Social Work Research & Abstracts,* 22:3, 3–10.

Orme, John G., & Hudson, Walter W. (June 1995). The problem of sample size estimation: Confidence intervals, *Social Work Research 19*:2, 121–127.

## Nonprobability Sampling

Nonprobability samples, the most common samples in social science and in social work research and practice, are samples with an unknown probability of representing any population larger than the sample. If not all population units are known or inventoried, located, or available, probability sampling is not possible. A nonprobability sample's representiveness to a population and its sample error cannot be determined. When you cannot use probability sampling, use nonprobability sampling. Any generalizations are tenuous and not based on the sampling methodologies. Whether they represent a population larger than themselves is not known. They have unknown margins of sample error. *Nonprobability samples are vulnerable to both inductive fallacies and deductive fallacies.* As we discussed in Chapter 4 on theory construction, the social worker who generalizes from a limited number of case studies, drawing on practice wisdom, often commits the same inductive fallacies when generalizing to whole populations. The social worker does not know the sample error commits deductive fallacies when using these cases to infer that the condition exists for a specific client simply because the client shares some of the traits—that is, is in the same "population" as the prior cases—without knowing population diversity.

Statistical power analysis cannot be appropriately done with nonprobability samples if the homogeneity-heterogeneity range and values for the population traits are unknown. Sample error cannot be estimated. As a rule of thumb, however, population heterogeneity, small effect sizes, low sampling error tolerance, and low alpha levels call for large sample sizes, whether probability or nonprobability sampling is used. Unfortunately, you cannot use statistical power analysis with nonprobability samples for more precise numbers on sample sizes.

Nonprobability samples are usually **samples of convenience.** They are used because of convenience and availability. Clinical trials, when the researcher puts out a call for patients or subjects, are samples of convenience. Mail-in surveys in magazines are samples of convenience. Technically, inferential statistics are prohibited as the sample's representiveness to a larger population is suspect. Caution and repetition is required for inferences and generalizations to a larger population from the single or limited sample.

Nonprobability samples also include a range of variations of the convenience sample. You may use **purposive, quota,** and **cluster samples.** As set forth in the table (page 177), purposive, quota, and cluster samples try to obtain representativeness on the heterogeneity of the values for known variables and their distributions. Cluster samples are larger units known to contain the elements for analysis and then sampling within those clusters for the units, or using all units in the sampled clusters. For example, a sample of child abuse clients might be obtained by randomly sampling clusters of child abusers as represented by the clients of various caseloads of a child protective services agency, or a second stage random sampling of the clients within the clusters.

## Comparison of Nonprobability Samples to Populations and Sample Frames

A nonprobability sample's population representativeness can be tentatively established by comparing its profile on some variables to a distribution of values known to exist for the population or sample frame. You can place confidence in generalizing from the sample to the population if the sample's values distribution lies within the confidence intervals of the population. If, for example, the population's distribution of values is known for gender, ethnicity, and age, and the comparison of the sample's distribution on the same variables reveals essentially the same distribution for sample and population, confidence in generalizing all sample values back to the population is increased.[3]

## Matching

Matching and the use of matched assignments and matched pairs between a treatment and a contrast group is not sampling. But it has relevance for external generalization and causal validity similar to random assignment. Matching is intended to enhance precision in the similarities between the treatment and contrast groups by matching and equalizing the units in the two groups on relevant traits. If the groups are the same, you can more readily attribute differences to treatment effects with enhanced causal validity. External validity and capacity to generalize is increased only if the final assignments represent the population.

Matching has many problems and may only provide a spurious precision. Matching requires a very large number of units if there is any appreciable variance on the traits and with more than a few traits for matching. But without appreciable and meaningful variance and a number of traits, there is no need for matching. While matching may give greater precision on a few traits than random assignment, as the number of traits and variation of traits used for matching goes up the sample size or pool of available subjects necessary for matching increases geometrically. If a treatment is tried with matched pairs and ethnicity, gender, and age are considered important, matched pairs must be found for each combination. For example, the pool must contain an even number of female Hispanics, age 25, if any subject with these traits is included. They must be "clones" on these traits distributed between treatment and contrast groups. As the number of traits increases, the difficulty in "cloning" and the pool size also must increase. If variances in traits are collapsed, any precision and reason for matching are lost.

Matching is done only on known variables or traits considered important. The groups cannot be matched on unknown but perhaps equally important traits that interact with the known traits or with other unknown traits. Random assignment, then checking the fit on known traits between the treatment and contrast groups, is generally preferred once the important traits for matching go beyond one or two traits.

## Using Time Sampling and Measurement Time Points in Practice

As a practitioner you are faced with sampling decisions throughout the intervention process. Decisions on the length of the baseline and follow-up and on what and when to measure are sampling decisions. Time and events sampling represent a larger population of times and events in the client's life. Practitioners observe or have clients or others report on observations

---

[3]See the earlier comparisons of the Great Deeds College sample, population, and sample frame.

of client behavior. Child protective services workers observe interactions between parent and a child at a few times and then generalize as to whether the parent has abusive interactions with the child. The times and interactions observed become a sample for the "population" of all the times the parent and child interact. Time sampling is used in combination with systematic observations to observe the behavior of people within specific time periods or in response to specific stimuli. Bloom (1983, pp. 560–582) holds that a client is a "population of events" and that the practitioner is sampling from the events. Unless all the times and events are measured, time and event sampling is used. Certain events are measured at certain times and then generalized to the entire intervention process and the case's life.

Bloom (1983) again advises:

> The issue is to identify patterns of behaviors and characteristics in one client-system, including what is normative for that person—that is, his or her own norms of typical behavior. These individual norms can be compared with group norms for applicability of interventions devised in relation to classes of persons, but the focus of clinical service is ultimately on the particular client system, not on clients in general.... what is being considered is a *population of attributes of one client-system over time* (emphasis original), as contrasted to a population of persons. This population idea allows the machinery of scientific probability to be applied. (p. 574)

Bloom, Fischer, and Orme (1995, pp. 337–338) suggest guidelines of at least three observations or sample points of times over a week or three baseline and follow-up points plus an additional observation for each 10% of variability (3 + 1 [highest rate – lowest rate / highest rate] n). The measurement or observation time points represent a sample of all possible measurement time points. They can be selected as a sample of convenience, another nonprobability sample, or by a random probability sampling strategy, probably a stratified random probability sam-

pling. Sampling theory and the need for generalizations guide the sampling protocol used. Samples of convenience and nonprobability samples, again, are limited in their capacity to generalize.

## Time Point Sampling

Time point sampling, according to Berlin and Marsh (1993) is used when "particular points of time are specified and the occurrence or nonoccurrence of a behavior at these points is recorded" (p. 109). The selection of time points can be done by stratified random sampling. The times are stratified into bands of days and times within the day of the most likely times for the events to occur, and disproportionate random sampling is done within each band. The most likely bands are oversampled and the least likely are under- or not at all sampled. If the event is abusive parent-child interaction, the bands are the days and times of day when the parent is most likely and least likely to abuse the child. Disproportionate random sampling is done within the bands, with the most likely times sampled more heavily.

## Time Interval Sampling

Time interval sampling is similar to time point sampling except that an interval of time is selected, such as 5 minutes, 10 minutes, or perhaps even an hour, rather than just a point in time. The time interval approach, like the time point approach, requires the observer to define the behaviors or events observed, recorded, and assessed. Then, at given intervals, the observer observes, records, and codes the client's behavior within the interval. Selection of times and time intervals used in client recordings of behaviors and events in client logs and diaries (client self-observation) is an application of time interval sampling unless continuous observation and recording are done. Intervals observed are selected by disproportionate random sampling time stratified by the most likely intervals for occurrence of the focal behaviors, as described above. Use simple random probability sampling only if you assume the events are equally distributed across time. A parent's child abuse behavior is not uniformly or even randomly distributed over all time points and intervals.

## Time Samples of Convenience

As a practitioner, stay alert to the limitations of time samples of convenience. A time sample of convenience is reliance on times most convenient and easiest to observe regardless of whether they are likely to contain the events. Visiting and observing a parent alleged to have abused a school-age child during times the child is in school because it is a convenient time for the social worker is unlikely to yield indicators of abuse. As we discussed the social worker Karen in earlier chapters, she must visit and observe Sharra, the mother, interacting with Trish, the child, in the morning and evening or other times they are together. These may be less convenient times for Karen, the social worker. Problems, limitations, and strengths of the different sampling strategies apply to time and event sampling within single case designs and case practice plans.

## Summary

Practitioners rarely use sampling strategies in selecting cases. Nevertheless, sampling has profound implications in practice, and knowledge of sampling theory improves practice proficiency. Practitioners observe or have clients or others report on observations of client behavior. Child protective service workers observe interactions between a parent and a child at a few times and then generalize whether the parent has an abusive relationship with the child. The times and interactions observed become a sample for the "population" of all the times the par-

ent and child interact. Systematic observations are used with the time sample to observe behavior of people within specific time periods or in response to specific situations.

Whenever a practitioner draws wider conclusions and makes generalizations from a limited number of cases, events, and times to cases as yet unserved or events and times unobserved, the practitioner has used a sample. Knowledge of sampling theory limits generalizations so the practitioner does not outrun the sample's limitations. Samples of cases, times, and events are likely to be samples of convenience with large and unknown sample error. Inferences and generalizations are always tentative.

Practitioners need knowledge about sample size and power that, coupled with design and causal validity knowledge, will allow them to better understand and use practice experience in developing and applying intervention theory. Conclusions about intervention effects are guided by sample power, size, and established causal validity. Increasing sample sizes, replicating the intervention with similar cases, will improve capacity to detect and defend small but real effect sizes. Cases can be compared on important traits to determine that they are part of the same sample frame. Practitioners can seek ways to improve a time and event sample's power by increasing its size or the number of observations and by using stratified probability sampling to select observation time units. Sample size for generalizations can be increased through replication and by using more powerful forms of nonprobability sampling, such as purposive samples.

In using the research and practice experience of others in development of case theories and more general theories, practitioners need to consider the research and practice generalizations, and theoretical propositions within limitations of the sample used. Were generalizations and propositions developed from a sample of units for a population of which the practitioner's case is a unit? What were the sample's characteristics? Was it a probability or a nonprobability sample?

Are there indicators that the sample potentially suffers from a high sample error? The sample error of concern is whether the research or practice experience of the sample represents the population of the current case. These considerations and questions are important to incorporate the research findings and practice experience into the case theory.

## Discussion Questions and Exercises

1. Use a random numbers table to select a sample of 50 units from a population of 500 units. What is the probability of each unit's selection? How many numbers were selected between 001 and 250 and 251 and 500? Record the numbers. Repeat the process by selecting another 50 numbers. Record the numbers. Is there a difference in the two distributions of numbers drawn between 001–250 and 251–500? What does this difference represent? (A sample without sample error will have 25 units in each stratum.) Now assume that 001–250 represents males and 251–500 represents females. Is any gender overrepresented?

   Now assume that 200 of the units have Z value on trait X and these units all fall within the numbers between 100 and 299. They constitute 40% of the population. What is their proportion in each of the two samples? *Was 40% of each sample composed of Z units with X traits? If not, what does this difference represent?* How might you improve the sample's precision to represent the population?

   Now assume that 50 units also have a y value on trait X. These units have numbers between 200 and 299 with every other number being one of this type of unit (200, 202, 204, etc.). They constitute 10% of the total population units and 25% of the X trait units. How many were in each sample? Were there the same number in each sample? Did they constitute 10% of the overall sample and 25% of the X trait units selected? What do any differences represent? Were the two samples on the y value for the X traits within 5% of the population's distribution (within 5% of 25% of the distribution of y values on the X trait and 10% of the total number of sample units)? How might you improve the sample's precision?

2. Take a group of any 50 real people and divide the group into two matched groups matching a person assigned to each of the groups with a matched partner in the other group on gender, age, and ethnicity. Remember, a person in one group must have an exact "double" in the other group on age (years), gender, and ethnic identification. How many "matched pairs" are there? Now add a fourth variable such as religious identification. Do the matches remain? Can you obtain matched pairs by collapsing categories? If so, what does this do to the comparability of the pairs?

3. Develop a sample frame for the most likely time intervals for observing the parent-child interaction to detect potential abuse between a mother and her 7-year-old son. The mother is suspected of child abuse. The mother works from 9:00 a.m. to 5:00 p.m. Tuesdays through Saturdays. What are the population units being sampled? What is the most appropriate sampling strategy? How long should a baseline (preintervention phase) be? What information do you need to guide the sampling strategy? How might you obtain this information?

# CHAPTER TWELVE

# Analyzing the Data: What Do You Know about the Success of the Practice Plan and How Do You Know You Know It?

Analysis in research or practice is judging the meaning of information collected. Practice assessment, reassessment, and practice evaluation make sense of the case by examining available information to determine whether or not it supports the theory, either case or general. Other than relying on pure intuition, analysis is necessary for case decision making. *Analysis uses the information collected from clients, subjects, or respondents to answer the research questions, affirm or reject the hypothesis, and determine the degree of change on variables of the case objectives.*

Analysis is a necessary part of the pre- and post-intervention assessment and follow-up to build or verify case theory and develop and test the intervention hypothesis. Analysis determines the degree that case objectives are achieved, whether case objective significance has been obtained, and the processes of evaluating any causal relationship between the inter-

vention and the objectives. Analysis is also necessary to determine an intervention's effectiveness. Specifying and limiting generalizations, inferences, induction, and deduction that reasonably can be made about the intervention's effectiveness and usefulness to a population of cases not yet served are only some of the relevant practice concerns requiring analysis.

The research design or practice plan guides the analytical approaches, models, and methodologies used in a particular case or research project. *The quality of the analysis is limited by the nature and availability of data yielded by sampling strategies and measurement and data collection processes.* Only actual available information is analyzed. "GIGO," or "garbage in—garbage out," defines analysis performed on shoddy information gathered by unreliable or spurious measurement and data collection processes. Shoddy data cannot accurately assess change, case objective significance,

Parallels of Practice and Research

| Practice Component and Tasks | Research Epistemologies and Methodologies |
|---|---|
| **Case evaluation** | **Analysis** |
| Impressions and judgments of indicators of client change and achievement of case objectives by interventions; | Analysis of information collected; ethnographic, nomothetic, and group data analytical models appropriate to case design; |
| case, process, case theory, and statistical significance; | charting and other visual analysis; descriptive and inferential statistical analysis; |
| informed consent and accountability | statistical significance |

or the intervention's contributions to changes and case objective significance. No sophisticated statistical analytical models will overcome prior errors in design, sampling, measurement, and data collection.

This chapter examines various analytical approaches and the transformation by content analysis of qualitative information into quantitative data. We devote particular attention to approaches in establishing significance and their relevance for case evaluation.

## General Approaches and Uses of Data Analysis in Practice

Analysis of data and information describes things, relationships between things, or relationships between traits of things. Analysis is *qualitative or quantitative.* Practitioners need to describe clients and relationships among many factors and to appraise connections of interventions to client behaviors and elements in clients' lives. The incidence rate of abusive behavior by child abusers can be described and related to variables such as socioeconomic classes, life stressors, drug use, or all of them. Changes in abuse incidence rates are related to differences in intervention types, duration, and intensity.

**Analysis** *is largely descriptive, even when describing the relationship among things.* Examining changes in levels of abusive behavior before and after intervention requires describing the pre- and postintervention levels. Inferring change as a function of intervention in analysis requires theory to guide the analysis and the implementation and control of an appropriate practice plan as well as analytical processes appropriate to the particular design used. Generalizing from case studies to other cases requires analytical models based on appropriate sampling strategies.

In *"natural* (i.e., *quasi)* experiments of practice," analysis is most often done, as Jayaratne and Levy (1979, p. 297) assert, by **"eyeballing"** or comparing the pre- and postintervention mea-

surements of the relevant outcome variables. Eyeballing includes visual examination of graphs, charts, and tables of the pre and post phases by levels of frequency, intensity, magnitude, duration, and comparing the pre- and postintervention measures to normative standards. Eyeballing is reinforced by using other analytical techniques, although the ability to make definitive inferences of causal validity and generalizability is limited in these "natural experiments."

Either qualitative or quantitative data analysis can describe things, but only quantitative measures or information can apply statistical analysis to make probabilistic inferences from a sample of cases to a larger population as yet unexamined. Regardless of the analytical model and tools, analysis is intended to describe variables, traits, conditions, and things, and relationships between variables, traits, conditions, and things.

## Types of Significance

Practitioners are fundamentally concerned with achieving case objectives and using interventions to that end. *Do not confuse achieving case objectives with statistical significance.* Significance comes in a variety of different forms. Statistical significance is only one and perhaps not the most relevant type of significance in social work practice. Statistical significance is not the same as the more practice-relevant and related forms of significance: case objective or clinical significance, process significance, and case theory significance. These are concerned with the actual changes in the case, the intervention, and the relationship between the intervention and change.

### Statistical Significance

Statistical significance is a probability expression arrived at by application of statistical models establishing a demonstrated relationship between or among variables that is unlikely to be a chance relationship at a given probability level. Statistical significance is a statistical test's results that a relationship between sets of numbers is unlikely to have occurred by chance, and a statistically significant relationship is probably a real relationship at the level of statistical significance applied. The relationships, however, are those between the numbers used in the test.

## Case Objective Significance

Case objective significance, often called clinical significance in direct practice, consists of quantitative and qualitative changes in case objective variables, in a planned direction, to a desired and meaningful level in the judgments of client, practitioner, and other stakeholders (Blythe & Tripodi, 1989, pp. 112–113).

> Action + intention + disposition (the change) = case objective significance

Case objective significance occurs when variables of an objective and their values move from unacceptable into acceptable ranges specified by the case plan's SMARRT objectives statement. Bloom, Fischer, and Orme (1996, pp. 484–485) refer to case objective significance as *practical significance*, reflecting the fact that change is meaningful and practical to the client and other stakeholders. Rubin and Babbie (1997) liken substantive significance to our concept of case objective significance. "By substantive significance of a relationship we mean its *importance* from a *practical standpoint*" (p. 518).

The somewhat clumsy label "case objective significance" is used here to cover the range of social work practice and cases, although all these labels connote essentially the same concept. Whether labeled clinical, practice, substantive, practical, or case objective significance, determining this effect generally involves comparing achievements against the preset normative standards specified in the case's SMARRT objectives. Jayaratne (1990) adds to the conception of clinical significance, or case objective significance by our labeling, a case theory relevance: "Clinical significance is the perception of an important change in an attribute or behavior in oneself or another as the result of treatment" (p. 273). The change is intended and the result of intervention; it is not a random change, changes in other than intended directions, or changes primarily resulting from causes other than the intervention. Good things should be assessed regardless of the source of change. Regardless of statistical significance, however, *the "good things" that happen to the client or case do not constitute case objective significance unless they are the good things that were intended to happen to the client.*

Case objective significance and statistical significance are separate concepts, arrived at separately and achievable independently of each other. Do not assume, as Tripodi (1994, p. 128) does, that "if there are statistically significant differences in the direction of reducing the problem, then the social worker has met the basic criteria [for significance]." The bottom line for case evaluation is case objective significance.

## Process Significance

Process significance is an analytical determination of contributions by the intervention *processes* to case objective and clinical significance outcomes. Process significance supports predictions by the case theory that the intervention will effect the case's SMARRT objectives. Process significance means that the model and "expectations of treatment are congruent with activities that occur within the context of treatment" (Jayaratne, 1990, p. 275). *Process significance and case objective significance are not required for statistical significance, nor is statistical significance necessary for process and case objective significance.*

## Case Theory Significance

When there is both case objective and process significance, there is case theory significance, or as Bloom, Fischer, and Orme (1995) label it, **theoretical significance.**

> Process significance + case objective significance = case theory significance

Case theory or theoretical significance is the perception established by the analysis that achieving the case's SMARRT objectives is a result, at least in part, of the intervention. There is support for the case theory's intervention hypothesis that the intervention will cause or contribute to significant change in case objectives. We label it case theory significance because when it is established, it supports the case theory. It requires determining the intervention's effect size, or strength of effect of a given intervention on outcomes.

## Effect Size and Significance

Effect size, simply put, is how much the intervention effects outcome or dependent variables. Effect sizes of group comparison research designs are differences between group scores on the dependent variables after the treatment group receives treatment.

> Effect size in group comparison designs = (treatment group mean − contrast group mean)/contrast group standard deviation)

It is determined by comparing group performance of contrast and treatment groups. With group comparison designs, statistical significance is affected by size of group differences and sizes of the groups (see the discussion under sample power on p. 182).

While single case designs and most practice plans lack comparison groups for isolating the intervention's strength of association with changes in outcome or dependent variables, an approximation of effect size are measurement differences between the baseline phase and the postintervention follow-up phase in the dependent or outcome variable.

> Single case design effect size = (follow-up mean score − baseline mean score)/(baseline score standard deviation)

Because of this inherent design weakness, any causal effect attributed to an intervention-based single case experience is highly tenuous.

## Significance and Practice

All four types of significance are relevant to practice, but they are not equally important. *Process, case objective, and case theory significance take precedence and are necessary prerequisites in practice to computing statistical significance.* Whether sets of measurements have statistically significant relationships and differences is less important than establishing whether outcomes are clinically or case objective significant, the intervention is process significant, and the relationship between the intervention and outcomes is case theory significant. **Case objective significance is primary.**

Our position is that statistical analysis and use of statistical significance are useful in making case objective significant judgments, but they do not constitute case objective significance, and are only limited factors in the judgment. An outcome has significance for practice if it is the *intended*

Practice Importance Ranking of Forms of Significance

| Type of Significance | Processes |
| --- | --- |
| 1. Case objective (most important) | Measurement of actual outcome levels compared to projected levels and preintervention levels |
| 2. Process | Measurement of actual intervention processes used compared to the case plan model |
| 3. Case theory | Inferred causal relation of process significance to case objective significance |
| 4. Statistical (least important) | Application of statistical tests and models to measurements |

outcome. The level of statistical significance is inconsequential if intervention results and outcomes are trivial. Results, relationships, and differences can be statistically significant and practically and clinically inconsequential. *Statistical significance does not replace practice judgments, rather practice judgments and case objectives guide any use and interpretation of statistical significance.* Statistical significance can corroborate, complement, or challenge a practice judgment, but it does not become that judgment.

Measurements, the information used in analysis and judgments, are as critical in process and case objective significance determination as in statistical significance. Relevance of the numbers depends on: how these numbers were obtained, and on how data collection, the practice plan, and case theory guided the practice plan and measurement.

## Relevance and Relationship of the Establishment of Four Significance Types in Practice[a]

| Case Objective | Process | Case Theory | Statistical | Practice Relevance Rank |
|---|---|---|---|---|
| Yes | Yes | Yes | Yes | 1 |
| Yes | Yes | Yes | No | 2 |
| Yes | No | NA | Yes | 3 |
| Yes | No | NA | No | 4 |
| No | Yes | NA | Yes | 5 |
| No | Yes | NA | No | 6 |
| No | No | NA | Yes | 7 |
| No | No | NA | No | 8 |

[a]*Yes* or *no* indicates whether or not significance form established. NA indicates that case theory cannot be established.

1. This ranking indicates the optimal practice relevant situation with all areas significant: achievement of SMARRT objectives, intervention adheres to the case plan's intervention model and effects outcomes in the manner predicted by case theory, with relationships between baseline and follow-up measures at a low chance probability level.

2. A less optimal but still very desirable and relevant practice outcome is case objective and process significance, indicating case theory significance. However, the postintervention achievement and change, compared to baseline measurements, does not meet conventional 0.01 or 0.05 levels for statistical significance. Nevertheless, the outcomes are meaningful.

3. A desirable level of change on the case objectives is obtained, so the results have case objective significance. As determined by pre- and postintervention measures, outcomes are statistically significant at conventional probability levels. Process significance is not determined because the intervention model is not followed or the intervention was not adequately monitored and measured. This failure occurs when intervention is characterized by drift, lack of monitored shifts, or lack of any model or discipline. Without both case objective and process significance, you cannot establish case theory significance or relate changes on outcome variables to the intervention. Case theory significance is only possible with the presence of both case objective and process significance.

4. A desirable level of change on outcomes and objectives is obtained, indicating case objective significance. The intervention is not adequately monitored or measured, eliminating establishment of process and case theory significance. Statistical significance is also lacking at conventional levels for pre- and postoutcome variable differences.

Rows 5 through 8 in the table are not practice relevant because they reveal a lack of case objective significance, although rows 5 through 7 indicate either process or statistical significance. Rows 5 and 7 demonstrate that statistical significance is possible without case objective significance. Row 5 occurs when a practitioner adheres to a practice model and has measurements on outcomes across many cases or many time points for a single case, although changes are trivial and not at the case objective significant level. *Outcomes in row 5 are not meaningful to the case stakeholders.* Row 6 exemplifies that a practitioner is adhering to a specified practice model without achieving case objective significance or statistical significance on any changes. *Slavish and dogmatic adherence to a specified practice model when the model does not produce any meaningful change, or when a practitioner does not assess change, is intervention for the sake of intervening or for the sake of the practitioner, not the case. Adherence to ineffectual practice models is not practice relevant.* Rows 5 and 6 characterize the lackadaisical practitioner who engages in rote interventions and follows bureaucratic routine or ideological preferences without regard to effects on the case.

Statistical significance can be found, as in row 7, with trivial case results but with a large number of cases or measurements with trivial effect size in the postintervention phases. The intervention is not monitored.

## Professional Values and Significance

Professional values have a meaningful role in establishing case objective and process significance. Values direct the definitions of problems and constrain the definitions and acceptability of outcomes and their levels as well as selection of interventions. Values are involved in cost-benefit studies in the use of monetary values, specifications of costs, and valuations or assignment of weights to benefits. *Values are also reflected in determining case objective, process, and theory significance.* Values, however, are not a factor in determining statistical significance.

## Data Coding

Data coding is the "process of taking data from data collection instruments and putting it into a form that can be digested by a computer. Coding translates a verbal or written response into a nu-

merical value" (Royce, 1991, p. 175), and is done through content analysis of qualitative descriptive narratives or by "precoded" measurements with numbers already assigned to response values. Assigning numerical values to a unit's variables and values allows for statistical description and analysis of units and variables, along with direct comparisons of variables across units, and of units and variables across time. Quantitative data allow more direct determination of change than do qualitative data. Numbers are basically concerned with relationships when they are used in other than a nominal manner. Numerical information, whether the numbers represent nominal, ordinal, interval, or ratio measures, can be analyzed by statistical tests applied through software computer programs. Coding, then, is the process of transforming impressions and information of measurement processes, whether collected in qualitative or quantitative forms, into analyzable information.

## Codes, Code Books, and Coding

Statistical analysis, whether it is done manually or by computer, requires developing codes and a code book. Codes are numbers standing for labels and values of things, the unit of analysis and its traits; they reflect variation and range. Number assignment is by a content analysis process for qualitative information or by precoded instruments and measures with codes determined prior to data collection. The code book guides the coding of the variables and explains the codes and their subsequent interpretation. Develop the codebook as soon as you know the characteristics of the variables.

The logic and format structure of coding for computer data entry is based on the now-antiquated IBM cards, 10 rows and up to 80 columns. Each row represented a single digit (numeric) or letter (alpha). If a digit, the first row was 1 and the last row was 0. The combination of rows and columns represented the unit and variable, and value of the unit or variable. Currently, data entry is directly into the computer software files, allowing full-screen editing of files. The

Code Book Format

| Column Number | Item Description | Codes[a] |
|---|---|---|
| 1–3 | File identification number | Enter file identification number from 001 to 999 |
| 4 | Gender | Male = 1<br>Female = 2 |
| 5 | Ethnicity | African Amer. = 1<br>Asian Amer. = 2<br>White = 3<br>Other = 4 |
| 6–7 | Age | Enter age in years |

Columns 1 ......................... / / / ...................... 80

| 1 | 2 | 3 | 4 | 5 | 6 | 7 | 8 | ... | 80 |
|---|---|---|---|---|---|---|---|---|---|
|   |   |   |   |   |   |   |   |   |   |

[a]Enter 0 for missing data.

computer monitor and direct entry does away with the card's rows, and each row on the monitor serves the same function as a card.

## Protocols for Coding and Code Book Construction

1. Assign a file identification number, a nominal code, to the case. This is usually the case identification number. Identification numbers range from 1 to the number corresponding to the total number of cases. All identification numbers as nominal codes must be mutually exclusive. Two cases cannot have the same identifier. If there are 200 cases, 200 distinct identifiers are required. Although any unique identifiers are acceptable, a simple sequential assignment of identifiers from 001 to 200 will prevent confusion. Consider that one of 200 cases is a 27 year old white female—you will require three columns for the identifiers. Cases with identifiers

below 100 will have 0s preceding the case number, such as 001, 099 so that all columns assigned are used. The case is case 1, the identifier is 001, and 001 is entered in the first 3 columns.

| 1 | 2 | 3 | 4 | 5 | 6 | 7 | 8 | ... | 80 |
|---|---|---|---|---|---|---|---|---|---|
| 0 | 0 | 1 |   |   |   |   |   |   |   |

2. Determine the number of columns required for each variable based on the variable's possible range of variation. If the variable has less than 10 variation points, assign one column. If it has 10 to 99, then assign two columns. A column must be assigned for each additional 9 points of variation. (If there are more than 9 variations, assign 2 columns; if more than 99, three columns; if more than 999 variations, four columns, etc.) The numbers or codes represent the variation point values.

3. The columns used for each variable must be mutually exclusive. Two variables cannot share the same columns. Values must also be mutually exclusive and represent the value's underlying numeric system.

4. When a variable requires multiple columns to reflect all the variation for different units, the implicit decimal point lies to the right of the farthest righthand column assigned to the variable. A value of 9 for a variable that possibly has values ranging between 1 and 300 is coded as 009, as indicated in the discussion with the identifier. Always enter a digit in every column assigned to the variable for the unit.

Case 1 is a white, 27-year-old female. The value variations for gender and ethnicity are less than 10, so only one column is required for the codes. Age can logically vary by more than nine years and will require two columns. It is unlikely that it will vary in the caseload by more than 99 years to require three columns. Case 1's information is coded and entered as:

| 1 | 2 | 3 | 4 | 5 | 6 | 7 | 8 | ... | 80 |
|---|---|---|---|---|---|---|---|---|---|
| 0 | 0 | 1 | 2 | 3 | 2 | 7 |   |   |   |

5. Use a consistent number, such as 0 or 9, for missing data. "Missing data" can be any unusable data. The code used is one that will not be frequently used for real values. This will reduce coding errors and hence subsequent analysis errors. Remember, the codes entered for the data now represent the data for subsequent analysis. If the data are erroneously coded and entered, the analysis will be erroneous.

This code book uses "0" for missing data because 0 age, gender, ethnicity is not possible as an existing value. The use of 0 then logically connotes a missing value. If for some reason ethnicity was not recorded for case 1, the codes will be:

| 1 | 2 | 3 | 4 | 5 | 6 | 7 | 8 | ... | 80 |
|---|---|---|---|---|---|---|---|-----|-----|
| 0 | 0 | 1 | 2 | 0 | 2 | 7 |   |     |     |

6. Precoded instruments with direct computer entry by respondents reduce potential coding and data entry errors. Consistency in codes reduces transferring errors. For example, if gender is coded as males = 1 and females = 2, be consistent in all codings of gender. Do not code males as 2s and females as 1s in a subsequent coding.

7. Verify or "clean" the coding's data entry by random sample data entries and compare the codes entered to the code book and original data source, such as the original questionnaire or case record. If you detect errors, determine the source of error because it may be a consistent error made across cases, coding, and data entry. Recode and reenter the data for the case and repeat the process of checking for other randomly selected cases. There are other ways to check and clean the data, such as dual entry of the data and comparing entries for the case. However, the method described is probably the simplest, most practical, efficient, and easy.

## Content Analysis

Content analysis transforms qualitative narratives into quantitative data and is used with qualitative information gathered by observations and interviews in natural settings such as practice situations. Qualitative methods are information-gathering methods that are not highly structured with predetermined response categories or that rely on standardized measurement instruments and approaches (Tutty, Rothery, & Grinnell, 1996, p. v). Use content analysis with virtually any form of narrative information: case records, client diaries and logs, interviews, and observations recorded as narratives. It is particularly well suited to social work practice observations and communications dealing with questions of "Who said what to whom, why, how, and with what effect?" (Rubin & Babbie, 1997, p. 422)

While not all content analysis needs reduction of information into numbers, a fundamental aim for translating qualitative narratives into quantitative data is to allow for more direct comparisons, use of descriptive statistics, and possibly application of statistical tests for comparisons of normative or postintervention and preintervention measurements. Content analysis transforms qualitative data into quantitative data (numbers) to determine and describe relationships between things to enhance our understanding of their meaning. Content analysis is a deconstruction-construction process—finding out how the variables and their values fit together in the minds of the case as well as the meanings, interpretations, and explanations.

## Content Analysis Protocol

While there are obvious differences between the information collection methods of observations and interviews, and case logs and client diaries, the protocols of content analysis follow similar and related steps (Alter & Evens, 1990, p. 124; Tripodi, 1994, p. 51). Observations and interviews, whether done separately or together, are recorded in some narrative format for content analysis.

1. *Specify the research or practice questions and variables for examination.*

Select concepts of interest and clearly define ideas and their referents or indicators. In practice, these questions concern information needed to understand the case, complete the assessment, develop case theory, understand the case's ecology, and determine the various forms of significance discussed earlier. Basically, as with data collection, the information relates to the *what, who, when,* and *how* questions.

2. *Define the unit of analysis (the case, or* who).

Both the individual case boundaries and ecology need definition and assessment.

3. *Determine the most appropriate and available sources of data to answer the questions or examine relationships.*

Relevant information sources are determined by protocol 1; where is and who has the information to answer the questions. Information sources can include available data sources, such as case records, clients, case stake holders, and other key informants. See Chapter 7 for possible information sources.

4. *Specify and secure the data and information.*

Recording and subsequent content analysis, whether research or practice, begins with the first encounters, because their analysis will guide and shape subsequent observations. Harkening back to Rubin and Babbie's (1997, p. 422), "Who said what to whom, why, how, and with what effect?" we can see that in any given case observation and interviews, both recording and subsequent analysis include who was present, where, at what time, and under what circumstances. People behave differently in different contexts. Understanding the meaning of content requires understanding context.[1]

5. *Determine authenticity and trustworthiness of data sources, documents, and narratives as valid*

*data sources for answering the research or practice question.*

Authenticity and trustworthiness refers to reliability and validity of the measurement and data collection processes for the narrative material (Lincoln & Guba, 1985, pp. 289–331). Lincoln and Guba (p. 290) list four components: (a) "Truth value," or confidence in the narrative's truth. This component is similar to measurement validity. (b) "Applicability," or extent to which a particular finding will have applicability to other contexts. Applicability is similar to external validity. (c) "Consistency," or whether we would get the same information if the inquiry were replicated with the same or similar cases. Consistency is the reliability of measurement and data collection processes. (d) "Neutrality," or whether the information reflects the information sources or biases, ideology, and motivations of the narrative's author. Neutrality refers to the information's objectivity. If the processes used to collect and record information for subsequent content analysis are not reliable and valid, rigorous content analysis will not yield valid information. The GI-GO principle is operating.

6. *Operationally define the analytical categories (words, ideas, themes) relevant to the research or practice questions).*

Analytical categories range from words to ideas. Content of the narrative is analyzed by word, phrase, or ideas. Categories are mutually exclusive and sufficiently precise to allow discrimination. Examine content to discover patterns that best describe relationships between variables better than alternative and rival explanations. If no single explanation best elucidates variables and their relationships, develop multiple explanations with special attention to negative cases that do not fit the pattern. Examine patterned variables prior to, during, and after intervention for pattern changes. Chart or map patterns in ecograms, maps, or matrices. Content analysis transforms narrative descriptions (words, phrases, or themes), into summary

---

[1]See the discussion of context under "Observation" in Chapter 7.

ideas and quantified symbols, (numbers) for statistical analysis. If different levels of data are available, often they are used to triangulate qualitative analysis.

7. *Determine reliability and validity of the analytical categories used.*

Content analysis can be a rich source of information, but there are significant issues of reliability and validity. *Reliability and validity in content analysis involve consistency in coding and analysis.* Consistency is established and improved by repeated independent coding and analysis of the narrative's content according to the analytical categories established in response to protocol 6 by the same analyst and by different analysis. Reliability increases when the analytical categories used are limited to words, but potential validity declines. Consistency is more difficult to obtain when the analysis uses ideas and themes.

For example, a client responded to open-ended questions requesting a narrative of the client's self-perceived well-being prior to, at different points in, and after treatment. Self-perception of well-being is a subjective condition. The client's interview narrative is analyzed to determine any changes in the client's self-perception of well-being. Accordingly, understanding the client's meaning of well-being is essential. Meaning cannot be determined by merely counting the number of times the client uses words like "feel good" as indicators of well-being. The client can say "I feel good," "I don't feel good," "I'd like to feel good," or "It's been a long time since I've felt good." If the content analysis is based on word counting of the number of variants of "feel good" statements during the pre- and postintervention phases, the scores are consistent after repeated countings—without any valid determination of changes in the client's self-perception of well-being. The meanings of the statements "I feel good," "I don't feel good," "I'd like to feel good," and "It's been a long time since I've felt good" are quite different.

## Validity

For *construct validity* examine categories of words, phases, and ideas that appear to be indicators of what is wanted for measurement and analysis. Do the "thematic" categories examined agree and capture the meaning intended? The intent is to determine whether the client's self-perception of well-being has changed, not the number of times certain words appear in the narrative. We are concerned here for the meaning of the construction of the coding scheme rather than its application. Agreement between client and users that "these are the indicators of well-being" is the **thematic validity.** Agreement that "this content indicates the existence of the indicator, whether or not the indicator is an indicator of well-being" is **reliability.**

**Content analysis** *of practice narratives is enhanced by formal or informal member checking— "checking with" or presenting the analysis, conclusions, and interpretations to original information providers to determine if it reflects their intended meaning.* Member checking provides feedback opportunities for correcting possible erroneous interpretations (Lincoln & Guba, 1985, pp. 314–315). As Lincoln and Guba explain, "Member checking is directed at a judgment of overall credibility" (pp. 315–316). Member checking in analysis addresses the validity of the presentation of the data's meaning.

## Reliability

Training and independent replication of analysis is required to achieve reliability with ideas and themes. Once consistency is established, ideas and themes are more likely to reflect meaning than is analysis limited to word countings. When multiple independent raters code and achieve the same results, **intercoder reproducibility** similar to independent test-retest is achieved. **Stability** is the extent that results of coding are the same over time when the same person recodes the same narrative. Coding reliability is achieved by reviewing and revising the categories and repeated training until suitable intercoder reproducibility and stability is established.

8. *After information is collected and the narrative is available, code and check coding for reliability, tabulate, and record and enter the data for analysis.*

The protocol involves operational coding of the information to transform qualitative narrative information into quantitative data categories. This is the encoding process. Samples taken from long narratives, if used for efficiency, need to adhere to appropriate sampling methodologies for generalizations. A simple random probability sampling, or stratified probability sampling protocol, can be used to select entries from all case record entries. This requires that all entries are known and available for sampling if the analysis is to represent the entire case. The sample is a simple random sample of narrative entries as sources of information on some variable, trait, or descriptor of the unit of analysis and not a random sample of the units of analysis. Case narrative sampling also can use a stratified sampling strategy based on important case events and phases.

9. *Apply appropriate statistical analysis for determination of relevant significance.*

The narratives now are transformed into quantitative data, and you can subject them to a variety of statistical analyses for determining case objective, process, case theory, and statistical significance. They can be plotted as graphs, charts, and tables for visual analysis and used in statistical models for statistical analysis.

10. *Compare the findings against normative standards.*

Once the data are transformed into quantitative indicators, you can compare with normative standards. These are the standards set forth in the case plan's case objective, process, or case theory significance. You can compare baseline, outcomes, and social standards to discover if the case falls within the normative ranges for a comparison population.

11. *Present the analysis to the relevant audiences.*

Presenting the analysis to relevant audiences is vital. Audiences vary. The most common audiences of stakeholders at the individual case level include clients and relevant others in clients' primary support systems, employing agencies, funding sources and client sponsors, and policy and community decision-makers. Tertiary stakeholders with a potential interest in the analysis include other social work practitioners who deal with similar case problems, social work theoreticians and researchers, and potential clients. Reporting is covered more completely in the following chapter.

## Descriptive Analysis

Descriptive analysis portrays the characteristics of things such as cases, clients, samples, or populations of units. In *qualitative analysis*, the descriptions are in words. The words can subsequently be transformed into quantitative descriptors by content analysis protocols. Qualitative analysis can provide richer, more vivid and lively descriptions of variables and patterns between variables that are often more engaging to a lay audience than are quantitative descriptions. However, qualitative descriptors often have suspect precision.

*Quantitative analysis* describes numerically in ordinal, equal interval, or ratio terms. Quantitative measures can describe clients by physical and social characteristics such as income, network characteristics (density and number of relationships), and eco-gram characteristics (types and strengths of relationships). Quantitative and number descriptors are called *statistics* if they describe a sample and *parameters* if they describe a population. Quantitative descriptions often sacrifice richness for specificity. They reduce the array of data into a succinct summary portrait of the information. Quantitative descriptors can portray the case, sample, or population and its traits and variables by averages and central tendencies such as mean, median, and mode, range of values, and the dispersion and shape of the distribution of measures such as average deviation, standard deviation, frequency distribution or frequencies within value categories.

- **Mean:** the average score in the distribution of scores, arrived at by totaling all scores and dividing by the number of scores in the distribution.
- **Median:** the middle point in the distribution of scores, where 50% of a set of scores lie above it and 50% lie below it.
- **Mode:** the most frequent score in the distribution of scores.

Although quantitative descriptors tend to be more precise than qualitative descriptors, the process can be fraudulent. For example, of the central tendency descriptors of mean, median, and mode, *only the mode needs to exist empirically.* The mean and median embody mathematical relationships between values rather than concrete empirical entities. For example, a group of people have the following annual incomes.

| Person | Income |
|--------|--------|
| 1 | $7,000 |
| 2 | $7,000 |
| 3 | $7,000 |
| 4 | $7,000 |
| 5 | $7,000 |
| 6 | $15,000 |
| 7 | $15,000 |
| 8 | $18,000 |
| 9 | $20,000 |
| 10 | $1,000,000 |

The $7000 annual income occurs most frequently and is the *modal* income. Empirically, 50% of the group's members have this poverty-level income. The *median* income, the point in the income distribution at which half of the group members' income falls below and half falls above is between $7000 and $15,000. If we assume a midpoint between these numbers as the median—although the midpoint does not constitute a "real limit" between the numbers, as assumed with continuous numbers such as 7 goes to 7.5 and 8 from 7.51 to 8.5—the midpoint is $11,000, which is empirically a nonexisting income. Any report of the group's "average" income using the median income rather than a modal presents a far more affluent group. *Medians are influenced by range and distribution. Modes indicate distributions.*

Additionally, use of the group's mean income as the average income portrays a distorted picture of the group's income. Mean annual income for the group is $110,300. The mean as an average exceeds 9 of the 10 group members' combined annual income, and it is also not empirical. The mean is greatly influenced by the skew and extreme distribution scores. This is why most Americans suffered a real income decline over the past decade while the per capita income, the mean income, increased. The *average* income of Americans increased while most got poorer.

## Grouped Data

Quantitative descriptors of central tendency and dispersion lose precision and specificity when ordinal, equal interval, and ratio data are grouped to compute descriptors rather than computing from raw or disaggregated data. Grouped data are usually grouped into categories for ease of data handling and management. Grouped data are commonly used with measurements such as age and income in frequency distributions.

| Income | Age | Height |
|--------|-----|--------|
| $000–$1000 | Under 21 yrs. | Under 48 in. |
| $1001–$2000 | 21–25 yrs. | 48.1 to 60 in. |

| Income | Age | Height |
|--------|-----|--------|
| $2001–$3000 | 26–30 yrs. | 60.1 to 72 in. |
| etc. | etc. | etc. |

Precision is lost for any case falling within each band and for comparing cases that fall within or between bands. A case between $1001–$2000 can fall at any point within this range. For a case with income of $2000, it is closer to a case with $2001. This is a different band with a different value than a case with $1001, yet that is the band where it is placed.

Grouped data are appropriate with a large numbers of cases and measurements with a fairly even distribution within the categories. With the advent of computers for data storage and analysis, it is generally better to collect and keep information as disaggregated as possible, as long as possible, to maintain detail. As we discussed in data collection, you can always disaggregate data in a variety of ways to satisfy a range of analytical needs. Once you lose disaggregation you cannot regain it.

## Which Descriptors

Questions for determining appropriate descriptors are:

1. **What descriptive statistics are most appropriate to describe the phenomenon?** Appropriateness relates to the description's intent and the statistics' ability to capture that intent. If intent for the earlier 10-person groups is to describe the income distribution, then the range, average deviation, and modes are preferable to simply using the range and mean. If deception is an intent—it is never an ethical practice intent—then the use of the mean will admirably deceive.

2. **Which descriptors help to clarify this unit of analysis, case and client?**

3. **Are the descriptors discrete or continuous?** If continuous descriptors are used, the description implicitly relies on measurements that are ordinal or above.

4. **What is their measurement level?** Descriptive narratives, descriptions, and content often can be coded and analyzed quantitatively if the description are, at the least, ordinal, describing frequency, duration, magnitude, or intensity.

## Visual Analysis

The most basic and often most dramatic analysis is visual, using time series graphs, bar graphs, pie charts, charts, tables, and other visual models. **Time series graphic analysis** critical to determining change entails plotting values of a variable, such as a dependent variable reflecting a case's SMARRT objective, at designated times points prior to, during, and after intervention. Plotted over time points, graphic analysis allows a relatively easy way to visually analyze any changes on the variables over time. If desired case objective significance levels are also plotted on the vertical axis for the horizontal axis's time points, a chart provides a visual comparison of actual changes over time with desired case significance levels. Qualitative data's transformation into quantitative data is necessary if data are presented in graphs or tables.

Figures 12.1 and 12.2 indicate change with introduction of the intervention and during follow-up. The plot line moves into the case objective significance range in both charts. Figures 12.3 and 12.4 reveal that the intervention has no discernable effects. The actual values do not fall into the case objective significance range during or after the intervention, nor do the plottings reveal any relevant pattern.

### Protocols for plotting time series charts

1. **Define the units of change for the case's SMARRT objectives or other indicators.** Plot the measurement indicators of changes in magnitude, frequency, or intensity on the vertical axis. The unit of change used should be relevant to case objective significance.

2. **Determine the relevant time points for the case that will best reflect change.** The relevant time points can be in minutes, hours, days,

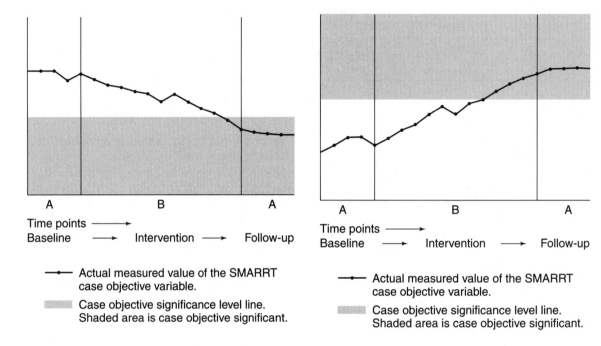

**FIGURE 12.1** Declining SMARRT case objective variable value in case objective significance zone during the intervention phase (B) and remaining during the follow-up phase (A)

**FIGURE 12.2** Accelerating SMARRT case objective variable value in case objective significance zone during the intervention phase (B) and remaining during the follow-up phase (A)

weeks, or other time units that have sufficient sensitivity and precision to capture the meaning of changes without being spurious or presenting a false picture. Plot time units on the horizontal axis. Indicate the time length of the baseline (A), intervention (B), and follow-up (A) phases on the graph's horizontal axis.

3. **Determine and plot the case objective significance zone.** This will require determining if changes achieve case objective significance through an increase or decrease in value. Plot the significance for each time point indicated on the horizontal axis. Connect the plotting to determine if case objective significant change is a decelerating ($\downarrow$) timeline, an accelerating ($\uparrow$) timeline, a constant ($\rightarrow$) timeline, or some other timeline pattern.

4. **Plot the case objective variable's measured values corresponding to the vertical axis above the relevant horizontal axis time points.** Measurement entries reflect the relevant time points during the baseline, intervention, and follow-up phases. Meaningful proceduralized intervention activity and other significant events or occurrences for the case are plotted on the case objective chart or overlay, on another chart, or in an accompanying narrative.

5. **Describe the case objective variables' patterns during the preintervention, intervention, and follow-up phases and compare this trend line to the case significance zone.** The trendline can be decelerating, accelerating, constant and unchanging, or erratic. Assess if trendline is in the desired and predicted direction during in-

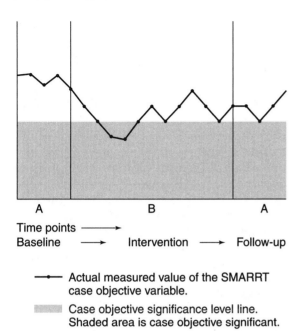

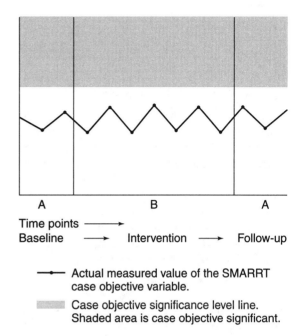

**FIGURE 12.3** Erratic SMARRT case objective variable value not remaining in case objective significance zone during the intervention phase (B) or the follow-up phase (A)

**FIGURE 12.4** Stable SMARRT case objective variable value not entering case objective significance zone during the intervention phase (B) or the follow-up phase (A)

tervention and follow-up phases. Is it at, within, or outside the case significance zone? Rubin and Babbie (1997, p. 333) call this determination of case objective significance **visual significance.** Determine visual significance "not through the use of fancy statistics, but by merely 'eyeballing' the data patterns" (p. 333) of the dependent or case objective variables.

7. **Compare and describe plotting patterns of the dependent or case objective variables with the significant intervention activity as proceduralized and other significant events or occurrences.** Was process significance indicated? It moves toward case theory significance when process significance accompanies case objective significance.

Time series graphs are appropriate for comparing the relationship between changes in any two ordinally measured variables over time, such as a youth's self-esteem level by the *Coopersmith Self-Esteem Inventory* (Coopersmith, 1959; Gurney, 1988) and frequency of drug use, or comparing measures on two self-esteem scales for concurrent validity. Indicate measurement units on the vertical axis. If the intent is visual analysis, however, graphs and charts should not be so busy that they lose visual clarity.

## Contingency and Frequency Tables

Contingency and frequency tables, like graphs, provide visual presentation and description of the information. Contingency tables can provide *univariate* (one variable) and *bivariate* (two variables) description and *multivariate* (many variables) description and analysis of relationships among multiple variables.

### Univariate contingency tables

A univariate table provides a frequency distribution of values for a variable across many units or the distribution or frequency of a behavior occurring across time for a single case. The value categories used should best distribute visually the variable's values across the units to make the units on this variable understandable. You can always use descriptive statistical analysis such as central tendency and frequency distributions with univariate contingency tables.

### Bivariate contingency tables

The bivariate contingency table presents the relationship between two variables across a number of cases or observations. Any two variables or things, including the intervention and case objectives, can be compared by frequency, intensity, duration, and magnitude if the variables' traits are quantifiably measured. The labels and value categories for the two variables and their values comprise the top row and the left column. The distribution of the units according to the values on the two variables fills the remaining cells. As with univariate tables, the value categories and the number of categories used are those that best visually present the relationship distribution of values across the units to make the relationship of the variables for the units understandable.

Parametric and nonparametric statistical models can be used with bivariate contingency tables depending on the nature of the sample, relationships of variables, level of the measurement system used, and distributions of variables in a population and sample. Bivariate contingency tables are used with any measurement level, nominal through ratio. Two nominal-level variables can be compared if numbers in the cells represent the number of cases that fall within that combination on variable values.

### Protocols for constructing bivariate contingency tables

1. Determine the two variables for comparison.
2. Code each variable's distribution of values into intervals that will best describe the variable conceptually to capture its empirical distribution. An examination of each variable's value frequency distribution aids in this task.
3. Determine the value and code of each unit of each variable.

Relationship of Frequency of Client's Aggressive Physical Behavior to Time Bands

Distribution of an Agency's Clients by Age

| Variable Descriptor Code Values (such as age bands or categories) | Distribution of the Units, Clients, with the Category's Value |
| --- | --- |
| Clients under 35 | 20% |
| 36–45 | 30% |
| 46–55 | 30% |
| 56 and over | 20% |
| Missing data | –0– |

| Time Units | Distribution of Units of Aggressive Behavior by Time Units |
| --- | --- |
| 6:01–9:00 a.m. | |
| 9:01–12:00 a.m. | |
| 12:01–3:00 p.m. | |
| 3:01–6:00 p.m. | |
| 6:01–9:00 p.m. | |
| 9:01–12:00 p.m. | |
| 12:01–6:00 a.m. | |

Contingency Table for Bivariate Analysis of Two Variables with Variable:
Self-Esteem Scale Scores and Frequency of Drug Use

|  | *High Frequency of Drug Use* | *Medium Frequency of Drug Use* | *Low Frequency of Drug Use* |
|---|---|---|---|
| High self-esteem scale scores | Number and/or % of cases high on both variables (1) | Number and/or % of cases with high self-esteem scores and medium drug use frequency (4) | Number and/or % of cases with high self-esteem scores and low drug use frequency (7) |
| Medium self-esteem scale scores | Number and/or % of cases with medium self-esteem scores and high drug use frequency (2) | Number and/or % of cases with medium on both variables (5) | Number and/or % of cases with medium self-esteem scores and low frequency of drug use (8) |
| Low self-esteem scale scores | Number and/or % of cases with low self-esteem scores and high drug use frequency (3) | Number and/or % of cases with low self-esteem scores and medium drug use frequency (6) | Number and/or % of cases low on both variables (9) |

4. Determine vertical or horizontal axis placement of two variable labels that will present the best visual description of their relationship.
5. Place the unit in the contingency table's cell corresponding to each variable's value.

Bivariate Contingency Table by Ethnicity and Gender (Nominal Variables and Ratio Measures)

|  | *Gender* | |
|---|---|---|
| *Ethnicity* | *Males* | *Females* |
| African American | Number of Males for Each Ethnic Label | Number of Females for Each Ethnic Label |
| Asian American | | |
| American Indian | | |
| Hispanic | | |
| White, not Hispanic | | |
| Other | | |
| Missing data | | |

## Multivariate contingency tables

Multivariate contingency tables are used to isolate, analyze, and visually present the relationship between two or more variables while holding a third variable constant. Examples include comparing age and severity of depression while holding gender constant, or demonstrating the relationship and interactions of three or more variables, such as age, severity of depression, and socioeconomic status. Protocols for constructing multivariate tables are similar to the bivariate contingency table construction protocols.

### Protocols for constructing multivariate contingency tables

1. Determine the variables and relationships for comparison. Which variable(s) is to be "nested" or placed within another other variable? Is age to be placed within severity of depression while holding gender constant, or will you rotate the variables? While a multivariate contingency table conceptually can include a great many variables, including too many variables makes the table busy and confused. These decisions are important because the presentation is visual.

Contingency Table of Ethnicity by Gender and Severity of Depression (Nominal Variable Compared to Nominal and Ordinal Variables)

| | Gender | | | | | |
| *Ethnicity* | *Males* | | | *Females* | | |
| | Severity of depression | | | Severity of depression | | |
| | High | Mod. | Low | High | Mod. | Low |
| African American | | | | | | |
| Asian American | | | | | | |
| American Indian | | | | | | |
| Hispanic | | | | | | |
| White, not Hispanic | | | | | | |
| Other | | | | | | |
| Missing data | | | | | | |

2. Code each variable's distribution of values into intervals that will best describe the variable conceptually and present the empirical distribution.

3. Determine the value and code for each unit on each of the variables.

4. Determine the vertical or horizontal axis placement of variables that will present the best visual description of their relationship, including the "nested" relationship.

5. Place the unit in the contingency table's cell corresponding to each variable's value.

## Statistical Analysis

Statistical analysis allows a mathematical examination of relationships between values of variables and changes in values. Statistical models calculate the probability that a relationship found between variables is one of chance. **Probability** is the mathematical likelihood of an event or relationship occurring by chance. It can range from 0.00 (never) to 1.00 (always). Tests can examine the strength of relationship, as in correlations. Statistical analysis can compare two or more groups' pre- and postintervention measurements of dependent variables.

Technically, with group differences or, more precisely, group differences on measurement scores of variables, the examination is to refute the alternative or null hypothesis. *The null hypothesis asserts that any relationship found between the groups or scores is probably due to chance at least as strong as the probability level used to reject it.* For example, if the chi square test is used to examine the relationship, as:

$$\chi^2 = 3.9 \ (1 \ df) \ P > .05$$

the statistic means that the strength of this relationship, 3.9 with 1 degree of freedom, as determined by the chi square test of association, will be found by chance less than 5% of the time. The 0.05 is the level of statistical significance. Research convention deems this as an acceptable level of statistically significance.

### Statistical Power

**The power of a statistical test is its ability to reject a false null hypothesis**—that is, the assertion that no relationship exists between two variables when, in fact, a relationship exists. More powerful models are more stringent. As discussed under sampling, statistical power is related to sample size with larger samples more likely, other things equal, to reject a false null hypothesis. Parametric statistical tests are generally more powerful than nonparametric statistical tests.

The power is represented by the Type I and Type II error relationship.

### Type I error

A type I error is accepting a false relationship between two things as a true relationship or making a false positive judgment about a relationship that is null or not real. A relationship is assumed to be real at a given probability level. *A common type I practice error is affirming the effectiveness of an intervention, such as a couple's counseling intervention, in contributing to the couple's satisfaction when in fact the intervention is not effective.*

### Type II error

A type II error is when a true relationship exists and the null hypothesis is false, but the null is accepted and the true relationship between the variables is rejected. *In practice a type II error is denying the effectiveness of treatment, such as a parent education program capacity to reduce child abuse, when in fact it is effective.*

## Power and the Alpha Level

The errors represent a dilemma. Since there is always a risk of one or the other type of error at some level, *avoiding one error may increase risk of the other.* To guard against type I error, you can move the statistical acceptance level to a higher, more stringent level of statistical significance, as from .05 to .01 or even .001 level. The level of rejection of the null hypothesis is the **alpha level.** Acceptable alpha levels of statistical significance relate to the dangers of making a mistake in rejecting a null when in fact no relationship exists, or accepting the null when a relationship does exist. A 0.05

alpha level indicates that there is a 95% probability that the event or relationship occurred not by chance, and a 5% probability that it did occur by chance. The social science conventions in using the 0.05 and 0.01 alpha are arbitrary and rooted in custom. At an 0.05 alpha level, relationships that have a 5% probability of being chance are acceptable, and relationships that have a 6% probability level of being chance are conventionally not acceptable as statistically significant.

Moving to more stringent alpha level, such as to 0.01 from 0.05, lowers the probability that the event occurred by chance from 5 in a 100 to 1 in a hundred. It reduces the probability of a type I error, but correspondingly increases the possibility of a type II error in that true relationships are more likely to be classified as chance relationships. To minimize type II errors (rejecting a true relationship and assuming it is a chance relationship), a less stringent alpha level can be used, such as 0.10 instead of 0.05. Short of moving to a less exacting alpha level, such as 0.10 for 0.05, more powerful statistical tests (tests that are more likely to reject the null), such as parametric statistical tests, when assumptions are met, rather than nonparametric tests, can be used along with a larger sample size, if possible.

In selecting the appropriate alpha level, the practitioner needs to consider the pragmatic risks involved in making each type of error. The real risks involved are false positives and false negatives. What are the risks in assuming a relationship exists between two things when the discovered relationship is only chance or assuming the false positive position? What are the risks in

Type I and Type II Error Risks

| Real World Condition | Decision to Reject Null Hypothesis | Decision to Accept, Not Reject, Null Hypothesis |
|---|---|---|
| Null is false | No error | Type II error |
| Null is true | Type I error | No error |

assuming an intervention is effective, that the apparent relationship between intervention and achievement of case objectives is true, when it is not? What are the risks in assuming a trait found among people with a certain syndrome is an indicator of that syndrome when it is not? Accepting the false indicator risks overlooking more valid indicators, leading to false diagnosis and assessments, invalid case theory, and inappropriate interventions.

Perhaps even more pragmatically risky for a practitioner faced with a need to intervene in a case is the risks of the type II error, or false negative judgments, when few alternatives are available. The relationships may not be significant at a particular alpha level because of sample size or test power. Without available alternatives with a stronger statistical relationship, the selected intervention is accepted with its alpha level. Acceptance of a "false treatment" risks not using a more effective treatment if available, but the rejection of "true treatments" may mean no treatment is available. If the risks resulting from a "false treatment" are high, you need a stringent alpha level. If the risks are low and no alternatives exist, a stringent alpha level may represent false rigor and obeisant compliance to scientific tradition.

## One-Tailed or Two-Tailed Tests and Alpha Levels

**Type I and type II errors** *are affected by whether you use a one-tailed or two-tailed test of the relationship between the variables.* The probability of a type I or type II error increases or decreases depending on application of a one or two tail test to the statistic. Tails refer to the normal distribution curve. **The alpha level** *indicates the location of the statistic representing the probability of the relationship in relation to the mean of the normal distribution curve.* **The statistic is called a z-score.** The normal or classic bell-shaped curve represents a symmetrical distribution of scores with a coincidence of mode, median, and mean (see Figure 12.5). Areas trailing away from the mid-

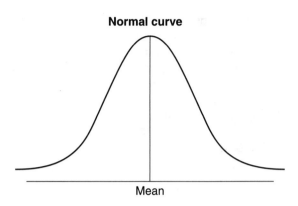

**FIGURE 12.5**

point are the tails. The area of the curve between the z-scores for a two-tailed test represent the rejection confidence region, and areas beyond the z-scores contain the acceptance regions. Farther out from the midpoint is the z-score, the more stringent the probability level reflected by the alpha level. An alpha level of 0.01 is farther out and more stringent than an alpha level of 0.05. The farther out the z-score and alpha level, the more likely it is that a type II error may occur. Z-scores that are closer in are more likely to produce type I errors. For the same alpha level, more or less of a curve from the midpoint will be accepted depending on whether the test is one or two tailed. A two-tailed test uses both tails or sides of the curve; a one-tailed test uses only one side.

On the baseline of a normal curve for an alpha level of 0.05, the distance from the mean of the curve on the tail is 1.96 z-scores on the baseline from the mean of the curve on both sides of the mean for a two tail test (see Figure 12.6). The amount of the curve above 1.96 z-scores, or both sides of the mean, will include 47.5% on each side, 95% of the total curve, as the rejection zone. The acceptance zone is the amount of the curve and the scores beyond, farther out on the baseline than 1.96 z-scores, or 2.5% on each side and 5% of the total curve.

A one-tailed test's 0.05 alpha level is at 1.65 z-scores along the normal curve's baseline in one direction or the other, depending on whether you

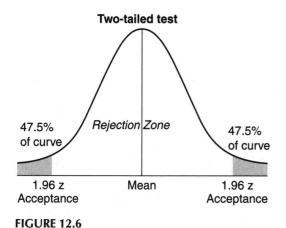

**FIGURE 12.6**

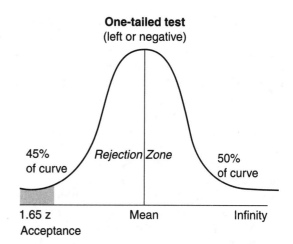

**FIGURE 12.8**

hypothesize a positive or an inverse relationship between the variables (see Figures 12.7 and 12.8). Depending on the direction, 50%, all of the curve on one side of the mean, and 45% of the curve or tail on the other side constitutes the rejection zone. A full 5% in the direction of the hypothesis constitutes the acceptance zone. Compared to the two-tailed test, one tailed tests are more like to accept the hypothesized relationship in direction of the tail. The z-score is 1.65 compared to 1.96, and the acceptance zone is the full 5% of the curve's tail compared with 2.5% of that tail for the two-tailed test.

The one-tailed test provides more acceptance room in direction of the hypothesis, but all relationships in the opposite direction are rejected regardless of how far they are along the baseline. Lower strengths of relationships are accepted as statistically significant with one-tailed tests more than with two-tailed tests if they are in the hypothesized direction. For example, using the $t$ test with 5 degrees of freedom to look at differences between means of two groups, a one-tailed test will accept a relationship of 2.015, while a two-tailed test requires a strength of relationship of 2.571 before you reach statistical significance.[2]

One-tailed tests are appropriate whenever change is hypothesized in a particular direction. The interventive hypothesis, the hypothesis that the intervention will affect the case objectives and reduce problematic conditions or improve other conditions, are reasonably one-tailed hypotheses: *Couples counseling will improve communication in a relationship between couples.* One-tailed and directional tests, however, will

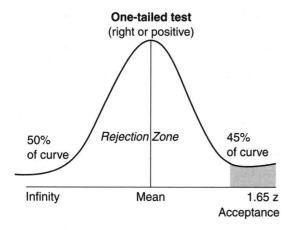

**FIGURE 12.7**

[2]The number of measurements units will affect statistical significance. Measurement units can be the number of units of analysis measured, the number of times a unit is measured, or both.

not test the strength of the relationship in the opposite direction.

Two-tailed tests are used with nondirectional hypotheses: *There is a relationship between the quality of communication between couples and couples counseling.* Implicitly this appears to be an inappropriate intervention hypothesis. Nondirectional hypotheses are appropriate when the knowledge base is insufficient to predict a direction of change or association between variables. Case theory needs to provide a sufficient knowledge base to predict that an intervention will be helpful. *Because interventive hypotheses are generally directional, one-tail tests are more appropriate than are two tailed tests.* All hypotheses positing a causal relationship are directional, making one tailed tests appropriate.

## Inferential Statistical Tests

Statistical analysis is applicable *only to numeric data.* Statistics and statistical analysis can be descriptive, as discussed, or *inferential*, to make inferences or generalizations from a sample to a population. Inferential statistics *reveal whether the apparent relationships between or among the variables in the sample measurements are indicative of true relationships.* Inferential statistics have practice relevance in shaping our confidence in the practice generalizations forming practice wisdom. This allows generalizations beyond the specific cases or time points sampled and also allows the practitioner to assess the information drawn from social science research in forming the case theory.

Statistical tests are of two general types: (1) parametric, and (2) nonparametric. Use **parametric statistical tests** to make inferences to larger population parameters from sample statistics. *They are called parametric because they make inferences from samples to populations.* In making inferences, parametric statistical tests can deal with random sampling errors but not with systematic sampling errors and biases. Parametric statistical tests technically require random probability samples drawn from populations with normally distributed variables, at least ordinal

measurement data, and preferably an interval level on at least one of the variables. These technical requirements are necessary if the sample's statistics are to have external validity. Conceptually, external validity's purpose is for the statistic to represent the parameter: whether an inference can be made from the sample to the larger population that both the sample and statistic are believed to represent. The technical requirements are often violated, sometimes with appreciable damage to the analysis.

**Nonparametric statistical** tests are used with nonrandom samples, nonnormally distributed variables, and measurements and comparisons of variables when one or more of the variables are nominal measures. Generally there are nonparametric tests corresponding to the parametric tests. Nonparametric tests are the more common analytical tests used in social work research. They generally have less power.

### Using statistical tests

Statistical analysis, other than purely description statistics, can use a range of specific statistical tests to assess the strength of relationships and differences between variables. It is not our purpose here to explore the range of specific statistical tests but instead to present a general overview of the purposes and practice uses of statistical analysis. It is useful in practice after case objective significance has been established and sometimes in the process of establishing case objective significance. For a more complete introduction to the analytical use of statistical tests and models, consult one of the many introductory statistical texts developed specifically for social work.[3] Additionally, many of the laborious computations required for statistical analysis can be performed by a range of computer software programs, provided the practitioner has access to the programs and a

---

[3]For example: Craft, J. L. (1990), *Statistics and data analysis for social workers* (3rd ed.) Itasca, IL: F. E. Peacock; Weinbach, R. W., & Grinnell, Jr., R. M. (1995), *Statistics for social workers* (3rd ed.) White Plains, NY: Longman.

personal computer, can use both, and knows the purposes and limitations of each statistic.

Some final caveats are offered. Although you can apply a statistical test to any set of numbers, *the results are meaningful only if you meet the assumptions of the particular test.* Relevance is determined by the test's contribution to determining case objective, process, and case theory significance, not the statistic itself. As we have said before, no amount of statistical methodology sophistication will overcome problems in measurement, design, sampling, and data collection. **Statistical tests are only analytical models, not the empirical phenomena.**

## Single Case Design and Statistical Analysis

Several statistical tests are applicable to single case design. Used in conjunction with visual analysis for case objective significance, they support and contribute to, rather than replace, the determination of case objective significance. Tests include the (1) two standard deviation procedure, (2) relative frequency procedure, (3) computing the chi square from pre- and postintervention medians and mean differences, and (4) binomial distribution analysis, among others.

Generally, they compare the relationship of baseline and follow-up measurement scores plotted on a time series graph. This is to determine if postintervention measurements are appreciably different from preintervention or baseline measurements by mathematically assessing any differences in the probability level of statistical significance. The more postintervention scores lie in the predicted direction within the case objective significance zone and deviate from the baseline scores, the more likely progress of the case is statistically significant.

Statistical significance in single case designs, as in group comparison designs, examines the probability that a relationship between variables is chance. As with group comparison designs, it is affected by the magnitude of relationship between the variables and the change, effect size that is practice relevant, and number of times

measurements are taken on the variables. In group comparison designs, the number of measurements is largely determined by group size. In single case designs, the more times measurements are taken on a subject, the more times the measurement is taken in a pretreatment phase and a posttreatment phase, the more likely pre–post differences on a variable for an effect size will indicate a statistically significant difference. The number of times something is measured in single case design is similar to the relationship of sample size to effect size in a power analysis of sample size for group comparison designs. *The more stable a change is over many measurement time points, the more likely that change will be statistically significant and the more confidence can be placed in a change as real.*

The computation of tests applicable to single case design is also beyond our scope. Interested readers are referred to the following texts in the References section at the end of this book, which contain detailed instructions for their computation: Berlin & Marsh, (1993), pp. 111–139; Bloom, Fischer & Orme (1995); Blythe & Tripodi (1989); Blythe, Tripodi & Briar (1994); Jayaratne & Levy (1979); Tripodi (1994); and Tripodi & Epstein (1983), among others.

## Computers in Research and Practice

Computers have made varied, useful, and ever-expanding contributions to research. We have indicated in earlier chapters the computer's uses in measurement, data collection and storage, and in computing a sample's power. Computers are most useful in performing repetitive tasks, in storing and retrieving immense amounts of qualitative and quantitative information efficiently, and in analyzing quantitative information. They retrieve specific information from extensive and complex data files or data bases with relative speed and ease. Computers contain data bases (data storage), reporting formats, and organize data by these formations. They can be programmed to provide planning and monitoring schedules useful in proceduralization of interventions. Communication systems are enhanced with electronic mail (e-mail) and local area networks of computer stations (lans). Computers allow respondents to directly respond and enter data for information ranging from biographic through questionnaires and measurement inventories (Butterfield, 1983). Respondents directly imputing the responses into the computer can, though not inevitably, reduce processing errors and increase data's reliability.

Perhaps the most significant contribution of the computer to research and knowledge development is quantitative data analysis. This is the basis for the derivation of the name *computer*—to compute. The computer's software can rapidly analyze vast amounts of data, not possible in a pre-computer era. Software is the set of programmed instructions that direct the equipment, hardware and other software, to perform specific functions and tasks in processing information (Taylor, 1981, p. 63; Valancy, 1985, p. 250). Software analytical statistical packages exist for almost all statistical computations. These packages require minimal statistical and computer competency and are deemed in computer argot to be "user friendly." But we must remember in using software, it does what it is programmed to do whether or not it is relevant to a particular analysis or question. An analytical statistical software will analyze nominal data as ratio data if told to do so, whether or not the analysis is legitimate. Be aware of the limitations of each analytical model and use the packages within these limitations. A second weakness in knowledge development in the era of fast and easy analysis is the decline of rigor in theory construction and gross naive empiricism. It often is easier and cheaper to analyze everything than to be guided by well thought out a-priori developed theoretical models.

## Practice and Computers

Computer and electronic technologies use will allow wider distribution of human and social services. Fewer professionals can serve more people. To date computer practice uses primarily include information storage, processing, and management. As with research, computers provide practitioners with assistance: in planning and monitoring intervention schedules and proceduralization, for storing and charting case process notes and records, and in providing communication systems. E-mail and Web pages on the internet offer more opportunity for public information distribution, marketing, and case coordination. Internet chat rooms are used for information sharing and emotional support groups (Finn, 1996). Computerized library reference services such as *Social Work Abstracts* and *Psychlit* allow more rapid and timely literature searches in developing case theory. Case records can be stored in computer files that allow for ease of retrieval and for the examination of traits and relationships across cases to develop treatment approaches. Spreadsheet software enables greater ease in fiscal management necessary in a competitive practice arena (Baskin, 1990, p. 6; Benbenishty & Ben-Zaken, 1988; Brod, 1987; Clark, 1988; Finn, 1988; Kreuger, 1987; Lohmann & Wolvovsky, 1979; Schinka & Smith III, 1984; Zysman, 1989).

Computer uses are commonly limited to providing auxiliary functions to practice and for information management and analysis rather than as direct intervention tools. Clients are able to make direct data entry to computers for eligibility determination, computation of benefits, and through debit cards make electronic transfers of cash assistance and food stamps at bank automatic teller machines (Peyrot, Harris, Fenzel, & Burbridge, 1997).

Computers as practitioners or as virtual therapists are promising, but currently mostly just promise. The computer is impersonal and potentially can be a non-judgmental "listening ear," although not necessarily, depending on its software programming.[1] As a non-judgmental listening ear, it may obtain very personal and intense information more readily from respondents because it is seen as less threatening than face-to-face disclosing to another person. Potentially it can deal with more client information—receive, store, sort, analyze, and respond—more rapidly and reliably than can a human (Baskin, 1990, p. 6).

The limiting factors to the computer as virtual therapist is its rigidity. It can only respond within its programmed options. As Hardcastle and Harkness (1982) pointed out almost two decades ago, and it still remains cogent, the practical analysis of qualitative and narrative data remains more a promise than a reality. It is limited by its ability to analysis of the meaning of qualitative data (see content analysis discussion). For widespread computer uses in therapies as virtual therapists, computers will need software that allows the use of, and enables responses to and in, the ordinary natural languages used by different clients. Presently the computer's language and logic is paramount. If the computer is to engage clients in therapies, software will have to use the natural languages of clients (or clients trained in the software's language) and understand the meanings of clients' inputs, and translate outputs into clients' natural languages. The task, a content analysis task for the computer, is to understand and communicate meaning of ideas rather than just words or even phrases (Plutchik & Karasu, 1990, p. 64; Stuart & LaRue, 1996).

Experience with translation programs between one language and another have demonstrated only very limited success. Idioms and cultural variances are lost with the translations often conveying meanings different from the intent. For example, translation by *Alta Vista's Babelfish,* a translation program, of the simple email announcement that "You have mail" when translated from English to German back to English ends up as "They have a post office" (Kelley, 1998, p. E7). Determinations of the subtle meaning in client communication by a virtual computer therapist is a distant event.

---

[1]Judgmental responses can be programmed. One of the authors during an earlier era of computer use, the era of mainframes, had made a mistake in the program cards. The University's computer staff had programmed in the response "STUPID! STUPID! STUPID!" for simple programming mistakes. The print-out did not contain an explanation of the error, but simply a repetition of STUPID! STUPID! STUPID!

Early treatment software such as *Eliza* have not been particularly successful as treatment programs. *Eliza* scanned and responded to key words and phrases according to programmed input-out rules. Certain words or phrases directed certain outputs or responses from a range of possible pre-set outputs. *Eliza* had difficulty with compound and complex sentences and with all cues other than verbal, and written, so necessary to assessing complex ideas and meanings (Plutchik & Karasu, 1990, p. 66).

Some software allows computers to use a range of speech-based natural languages of 50 to 80 words per minute. These are appropriate with limited communication patterns and information such as airlines and hotel reservations (Eisenberg, 4/23/98, pp. E1, E8). They are not appropriate for the complexities and variations of client interactions.

HMOs and other third party payers are highly motivated to develop computerized speech based natural language virtual therapies. Once developed, the interventions will be economical, consistent, have perfect memory and recall, and not make or communicate unprogrammed moral judgments, work any time and not represent a cost when not working, and not get bored (unless programmed to be bored). This is not true with the human professional.

## Why Computer Knowledge for Social Workers

Social workers have been resistant to developing computer knowledge and computer assisted practice, although this stance may be attenuating (Finn, 1988, Zysman, 1989). Social workers need to understand the growing use of and intrusion of computers into the practice arena. If they do not understand and control the technology, the technology will direct and control the social workers. Specific and precise technologies such as the computer historically have tended to drive out more general and diffuse technologies such as those used by social workers in their interventions.

The social work labor market reflects society and will continue its movement toward commercialization, privatization, and competition. Competition between professions and professionals will increase. *Social workers will more immediately go into "private" and "self-managed" practice as associate, contract, and contingent employees.* As with managed care/cost, interventions will emphasize short-term and computer assisted therapies and treatments. Computer, electronic information, and communication management skills necessary for the internet, the Web, self-help videos and Web sites, closed circuit telenets, interactive computer and video bases, interactive online/WWW sites, and the "virtual clinics" on the internet will become more crucial. Skills are needed for both managing and conducting a practice in the environment of the future.

Our conviction is not that computer-assisted and virtual therapies and interventions will produce better interventions. There is little, if any, evidence that the computer has improved quality or even the efficiency of services (Madrick, 1998). Remote, electronic, "canned," and "distance therapies" and education have a "touch" lacuna and lack a more personal or primary relationships necessary for emotion-based interventions. The Web truly moves the social work helping relationship and bonding to a tertiary union similar to an "Oprah" style radio talk show with little true sense of the client (respondent) involvement at the other end of the line. The ability of both helper and client to triangulate messages from the range of cues of voice tone and inflection to non-verbal cues is limited if not lost. Clients become an audience in short attention span venues and require entertainment as much as education or therapy. Fantasies as well as attention run wild. Chat room support groups are fraught with fraud, factitious illness and disorders, and aggrandizement (Grady, 1998). There is some evidence that significant time on the Web contributes to clinical depression. Interstate licensure issues, the ability to verify credentials of the electronic service provider, and a lack of a definition of an electronic professional relationship or the fiduciary responsibility of the virtual therapist are still unre-

solved. Electronic technology presents ethical questions for informed consent, privacy, and confidentiality from hacker access to the communication and files. Chat-room conversations and support groups with messages moving between a central location and several users' servers are especially insecure to electronic eaves-dropping. Chat-room visitors can never be sure who else is present nor are other cues to assess voracity available. Privacy controls should be at least as great for computer records and sessions as for face-to-face sessions and hard copy records (Levenson, 1997a; *Linkages*, 1997).

Computer and electronic technologies, however, are a complex arena for which social workers should be prepared. They need skills to compete in a labor market riddled with computerization. Without this knowledge and these skills, the practitioner will not be competitive just as a researcher without computer skills is at a disadvantage.

## Summary

The use of research tools in practice is a significant challenge. They can add much to practice effectiveness when appropriately used. Applicable design, measurement, data collection, and sampling are essential in analysis to test case theory and practice effectiveness. The use of statistical tests can reinforce analysis. They can also cloud decisions about practice and its effectiveness. There are challenges in developing appropriate measures and data collection protocols as well as time demands of these procedures, possible reflexivity and reactive effects.

Particularly problematic is letting measurement dictate and constrain problem definition, assessment, case theory development, and selection of interventions rather than the reverse. Appropriately meeting these challenges will enhance practice. Just as availability of particular measurement tools, especially the quantified paper-and-pencil scales become the deciding force in selecting outcomes or measuring them, there is the related danger of trivializing the analytical process and substituting statistical significance for case objective significance. Measurements may be selected based on the contemporary popularity of using the manipulation numbers as a substitute for wisdom. The more relevant analysis of intervention success has to do with case objective significance and achieving the appropriate (but not necessarily the most conveniently analyzed) outcomes.

## Discussion Questions and Exercises

*Susan Probity, a social worker employed by Hustle Mental Health Agency, was the worker for Doa Downs, a 12-year-old African American girl, who suffered from childhood depression. Susan and Doa engaged in treatment, counseling, and drug treatment for one year. They had weekly hour sessions for a year. Susan audiotaped the sessions. Case objectives were to reduce the depression level by 20% and improve school attendance to no more than two absences a month. After the year of treatment, Doa reported that she was happier and less moody.*

*Susan had administered the Depression Self-Rating Scale (DSRS) (Fischer & Corcoran, 1994, pp. 464–465) to Doa every other week. The range of possible scores is 0–36, with positive items scored 0 to 2 and negative items –2 to 0. Lower scores indicate higher depression. The table shows Doa's scores and school attendance record (days absent) for the previous month. Treatment began week 2 and continued through week 50. There was no school attendance for weeks 24 through 34 because of the summer break. Susan was on vacation for weeks 26–28.*

| Week | DSRS | Attendance | Week | DSRS | Attendance |
|------|------|------------|------|------|------------|
| 1 | 12 | 6 | 30 | 14 | — |
| 2 | 10 | — | 32 | 16 | — |
| 4 | 11 | 6 | 34 | 16 | — |
| 6 | 12 | — | 36 | 18 | — |
| 8 | 14 | 5 | 38 | 17 | 3 |
| 10 | 14 | — | 39 | 16 | — |
| 12 | 18 | 5 | 40 | 18 | — |
| 14 | 16 | — | 42 | 18 | 2 |
| 16 | 14 | 4 | 44 | 20 | — |
| 18 | 15 | — | 46 | 22 | 0 |
| 20 | 15 | 4 | 48 | 21 | — |
| 22 | 16 | — | 50 | 20 | 0 |
| 24 | 15 | 2 | 52 | 18 | — |
| 26 | — | — | 54 | 18 | 0 |
| 28 | — | — | | | |

1. Chart the data to determine case significance. Was case significance achieved on reduction of depression and for school attendance?

2. How might Susan have strengthened the case evaluation?

3. Is the length of baseline and follow-up measurement time points adequate for depression and school attendance to determine stability as well as case objective significance?

4. How can the case narratives be analyzed and triangulated to reinforce the analysis?

5. How can Susan establish process and theory significance?

# CHAPTER THIRTEEN

# Reporting

Reporting is an indispensable and continuing component of both research and practice. Research contributes to a discipline's or profession's knowledge only when it is reported. Reporting by practitioners to clients and various stakeholders and constituencies is essential for accountability to clients, agencies, funding sources, and the public. Reporting on case experience to the profession, other practitioners, and social scientists contributes to the profession's knowledge base. Knowledge development and transmittal responsibilities for both research and practice require reporting or diffusion and often conversion, allowing use of practice- and research-generated knowledge by the profession, other practitioners, and clients.

This chapter examines the various targets for reporting by practitioners and considers means to improve the communication and accuracy of reporting. We review the twin responsibilities in practice of diffusion and conversion in reporting, and present a generic report model.

## Clients, Informed Consent, Member Checking, and Reporting

The practitioner's reporting of knowledge development to clients is an ethical responsibility. The practitioner needs to inform clients of their progress, problems, and achievement or failure to achieve case objectives. Assessment is a joint activity with clients and requires reporting. *Reporting is integral to informed consent.* For clients to provide informed consent, they must be kept informed at each step of the intervention. Reporting

Parallels of Practice and Research

| Practice Components and Tasks | Research Epistemologies and Methodologies |
|---|---|
| **Reporting and reassessment** | **Reporting** |
| Reassessment of the case theory; report progress toward goals to the client and other components of the action and change system; establish new goals; recontract with the client; clinical, process, case theory, and statistical significance reporting for accountability and informed consent | Construct shared reality with member checking for case study reporting; knowledge conversion, publication, and diffusion |

and the capacity for informed consent are fundamental to client empowerment. **Empowerment** is
a process of increasing personal, interpersonal or
social, and political power so that empowered individuals can take action to improve their life situation. It is a process reflecting an increasing
sense of self-control and choice through which
people gain mastery over their own affairs and in
interactions with their social environment (Lee,
1994). Clients must have information and a
knowledge base to make rational choices.

Reporting to clients is a continuous form of
member checking (Lincoln & Guba, 1985, pp. 236,
314–316; Tutty, Rothery, & Grinnell, Jr. 1996,
p. 113) and, according to Grinnell (1997), an "integration of evaluative activities with normal day
to day service delivery" (p. 590). Member checking can be both formal and informal. *Prior to any
final conclusions and "external" reporting stages it is
crucial to determine whether the data and report have
captured the informants' constructions.* Providing
them with opportunities for corrections, amend-
ments, and additional interpretations, it aids in
establishing reporting credibility. "The member
check, whereby data, analytic categories, interpretations, and conclusions are tested with members of those stakeholding groups from whom the
data were originally collected, is the most crucial
technique for establishing credibility" (Lincoln &
Guba, 1985, p. 314).

## Audiences, Stakeholders, and Language

The purpose of reporting is to communicate information to a target audience in a manner that
presents (1) what is important about the information for the target audience, (2) the confidence the
target audience can place in the information, and
(3) any limitations the target audience should
place on the information. While reports must always be truthful, different audiences will have
different information needs. Research report audiences include other researchers, the discipline
or profession, sponsors, policy makers, the media, potential and current clients, and the general

or lay public. Reporting's language varies according to each audience's language, information needs, and interests.

Practice case report audiences also vary. The
most common are stakeholders at the individual
case level, including clients and relevant others
in clients' primary support systems, agencies,
funding sources and client sponsors, and policy
and community decision makers. Tertiary stakeholders with a potential interest include other social work practitioners who deal with similar
case problems.

Practitioners need to know the language of
each of the specific constituencies or audiences in
order to express the report's content in the audience's language. Each target audience may not
know the language of the other audiences. In reporting to clients and nonprofessional stakeholders and audiences, avoid clinical jargon. Translate
the label "bereavement therapy," for example,
into lay language with emotional impact such as
"learning to live again" or "getting over the
grief" (Levenson, 1997b, p. 3).

As more and more services fall under the pro-
visions of managed care/cost companies, Maryland proprietary practitioner Britt Rathbone
(Levenson, 1997b) advises practitioners to use
appropriate language with managed care panels
and case managers, which emphasizes measurement and quantification:

> [The practitioner] must speak the language of
> the reviewers.... Treatment goals presented to
> managed care companies should include some
> numerical measure of success illustrating your
> intervention has worked and the company's
> money has been well spent. "Clients feel hap-
> pier" does not work as well as writing, "Clients
> feel happier as evidenced by attending school
> 90 percent of the time."
>
> Managed care companies want evidence to
> justify diagnosis, treatment, and treatment suc-
> cess, preferably numerical measures that justify
> that the treatment works and the company's
> money has been well spent. (p. 3)

A report's language is critical as the means of
conveying the meaning that is the intent of the

communication. The task is not to just learn the audience's words and the symbols but the meaning of the words and symbols, the ideas and conceptualizations.

## Public Reports

The 1971 Council of the American Anthropological Association's *Principles of Professional Responsibility* emphasizes the public nature of research and the importance of reporting to all audiences (Spradley, 1980).

> In accordance with the Association's general position on clandestine and secret research, no reports should be provided to sponsors that are not also available to the general public and, where practicable, to the population studies. (p. 25)

Individual case reports do not have a general mandate and are protected by the client's privilege. However, aggregate case information needs to be public, if the public is to understand conditions facing social work clients. *Practitioners need to accept this public information responsibility.*

## Practitioners as Target Audiences

A primary audience for information gained from practice experience and research is, reasonably, other practitioners. *A profession's fundamental reporting task is the transmission of useful and valid information for practice.* To date, if the research on research utilization is credible, this purpose has not been fulfilled in the transmission of knowledge from research to practitioners. As reviewed earlier, social workers have not made the professional literature a high priority in informing their practice. While scientific journals may be a viable venue for reaching social scientists and other researchers, it has not been as successful in reaching practitioners. Practitioners also rarely use, or perhaps have little access to, sharing practice experience in the professional literature. A cursory review of the major social work journals indicate

that most authors have academic or research affiliations. Dissemination of the knowledge to practitioner target audience will require other forums and venues.

## Accuracy in Reporting

Some skepticism about use of research information is probably in order. In this electronic and sound bite age, with widespread touting of the World Wide Web, the information superhighway, and the Internet, diligent attention to accuracy and a concern for lowering sensational rhetoric is needed. This is particularly true for reporting to the lay public through the mass media and the Web. Reporting in the mass media and on the Web is becoming better known for its sense of urgency than fidelity to accuracy. The Web and the Net have given potentially everyone access to information and the capacity to widely communicate information, no matter how bogus, as genuine. Anything once sent over the information electronic networks, broadcast on television, or published in the print media or professional journals has an aura of credibility. Research reports have often been sensationalized to have more impact on the public's fleeting attention span, promote continued funding, and impact public policy.

A *New York Times* report (Holmes, July 6, 1997, p. e3) reveals several sound bite sensationalisms, some the fault of slothful journalism and others the shortcomings of overly ambitious researchers combining research with ideological advocacy[1] to convince their audiences that the research is important. One example was the 1995 report by several research organizations that a hefty percentage, as high as 65%, of teen-age mothers had babies by adult men: "Innocent young girls are

---

[1]We have no problem with ideological advocacy when it is ethically done. As stated earlier, we believe most social science is ideological. We trust the reader of social science research reports will search for the report's ideology.

sexual prey to lecherous men." This made a good sound bite that led to several social action campaigns to end the practice of older men preying on young girls. While the ends are good, the sound bites did not represent reality. The full information from those and subsequent studies indicated that 62% of the teenage mothers were 18 to 19 years old and were legally adults; many were married teenage mothers; and of the 15- to 17-year-old mothers, only 8 percent were unmarried girls made pregnant by men at least 5 years older. The unmarried pregnancies, perhaps all pregnancies, of teenagers and especially those caused by older men, constitute a social and personal problem, but not the one reported. As Kristen Moore, president of Child Trend, Inc., a Washington-based adolescent sexual issues research organization, commented (Holmes, July 6, 1997, p. e3), "people are always looking for a single-bullet answer. But things are more complicated than people want them to be."

The people looking include social work researchers and practitioners. These sound bite reports and ensuing overweaning policies and practices cloud the condition's true complexities; divert our capacity to rectify the actual condition to grasping popular, faddish, and cheap solutions; and make us impatient with gradual, complex solutions.

The research literature unfortunately is often replete with conclusions that outrun the data, the samples, and the designs. Overgeneralizing from nonprobability samples and attributing causal validity from poorly controlled designs are common.

**Accuracy** is critical in practice reporting, whether to clients or "for the record." Case records are used for administrative and fiscal accountability, supervisory consultation and monitoring, treatment study, teaching and research, and practitioner self-evaluation. *The record is the official history of the case.* Unfortunately, often it allows limited privacy for the information. Official records contain the client's social histories, case assessments, goals and objectives, treatment plans, progress notes, progress measurements,

and outcomes (Kagle, 1983). As the profession gains in stature, its fiduciary responsibility and legal liability increases (Kutchins, 1991; Reamer, 1994, 1995b). The record reports on both the client and the professional's intervention. Prudence compels accuracy for legal protection.

## Report Diffusion and Conversion

It is important to view reporting targets much more broadly than only clients and other immediate case stakeholders, sponsors, and professional journals. In an era of pernicious social welfare and health policies, with an overriding deleterious emphasis on cost containment and managed costs, downsizing, outsiding, privatization, commercialization, and competition, social work practitioners need to establish effectiveness for their interventions and tell their stories broadly. Policies and policy makers' constructions and the public's perceptions of what is good and bad is heavily formed by the media (Mazmanian & Sabatier, 1981). *Staging discussion and influencing public attitudes are vital contributions of reporting.*

### Developing and Assessing Reports

Like all communication, the reporter, whether researcher or practitioner, wants the message or report to reach the target audience in the manner intended in order to influence understanding and reactions. Considerations must be given to adapt each report to each target audience. The journalistic criteria of the five Ws—*who, what, when, where,* and *why* (and sometimes the H of *how*) are used to shape the report (Hardcastle, Wenocur, & Powers, 1997, pp. 335–336; Rose, 1995). These criteria apply both to the content and distribution of reports.

1. *Who* are you? *Who* is interested in the information (the audience)? *To which* specific public or target audiences are you aiming the report? Does the target operate under any special cir-

cumstances and have traits; location, demographic and ethnic characteristics, culture and other factors that distinguishes it from other audiences and require separate consideration in the reporting? Know the barriers and facilitating conditions to information exchange. *Who* is the audience in terms of its comprehension capacity? Does the report fit that capacity?

2. *What* is the intended purpose of the report? *What* will the audience know and/or be able to do after receiving and reading or hearing the report than before the report? *What* specific actions or responses are sought from the audience? *What* specific information is needed by each specific audience to use the information and perform any behaviors or actions sought by the report?

3. *What* is significant about the research or practice for the particular target audience? *What* events, occurrences, or findings are or should be of interest to the target audience? *What* will the audience gain by the information contained in the report? *Why* will the target audience incorporate the information into the knowledge base for practice, compliant behavior, or policy? *Why* will the information or report motivate the venue to transmit the information?

4. *When* will or has the research or practice occurred? And, very important, *when* does the target audience need to receive the information for it to have an impact on their behavior? *When* does the venue need the report to best transmit it? For example, information-shaping public policy has to be very dramatic to compel policy makers to reconsider a legislative decision once made.

5. *Where* will or did the event occur? *Where* does the target audience receive its information? Context as well as content influences a target audience's capacity to use information. *Where* are the information venues located?

6. *How* did the event come about? *How* does each target audience obtain its information? *What* are the primary information sources and venues for information sources for each audience? When possible, assess and use specific venues of print media; television programs and times; radio, including "talk radio"; and word-of-mouth information and opinion leaders' networks used by the particular targets.

7. *How* will the reporting researcher or practitioner know that the report has been received and understood by the target audience? Know the feedback mechanisms. A report is only communication when it has been sent and the message received and understood by the targeted recipients as intended by the sender.

Reports written and presented in a manner requiring the least work and cost to the venue are more likely to be passed on. It is critical to follow deadlines in formal print or broadcast venues. Venues should be surveyed and relationships developed with the appropriate editors and contacts to discover the preferred length, timing, style, and format. The report writer needs to be available to the venue in case follow-up is necessary. Similar consideration is helpful in working with informal communication venues and opinion leaders.

Obtain information on media outlets from the white and yellow pages of the telephone directory and media directories. Additionally, potential classes and types of venues and relevant approaches to their use can be discovered in texts and other resources on marketing, promotion, and public relations (Brawley, 1983; Hardcastle, Wenocur, & Powers, 1997, pp. 309–345; Kotler & Roberto, 1989; Richan, 1996, 279–319). Many outlets provide media kits to promote their use.

## Assessing Written Communication

A challenge in developing written and verbal reports is to assess the match between audience comprehension and the comprehension required to understand the communication. This is one of the values of member checking with clients and other stakeholders. Advisory panels from differing target audiences are helpful. While the capacity to read a written message and understand its individual words is not sufficient to understand the message, it is a necessary prerequisite. A number of computer software programs test the readability levels required for written communications. The written message is entered into the software, which then assesses the message for the readability grade level necessary to comprehend it. The SMOG Readability Formula (Office of Cancer Communication, 1992, p. 77) discussed in Chapter 6 offers an inexpensive and expedient set of techniques to assess the report's readability level. However, these approaches do not address *rhetoric and jargon considerations* for each target audience. This requires a more intimate relationship with the target audience and is another area where member checking and advisory groups are helpful.

## Diffusion and Conversion

Different target audiences, as indicated, have different information needs, require different communications, and use different information venues. *Shaping reports on the same practice or research project requires conversion to carry the desired message to each audience.* Rothman and his colleagues (Rothman, 1980; Rothman, Teresa, Kay, & Morningstar, 1983) review differences in communication venues in their discussion of diffusion and conversion of social research and development (social R and D) products. **Diffusion** in Rothman's social R and D model is basically *promotion and dissemination of the products*—the findings of the social R and D, such as the new knowledge or skills—in ways that a particular target audience or information consumers can evaluate and use.

Reporting diffusion can range from **low-intensity** mass communication to **high-intensity** individualized communication (Rothman, 1980, pp. 189–213). An example of low-intensity mass communication is reporting in general-purpose media such as newspapers and television through general media press releases and announcements of the results of a practice demonstration or research project. Middle-intensity diffusion might range from radio and television talk shows with an interactive "call-in" component, magazines

with targeted audiences, and interaction electronic "chat rooms" and Web sites to professional and scholarly journals with a limited professional or scientific audience, and practice manuals. High-intensity reporting is targeted, individualized, personalized, and often features direct contact with specific recipients to provide high-intensity interaction and feedback. Workshops, conference presentations, and reports to clients are examples of high-intensity communication.

**Conversion** *requires adapting the knowledge to the target audience's need and capacity to use it.* Knowledge of the target audience's language and translation of information into this language enhances its use by the target audience. Messages that require a lot of work to receive and understand are more likely to be discarded by the targets. Conversion brings generalizations down to specific applications relevant for a target.

· · · · · · · · · · · · · · · · · · · · · ·

*Considering Elana's practice from earlier chapters, at least twice a year Elana facilitates workshops in the community to inform its residents about domestic violence and the available resources to address it. She also makes presentations at the local high schools discussing how to achieve positive relationships and avoid violence. Elana maintains detailed records of her work with families and tapes sessions at least twice a month, with written informed consent by Bill and Sharon and her other clients, to aid her analysis and in assessing and developing both case and general theory. The analysis and theory are presented at professional conferences and to lay audiences.*

*Karen, another of our social workers, writes a column for a local newspaper. Karen reviews child abuse issues, successes in interventions, and resources available to parents, children, and the community. She is alert to negative reports as opportunities to inform the public of the importance of professional intervention. With informed consent of clients such as Sharra and a respect for client privacy, she also uses the column to diffuse reports of client success. Karen writes using lay terms, sensitive to use of conversation to capture her audience.*

• • • • • • • • • • • • • • • • • • • •

All promotion requires assessment of the target audience's preferred method of obtaining information, accessibility to high- and low-intensity venues, concentration or dispersion, strength of control of communication and information channels, homogeneous or heterogeneous reference groups, and environmental constraints to and controls on information. This assessment guides the diffusion strategy.

## Reporting to Potential Clients

Reporting and reaching potential clients is vital for maintaining a caseload. But reporting goes beyond marketing for fiscal purposes to embrace *social marketing.* If particular interventions have value for certain conditions, their use is in the public good. Potential clients, people who can reasonably use these interventions, need to be made aware of the interventions. More intense communication strategies and techniques to reach potential clients through mass communication includes: feeding information into client networks and support systems, providing key informants with information and using other word of mouth techniques, and holding community forums and special events for target client groups.

## Generic Report Outline

The following generic report outline of content areas is a composite of many resources (Blythe, Tripodi, & Briar, 1994, pp. 205–222; Lincoln & Guba, 1985, pp. 357–381; Marlow, 1993, pp. 248–267; Royce & Thyer, 1996, p. 292; Singleton, Straits, & Straits, 1993, pp. 502–507; Tutty, Rothery, & Grinnell, 1996, pp. 123–150). It provides a comprehensive guide for reporting to a variety of venues, can serve as a general research report

outline, and can be adapted for practice case reports. Content and areas used, but not truthfulness, vary depending on the needs and interest of the *report's* target. Truthfulness is a constant in all reporting. As previously indicated, observe each venue's requirements.

**Title:** The title is clear, concise, descriptive, and reflective of the report's contents and purpose.

**Authorship and sponsorship:** The report provides complete authorship and sponsorship.

All contributors to the research or intervention project are acknowledged and given due recognition. This reflects courtesy, fairness, and honesty and may prevent accusations of plagiarism and future liabilities. In academia, it is too common for the senior researcher to take full credit when equity called for sharing it more widely with junior associates and assistants.

Sponsorships also are fully reported. Sponsorship reporting is important to credit those funding the research or intervention project, and it can enhance the report's credibility. Research or practice conducted under the aegis and sponsorship of prestigious agencies accrue some of the sponsor's stature. Knowledge of sponsors also helps the report's audience and potential users better evaluate and understand any latent biases in the report. Reports of the positive effects of red wine consumption on heart attacks might be evaluated differently depending on whether the research was sponsored and funded by a wine marketing association or by a heart disease prevention group.

Assessing sponsorship often is tricky. While recognizing the National Institute of Mental Health as a federal agency is straightforward, other affiliations are not so direct. Some sponsors are Potemkin or false-front groups. *Potemkin* organizations are hollow organizations that give the impression of representing the public interest. *False-front* organizations are organizations with names that disguise real interests and convey a positive public interest connotation (Rubin, 1997, pp. 202–212). *The Coalition for Health Insurance Choices* (CHIC) sponsoring the "Harry and Louise" television commercials against the 1995 Clinton health care proposals was a false-front organization, solely funded by the Health Insurance Association of America. A Potemkin or false-front organization's aim is to alter the target's view of the position stated from that of narrow economic self-interest to a position with a broad public good interest—choice in health insurances and health care. While the name may not technically be a misrepresentation, its intent is to deceive.

It is not necessary to adhere to the American Anthropological Association's 1980 position that "no reports should be provided to sponsors that are not also available to the general public and, where practicable, to the population studied" (Spradley, 1980, p. 25) to recognize that projects with clandestine sponsors are more likely to have hidden biases than projects with public sponsors. The report needs to indicate when sponsorship carries with it the right of the sponsor to censor the report, even when the right has not been exercised. When the right exists, the report writers may engage in self-censorship to prevent anticipated sponsor censorship. The censoring effects are similar: altering, eliminating, or biasing the information for compatibility with sponsors' interests.

Authorship and sponsorship information is helpful in allowing the audience to locate and communicate with authors. Often members of the audience may wish to pursue knowledge development efforts with the authors, debate and challenge them, or use any research or practice tools described. Many scholarly journals now include their authors' academic or employment affiliation and email or another address of a contact person. If the development and use of intervention knowledge and techniques is a collective enterprise, practice reports require similar information.

1. **Introduction:** The introduction prepares the reader for the body of the report. It contains:

   a. a statement of problem or questions for exploration
   b. a description of the problem
   c. the problem's significance and rationale for studying it

The analogous practice model is the recognition of a problem and establishment of the need for change. Problem solving and interventions begin with the recognition of a need for change by someone. Case reports describe the presenting problem and the process of recognition.

2. **Literature review:** The literature review determines the current state of knowledge and develops the theory guiding the research or the case theory guiding the intervention. It generally covers three parts:

   a. Theoretical and historical perspectives
   b. Identification of gaps in the knowledge and theory
   c. Reiteration of research or intervention's purposes

Royce and Thyer (1996) remind us that a "well-developed literature review helps explain the underpinnings of the intervention by identifying major theoretical explanations of the social problem or phenomenon that prompted a human service program" (p. 296). The literature review avoids being pro-forma and cursory. Resources are too scarce to unknowingly research what is well known or to expend on ill-conceived explorations or theories. The literature review in social work practice is used to develop the case theory. In social work practice, the risks to clients are too great to have interventions guided by ignorance.

Literature reviews are ethical practice requirements. The NASW's Code of Ethics' (*Code of Ethics*, 1997) Ethical Standard 1.04 (b) under "competence" states that social workers "use intervention techniques or approaches that are new to them only after engaging in appropriate study" (p. 8). Ethical Standard 4.01 (b) asserts that social workers "should critically examine and keep current with emerging knowledge relevant to social work. Social workers should routinely review the professional literature" (p. 22).

Whenever materials are used in the literature review and elsewhere in the report, appropriate citations and referencing are needed. The citation's purposes are reflected in its content: (1) To meet legal and ethical considerations by giving credit where credit is due and not to claim the intellectual work of others as one's own. Such intellectual theft is considered plagiarism. (2) To enable a reader to pursue the complete work or literature if desired.

A good reference or citation format satisfies both requirements. A good format provides the appropriate credit and contains sufficient information to allow the reader to follow up. The publication's author or authors, title, source, date, and publisher's location and name are customarily provided. Many formats are possible, although the American Psychological Association's *Publication Manual* (1994) currently predominates in the social work literature. The latest version should be reviewed because the APA manual periodically undergoes revision.

3. **Methodology:** This section covers the research or equivalent practice plan methodologies of design, measurement and data collection, sampling and subjects, and analysis plan.

The design is described in sufficient detail to allow for replication. The reader needs to understand and evaluate any claims the report makes for the research's causal validity. The practice case plan is analogous to the design and is explained in similar detail.

A research report contains the sampling strategy as well as any time and events sampling procedures. Similarly, case reports include the times and rationale and limitations for the time and events sampling used. Whether samples of convenience or a more probabilistic sampling strategy was used needs explication. This information is critical for the audience to place the appropriate confidence in any generalizations drawn from the sample to times, events, populations, and people not sampled or a part of the study.

The subjects, sample frame, clients, or cases are described within the constraints of their right to privacy and confidentiality. Generalizations will relate to units with these traits as limited by the sampling strategy.

Include brief but sufficient descriptions of measurement tools and processes and data collection procedures to allow replication. Present the protocols used to establish reliability and validity, including triangulation, and how they are applicable to the research or practice case reported. It is insufficient to merely state that the measurements are reliable and valid. Reporting reliability and validity is essential even when previously developed, standardized instruments were used. The test is always applicability to the research project or case under consideration, not to any other research effort.

Report the logic and rationale for the data analysis procedures along with the analysis. If you use member-checking panels and procedures with qualitative data, include descriptions of the panel and procedures in the report. A part of reporting's task is to establish and report on the data's "trustworthiness." When member-checking panels are used to establish trustworthiness, consensus and descensus on meaning is sought from the review panel, which represents the range of stakeholders. The review panel fulfills its function best when there is a range of perspectives within each set of stakeholders which the panel can review during each stage of the research and the report development (Lincoln & Guba, 1985, pp. 374–376). If consensus is not obtained, report the descensus.

4. **Results:** The results section contains a descriptive analysis of the factual data; any statistical analysis; whether hypotheses are supported; and case objectives, process, case theory, and statistical significance.

The results present a brief summary of the findings or what Singleton, Straits, and Straits (1993, p. 507) label a "caboose abstract." The use of visual aids such as charts, graphs, and tables in the report provides the audience with an opportunity to perform their own visual analysis. In case reporting for practice, the analysis focuses on case objective significance, process significance, and case theory significance and their meaning to clients and other stake holders. The results and the subsequent discussion sections must be concerned with the conversion issue, enabling other practitioners to use the knowledge in their practice.

5. **Discussion:** The purpose of the discussion section is to present the meaning of the data and findings and their contribution to theory, whether it is a general theory or a case theory.

The discussion section is most concerned with the findings' support of the theory and with the conversion of findings to enable other researchers and practitioners to understand how the knowledge is applicable to practice. The section is a discussion of the case's meaning to the target audience. Since professional knowledge is most meaningful in its application, *all social work research and practice reporting needs to address conversion.* The discussion section also needs to address and incorporate any unexpected findings into a revision of the theory. A well-developed discussion section explicitly confronts the weaknesses and limitations of design, sampling, measurement, and data collection and how they limit generalizations and practical use of the findings. The report recognizes and stays within the design and sample's limitations of causal validity and external validity.

6. **References:** The reference list consists of the references cited in the body of the report.

Often the list of references directly cited in the body of a report is supplemented by references not directly cited that will help the reader understand the topic and theory. Inclusion of references beyond those directly cited is generally governed by the publication source's style preferences. The reference list completes the citation information. A good format contains sufficient information to allow the reader to locate the citation: the publication's author or authors, publication or citation title, publication date, and publisher's location and name. Standard reference models for a range of reference formats is provided by the American Psychological Association's *Publication Manual* (1994, pp. 118–133).

7. **Appendices:** Appendices contain copies of measurement instruments and other information that better enable the audience to understand and use the report but that are not essential to a basic understanding of the report.

Appendices customarily contain the measurement instruments, especially paper-and-pencil instruments, informed consent statements, complete sampling strategies, and raw data presentations that enable readers to better understand and replicate parts of the effort. Each appendix clearly labels its purposes and uses.

## Summary

Reporting is essential for the profession's knowledge development, and important for practitioners and clients. Without reporting, there is no knowledge sharing. A profession does not continue its development if each individual practitioner must uniquely replicate the efforts and experiences of other practitioners. At the same time, reporting is the essential component for accountability and client self-determination and empowerment. Clients cannot make informed judgments unless they have informative reports.

Reporting is vital for public support of the profession. Without usable information, the public is asked to embrace the profession and its mission in ignorance. Conversion and diffusion are necessary processes in public reporting. Successful interventions and cases, with a respect for privacy, need to be reported in language understandable by the target audiences. The diffusion of successes in a competitive professional arena is important if the profession is to remain vital. Diffusion of information on successes is necessary to balance the diffusion of information on the practice failures appropriately reported by the media.

## Discussion Questions and Exercises

Take a case plan where case objectives were met and develop reports for:

1. the case or clients
2. the sponsor or funding source if different from the case
3. professional colleagues
4. a professional journal
5. a media release for the general public

    a. Do the reports differ based on the interests of the targets?

    b. How will the reports' language and construction differ?

    c. How might you reach potential clients who could benefit from the invention?

# CHAPTER FOURTEEN

# Using Research Methodologies for Practice Effectiveness

Throughout these chapters we have emphasized the inherent use of research in practice tools and thinking by social work practitioners. In our model for effective practice, practitioners use research methodologies, including measurement, data collection, design and single case design, control of interventions, sampling, analysis, and reporting. At the same time they employ practice skills by developing helping relationships, communication, and practitioner observation. Social workers intervene to achieve client change guided by case theory and treatment goals based on sound, valid, and reliable information about the client, drawing from normative behavioral and social theories. Intervention in social work is a prediction that a set of behaviors by the practitioner, client, and other components of an action system will produce desired effects and make a positive difference in the client's life.

In this final chapter we present a case example through which we illustrate some of the major points from all the preceding chapters, including the overriding service mission and multilevel nature of social work practice, impacts of values and ethics, and use of multiple sources and methods of knowledge development. To highlight their illustration we use bold type for the practice components and research methodologies presented in earlier chapters. The major principle that guides our practice is this: The client problem and situation determine the methods, theories, and skills used by the social worker.

### PRACTICE CASE   SALLY'S SOCIAL WORK PRACTICE WITH CARMEN RUIZ

Carmen Ruiz is 48 years old and lives by herself in a public housing project. Located in a large Eastern city, the project is old, with many broken windows and hallways filled with debris. Drug dealing leaves empty vials littering the streets.

Referred by a hospital social worker for follow-up after her recent mastectomy, Carmen is seen by Sally, employed by an outpatient facility providing mental health services to residents of the project and surrounding low-income area.

Committed even as a child to "help others," Sally sought out **social work as a profession with a mission to redress inequality, fight oppression, and help individuals live better lives in healthier communities.** Never wanting to be poor again (she too had grown up in public housing), Sally knew she would not become rich as a social worker. Desirous of providing services to those who are poor and seemingly cut off from benefits enjoyed by others, she wanted to work for a publicly funded agency offering a range of services to residents and the community. Sally resonated to the **altruistic and service nature of professional social work practice.**

Since Carmen is recovering from surgery, Sally visits in Carmen's home. Though social workers began as friendly visitors, providing services in client's homes and communities, it is now common for some agencies to provide only in-office services. In order to treat Carmen's problems, however, Sally knows she needs information about Carmen's community and environment. Just as **anthropologists study culture by immersing themselves in the field,** Sally acquires a richer picture of Carmen and the resources available to her by meeting at her home (**participant observation, interviewing time sampling**).

Sally builds towards **belief bonding of the helping relationship,** recognizing it as a "necessary, though not sufficient, condition for the accomplishment of the client's goals and objectives" (Bisman, 1994, p. 79). Presenting herself as competent with expertise to help Carmen, she is respectful, conveying belief in Carmen's worthiness and capacity to change.

Informing Carmen of her role and experience at the agency, she explains that concern by the hospital social worker about Carmen's sadness and anxiety initiated this visit. Asking Carmen to meet with her for two sessions to talk together, Sally informs her that in some situations clients have felt better and have not needed any further visits, but that in others visits were scheduled for a three-month period, in which case they regularly evaluate progress and achievement of goals. They will work together to figure out Carmen's problems and plan ways to help her feel better (**informed consent**).

Advising Carmen that their talks are private, she also explains that she meets regularly with her supervisor and team at the agency. Should there be concern that Carmen was at risk of hurting herself, Sally is obligated to provide her with protection (**limits to confidentiality, duty to protect, and informed consent; relationship with supervisor and peers and member checking; triangulation and guarding against false positives and negatives**).

When Carmen describes a series of losses including ending a 20-year relationship two months ago because of her boyfriend's alcoholism; losing vision in her right eye two years ago, which stemmed from her diabetes; menopausal symptoms of hot flashes with extreme sweating and very heavy blood flows; and the mastectomy three weeks ago, with continuing weakness in her right arm (**baseline information from available data**), Sally affirms the many serious losses and asks if there is one that bothers her the most. Carmen responds that she feels most bad about her mastectomy and is reminded of it every day when she looks in the mirror. These persistent thoughts (lasting for several hours) lead to more thoughts about her other problems. Concerned that **they construct a shared conceptualization of reality,** Sally shares with Carmen the meaning she attributes to the statements Carmen expresses (**respondent validation**). Together they identify the terrible feeling resulting from these thoughts as "depression."

Central in Sally's approach to her practice with Carmen are her beliefs in **client self-determination**. This value mandates **informal consent** at each step. This means that Sally struggles to increase Carmen's opportunities for functioning as an independent and autonomous adult. Sally understands that societal ideas about cancer and beauty helped shape Carmen's extreme fear and discomfort with her mastectomy.

Sally often has trouble hearing Carmen, who speaks very little about herself, and when she says something it is usually in a monotone with no indication of any feelings about what she says. Sally reflects on and validates Carmen's experiences with comments such as, "I know you are managing many losses all at one time. Most people would feel sad and overwhelmed facing all these problems—is that how you feel?" (**respondent validation**) She also uses silence to encourage Carmen's talking, looks directly at her with attention and interest, and asks open-ended questions to obtain more information (**semistructured interview for data collection and communication**).

To construct a valid case theory to explain, understand, and plan an intervention for Carmen's problems and determine whether "depression" captures the situation, Sally **collects data through observation and focused interviews with Carmen,** talks with the hospital social worker (**construct and concurrent validity, triangulation, reduction of false positives and enhancement of true positives**) and gains a historical perspective by encouraging Carmen to talk about her life as a younger person as well as about when she first began to experience these feelings she calls "depression" (**baseline from available data, construction of reality**).

She learns that Carmen quit her job as a cashier in a local grocery store about four years ago when she began to have problems with her vision. Things never became "right" after then. Her boyfriend's drinking increased and he seemed uncomfortable around her.

Sally knows that her **measurement and data collection processes determine the integrity and validity of her data,** so she always considers the kind of information she needs and the best available means to gather it. This will greatly affect the possibilities of making **true positive and negative judgments in assessment. For systematic observations in the data collection,** Sally and Carmen agree to meet one hour weekly for twelve sessions to discuss her feelings and work out resolutions for some of her problems. At least 45 minutes of every hour will focus solely on Carmen and her feelings and problems since she is very reluctant to talk about herself, preferring to discuss neighbors and family. They consider **specific problems in func-**

**tioning,** including: sleep disturbance, with sustained sleep of less than two hours at night; poor concentration, with inability to sit and read or engage in any sustained activity for more than a few minutes other than sitting before the television; extreme fatigue, with little energy to prepare meals or clean up around the apartment; little contact with others except for one or two chats a week with a neighbor and two phone calls from her sister; frequent bad thoughts daily about the mastectomy and feeling at times she did not want to go on this way much longer **(case theory guidance for intervention proceduralization, time sampling strategy for client available data, operationalization of concepts).**

At their very first meeting, Carmen agrees that before their second meeting she will **record in a log** her hours of sleep, frequency of bad feelings, and amount of food eaten to provide measurements of some of the problematic behaviors **(measurement and data collection, sampling, baseline).** Carmen enters the number of hours of bad and good thoughts and rates the severity of the thoughts on a five-point scale: 1 equals very bad, and 5 equals wonderful **(interval time sampling, ordinal scale with respondent self-anchoring).**

Recognizing that the act of observing these behaviors may alter them **(reflexivity)**, Sally asks Carmen to continue with her usual behaviors and merely record them for this next week. Moreover, in addition to the interviews she has Carmen complete the **Beck Depression Inventory (measurement, triangulation, reliability, social desirability bias).**

She also requests Carmen's permission to audiotape their interviews to help her better prepare with her supervisor and provide Carmen with the best possible social work services **(informed consent).** Teams at Sally's agency meet regularly, offering each other **expertise in a peer review process** as they construct their case theories **(triangulation, member checking, measurement, expert validity, intervention measurement, monitoring).** The team reviews the audiotape and assesses the client and intervention using checksheets. Sally compares these with her own, providing a guide for narrative content analysis **(interview narratives using content analysis, interrater reliability, intervention integrity, reliability, prevent drift).**

After the first visit, Sally takes a walk in Carmen's immediate neighborhood to collect data on the community resources and check out the proximity of grocery stores, pharmacies, churches, and medical offices **(community survey).**

After the second session, using **measurements** from the log, scores on the Beck inventory and gaining **expert validity through member checking with her team and supervisor (triangulation),** Sally develops the following case theory:

> Carmen may be clinically depressed. Her feelings of sadness, at times despair, probably result from her many serious losses over a period of time. Since ending the relationship with her boyfriend, she lacks any meaningful relationships except occasional calls with her sister. Carmen is isolated and lonely and is at risk of suicide. She feels bad that she is not properly taking care of herself yet seems to have no interest in functioning more autonomously.
>
> Health problems add to Carmen's lack of independence. Should she go out on her own, she worries about inability to manage without vision in the one eye and the heavy bleeding. These fears are exacerbated by high crime in her neighborhood. She does not see herself as an autonomous adult.

Sally acquires knowledge from general theories to help explain Carmen's behaviors and learns that some of these changes occur to women about her age.

Pearlman (1993) posits there is a developmental stage of "late mid-life astonishment" that occurs between the ages of 50 and 60 and is marked by a series of losses including menopause, declining health, and changes in physical appearance. Jue (1994) admonishes that individuals may not experience all stages or in the order theories suggest, while from Simos (1979) Sally learns that loss is a universal human experience and that its exploration is deeply personal and complex (**case theory assessment for deductive fallacies, false positives, and false negatives threatening its valid incorporation of general theories**).

Carmen needs to separate and address problems that can be changed, acknowledge and grieve her losses, and learn to expect continuing feelings of sadness as a part of her life (**case theory, case objectives**).

Recognizing that case theory construction is a joint activity between her and Carmen, Sally and Carmen develop these hypotheses together, increasing the **belief bonding of the relationship and building ground for the intervention (mutuality in assessment process, client self determination).**

Sally also turns to literature to help her better understand issues of loss. In *One True Thing* (1994), Anna Quindlen poignantly portrays a woman dying of cancer and the effects of the dying on her daughter and husband. Gloria Naylor has helped Sally understand issues facing women of color, particularly in *The Women of Brewster Place* (1983).

Sally is Black, while Carmen is Latino, and Sally knows she must not assume that they share similar experiences even though they are both women from the projects and members of minority groups (**practitioner observation to gain objectivity and develop shared constructions of reality**). Often hearing her father's expressions of hostile feelings towards Puerto Rican and other Latino neighbors, she knows she must be attentive to any of her own prejudiced reactions. It is also possible that Carmen may resent her as a black professional woman and bias her responses (Bachman & O'Mally, 1984; Cotter, Cohen, & Coulter, 1982), so Sally considers issues of difference and the complexities of similarities.

Again she turns to literature for understanding and guidance. In college she read *The Autobiography of an Ex-Colored Man*. Johnson's (1927) portrayal of "passing" with light skin provided her with a deep comprehension of the horrible effects of race on identity formation and belonging. To retain her compassion and enhance her understanding, Sally continues to read authors of color, Latinas, and others who address issues of race in their work. She recently read *White Boys*, a collection of stories by Reginald McKnight (1997), offering her a powerful affirmation of the racism experienced by middle class Blacks. Many of her clients are Latino and she has found books by Gabriel Garcia Marquez enlightening. In his *News of a Kidnapping* (1997) she learned much about resilience and its importance in sustaining people through difficulties. A female Latino author, Ferre, in *Eccentric Neighborhoods* (1998), chronicles some of the changes in Puerto Rico with the arrival of Americans through telling the story of family alienation juxtaposed with class differences. Sally prefers female authors, and particularly likes Louise Erdrich's *The Antelope Wife* (1998), which addresses the mysteries and strength of family bonds.

The case theory directs the intervention and forms the **problem statement.**

Carmen has *problems in functioning,* including: poor sleep patterns, lack of concentration, frequent feelings of fatigue, minimal social contact, frequent bad thoughts about her recent mastectomy, and considerations of suicide (**operationalization of concepts**).

Sally knows the importance of *clarity in goals formulation.* Just as she needed an **operational definition for depression in the case theory,** she and Carmen now need **clear indicators of change (SMARRT case objectives, case objectives' significance).**

In complex situations with several problematic areas (which describes most of her cases), Sally has found that prioritizing the more immediate changes sets destinations and time frames for her and the client. She and Carmen break their work into **short-term** and **long-term case objectives.**

They agree the **long-term case objectives** are to reduce Carmen's feelings of depression and increase her overall feelings of well-being, including a sense that she is taking care of herself as an autonomous and independent adult. Indicators include: ability to sleep at least six hours per night; enhanced concentration, with ability to sit and read for at least one hour at a time at least nine times per week; no suicidal thoughts; eating three meals of healthy food each day; no bad thoughts about the mastectomy for an hour each day; increased social interaction with others; and exploration of possibilities of return to employment (**concurrent and empirical validity, case objectives**).

**Measurements** will vary depending on the particular **case objectives.** However, if the case theory is valid, if improvement occurs on one objective, Sally expects improvement on the other indicators, although perhaps not uniformly. **Client logging** will measure and collect data collection for the behavioral indicators. **Respondent-anchored scales** and **interview narratives** will **measure the indicators** that are feelings and thoughts. Increased social interaction by Carmen with others indicates she is achieving this objective, and Carmen **logs the interactions.** Exploring possibilities of return to employment requires Carmen to also log the number of and amount of time spent reviewing classifieds in the local newspaper. Sally and Carmen will briefly discuss the classifieds reviewed during their interview sessions. **The Beck Depression Inventory provides a criterion (triangulation, SMARRT case objectives, case significance).**

While Sally does not always develop formal written contracts with her clients, she does with clients like Carmen who seem suicidal. In the **contract** Carmen agrees not to hurt herself and to call Sally or a hot line if she has that feeling. They also include what they each will do and plan for the length of time needed to achieve the objectives (**intervention compliance or control of intervention, case objective significance**).

They agree that they have already begun solid work on their first **short-term objective**—building a relationship with trust and confidence so that Carmen will more freely talk about herself and her situation. Evidence is their decision to meet weekly and spend 45 minutes discussing Carmen's feelings. They both agree to audiotape the sessions and evaluate the session by a checksheet (**measurement and monitoring of intervention and case objectives during the intervention phase, narrative content analysis**).

Sally's second objective is a psychiatric consultation for medication assessment (**triangulation, risk of false negatives**). At first Carmen refuses, stating she does not like medicines and is afraid they could activate dormant cancer. Sally expresses her concern about the risk of suicide, explains the biological basis of many depressions, and reminds Carmen that her mother and sister both exhibited signs of depression (they discovered this in the **available data collection about family history**). After Sally advises Carmen of her potential risks and poor prognosis without considering medication as one component of her treatment (**informed consent, duty to protect**), Carmen finally agrees to a psychiatric consultation.

The third objective is to increase Carmen's social interaction with family and others in the community while the fourth focuses on improving Carmen's nutrition.

**Procedures** and **protocols** make clear each of their activities to achieve the objectives and include: twelve weekly hours of talk therapy, with 45 minutes of each session devoted to examining Carmen's feelings; referral by Sally to a psychiatrist for medication assessment; Carmen obtaining information about the breast cancer survivors' support group offered at the hospital (which can also offer exercises to strengthen her arm); Carmen renewing contact with her sister who lives in another part of the city; Sally obtaining services from Meals on Wheels for the next two weeks; and, following further recovery from her surgery (at the end of the month), participation in church activities or volunteering, where Carmen would spend at least 10 hours per week outside the home. The intervention procedures and protocols are laid out in a checksheet schedule for both Sally and Carmen. Each independently enters the date when each event in the protocol is completed (**intervention proceduralization, measurement and data collection, triangulation**).

Sally knows from experience the importance of preventing drifts from the intervention. To maintain focus on changing two of the **dependent variables**—the bad thoughts and the lack of concentration—Sally draws from a cognitive approach. Advocating challenging clients' unrealistic "automatic thoughts," Beck (1979) calls for engaging them in "constructive" activities to dispel some of those thoughts (**case theory guides intervention**).

Carmen agrees to record her efforts to arrange for volunteer or church activities. In the third week of treatment, she spends a half hour for one day and an hour on two more days making phone calls. During the fourth week, she spends an hour a day for four days. By the end of all this calling, she finds a church needing volunteer help to mark prices on clothing and household items in preparation for a fundraising flea market. They ask her to give them two hours a day, four days a week, and will arrange for another volunteer to pick Carmen up and take her home.

Sally also has Carmen continue charting her bad feelings, which they initiated during the very first week of treatment (**charting for intervention monitoring and measurement, case objectives measurement, A–B measurements**). Considering the first week as baseline, Carmen's chart for that period indicate six hours per day of bad thoughts in the severity range of 1s and 2s, for an average of 1.3. For week 2, bad feelings reduce from six to four hours per day with an average severity of 1.9. By weeks 3 and 4, the average severity is 2.5 and a reduction of bad feelings to three hours per day.

As Sally and Carmen discuss the chart together, it becomes clear to both of them that even Carmen's calling around about activities and the act of charting reduce the severity of the bad thoughts (**analysis for case objective significance**). Weeks 7 to 12 indicate further improvement, with more positive thoughts than negative and an average of 3.5.

Deciding against continuing charting insomnia because Sally observed that the attention to the number of hours slept has been counterproductive— Carmen reports a focus at night on trying to keep track of the time—this keeps her awake (**reflexivity and intervention shift**). Drawing from literature on loss and grieving, Sally and Carmen engage in grief therapy for six sessions. Sally gives Carmen permission for her bad feelings, validates the serious losses, and normalizes them by acknowledging that most persons would be depressed in these circumstances (Jensen, 1994; Shulman, 1984).

In addition to their audiotapes, they both use a **check sheet (intervention measurement)** to assess topics covered. Carmen measures sleep patterns by logging on a **simple respondent-anchored scale** upon awaking in the morning if she feels well rested (5) or tired (1). This logs the subjective need for sleep.

Sally also comments about Carmen's monotone and barely audible voice, and they discuss other possible effects on body and functioning from these continual bad feelings.

Audiotaping sessions from both the pre- and treatment phases, Sally chooses a few minutes from the start, middle, and end of each session to review with her supervisor (**stratified random probability time sampling) to monitor, evaluate, and analyze the intervention and measure by content analysis** Carmen's expressions of feelings. From listening to the early tapes, Sally and her supervisor notice Carmen's extremely low monotone, with frequent sighing.

Considering this behavior an indicator of Carmen's depression and bad feelings, Sally decides to play back segments of the tape with Carmen. They listen together and pay close attention to tone and intensity of voice (**treatment shift**).

From what they hear, they construct a chart to indicate for each session the amount of audible speaking, number of sighs, and changes from the flat monotone quality (**measurement, content analysis**).

For the last six sessions Carmen speaks in a loud and clear voice for over three-quarters of the session, sighs two or three times instead of the twelve or more from the beginning, and in the last three sessions laughs once or twice (**content analysis, case objective significance**). Use of the audiotaping has proven extremely useful to Carmen for measuring and assessing her own change as well as to Sally and her supervisor. In their discussions together, Carmen reports having more energy and greater concentration (**intervention, case objective, process, case theory significance, member checking, reporting**).

As part of their team approach and **peer review process**, Sally **reports** to her team at the same time she **reassesses** with Carmen (**reporting and diffusion**). When she talks with either Carmen or colleagues, Sally works hard to not use jargon. Often she cannot understand what other social workers say to her and worries that she places a different meaning than they do on terms such as depression or anxiety. Though they are frequently used, she knows these terms convey different meanings based on personal experiences and interpretations and can result in a false sense of understanding. Sally forces herself to be precise and **quantifies Carmen's problems in her presentation to the team outlining the specific and measurable outcomes they achieved (member checking, operationalization).**

Sally recognizes the importance of disseminating information about social work, both to other practitioners and to the larger society. She submits papers on her practice with clients who have depression to professional conferences, and has published two of these in professional journals. She provides community workshops through her agency with information about depression and available community resources. **Reporting and diffusion** is important to the client and to the community.

## Summary

Sally's practice plan with Carmen is basically a *single case design*. Sally obtains baseline and follow-up measures to assess case objective significance, which along with Carmen's feelings and functioning have **critical, significance though not statistical, significance.** Sally proceduralizes, measures, and monitors her intervention. Her practice with Carmen illustrates the major points in this book: *Driven by a practice perspective, practitioners use research methodologies for effective practice. Social work has extraordinary breadth, with deep roots in social norms and mores. Social workers need humility to place their struggles for meaning and precision within the more universal struggle by most disciplines to develop and understand knowledge. This is a process of dynamic evolution, filled with continual change and challenges to well established traditions.*

Practitioners need to use research methodology and epistemology in practice, to develop case theory and achieve case objectives. The ideological base of paradigms shapes our assumptions of the world. Client problems must guide social work methods and social work intervention, the methodologies of the case plan, measurement, data collection, and assessment. We develop our questions and measurements and data collection processes to answer our concerns. Social work's broad service paradigm of person and environment requires multiple approaches to knowledge development and multiple methodologies for practice interventions.

## Discussion Questions and Exercises

1. In what ways did Sally's view of the world shape her approach to practice with Carmen?

2. Critique the data collection processes that Sally used.

3. Evaluate Sally's case theory and its ability to predict intervention.

4. Consider other potential case theories to explain Carmen. What interventions would follow?

5. If the intervention is successful and SMAART objectives achieved to whom and how should the information be diffused.

# References

Abbott, A. (1988). *The system of professions. Chicago: University of Chicago Press.*

Achienstein, P. (1971). *Law and explanation: An essay in the philosophy of science.* New York: Oxford University Press.

Addams, J. (1902). *Democracy and social ethics.* New York: Macmillan.

*Administrative systems for church management.* (n.d.). Colorado Springs, CO: Systemation, Inc.

Alter, C., & Egan, M. (1997). Logic Modeling: A tool for critical thinking in social work practice. *Journal of Social Work Education, 33:*1, 85–102.

Alter, C., & Evens, W. (1990). *Evaluating your practice: A guide to self-assessment.* NY: Springer.

American Psychological Association. (1994). *Publication manual of the American Psychological Association* (4th ed.). Hyattsville, MD: Author.

Anderson, R., & Carter, I. (1984). *Human behavior in the social environment: A social systems approach* (3rd ed.). New York: Aldine.

Aronson, S. H., & Sherwood, C. C. (1967). Researchers versus practitioners: Problems in social action research. *Social Work, 12,* 89–96.

Austin, D. M. (1983). The Flexner myth and the history of social work. *Social Service Review, 57,* 357–77.

Bachman, J. G., & O'Malley, P. M. (1977). Self-esteem in young men: A longitudinal analysis of the impact of education and occupational attainment. *Journal of Personality and Social Psychology, 35,* 365–380.

Bachman, J. G., & O'Malley, P. M. (1984). Yea-saying, nay-saying, and going to extremes: Black and white differences in response styles. *Public Opinion Quarterly, 48,* 491–501.

Bailey, C. L. (1996). *A guide to field research.* Thousand Oaks, CA: Pine Forge Press.

Baldwin, J. (1998a). *Collected essays.* (Selected by T. Morrison). New York: The Library of America.

Baldwin, J. (1998b). *Early novels and stories* (Selected by T. Morrison). New York: The Library of America.

Barnum, B. J. S. (1990). *Nursing theory: Analysis, application, evaluation* (3rd ed.). Glenview, IL: Scott, Foresman/Little, Brown Higher Education.

Bartlett, H. (1958). Toward clarification and improvement of social work practice. *Social Work, 3:* 2, 3–9.

Bartlett, H. (1970). *The common base of social work practice*. New York: National Association of Social Workers.

Barzun, J. (1943). History, popular and unpopular. In J. Strayer (Ed.), *The interpretation of history*. Princeton: Princeton University Press.

Baskin, D. B. (1990). *Computer applications in psychiatry and psychology*. New York: Brunner/Mazel.

Batchen, G. (1997). *Burning with desire: The conception of photography*. Cambridge, MA: The MIT Press.

Bateson, G. (1972). *Steps to an ecology of mind*. New York: Ballantine Books.

Bellah, R., Madsen, R., Sullivan, W., Swidler, A., & Tipton, S. (1991). *The good society*. New York: Vintage Books.

Benbenishty, R., & Ben-Zaken, A. (1988). Computer-aided process of monitoring task centered family intervention. *Social Work Research and Abstracts, 24:1,* 7–9.

Berger, P. L., & Luckmann, T. (1967). *The social construction of reality: A treatise in the sociology of knowledge*. New York: Anchor Books.

Berlin, S. B. (1990). Dichotomous and complex thinking. *Social Service Review, 64:* 1, 46–59.

Berlin, S. B. (1983). Single-case evaluation: Another version. *Social Work Research and Abstracts, 19,* 3–11.

Berlin, S. B., & Marsh, J. C. (1993). *Informing practice decisions*. New York: Macmillan.

Bernard, H. R. (1994). *Research methods in anthropology: Qualitative and quantitative approaches* (2nd ed.). Thousand Oaks, CA: Sage.

Bernstein, N. (1995, December 4). Caseworkers pressured to close children's files. *The New York Times*, pp. 1, 26.

Birdwhistell, R. (1973). *Kinesics and Context*. Great Britian: Penguin Press.

Bisman, C. (1994). *Social work practice: Cases and principles*. Pacific Grove, CA: Brooks/Cole.

Blake, J., & Davis, K. (1964). Norms, values and sanctions. In R. E. Faris (Ed.), *Handbook of modern sociology* (pp. 456–484). Chicago: Rand McNally.

Blankenship, R. (1977). *Colleagues in organization*. New York: John Wiley & Sons.

Bloom, M., (1983). Empirically based clinical practice. Aaron Rosenblatt & Diana Waldfogel (Eds.), *Handbook of clinical social work*. (pp. 560–582). San Francisco, CA: Jossey-Bass.

Bloom, M., Fischer, J., & Orme, J. (1995). *Evaluating practice: Guidelines for the accountable professional*, (2nd. ed.) Boston: Allyn & Bacon.

Bloom, M., & Orme, J. (1993). Ethics and single-system design. *Journal of Social Service Research. 18:1–2,* 161–180.

Bloom, M., Wood, K., & Chambon, A. (1991). The six languages of social work. *Social Work, 36:6,* 530–534.

Blumer, H. (1969). *Symbolic interactionism*. Englewood Cliffs, NJ: Prentice-Hall.

Blundo, R., Greene, R., & Gallant, P. (1994). A constructivist approach with diverse populations. In R. Greene (Ed.), *Human behavior theory: A diversity framework* (pp. 115–132). New York: Aldine de Gruyter.

Blythe, B. (1990). Inproving the fit between single-subject designs and practice. In L. Videka-Sherman & W. Reid (Eds.), *Advances in clinical social work research* (pp. 29–32). Silver Springs, MD: NASW Press.

Blythe, B., & Tripodi, T. (1989). *Measurement in direct social work practice*. Newbury Park, CA: Sage.

Blythe, B., Tripodi, T., & Briar, S. (1994). *Direct practice research in human service agencies*. NY: Columbia University Press.

Bok, S. (1982). *On the ethics of concealment and revelation*. New York: Pantheon.

Bostwick, G. J., Jr., & Kyle, N. S. (1985). Measurement. In R. M. Grinnell, Jr. (Ed.), *Social work research and evaluation*, 2nd ed. (pp. 149–160). Itasca, IL: F. E. Peacock.

Bowen, M. (1978). *Family therapy in clinical practice*. New York: Aronson.

Bowlby, J. (1977). The making and breaking of affectional bonds. *British Journal of Psychiatry, 130*, 201–210.

Brawley, E. A. (1993). *Mass media and human services: Getting the message across*. Beverly Hills, CA: Sage.

Briar, S. (1973). The age of accountability [editorial]. *Social Work, 18*:2, 233.

Briar, S. (1990). Empiricism in clinical practice: Present and future. In L. Videka-Sherman & W. Reid (Eds.), *Advances in clinical social work research* (pp. 1–7). Silver Springs, MD: NASW Press.

Brod, S. J. (1987). Coordinating and distributing emergency medical information by computer. *Social Work, 32*:6, 42–543.

Bulmer, M. (Ed.) (1982). *Social research ethics: An examination of the merits of covert participant observation*. New York: Holmes & Meier.

Butterfield, W. H. (1983). Computers for social work practitioners. *Practice Digest, 6*:3. [entire issue]

California Task Force to Promote Self-Esteem and Social Responsibility. (1990). *Toward a state of esteem: The final report of the California task force to promote self-esteem*. Sacramento, CA: Bureau of Publications, California State Department of Education.

Camasso, M. J., & Jagannathan, R. (1995). Prediction accuracy of the Washington and Illinois risk assessment instruments: An application of receiver operating characteristic curve analysis, *Social Work Research, 19*:2, 174–183.

Campbell, D. T., & Stanley, J. C. (1966). *Experimental and quasi-experimental designs for research*. Chicago: Rand-McNally.

Carr-Saunders, A. M., & Wilson, P. A. (1933). *The professions*. Oxford: Clarendon Press.

Chambers, C. (March 1986). Women in the creation of the profession of social work. *Social Service Review*, 1–33.

Chomsky, N. (1968). *Language and mind*. New York: Harcourt, Brace & World.

Chubb, N. H., Fertman, C. I., & Ross, J. L. (1997). Adolescent self-esteem and locus of control: A longitudinal study of gender and age differences. *Adolescence, 32*:125, 113–129.

Clark, C. F. (1988). Computer applications in social work. *Social Work Research and Abstracts, 24*:1, 15–19.

Cobb, S., & Jones, J. (1984). Social support, support groups, and marital relationships. In S. Duck (Ed.), *Repairing personal relationships*. London: Academic Press.

Code of Ethics Revision Committee. (1996, January). Proposal: Revision of the Code of Ethics. *NASW News*, 19–22.

Cohan, N. (1997). AIDS and the family narrative: Reconstructing a story to encompass an illness. In J. Atwood (Ed.), *Challenging family therapy situations: Pespectives in social construction* (pp. 71–98). New York: Springer.

Cohen, N. (1958). *Social work in the American tradition.* New York: Dryden Press.

Cohen, S., & Syme, S. (1985). *Social support and health.* Orlando, FL: Academic Press.

Cole, S. (1992). *Making science: Between nature and society.* Cambridge, MA: Harvard University Press.

Cook, T. D., & Campbell, D. T. (1979). *Quasi-experimentation: Design and analysis issues for field settings.* Boston: Houghton Mifflin.

Coopersmith, S. (1959). A method for determining types of self-esteem. *Journal of Abnormal Social Psychology, 59,* 87–94.

Cotter, P. R., Cohen, J., & Coulter, P. B. (1982). Race of interviewer effect in telephone interviews. *Public Opinion Quarterly, 46,* 278–284.

Council on Social Work Education. (1992). *Curriculum policy statement for master's degree programs in social work education.* Arlington, VA: Author.

Cowger, C. D. (1994). Assessing client strengths: Clinical assessment for client empowerment. *Social Work, 39,* 262–268.

Craft, J. L. (1990). *Statistic and data analysis for social workers* (2nd ed.). Itasca, IL: F. E. Peacock.

Derrida, J. (1972). *Positions.* Trans. A. Bass. London: Athlone.

Derrida, J. (1977). *Of grammatology.* Trans. G. C. Spivak. Baltimore: Johns Hopkins Press.

Deutsch, K. (1952). Communication theory and social science. *American Journal of Orthopsychiatry, 22:*469–83.

Donner, S., & Sessions, P. (1995). *Garrett's interviewing: Its principles and methods* (4th ed., rev.). Milwaukee, WN: Families International, Inc.

Drucker, P. F. (1974). *Management: Tasks, responsibilities and practices.* New York: Harper & Row.

Dubin, R. (1978). *Theory building.* New York: Free Press.

Dunlap, K. M. (1993). A history of research in social work education: 1915–1991. *Journal of Social Work Education, 29:*3, 293–302.

Durkheim, E. (1938). *The rules of the sociological method.* Chicago: University of Chicago Press.

Dyson, F. (1995, May 25). The scientist as rebel. *The New York Review of Books,* pp. 31–33.

Ehrenreich, J. (1985). *The altruistic imagination.* Ithaca, NY: Cornell University Press.

Eighner, L. (1993). *Travels with Lizbeth.* New York: St. Martin's Press.

Eisenberg, A. (1998, April 23). Computers are starting to listen, and understand. *The New York Times,* pp. E1, E8.

Erdrich, L. (1998). *The antelope wife.* New York: HarperCollins.

Etzioni, A. (1993). *The spirit of community: Rights, responsibilities and the communitarian agenda.* New York: Crown.

Everdell, W. (1997). *The first moderns.* Chicago: University of Chicago Press.

Fanshell, D. (Ed.). (1980). *The future of social work research.* Washington, DC: NASW.

Fawcett, J., & Downs, F. (1992). *The relationship of theory and research.* Philadelphia: F. A. Davis.

Ferre, R. (1998). *Eccentric neighborhoods.* New York: Farrar, Strauss & Giroux.

Fine, S. F., & Glasser, P. H. (1996). *The first helping interview: Engaging the client and building trust.* Newbury Park, CA: Sage.

Finn, J. (1988). Microcomputers in private nonprofit agencies: a survey of trends and training requirements. *Social Work Research and Abstracts, 24:*1, 10–14.

Finn, J. (1996). Computer-based self help groups: On-line recovery for addiction. *Computers in Human Services, 13:*1 21–41.

Fischer, J. (1981). The social work revolution. *Social Work, 26:* 199–207.

Fischer, J. (1993). Empirically based practice: The end of ideology? *Journal of Social Service Research, 18:*1–2, 19–64.

Fischer, J., & Corcoran, K. (1994). *Measurement for clinical practice: A sourcebook,* Vol. 1 (2nd ed.). New York: The Free Press.

Flew, A. (1984). *A dictionary of philosophy* (2nd ed.). New York: St. Martin's Press.

Flexner, A. (1915). Is social work a profession? *Proceedings of the National Conference of Charities and Correction* (pp. 576–590). Chicago: Hildmann.

Fong, R., Spickard, P. R., & Ewalt, P. L. (1995). A multiracial reality: Issues for social work. *Social Work, 40:*6, 725–728.

Foucault, M. (1969). *The archaeology of knowledge.* Trans. A. Sheridan. London: Tavistock, 1972.

Frankel, C. (1966). The moral framework of the idea of welfare. In J. S. Morgan (Ed.), *Welfare and wisdom* (pp. 147–164). Toronto: University of Toronto Press.

Franklin, C. (1995, September). Expanding the vision of the social constructionist debates: Creating relevance for practitioners. *Families in Society,* pp. 395–407.

Freidson, E. (1974). Dominant professions, bureaucracy, and client services. In Y. Hasenfeld & English (Eds.), *Human service organizations* (pp. 428–448). Ann Arbor, MI: University of Michigan Press.

Gambrill, E. (1968). Social study, past and future. *Social Casework, 49,* 403–409.

Gambrill, E. (1983). *Casework: A competency-based approach.* Englewood Cliffs, NJ: Prentice-Hall.

Geertz, C. (1995). *After the fact.* Cambridge, MA: Harvard University Press.

Gergen, K. (1985). The social constructionist movement in modern psychology. *American Psychologist, 40:* 266–275.

Gibbs, L., & Gambrill, E. (1996). *Critical thinking for social workers: A workbook.* Thousand Oaks, CA: Pine Forge Press.

Gingerich, W. (1990). Rethinking single case evaluation. In L. Videka-Sherman & W. Reid (Eds.), *Advances in Clinical Social Work Research* (pp. 11–24). Silver Springs, MD: NASW Press.

Gleick, J. (1987). *Chaos.* New York: Penguin.

Goldstein, E. G. (1995). Working with persons with AIDS. In E. Goldman (Ed.), *Ego psychology and social work practice* (pp. 274–281). New York: Free Press.

Goldstein, H. (1986). Toward the integration of theory and practice: A humanistic approach. *Social Work, 31,* 352–357.

Goode, W. A. (1969). The theoretical limits of professionalization. In A. Etzioni (Ed.), *The semi-professions and their organization* (pp. 266–313). New York: Free Press.

Gordon, W. (1965). Knowledge and value: Their distinction and relationship in clarifying social work practice. *Social Work, 36:* 2, 106–113.

Gordon, W. (1983). Social work revolution or evolution. *Social Work, 28:*3, 181–185.

Gordon, W., & Bartlett, H. (1959). Generalizations in medical social work: Preliminary findings. *Social Work, 4,* 72–76.

Gould, S. J. (1983). *Hen's teeth and horse's toes*. New York: Norton.

Grady, D. (1998, April 23). Faking pain and suffering in Internet support groups. *The New York Times*, pp. E1, E7.

Greene, R. (1991). General systems theory. In R. Greene & P. Ephross (Eds.), *Human behaviors theory and social work practice* (pp. 227–259). New York: Aldine de Gruyter.

Greene, R., & Saltman, L. E. (1994). Symbolic interactionism: Social work assessment, meanings, and language. In R. Greene (Ed.), *Human Behavior Theory: A Diversity Approach* (pp. 55–73). New York: Aldine de Gruyter.

Greenwood, E. (July 1957). Attributes of a profession. *Social Work, 45–55*.

Griffin-Shelly, E., Sandler, K. R., & Lees, C. (1990). Sex-role perceptions in chemically dependent subjects: Adults versus adolescents. *International Journal of the Additions, 25*:12, 1383–1391.

Grinnell, R. M., Jr. (1997). *Social work research & evaluation: Quantitative and qualitative approaches* (5th ed.). Itasca, IL: F. E. Peacock.

Grinnell, R. M., Jr., et al. (1994). Social work researchers' quest for respectability. *Social Work, 39*:4, 469–470.

Gummesson, E. (1991). *Qualitative methods in management research* (rev. ed.). Newbury Park, CA: Sage.

Gurney, P. W. (1988). *Self-esteem in children with special education needs*. London: Routledge.

Gustafson, J. M. (1982). Professions as "callings." *Social Service Review, 56*, 501–515.

Gutierrez, L. (1990). Working with women of color: An empowerment perspective. *Social Work, 35*:2, 149–153.

Haber, S. (1991). *The quest for authority and honor in the American professions, 1750–1900*. Chicago: University of Chicago Press.

Hammersley, M., & Atkinson, P. (1983). *Ethnography: Principles in practice*. New York: Tavistock.

Hardcastle, D. (1987). *The social work labor force*. Social work education monograph series. Austin, TX: University of Texas School of Social Work.

Hardcastle, D. (1990). Legal regulation of social work. In *Encyclopedia of social work* (18th ed.) (pp. 203–217). Silver Springs, MD: NASW.

Hardcastle, D., & Brownstein, C. (1989). Private practitioners: Profile and motivations for independent practice. *Journal of Independent Social Work, 4*:1, 7–18.

Hardcastle, D., & Harkness, D. (1982). Organizational obstacles and facilitating conditions for information use. In C. A. Rapp (Ed.), *The management of information transfer for the employment and training field* (pp. 56–85). Lawrence, KS: The University of Kansas School of Social Welfare and the Human Resources Program.

Hardcastle, D., Wenocur, S., & Powers, P. (1997). *Community practice: Theories and skills for social workers*. New York: Oxford University Press.

Harkness, D., & Hensley, H. (1991). Changing the focus of social work supervision: Effects on client satisfaction and generalized contentment. *Social Work, 36*:6, 506–512.

Hartman, A., & Laird, J. (1983). *Family centered social work practice*. New York: Free Press.

Hawkins, J. M., & Allen, R. (Eds.). (1991). *The Oxford encyclopedic english dictionary*. New York: Oxford University Press.

Heineman Pieper, M. (1986). Some common misunderstandings of the heuristic approach [Opinions from the Field]. *Social Work Research & Abstracts, 22:*1, 2.

Heineman Pieper, M. (1989). The heuristic paradigm: A unifying and comprehensive approach to social work research. *Brown Foundation Lecture in Research at the Smith College School for Social Work,* 8–34.

Heineman, M. (1981). The obsolete scientific imperative in social work research and practice. *Social Service Review, 55,* 371–397.

Hempel, C. (1965). *Aspects of scientific explanation.* New York: Free Press.

Hess, H. (1997). HIV / AIDS: Issues in working with culturally diverse families. In E. Congress (Ed.), *Multicultural perspectives in working with families* (pp. 252–271). New York: Springer.

Hilts, P. (1997, September 21). Medicine remains as much art as science. *The New York Times,* p. 5.

Hobbs, J. (1990). *Literature and cognition.* Stanford, CA: CLSI.

Holmes, Jr., O. W. (1981). *The common law.* Boston: Little, Brown, & Co.

Holmes, S. A. (1997, July 6). The nation: It's awful! It's terrible! It's…Never mind. *The New York Times,* p. E3.

Home, A. (1997). Learning the hard way: Role strain, stress, role demands, and support in multiple-role women students. *Journal of Social Work Education, 33,* 335–346.

Horton, J. (1966). Order and conflict theories of social problems as competing ideologies. *American Journal of Sociology, 71,* 701–713.

House, J., & Kahn, R. (1985). Measures and concepts of social support. In S. Cohen & S. Syme (Eds.), *Social support and health* (pp. 83–108). Orlando, FL: Academic Press.

Howe, E. (1980). Public professions and the private model of professionalism. *Social Work, 25:*3, 179–191.

Hudson, W. W. (1982). Scientific imperatives in social work research and practice. *Social Service Review, 56:* 242–258.

Hudson, W. W. (1978). First axiom of treatment. *Social Work, 23:*1, 65.

Hudson, W. W. (1982a). Scientific imperatives in social work research and practice. *Social Service Review, 56:*2, 246–259.

Hudson, W. W. (1982b). *The clinical measurement package: A field manual.* Homewood, IL: Dorsey Press.

Ibsen, Henrik. (1965). *Three plays: An enemy of the people, the wild duck, Hedda Gabler.* New York: Heritage.

Imre, R. W. (1984). The nature of knowledge in social work. *Social Work, 29:*1, 41–45.

Ivanoff, A. M., Blythe, B. J., & Tripodi, T. (1994). *Involuntary clients in social work practice: A research based practice.* New York: Aldine de Gruyter.

Jayaratne, S. (1990). Clinical significance: Problems and new developments. In L. Videka-Sherman & W. J. Reid (Eds.), *Advances in clinical social work research* (pp. 271–285). Silver Springs, MD: NASW.

Jayaratne, S., & Levy, R. (1979). *Empirical clinical practice.* New York: Columbia University Press.

Jensen, C. (1994). Psychosocial treatment of depression in women: Nine single-subject evaluations. *Research on Social Work Practice, 4,* 267–282.

Johnson, J. W. (1927). *The autobiography of an ex-colored man.* New York: Alfred Knopf.

Jones, S. (1997, November 6). The set within the skull. *The New York Review of Books*, pp. 13–16.

Jue, S. (1994, June). Psychosocial issues of AIDS long-term survivors. *Families in Society*, 324–332.

Juhasz, A. M. (1985). Measuring self-esteem in early adolescents. *Adolescence, 20:80*, 877–887.

Kadushin, A., & Kadushin, G. (1997). *The social work interview: A guide for human service professionals* (4th ed.). New York: Columbia University Press.

Kagle, J. D. (1983). The contemporary social work record. *Social Work, 28*, 149–153.

Keefe, K., & Berndt, T. J. (1996). Relations of friendship quality to self-esteem in early adolescence. *Journal of Early Adolescence, 16:1*, 110–129.

Kelley, T. (1998, April 30). It is for you defective day of hats, no? Even helpful translation software sometimes weaves a tangled web. *The New York Times*, pp. E1, E7.

Kerlinger, F. N. (1986). *Foundations of behavioral research* (3rd ed.). New York: Holt, Rinehart, & Winston.

Kilty, K. M., & Meenagham, T. M. (1995). Social work and the convergence of politics and science. *Social Work, 40:4*, 445–453.

King, J. C. (1981). *The biology of race*. Berkeley: University of California Press.

Kinnier, R. T., Metha, A., Okey, J. L., & Keim, J. (1994). Adolescent substance abuse and psychological health. *Journal of Alcohol and Drug Education, 40:1*, 51–56.

Kirk, S. (1990). Research utilization: The substructure of belief. In L. Videka-Sherman & W. Reid (Eds.), *Advances in clinical social work research* (pp. 233–250). Silver Springs, MD: NASW.

Kirk, S. A. (1990). Research utilization: The substructure of belief. In L. Videka-Sherman & W. Reid (Eds.), *Advances in clinical social work research* (pp. 233–250). Silver Springs, MD: NASW.

Kirk, S. A., Osmalov, M. J., & Fischer, J. (1976). Social workers' involvement in research. *Social Work, 21:2*, 121–124.

Kirst-Ashman, K. K., & Hull, G. H., Jr. (1997). *Generalist practice with organizations and communities*. Chicago: Nelson-Hall.

Koeske, R., & Koeske, G. (1989). Working and non-working students: Roles, support and well being. *Journal of social work education, 25*, 244–256.

Kotler, P., & Roberto, E. L. (1989). *Social marketing: Strategies for changing public behavior*. New York: Free Press.

Krause, E. (1997). *Death of the guilds: Professions, states, and the advance of capitalism, 1930 to the present*. New Haven, CN: Yale University Press.

Kreuger, L. W. (1987). Microcomputers in private practice. *Journal of Independent Social Work, 1:2*, 55–66.

Kreuger, R. A. (1988). *Focus groups: A practical guide for applied research*. Newbury Park, CA: Sage.

Kuhn, T. (1970). *The structure of scientific revolutions* (2nd ed.). Chicago: University of Chicago Press.

Kutchins, H. (1991). The fiduciary relationship: The legal basis for social workers' responsibility to clients. *Social Work, 36:2*, 97–102.

Lakoff, G., & Nunez, R. (1997). The metaphysical structure of mathematics: Sketching out cognitive foundations for a mind-based mathematics. In L. English (Ed.),

*Mathematical reasoning: Analogies, metaphors and images* (pp. 21–89). Hillside, NJ: Erlbaum.

Lauffer, A. (1982). *Assessment tools for practitioners, managers, and trainees.* Newbury Park, CA: Sage.

Lee, J. A. B. (1994). *The empowerment approach to social work practice.* New York: Columbia University Press.

Lee, J., & Nisivoccia, D. (1997). Substance abuse and homeless mothers: Multiple oppression and empowerment. In E. Congress (Ed.), *Multicultural perpsectives in working with families* (pp. 288–310). New York: Springer.

Lee, P. (1929). Social work: Cause and function. In *Proceedings of the National Conference of Social Work* (pp. 3–20). Chicago: University of Chicago Press.

Leiby, J. (1984, December). Charity organization reconsidered. *Social Service Review,* 523–538.

Leiby, J. (1985). Moral foundations of social welfare and social work: A historical review. *Social Work, 30:* 4, 323–330.

Levenson, D. (1997a, Summer). Online counseling: Opportunity and risk. *NASW News,* p. 3.

Levenson, D. (1997b, November). In a volatile job market, know business: Attention to economics key for professional survival. *NASW News,* p. 3.

Levy, C. S. (1976). "Personal vs. professional values: The practitioner's dilemma," *Clinical Social Work Journal,* 4:2, 110–120.

Lewis, H. (1982). *The intellectual base of social work practice: Tools for thought in a helping profession.* New York: Haworth Press.

Lewis, M., & Wigen, K. (1997). *The myth of continents: A critique of metageography.* Berkeley: University of California Press.

Lewontin, R. (1994). Sex, lies, and social science. *New York Review of Books, 42,* 24–29.

Lincoln, Y., & Guba, E. (1985). *Naturalistic inquiry.* Beverly Hills, CA: Sage.

*Linkages* (1997). Institute for Distance Education, University System of Maryland. 6:1.

Living a life of giving. (1994, February 21–March 7). *The Voice:University of Maryland at Baltimore,* p. 6.

Lohmann, R. A., & Wolvovsky, J. (1979). Natural language processing and computer use in social work. *Administration in Social Work, 3:4,* 409–422.

Loneck, B., & Way, B. (1997). Using a focus group of clinicians to develop a research project on therapeutic process for clients with dual diagnosis. *Social Work, 42,* 107–111.

Luborsky, L. (1993). The role of the therapeutic alliance in psychotherapy. *Journal of Consulting Psychology, 61:4,* 561–573.

Lubove, R. (1977). *The professional altruist: The emergence of social work as a career, 1880–1938.* New York: Atheneum.

Lukus, S. (1993). *When to start and what to ask: An assessment handbook.* New York: W. W. Norton.

Lynn, K. (1963). *The professions in America.* Boston: Houghton-Mifflin.

Madrick, J. (1998, March 26). Computers: Waiting for the revolution. *The New York Review of Books,* pp. 29–33.

Magura, S., & Moses, B. S. (1986). *Outcome measures for child welfare services: Theory and application.* Washington, DC: Child Welfare League of America.

Maisto, S. A., McKay, J. R., & Connors, C. J. (1990). Self report issues in substance abuse: State of the art and future directions. *Behavioral Assessment, 12,* 117–134.

Malinowski, B. (1922). *Argonauts of the western Pacific.* London: Routledge.

Mancoske, R. (1996). HIV/AIDS and suicide: Further precautions. *Social Work, 3,* 325–326.

Maranto, G. (1998, May 26). On the fringes of the bell curve, the evolving quest for normality. *The New York Times,* p. C7.

Mark, R. (1996). *Research made simple: A handbook for social workers.* Thousand Oaks, CA: Sage.

Marks, J. (1995). *Human biodiversity: Genes, race, and history.* New York: Aldine de Gruyter.

Marlow, C. (1993). *Research methods for generalist social work.* Pacific Grove, CA: Brooks/Cole.

Marquez, Gabriel Garcia. (1997). *News of a kidnapping.* New York: Alfred Knopf.

Martin, M. & Henry-Feeney, J. (1989). Clinical services to persons with AIDS: The parallel nature of the client and worker processes. *Clinical Social Work Journal, 17*:14, 337–349.

Martinez-Brawley, E., & Mendez-Bonito Zorita, P. (1998). At the edge of the frame: Beyond science and art in social work. *British Journal of Social Work, 28*: 197–212.

Mattaini, M. & Kirk, S. A. (1993). Points & viewpoints: Misdiagnosing assessment. *Social Work, 38,* 231–233.

Mazmanian, D. A., & Sabatier, P. A. (Eds.). (1981). *Effective policy implementation.* Lexington, MA: Lexington Books.

McCormick, M. J. (1961). The role of values in social functioning. *Social Casework, 42:* 70–78.

McKnight, R. (1997). *White boys.* New York: Henry Holt.

Mead, G. H. (1930). Philanthropy from the point of view of ethics. In E. Faris, F. Laune, A. Todd (Eds.), *Intelligent philanthropy* (pp. 122–138). Chicago: University of Chicago Press.

Mecca, A. A., Smelser, N. J., & Vasconcellos, J. (Eds.). (1989). *The social importance of self-esteem.* Berkeley, CA: University of California Press.

Menaker, D. (1998). *The treatment.* New York: Alfred Knopf.

Merton, R. K., Fiske, M., & Kendall, P. (1952). *The focused interview: A manual.* (2nd. ed.). New York: Bureau of Applied Research, Columbia University.

Merton, R. K., Fiske, M., & Kendall, P. (1956). *The focus interview.* Glencoe, IL: The Free Press.

Merton, R. M. (1982). Institutionalized altruism: The case of the professions. In *Social research and the practicing professions* (pp. 109–134). Cambridge, MA: Abt Books.

Meyer, C. (1993). *Assessment in social work practice.* New York: Columbia University Press.

Miedaner, T. (1981). The soul of Martha, a beast. In D. Hofstadter & D. Dennett (Eds.), *The mind's I* (pp. 100–118). New York: Basic Books.

Monette, D. R., Sullivan, T. J., & DeJong, C. R. (1990). *Applied social research: Tool for the human services* (2nd ed.). Chicago: Holt, Rinehart & Winston.

Morrison, T. (1970). *The bluest eye.* New York: Alfred Knopf.

Mullen, E. (1983). Personal practice models. In A. Rosenblatt & D. Waldfogel (Eds.), *Handbook of clinical social work* (pp. 623–649). San Francisco, CA: Jossey-Bass.

NASW to urge tighter privacy guidelines. (1998, January). *NASW News*, p. 7.

National Association of Social Workers. (1996). *Code of Ethics*. Silver Springs, MD: Author.

National Association of Social Workers. (n.d.). *NASW policy statement 1, code of ethics of the National Association of Social Workers; As adopted by the 1979 NASW Delegate Assembly and revised by the 1990 and 1993 NASW Delegate Assemblies.* Silver Springs, MD: Author.

Naylor, G. (1983). *The women of Brewster Place.* New York: Ticknor & Fields.

Nelson, J. (1980). *Communication theory and social work practice.* Chicago: University of Chicago Press.

Netting, F. E., Kettner, P. M., & McMurtry, S. L. (1993). *Social work macro practice.* New York: Longman.

Nielsen, D. M., & Metha, A. (1994). Parental behavior and adolescent self-esteem in clinical and nonclinical samples. *Adolescence, 29:*115, 525–542.

Nugent, W. R. (1987). Information gained through integrated research approaches. *Social Service Review, 61:*2, 337–364.

Nugent, W. R. (1991). A mathematical model for analyzing single subject design replication series. *Journal of Social Service Research, 15:*1–2, 93–129.

Nugent, W. R., & Hankins, J. A. (1989). The use of item-response theory in social work measurement and research. *Social Service Review, 63:*3, 447–473.

Office of Cancer Communication, National Cancer Institute. (1992, April). *Making health communication programs work: A planner's guide.* Washington, DC: U.S. Department of Health and Human Services, Public Health Service, National Institutes of Health, NIH Publication No. 92–1493.

Orme, J. G., & Combs-Orme, T. D. (1986). Statistical power and type II errors in social work research. *Social Work Research & Abstracts, 22:*3, 3–10.

Orme, J. G., & Hudson, W. W., (June 1995). The problem of sample size estimation: Confidence intervals. *Social Work Research 19:*2, 121–127.

Pardeck, J. T. (1987). Micro computer technology in social work practice: An analysis of ethical issues. *Journal of Independent Social Work, 2:*1, 71–81.

Pardeck, J. T., & Murphy, J. W. (1986). Micro computer technology in clinical social work practice: Benefits and problems. *Arete, 11:*1, 35–43.

Parent, M. (1995, November 28). For Elisa, more than the system failed. *The New York Times*, p. 23.

Passmore, J. (1967). Logical positivism. In P. Edwards (Ed.)., *Encyclopedia of philosophy* (pp. 52–57). New York: Macmillan.

Pearlman, S. (1993). Late mid-life astonishment: Disruption to identity and self-esteem. *Women and Therapy, 14*, 1–12.

Peile, C. (1988). Research paradigms in social work: From stalemate to creative synthesis. *Social Service Review*, March: 1–19.

Peile, C. (1993). Determinism versus creativity: Which way for social work? *Social Work, 38:* 2, 127–134.

Peile, C., & McCourt, M. (1997). The rise of relativism: The future of theory and knowledge development in social work. *British Journal of Social Work, 27*, pp. 343–360.

Peyrot, M., Harris, W. L., Fenzel, M. L., & Burbridge, J. J. (1997). Welfare plastic: The transformation of public assistance in the electronic age. *Journal of Sociology and Social Welfare, 14*:2, 127–134.

Pinker, S. (1997). *How the mind works.* New York: Norton.

Plutchik, R., & Karasu, T. B. (1990). Computers in interviewing and psychotherapy. In D. B. Baskin (Ed.), *Computer Applications in Psychiatry and Psychology* (pp. 57–76). New York: Brunner/Mazel.

Pollock, N. L., & Maenpaa, M. (1990). How are psychologists using computers? *Canadian Psychology, 31*:2, 167–171.

Pope, A. W., McHale, S. M., & Craighead, W. E. (1988). *Self-esteem enhancement with children and adolescents.* New York: Pergamon Press.

Popper, K. (1982). *The open universe: An argument for indeterminism.* Totowa, NJ: Rowman & Littlefield. [From a postscript to *The logic of scientific discovery,* published as *Logik der forschung* in 1935 and revised 1959.]

Popple, P. (1985). The social work profession: A reconceptualization. *Social Service Review, 59*:4, 560–577.

Posner, R. (1990). *The problems of jurisprudence.* Cambridge, MA: Harvard University Press.

Powers, R. (1998). *Gain.* New York: Farrar, Strauss & Giroux.

Quindlen, A. (1994). *One true thing.* New York: Random House.

*Random House Dictionary.* (1966). New York: Random House.

Rawls, J. (1971). *A theory of justice.* Cambridge, MA: Belknap Press.

Reamer, F. G. (1979). Fundamental ethical issues in social work. *Social Service Review, 53*:2, 229–243.

Reamer, F. G. (1982). *Ethical dilemmas in social services.* New York: Columbia University Press.

Reamer, F. G. (1993). *The philosophical foundations of social work.* New York: Columbia University Press.

Reamer, F. G. (1994). *Social work malpractice and liability: Strategies for prevention.* New York: Columbia University Press.

Reamer, F. G. (1995a). *Social work values and ethics.* New York: Columbia University Press.

Reamer, F. G. (1995b). Malpractice claims against social workers: First facts. *Social Work, 40*:5, 595–601.

Reddin, B. A. (1971). *Effective management by objectives: The 3-D method of MBO.* New York: McGraw-Hill.

Reinharz, S. (1992). *Feminist methods in social research.* New York: Oxford University Press.

Rescher, N. (1972). *Welfare.* Pittsburgh: University of Pittsburgh Press.

Reynolds, P. (1971). *A primer in theory construction.* New York: Macmillan.

Rhodes, M. L. (1991). *Ethical dilemmas in social work practice.* Milwaukee, WI: Family Service of America.

Richan, W. (1996). *Lobbying for social change* (2nd ed.). Binghamton, NY: Haworth.

Richmond, M. (1899). *Friendly visiting among the poor.* New York: Macmillan.

Richmond, M. (1917). *Social diagnosis.* New York: Russell Sage Foundation.

Richter, S. S., Brown, S. A., & Mott, M. A. (1991). The impact of social support and self-esteem on adolescent substance abuse treatment outcomes. *Journal of Substance Abuse, 3:4*, 371–385.

Ricoeur, P. (1987). The teleological and deontological structures of action: Aristotle and/or Kant? in A. P. Griffiths (Ed.), *Contemporary French philosophy.* Cambridge: Cambridge University Press.

Roberts, S. (1995, August 27). Yes, a small town is different. *The New York Times,* pp. E1, E5.

Rodwell, M. K. (1987). Naturalistic inquiry: An alternative model for social work assessment. *Social Service Review, 61:2*, 231–246.

Rorty, R. (1998). *Truth and progress: Philosophical papers, vol. 3.* New York: Cambridge University Press.

Rosaldo, R. (1989). *Culture and truth: The remaking of social analysis.* Boston: Beacon.

Rose, R. (1995, Feb.). Marketing: Hook editors with a pro-caliber release. *NASW News, 40*, p. 5.

Rosen, A., & Mutschler, E. (1982). Social work students' and practitioners' orientation to research. *Journal of Education for Social Work, 18:3*, 62–68.

Rosenberg, M. (1979). *Conceiving the self.* New York: Basic Books.

Rosenblatt, A. (1968). The practitioner's use and evaluation of research. *Social Work, 13*, 53–59.

Ross, D. (1991). *The origins of American social science.* New York: Cambridge University Press.

Rothman, J. (1980). *Social r & d: Research and development in the human services.* Englewood Cliffs, NJ: Prentice Hall.

Rothman, J., Teresa, J. C., Kay, T. L., & Morningstar, G. C. (1983). *Marketing human service innovations.* Beverly Hills, CA: Sage.

Rothstein, E. (1997, December 20). The subjective underbelly of hard-headed math. *The New York Times,* pp. A17, 18.

Royce, D. (1991). *Research methods in social work.* Chicago: Nelson-Hall.

Royce, D., & Thyer, B. A. (1996). *Program evaluation: An introduction,* 2nd ed. Chicago, IL: Nelson-Hall.

Rubin, A., & Babbie, E. (1993). *Research methods for social work.* (2nd ed.). Pacific Grove, CA: Brooks/Cole.

Rubin, A. & Babbie, E. (1997). *Research methods for social workers* (3rd ed.). Pacific Grove, CA: Brooks/Cole.

Rubin, B. R. (1997). *A citizen's guide to politics in America: How the system works & how to work the system.* Armonk, NY: M. E. Sharpe.

Saleebey, D. (1979). The tension between research and practice: Assumption of the experimental paradigm. *Clinical Social Work Journal, 7*, 19–40.

Sawin, K. J., Harrigan, M. P., & Woog, P. (Eds.). (1995). *Measures of family functioning for research and practice.* New York: Springer.

Schilling, R. F. (1990). Commentary: Making research usable. In L. Videka-Sherman & W. J. Reid (Eds.), *Advances in clinical social work research* (pp. 256–260). Silver Springs, MD: National Association of Social Workers.

Schinka, J. A., & Smith, R. B. (1984). The computer in the psychotherapist's office: Present and future applications. In M. D. Schwartz (Ed.), *Using computers in clinical practice: Psychotherapy and mental health applications* (pp. 7–17). New York: Haworth.

Schlesinger, A. (1996, May 3). History as therapy: A dangerous idea. *The New York Times*, p. A31.

Schon, D. (1983). *The reflective practitioner.* New York: Basic Books.

Schutt, R. K. (1996). *Investigating the social world: The process and practice of research.* Thousand Oaks, CA: Pine Forge Press.

Schwartz, W. (1969). Private troubles and public issues: One social work job or two. In *Social Welfare Forum* (pp. 22–43). New York: Columbia University Press.

Selznick, P. (1996). Social justice. A communitarian perspective. *The Responsive Community: Rights and Responsibilities, 6:*4, 13–25.

Sexton, Joe. (1996, February 17). A failure to protect: How a school for child welfare workers fell apart. *The New York Times*, pp. 25–26.

Sherman, S., & Reid, W. (Eds.). (1994). *Qualitative research in social work.* New York: Columbia University Press.

Shulman, L. (1984). *The skills of helping individuals and groups.* Itasca, IL: F. E. Peacock.

Siegel, D. H. (1984). Defining empirically based practice. *Social Work, 29:*4, 325–331.

Silverlake, A. C. (1998). *Comprehending test manuals: A guide and workbook.* Los Angeles: Pyrczak.

Simos, B. (1979). *A time to grieve: Loss as a universal human experience.* New York: Family Services of America.

Singleton, R. A. Jr., Straits, B. C., & Straits, M. M. (1993). *Approaches to social research* (2nd ed.). New York: Oxford University Press.

Siporin, M. (1975). *Introduction to social work practice.* New York: Macmillan.

Siporin, M. (1982). Moral philosophy on social work today. *Social Service Review, December,* 517–537.

Souflee, F., Jr. (1993). A metatheoretical framework for social work practice. *Social Work, 38:*3, 317–331.

Spano, R. (1982). *The rank and file movement in social work.* Washington, DC: University Press of America.

Specht, H. (1994). *Unfaithful angels.* New York: Free Press.

Sperry, L. (1995). *Psychopharmacology and psychotherapy: Strategies for maximum treatment outcomes.* New York: Brunner/Mazel.

Spiegel, M. (1996). *The dreaded comparison: Human and animal slavery.* New York: Mirror Books.

Spiro, M. (1987). *Culture and human nature.* Chicago: University of Chicago Press.

Spradley, J. P. (1979). *The ethnographic interview.* New York: Holt, Rinehart & Winston.

Spradley, J. P. (1980). *Participant observation.* New York: Harcourt Brace Jovanovich.

Stakes, R. E. (1995). *The art of case study research.* Thousand Oaks, CA: Sage.

Staudt, M. (1997, January). Pseudoissues in practice evaluation: Impediments to responsible practice. *Social Work, 42:1,* 99–106.

Steinbeck, J. (1939). *The grapes of wrath.* New York: Viking.

Stokes, K., & Brasch, B. (1997). A view from the States: Case management and welfare reform in Nebraska. *Public Welfare, 55,* 33–41.

Strand, V. (1997). The impact of ethnicity and race on the treatment of mothers in incest families. In E. Congress (Ed.), *Multicultural perpsectives in working with families* (pp. 201–216). New York: Springer.

Straus, M. S., & Gelles, R. J. (1990). *Physical violence in American families: Risk factors and adaptation to violence in 8,145 families.* New Brunswick, NJ: Transaction.

Strayer, J. (1943). *The interpretation of history.* Princeton: Princeton University Press.

Stuart, S., & Larue, S. (1996). Computerized cognitive therapy: The interface between man and machine. *Journal of Cognitive Psychotherapy, 10:3,* 181–189.

Sullivan, W. (1995). *Work and integrity.* New York: HarperCollins.

*Tarasoff v. Regents of University of California.* 13 Cal3d. 177 (Sup. Ct. 1976).

Taylor, J. B. (1981). *Using microcomputers in social agencies.* Beverly Hills, CA: Sage.

Thomas, L. (1983). *The youngest science.* New York: Viking.

Thyer, B. (1986). Single-subject designs in clinical social work: A practitioner's perspective. In H. R. Johnson & J. E. Tropman (Eds.), *Social work policy and practice: A knowledge driven approach* (pp. 292–309). Ann Arbor: University of Michigan School of Social Work.

Thyer, B. (1990). Single-system research designs in social work practice. In L. Videka-Sherman & W. Reid (Eds.), *Advances in clinical social work research* (pp. 33–36). Silver Springs, MD: NASW Press.

Tran, T. V., & O'Hare, T. (1996). Congruency between interviewers' ratings and respondents' self-reports of self-esteem, depression, and health status. *Social Work Research, 29,* 43–50.

Tripodi, T. (1994). *A primer on single subject design for clinical social workers.* Annapolis Junction, MD: NASW.

Tripodi, T., & Epstein, I. (1983). *Research techniques for clinical social workers.* New York: Columbia University Press.

Turow, S. (1977). *One L.* New York: G. P. Putnam's Sons.

Tutty, L. M., Rothery, M. A., & Grinnell, R. M., Jr. (1996). *Qualitative research for social workers.* Boston: Allyn & Bacon.

Tyson, K. (1992). A new approach to relevant scientific research for practitioners: The heuristic paradigm. *Social Work, 37:6,* 541–556.

Tyson, K. (Ed.) (1994). *New foundations for scientific research social and behavioral science research: The heuristic paradigm.* Needham Heights, MA: Allyn & Bacon.

Valancy, J. (1985). *Microcomputers and your practice: A guide for physicians.* Chicago: Pluribus Press.

Warner, G., with Kreger, D. (1998). *Dancing at the edge of life.* New York: Hyperion.

Warnock, G. J. (1971). *The object of morality* . London: Metheun.

*Webster's Seventh New Collegiate Dictionary.* (1963). Springfield, MA: G. & C. Merriam Co.

Weinbach, R. W., & Grinnell, Jr., R. M. (1995). *Statistics for social workers* (3rd ed.) White Plains, NY: Longman.

Weiner, M. E. (1982). *Human services management: Analysis and applications.* Homewood, IL: Dorsey.

Wells, C. C., with Masch, M. K. (1986). *Social work ethics day to day: Guidelines for professional practice.* Prospect Heights, IL: Waveland.

Wenocur, S., & Reisch, M. D. (1989). *From charity to enterprise: The development of American social work in a market economy.* Chicago: University of Illinois Press.

Wexler-Vigilante, F. W. (1993). Work: Its use in assessment and intervention with clients in the workplace. In P. Kurzman & S. Akabas (Eds.), *Work and well-being: The occupational social work advantage* (pp. 179–199). Washington, DC: National Association of Social Workers.

What happened to Elisa? [Editorial]. (1995, November 28). *The New York Times*, p. A22.

Wilensky, H. (1964). The professionalization of everyone? *American Journal of Sociology, 70*, 137–58.

Williams, L., & Hopps, J. (1990). The social work labor force: Current perspectives and future trends. *Encyclopedia of social work* (18th ed.) (pp. 289–306). Silver Springs, MD: NASW Press.

Winawer, S. (1998). *Healing lessons.* Boston: Little, Brown & Company.

Winnicott, D. W. (1989). *Psychoanalytic explorations.* Cambridge, MA: Harvard University Press.

Witkin, S. (1998a). The right to effective treatment and the effective treatment of rights: Rhetorical empiricism and the politics of research. *Social Work, 43:1*, 75–80.

Witkin, S. (1998b). Human rights and social work. *Social Work, 43:3*, 197–201.

Wodarski, J. S. (1997). *Research methods for clinical social workers: Empirical practice.* New York: Springer.

Yegidis, B. L., & Weinbach, R. W. (1996). *Research methods for social workers* (2nd ed.). Boston, MA: Allyn & Bacon.

Yin, R. (1984). *Case study research: Design and method.* Beverly Hills, CA: Sage.

Zimmerman, J. (1989). Determinism, science, and social work. *Social Service Review, 63*, 52–62.

Zimmerman, M. (1994). *Interview guide for evaluating DSM–IV psychiatric disorders and the mental status examination.* Philadelphia: Psych Press Products.

Zuger, A. (1997, December 16). New way of doctoring: By the book. *The New York Times*, pp. c1, 7.

Zysman, S. H. (1989). Attitudes of alcohol/substance abuse practitioners toward utilizing computer-based information and communication systems in practice. Unpublished Ph.D. dissertation, Adelphi University.

# Index